THE HOLY KINGDOM

THE HOLY KINGDOM

Adrian Gilbert
Alan Wilson and Baram Blackett

BANTAM PRESS

LONDON · NEW YORK · TORONTO · SYDNEY · AUCKLAND

TRANSWORLD PUBLISHERS LTD
61–63 Uxbridge Road, London W5 5SA

TRANSWORLD PUBLISHERS (AUSTRALIA) PTY LTD
15–25 Helles Avenue, Moorebank, NSW 2170

TRANSWORLD PUBLISHERS (NZ) LTD
3 William Pickering Drive, Albany, Auckland

Published 1998 by Bantam Press
a division of Transworld Publishers Ltd
Copyright © Adrian Gilbert, Alan Wilson & Baram Blackett 1998

The right of Adrian Gilbert, Alan Wilson and Baram Blackett to be identified
as authors of this work has been asserted in accordance
with sections 77 and 78 of the Copyright Designs and
Patents Act 1988.

A catalogue record for this book is available from the British Library.
ISBN 0593 040627

Set in 11/13 pt Times by Falcon Oast Graphic Art

Printed in Great Britain
by Mackays of Chatham plc, Chatham, Kent

For all those who through the long centuries and
the many wars have fought to preserve Britain.

'To know nothing of what happened before you
were born is to remain forever a child.'

CICERO

CONTENTS

ACKNOWLEDGEMENTS

We would like to extend our thanks to all of the following people who have aided us in our quest over the years: Rodger Bird, William Currie-Laird, James B. Michael (President of the Ancient Kentucky Historical and Epigraphical Association), Professor Lee Pennington and Dr Joy Pennington, Professor Tom Watson, Dr Ian Crabbe, Michael Clark, Matthew Browning, John Battersby, Phillip P.E. Brown, Brian Heard, Terry DeLacy, Richard Wyre, Ed Silverstein, David Bushell, Richard Melbourne, Paul Tipping, John Wynne Hopkins, Lyndon Thomas, Bill Isaacs, Jayne Isaacs, David Watson, Councillor Clayton Jones, Councillor Gerald Edwards, R.T. Weightman, Brian Davies (Curator of Pontypridd Cultural and Heritage Centre), along with many others who, for positive reasons, require anonymity.

We would also like to thank the following for quotations from a variety of books: Penguin Books Ltd, London; Oxford University Press, Oxford; Weidenfeld and Nicholson, London; Phillimore and Company, Chichester and London; Covenant Books, London; Batsford Ltd, London; Ernest Brown, London. We should also not forget Edward Williams (Iolo Morganwg) and the other members of the Welsh Manuscripts Society, without whose dedicated work during the late eighteenth and early nineteenth centuries so many manuscripts, vital to our work, would have been lost.

Finally our thanks to Sally Gaminara, Katrina Whone, Simon Thorogood and everyone else at Bantam Press for keeping us on track with what has at times been a very difficult project and for producing such a splendid book.

LIST OF ILLUSTRATIONS

St Joseph of Arimathea
Maescadlawr on Mount Baedan, scene of Arthur II's decisive battle
The site of the Palace of Caermead
The dingle at Nash Point
Views of the estuary leading to the Ogmore and Ewenny Rivers, along which the body of the dead King Arthur II was brought for burial
View of the river confluence, where Arthur II gathered his forces before the Battle of Baedan
Ogmore Castle
The Ogmore stone
The first burial of King Arthur II
Alan Wilson outside the cave of St Illtyd, the probable site of King Arthur II's first burial
The 'anvil stone'
Sword mark on the 'anvil stone', reminiscent of the legend of the Sword in the Stone
The ruined Church of St Peter's
The 1990 excavation of St Peter's
Alan Wilson with the stone of Arthur II, and Baram Blackett with the stone of Arthur I
The coat of arms of London
A grille-protected fragment of the London Stone
The Liwell stone
Ancient sword, possibly the Sword of Constantine (© *Ralph Thomas*)

Unless otherwise stated, all photographs are the property of the authors.

PROLOGUE

In 1993 I read in one of the Sunday papers a lengthy article describing
how an historian called Alan Wilson, along with fellow investigator
Baram Blackett, claimed to have discovered the tomb of the legendary
King Arthur in the vicinity of an ancient Welsh church. Like most people who haven't really delved deeply into the subject, I had always
assumed that King Arthur, if he had existed at all as an identifiably real
character, had been buried in Glastonbury Abbey in Somerset. Indeed, I
had many times stood in front of his supposed resting place, close to the
site of what had been the high altar in that once magnificent building.
To read that this might not be the case was intriguing, but I approached
the article with a high degree of scepticism, not expecting to see anything more than idle speculation.

As I read on, though, my interest increased. It became clear that the
suggestion that King Arthur was buried in Wales and not in Somerset was
based not on idle fantasies but on decades of solid research. What gave the
story an extra dimension was that Wilson and Blackett had actually bought
the church in question and arranged an archaeological dig, so certain were
they of the truth of their arguments. There they had found treasure and
church artefacts of a most exciting nature, linking the site with the Dark
Ages and with King Arthur himself. Though they had not yet unearthed
the bodily remains of the man sometimes described as the 'once and
future king',[1] this, their article suggested, seemed now to be only a matter
of time. With a chuckle I wondered how the establishment would feel
when they realized that the Church Commissioners had sold off to two
independent researchers a place that could, if their discoveries were valid,
be seen to be one of the most important heritage sites in Europe.

As a fellow researcher on the fringes of academic acceptability, I knew what they must be feeling: excitement mixed with incredulity that nobody had discovered these things before. I could also tell from the tone of the article that they had stirred up a hornet's nest of scholarly disapproval, for if they were right, their conclusions presented a serious challenge to many reputations. The threat that they constituted to the academic world possibly explained why, outside their home in south Wales, hardly anyone had, until that article, heard of their work. Without the backing of the archaeological establishment and the powerful quango of the CADW (the Welsh Ancient Monuments Commission), it had been difficult for them to attract the attention of the local media, still less to get national coverage for what were undoubtedly major discoveries of interest to a very wide audience.[2] Intrigued, I made a mental note to get in touch with Wilson and Blackett at some future date to see how their work had progressed.

The next year was an extraordinary one for me. It saw the publication of *The Orion Mystery*, which I co-authored with Robert Bauval, and the production of a BBC documentary on the same subject called *The Great Pyramid: Gateway to the Stars*. Thanks to the programme the book became an immediate bestseller, provoking a vigorous debate among academics and the public alike as to the true nature and purpose of the pyramids of Egypt. Were they simply tombs of long-dead and nearly forgotten pharaohs, as the textbooks all taught, or were they, as we believed, meant to represent stars?

The success of *The Orion Mystery* brought me into contact with a number of interesting people – among them a clairvoyant called Ann Walker, who later visited me in Dorset. After discussing other matters, she gave me a clairvoyant reading and as she finished off the session, she made a strange prophecy.

'You'll see it on a wall, a shape like this,' she said, drawing a rather stylish cross on the pad in front of her, 'and behind it there is a real one.' I had little time to consider her words further, as a few days later my wife Dee and I were due to fly to Mexico. I knew that whilst there we would be visiting the ancient Mayan city of Palenque with its own collection of strange pyramids. One of these, the Temple of the Cross, contained a stucco relief depicting two chieftains standing at either side of an elaborate cross. I presumed that this was what Ann Walker had 'seen' and resolved to have a look to see if there was indeed another cross – 'a real one' – behind it. When we arrived in Mexico, on finding nothing there of note, I dismissed the prophecy as a figment of her imagination and put it out of my mind.

A month or two after I got back from Mexico, I had an unexpected phone call. It was Alan Wilson. I had all but forgotten about the newspaper article concerning his and Baram Blackett's discovery of King Arthur's grave and it took me a few moments to realize who he was. Over the course of the next half-hour he began to explain the course of their researches; how the story of the Arthur dig, which I had read about in the paper, was but the tip of a very large iceberg; and that Alan wanted me to work with them to co-author a book. I felt a sense of *déjà vu*, for in November 1992 I had been contacted on the phone by Robert Bauval, which led to our writing *The Orion Mystery* together. Now it seemed that history was about to repeat itself. Truth be told, I wasn't keen to enter into another joint venture. I was busy working on *The Mayan Prophecies*, I had a further title commissioned, this time a solo effort entitled *Magi: the Quest for a Secret Tradition*, and I had other projects in mind to follow this. The last thing I wanted was to commit myself to even more work. However, as much out of curiosity as anything else, I agreed to go and visit them a few weeks later.

Alan's house was in one of the older parts of Cardiff, a city richly provided with Victorian terraces of ample proportions. After decades of slump following the collapse of the coal and steel industries, Cardiff today is undergoing something of a transformation. This was evident as Dee and I drove into the city, which I could still remember vaguely from my childhood as a rather old-fashioned place of brightly polished steam trains and busy shopping streets. Though I am English and was born in the suburbs of London, my mother was Welsh and came from Merthyr Tydfil; she left the valleys at the age of sixteen. My mother's parents still lived in south Wales and during the fifties my sisters and I would most years spend a few weeks with them. In those days, before the building of the first Severn Bridge, it would take all day to drive down to Wales from London by car, so usually we would travel down by train. To reach Merthyr, once the capital of the south Wales mining and steel industries and still, even in the fifties, a thriving town with an omnipresent smog, we would have to change at Cardiff, before chugging up the Taff Valley to our destination.

I didn't know this then but the word 'Merthyr' means 'martyr' in Welsh and Merthyr Tydfil is named after a sixth-century British saint called Tydfil (Theodora), who was murdered during the Saxon wars that raged around that time. Though her statue stood in the middle of the town, as children we never gave her a second thought. She could have come from Mars for all we knew.

In that tightly knit community, it seemed that everyone knew who we were. In those days every Welsh family had a Bible and I remember my mother telling me how her grandfather used to read through it from beginning to end, before starting again at Genesis. He would boast that he had read the Bible in its entirety at least fifty times – but of course in those days they had no television.

One of the other primary functions of my grandmother's ancient Bible was to record the family tree. Our names too were inscribed in that venerable tome which lived in its own little chest in the hall. I thought little of such things at the time but now realize that what we witnessed as children was a last gasp of an ancient tradition, at one time common in Wales but now dying, perhaps still practised today only in some of the principality's more rural parts. Sadly, with the passage of the gener-ations, that Bible, with our recorded family tree, has disappeared.

With these happy memories turning over in my mind, my wife and I made our way up through the gate and rang the doorbell. It was answered by Alan himself, who turned out to be a gentleman in his early sixties, of stocky build and still boasting a full head of hair. Covering the walls of his front room were pictures of various Arthurian sites as well as certificates registering both him and Baram as 'Kentucky Colonels'. This honour had evidently been bestowed on them for services to the state of Kentucky in connection with their researches into the legend of Madoc, a Welsh prince who had apparently crossed the Atlantic in the sixth century. Piled up in heaps – on the floor, on the table and indeed on any and every horizontal surface – were papers, diagrams, maps and even whole manuscripts. There were also several books that he and Baram had published together over the years, with titles such as *Arthur and the Charters of the Kings*, *King Arthur of Glamorgan and Gwent* and *Artorius Rex Discovered*. It was clear to me, looking round the room, that these two were no slouches. They had obviously not only done much research into the subject but also done their level best to get their researches out into the world. Indeed, as I was to discover later, they believed so much in what they were doing that over the years they had invested almost everything they owned in the venture, including the proceeds from the sale of two houses. Given this level of commitment I felt I had to take what they said seriously.

Whilst Dee and I had been perusing the room, Alan had been busying himself in the kitchen. Presently he returned bearing two cups of tea and, clearing a space, beckoned us to sit down. It being a cold day he lit the fire which was already piled up waiting in the grate. In no time at all it was roaring away, the sparking and exploding Welsh anthracite filling the room with a pungent aroma of coal tar and ammonia. This brought back more memories of 1950s Merthyr. In those days the air was always heavy with the caustic breath of the foundries, whilst at night the valley sides would be lit up by the glowing iron-slag tips. Of course with the closure of the steel-works all this has changed. Today the landscape around Merthyr is rapidly reverting to its pre-industrial verdancy and once more it is becoming possible to imagine knights in shining armour riding through hills and valleys covered with trees rather than slag heaps.

Having seen to the comfort of his guests, Alan too sat down and, with all the gravitas of an ancient bard, began to tell us his story. He explained how as a young man, in the 1960s, he had worked as a management planner. In those days the port of Cardiff was still a flourishing concern. He had been employed in the shipbuilding industry and during the sixties and seventies had seen at first hand how a fatal combination of managerial incompetence and trade union intransigence had all but destroyed what had once been one of Britain's premier industries. As a senior manager, time and again he found himself having to negotiate with the unions for improved shop-floor pay and conditions which, if they did but know it, were already better than those received by the white-collar staff they envied.

By now his work was taking him all over the country and, to fill in long evenings spent in hotels away from home, he found he needed a hobby. Having graduated in economics and also studied history and archaeology for three years at Cardiff University, it was only natural that he should take up historical studies. At this time, in the mid sixties, the archaeological excavations of Leslie Alcock on the site of South Cadbury Castle in Somerset were very much in the headlines as the supposed location of Camelot. However, the supposition that this English hill fort was the legendary Arthur's capital was at odds with the local traditions that Alan had heard as a boy, which clearly held that the historical (rather than mystical) King Arthur came from south Wales. Having more than a passing interest in the subject he began, at first on a casual basis but later as an all-consuming passion, to research the

5

matter for himself. He quickly discovered that what passes for the 'history' of this period is, more often than not, the repeated opinions of one or two individuals who are themselves quite ignorant on the subject and whose motives are also often quite suspect.

Alan explained that he had found out that over the last couple of hundred years historians have constructed a false scenario about the whole of early British history. 'Until the eighteenth century the teaching of British history was based on the *Bruts*,' he began. 'These were chronicles of events, beginning with the arrival in Britain of Brutus and the Trojans, through the epoch of the Roman Empire to King Arthur and the Saxon takeover of England, and on to the Middle Ages. Respected historians such as Percy Enderbee, whose *Cambria Triumphans or Britain in its Perfect Lustre* was published in 1661 and dedicated to Charles II, used the *Bruts* as their base material. Geoffrey of Monmouth's twelfth-century text, *History of the Kings of Britain*, was also believed to be a substantially correct source. With the accession of "German George" in 1714 all this changed. Court historians were anxious to cool down any nationalistic feelings in Britain that could prejudice the safe rooting of the House of Hanover. The Scottish rebellions of 1715 and 1745, when the Stuarts came close to regaining the throne of Britain, the French Revolution of 1789 and the ensuing Napoleonic Wars probably reinforced the view that the *Bruts* should be suppressed.

'With the accession of Queen Victoria and her marriage to Prince Albert of Saxe-Coburg-Gotha, the process of historical "sanitization" was taken a stage further. Bishop William Stubbs, who was appointed Regius Professor of Modern History at Oxford University in 1866, set about a total reform of the teaching of British history on German lines, ruthlessly suppressing what he saw as heretical ideas. A staunch Anglican, Germanophile and notable historian of the Church of England, he established a new curriculum for the teaching of history in schools. His *magnum opus* was his three-volume *Constitutional History of England*, which traces the development of the English constitution from the Saxon invasions to 1485. He had little interest in King Arthur, still less in the Brutus dynasty from which he purportedly sprang, and based his approach on the emergent science of archaeology. Following his lead, historians at this time painted a new picture of pre-Roman Britain as a land of barbarians ignoring all evidence to the contrary in the traditional histories, which were now regarded as unreliable. Conversely the Romans, who for the main part were in fact crude adventurers intent on pillage, rapine and the enslavement of free peoples and who for entertainment liked to watch Christians being thrown to lions, were presented as "noble". Roman accounts of historical events, often distorted and written to be read by their fellow compatriots, were treated as gospel truth. As the Romans had little to say about Britain itself (or at least little that has been preserved), a large vacuum was created in the historical record. Since Stubbs's time this vacuum has been filled by an avalanche of speculation, wild theories and completely false assumptions which are themselves totally at odds with the traditions of the British.

'The reason for this baffling attitude of nineteenth-century British historians towards the history of their own country seems to be that subconsciously they equated the Empire of their own time with that of ancient Greece and Rome – the inevitable outcome of a public school and university system that for centuries was overloaded with an obsession with Greek and Latin classical studies. Seeing pre-Roman Britain in the same light as pre-colonial Africa, they looked upon the Romans as heroes bringing the light of civilization to "darkest Britain", which, they now believed, had until then been the preserve of unwashed tribes living primitive lives. The truth is that the scholars of the eighteenth and nineteenth centuries, in writing of ancient Britain, were not writing British history at all, but writing Roman history as it pertained to Britain, treating the subject from a totally Roman-orientated angle.

'With this distorted scenario in place, archaeological finds of today are all too often misinterpreted and mistaken attitudes and assumptions have ensued. For instance, the rude assumption seems to be that the Welsh were unable, without outside help, to place one stone on another, let alone build a castle. Thus any building in Wales of any worth that dates from the early centuries AD is labelled "Roman", even when there is documentary evidence to the contrary. Anything slightly later that cannot be fitted into this category is classified as "Saxon", or better still "Norman", despite the fact that the Saxons raided but never settled in Wales and that the Normans never penetrated beyond the coastal plain of Glamorgan. In the case of churches or other religious centres there is a tendency to push their origins forwards in time to be post-Augustine (c. AD 600), ignoring evidence of any earlier foundation. Many objects, such as memorial stones, which can be proved by inscriptions clearly identifying known individuals to date from the fifth and sixth centuries

7

or even earlier, are redated to several hundred years later to fit into the false scenario. This process has been taken to absurd lengths, so that many churches dedicated to fifth- and sixth-century Christian saints, who in the histories are said to have been the founders of these establishments, are nonetheless labelled "Norman" in origin.

'Another result is that the history of south Wales after the "withdrawal" of the Romans has been almost totally ignored, as though nothing was happening there, even though they were traditionally the first people in Britain to have been converted to Christianity. South Wales was the home of the powerful Silures, and Glamorgan, or Morganwg as it was once called, which enjoys the best climate, had the best natural communications and has always been the most densely populated part of Wales, is again ignored. Another false belief, with no basis in real history, has arisen, to the effect that north Wales, or Gwynedd – in reality always a poor neighbour – was the centre of Welsh culture. In fact the story arose from the intense rivalry between north and south Wales for hegemony, and from the heavy industrializing of Glamorgan during the last century, which led to massive immigration, with many Irish, English and Scottish labourers seeking work in the Glamorgan mines and steel mills. These people, now Glamorganers, couldn't speak Welsh, which anyway was under threat from other pressures, and they had little interest in the local history. To the "purist" north Welsh, the people of Glamorgan were foreigners hardly worthy of the title "Welsh" at all. Unable to read their own tongue and with little encouragement from the north, the Glamorganers all but lost touch with Welsh written histories, which languished in forgotten libraries. With the excitement of the nascent British Empire taking up their energies and under the spell of the new, non-conformist movements – mostly imported from England – they also had little incentive to look back to an often bleak past. Thus it was that north Wales came to be seen as the centre of Welsh culture and the carefully maintained and written tradition of south Welsh history was "lost".'

In relation to King Arthur, Alan found that there seemed to be a strange wall of silence surrounding the existence of a vast Welsh literature concerning both him and the dynasty from which he sprang. It soon became apparent that if he wanted to get to the truth of the matter, this wall would have to be breached: he would have to reach back beyond popular 'Arthurian' books to these earlier Welsh documents, some of which purported to have been written during or soon after the time of King Arthur himself. Accordingly he began searching anti-quarian bookshops, markets, libraries and museums for this all but lost literature.

Within a few years, in the mid seventies, he had assembled a large archive of material on the subject of Dark Age Britain and, unexpectedly, he had found dynastic links between the royal families of south Wales and the ancient kingdom of Northumbria. This, in ancient times, com-prised most of England north of the River Humber and much of what is now southern Scotland. By this time Alan himself was working in Newcastle, and as the premier city of Northumberland, Newcastle was ideally located to conduct research on this region. He began – it was by now almost second nature to him to do so – to explore the contents of its main library. He quickly discovered that he was not alone in his quest, as a local man, Baram Blackett, was also researching the Dark Age Northumbrian dynasty. As they were therefore competing for access to the same books, it was only a matter of time before they met. Recognizing that it might bring mutual benefits, they agreed to collab-orate on their researches. This decision resulted in their setting up a private publishing house called M. T. Byrd & Co. Ltd, and in the early 1980s they set about publishing the results of their researches in the form of the series of large hardbound books my wife and I had seen when we arrived. Since then they had made many other intriguing dis-coveries concerning not just Arthur or even early Britain but the entire history of Europe before, during and immediately after the Roman Empire. What they had painstakingly unearthed, in the form of archives, inscriptions and other documentary evidence, threw a new light not just on King Arthur but on the whole origins of Christianity. Their work had not, though, been without its difficulties, foremost among which was the problem of convincing a sceptical academic world of the startling discoveries they had made over the years.

I was stunned and impressed by all Alan said. I believed his charge of academics ignoring traditional histories in favour of pet hypotheses of dubious value, for it was a response I had met before in other contexts in my work on *The Orion Mystery* and *The Mayan Prophecies*. Robert Bauval, my co-author on *The Orion Mystery*, had frequently met with opposition from the Egyptological establishment when trying to prove that the pyramids were essentially linked to a stellar cult and were not solar symbols; whilst writing *The Mayan Prophecies* I had discovered similar levels of prejudice in Mexico, where to even suggest that there

9

might have been transatlantic contact between the Old and New Worlds was to be tainted with the heresy of 'diffusionism', despite substantial evidence to prove the point.

Alan spoke convincingly and his dedication to his research was awesome. I quickly began to appreciate that, though the archives they had amassed over the years were enormous and growing, these were as nothing to his own encyclopaedic memory for names, dates and events. Indeed he seemed to be the living embodiment of the ancient traditions of the bards, charged as they were with keeping alive the memory of the Welsh.[3] I was keen to know more and asked Alan some questions concerning the article I had read the previous year. 'Is it true that you and Baram now own a church that could possibly be the resting place of King Arthur?' I asked.

He looked at me thoughtfully for a moment, perhaps judging whether or not this was the appropriate time to discuss such a delicate subject, before giving his reply. 'Yes and no,' he said in a measured tone and went on to explain.

'In the 1980s Baram and I bought what had been a church, the Church of St Peter's, before it had been allowed to become a vandalized ruin. It was a scheduled monument, and should have been protected as such, but unfortunately the Church of England, backed up by the local archaeological establishment, did not consider it to be of any value. Convinced that it was of "relatively late" construction – though one might have thought that with a date of construction of c. AD 1200 it was old enough to be worth conserving – they were not at all bothered that people were using it as a convenient quarry. From our own historical researches we had reason to believe that even if the building was only about seven hundred years old, the site was ancient, going back to the very dawn of Christianity in Britain.

'This became a highly contentious issue. When we publicized this view we ran into opposition from the local academic "Taffia", who went to the press and tried to discredit us by insisting that as the present building was only Norman the site wasn't worth investigating. We therefore decided to bring in professional archaeologists from outside the Cardiff area to excavate the ruins. To do so we had to get permission from the relevant authorities, and this was withheld throughout the spring and summer. We were eventually granted just four weeks in September in which to carry out our investigations.

'As the church lies up on a mountain and is open to the elements, our opponents probably thought this would be enough to stop us; but they hadn't reckoned on Baram's pertinacity. With financial support from many English friends, he chartered a helicopter and flew up there everything that we needed, including a huge marquee which covered the entire church. Under canvas the team of professional archaeologists, led by Dr Eric Talbot, were able to work day and night, under all weather conditions. As a result of this work, we were able to show that although part of the present building dates only from the thirteenth century, it stands on top of a succession of earlier buildings going right back to the second century – confirming what is written in the traditional histories.'

They found much more of interest besides, which Alan promised to tell me if we agreed to work together. For now, he said he would show me a stone that they had discovered in the church, which, he thought, I could find of more than passing interest.

Rising from his chair and beckoning us to follow, he then led us into a shed at the back of the house. There, standing in one corner, was a large slab, about four to five feet long and shaped vaguely like a letter 'T' with one arm broken off. Closer inspection revealed that it carried a Latin inscription, faint but recognizable, and all written in capitals. Looking carefully I could make out the following words: 'REX ARTORIVS FILI MAVRICIVS'. Though the Latin was grammatically imperfect, it was understandable, translating as: 'The King Arthur the son of Maurice'.

I was amazed to say the least. It seemed that – though it was yet to be proved to me – here, standing before me in a shed at the back of a Cardiff terrace, was what could possibly have been the very gravestone of King Arthur. Naturally I asked what sort of reaction their discovery had aroused from the archaeological community.

'Their attitude was almost entirely hostile,' Alan replied in sombre tone. He then described an episode when the BBC came to see what was going on. 'Having asked around about us, the BBC sent down a team who, after examining the stone for themselves, telephoned a professor at Glasgow University, who told them that the stone was a fake. When asked how he knew, he said he had seen photographs which showed that the writing was definitely not sixth century. Baram and I were puzzled by this, for at that time we hadn't sent anyone any photographs of the stone. Accordingly the producer asked where they could see other examples of sixth-century Welsh stones; we pointed them in the right direction and off they went. They came back later in the afternoon and called the same professor again. The producer told him they had spent the whole day looking at sixth-century stones and as far as they could tell, the style of lettering on the one we had found was identical. The professor now changed his story, stating that in his opinion the reason for any similarity was that we were clever forgers. The BBC, realizing that he had never actually seen either the stone or a picture of it, weren't taken in by this, and went ahead and made a piece for the national news.

'But it may interest you to see,' Alan went on, 'what Dr Eric Talbot, a senior archaeologist from the same university and perhaps better acquainted with Welsh stones than the other professor, had to say when he actually saw the stone for himself for the first time.' He handed me a piece of paper which had clearly been part of the proposal for the archaeological dig at the church. It contained the following paragraph, signed by Eric Talbot BA, FSA: 'The discovery of the Arthur stone at St Peter's has led to much controversy. The writer is, he believes, the first person with relevant qualifications to have examined the stone at first hand. In the writer's opinion the inscription it bears is one in accord, by wear and lettering, with the period of Arthur.'

It was perhaps unfortunate that they found the stone before the church was excavated; had it been discovered during an excavation, there would have been no question of a forgery. Despite Dr Talbot's support and even though enough other evidence was found during the subsequent dig to show that the stone was genuine, the archaeological establishment continued not to accept that it was genuine. 'We can only believe,' said Alan, 'that the sceptics don't want to give support to the idea that King Arthur was connected with south Wales and not Somerset.'

Going back into the house Alan was anxious to stress that these artefacts were only a tiny part of the evidence that he and his colleague Baram had uncovered for the existence of King Arthur in south Wales. Then, trusting that I wouldn't divulge its location before they were ready, he showed us a videotape they had taken of a secret site in west Wales. It showed what appeared to be a steep cliff-face surrounded by woodland. However, closer examination revealed that whilst part of the cliff was natural, much of it was in reality man-made, a wall blocking what appeared to be a secret cave. What was most startling was that carved partly on this wall and partly on the solid cliff above it was a cross. Even more astoundingly, Alan then confided in us that he and Baram had good reasons for believing that within this cave was concealed a real cross, possibly that of Jesus himself. I remembered then the words of the clairvoyant: 'You'll see it on a wall, a shape like this, and behind it there is a real one.'

Before seeing this video I was not certain that this was work I should involve myself with. However, from that moment onwards it became a matter of destiny. I had little doubt that Alan's and Baram's extraordinary discoveries would be of great interest to a large and increasingly receptive audience. We agreed that together we would write a book that would at last reveal the real history of King Arthur and the 'Holy Kingdom' as we have come to call it – the early Christian realm over which he ruled. Once and for all, we hoped we would slay the dragon of ignorance that has for so long prevented access to this extraordinary treasure.

Leaving Wales and driving back home to Dorset I was in a state of high euphoria. I was itching to go and see the cross but I realized that first I would have to do a lot of research of my own before I could properly judge the truth of the matter. Armed with copies of Alan's and Baram's books and with promises to supply me with any other information that I needed, I began my quest.

In the course of the next two years I made a number of journeys to Wales, meeting up with both Alan and Baram. They showed me various sites, including the real Camelot, King Arthur's legendary capital, and the site of the Battle of Baedan, his most famous battle against the Saxons. Travelling with them around the principality was an education in itself, for, unlike England, Wales retains its old place names and with them its memory of events long past. I discovered that in Wales, where the old native language of Britain has been preserved, the name for almost every hillock, valley and field is still meaningful and records the history of the area. Gradually, over a period of time, I was able to piece together Alan's and Baram's extraordinary story. The process was an ongoing adventure which constantly threw up fresh challenges. It was history in the raw: the constant sifting and reinterpretation of data in the light of new evidence. They brought to my attention many other old books and documents, much of the material either unknown to or ignored by academics. Using these documents it has at last been possible to draw up correct family trees and recreate the historical scenario of Britain in the first centuries AD; to give a coherent account of not just the reign of King Arthur but of how he fits into the larger picture of British history. As we brought the evidence together and as they took me round Arthurian sites and explained their extraordinary significance, it became apparent that far from being a Dark Age, where

Britain was concerned this was a time of great religious creativity.

My own views on British history went through a profound change. Unwittingly I found myself on a path of initiation that led from King Arthur to a wider and deeper understanding of what he and his dynasty stood for. I discovered that once there had been a 'Holy Kingdom' in Britain, a Christian kingdom during the Dark Ages that followed the collapse of the Roman Empire. The heartland of this kingdom was in Wales and it was closely linked with the very origins of Christianity in Europe. Though the conquest of England, first by the Saxons and then by the Normans, destroyed it as a political power, the memory of this kingdom has never been totally erased. Here and there amongst the detritus of modern-day living, like the bones of some great dinosaur, were its fragmentary remains. Unearthed, cleaned and pieced together they told its story: its birth, its struggles and final oblivion.

The issue of the Holy Kingdom is a matter not just for Wales but for England too. The old idea that as waves of Saxon immigrants arrived on the eastern shores of England, so the settled, indigenous population was driven out to take up residence in the mountainous regions of Wales, Scotland and Cornwall is no longer accepted. Modern archaeology reveals that, except in the coastal regions of East Anglia, Kent and perhaps further north into Yorkshire, many of the ancient Britons, or at least those who survived the incessant wars and natural catastrophes of the sixth century, stayed put. Over a period of time they intermixed and intermarried with first the Saxons and then later the Danes and Normans, who arrived in the ninth to eleventh centuries. The English of today are therefore more Welsh than they realize.

The same process happened in Scotland too, where the indigenous population of Britons was added to first by the Picts, who came from Scandinavia, then by the Saxons, and finally by the Scots, who arrived from Ireland only in the sixth century AD. Though for historical reasons Wales preserves to this day the indigenous language and history of the ancient Britons, its legacy is relevant to the whole of Britain, the English and Scots too, being in part descended from the ancient Britons. So too, it must be said, are the Americans, Canadians, Australians, New Zealanders and others of the British diaspora. Indeed the seed of the Holy Kingdom has been spread worldwide. That the truth about this kingdom should emerge now seems to me to be more than fortuitous, for today, for the first time in centuries, Wales and Scotland are to elect their own assemblies. Suddenly what is often called 'the matter of Britain' is becoming more relevant, perhaps as part of a greater rediscovery of the past in preparation for the next millennium; this seems to be our *Zeitgeist*. In this spirit and in all humility we offer the reader the fruits of these researches.

Because the story we reveal is significantly different from the hotch potch of lies and misinformation that in the main passes for Dark Age history and differs substantially from what is currently written in history books, we expect criticism from academic quarters. We know that what we have said is controversial. The truth, though, has its own luminance and I know our readers will be as excited as we are when they discover that there is an extraordinary legacy in Britain: remains of King Arthur's Holy Kingdom are visible to this day. We can but hope that the revelation of the secrets of the ages will not be in vain and that future generations will be more careful than our own in preserving this extraordinary inheritance and in safeguarding the many important sites connected with it.

CHAPTER ONE

THE ONCE AND FUTURE KING

Our story begins in 1136 with Geoffrey of Monmouth.[1] Nephew of the Archbishop of Llandaff, Geoffrey translated from Welsh into Latin a manuscript dated *c.* AD 937 and now known as *The History of the Kings of Britain*. Covering the long period from the aftermath of the Trojan War to around AD 689, this contains the first Anglo-Norman account of the life of King Arthur and was the book that sparked the extraordinary outpouring of Arthurian literature in the Middle Ages. Geoffrey, like everyone else of his era, believed that the ancient Britons were, in the main, descendants of *émigré* Trojans. He narrates how in Greece, three generations after the fall of Troy, Brutus (or Brwth), a great-grandson of Aeneas, founder of Rome, led a successful rebellion of Trojans against their Greek masters. Realizing that they would never be safe from attack if they remained in Greece, they took to the sea and sailed to a then un-inhabited island Geoffrey calls Leogetia. Here, whilst sleeping in the ruins of a temple, Brutus met the goddess Diana in a dream. She told him to take heart, and that they should carry on their voyage and sail beyond the Pillars of Hercules (the ancient name for the Straits of Gibraltar), where they would eventually find a large, verdant island; there, she said, they would be safe from their enemies and able to live in peace and prosperity.

The island was Britain and Brutus, like Moses leading the Israelites, brought his people to this promised land. Here, on the banks of the river Thames, he established a new capital, called at first Troia Nova[2] or Trinovantum, its name being changed shortly before the Roman invasions to Kaerllud.[3] This, according to Geoffrey, was later corrupted to Kaerlundein and later still to London.

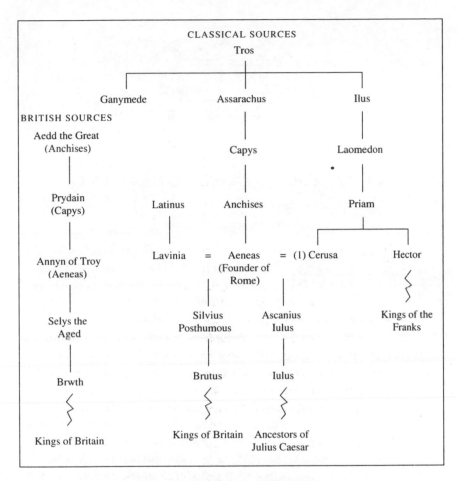

THE DESCENT OF BRUTUS
Diagram 1

Having lauded Brutus, the eponymous father of Britain, Geoffrey compresses centuries of history into a couple of chapters before coming to the next significant event in his history: the Roman invasions. He tells how Julius Caesar, who invaded Britain in 55–4 BC, was forced to make peace on honourable terms with the then ruler of south-east Britain, Cassivelaunus; and how nearly a century later Britain was again invaded by the Romans, this time by the Emperor Claudius. Though more successful than Caesar, according to Geoffrey, Claudius was able to bring to an end a disastrous war with Arviragus, then king over much of

17

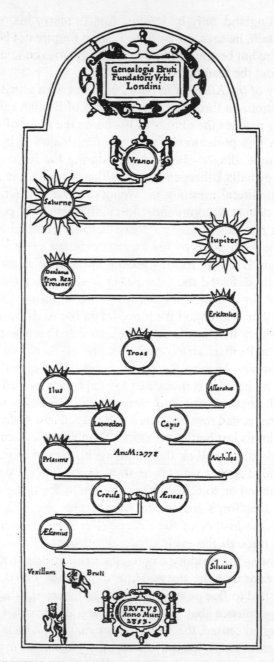

Genealogia Bruti
Fundatoris Vrbis
Londini

Vranos

Saturne

Iupiter

Dardanus
Prim Rex
Troianer

Erictonius

Troas

Ilus

Assaratus

Laomedon

Capis

Priamus

An:M:2778

Anchiles

Creula

Æneas

Ascanius

Siluius

Vexillum

Bruti

BRVTVS
Anno Mun:
2855.

THE BRUTUS TRADITION IN THE LATE RENAISSANCE
Diagram 2

what is now England, only by inviting him to marry his own daughter Genvissa. Britain, he says, entered the Roman Empire not because it had been conquered but because of this and other treaties concluded between the Romans and the leading royal houses.

The History of the Kings of Britain continues with a British-eye view of the occupation, on through to the collapse of Roman rule in AD 406, until Geoffrey reaches the climax of his book: the reign of King Arthur. Arthur's birth was portentous, for it was foreshadowed by the appearance of a strange, dragon-shaped 'star'[4] during the reign of his father, whom Geoffrey calls Utherpendragon (Utherpendragon is in fact a title not a name; its literal meaning is 'Wonderful Head of Dragons' and it was used to denote a commander-in-chief). Arthur is portrayed as a knightly king *par excellence*. As a true hero he excelled in all matters chivalrous, the high point of his career being his great victory at the Battle of Mount Baedan.[5] Here, wielding his sword Caliburn, he almost single-handedly defeated the then pagan invading Saxons and thereby saved Britain for Christ. Not content with securing his own land, Geoffrey's Arthur challenged the power of Rome itself by invading first Gaul (the territory that was later to develop into France) and then Italy. He defeated a Roman army at the Battle of Sassy and slayed the Emperor. However, he was forced to abandon these continental campaigns when he heard a rumour that his nephew Mordred, who during the King's absence abroad had been having a liaison with Arthur's queen, Guinevere, had revolted. Civil war ensued and Arthur returned to Britain to fight his last battle, the fateful Camblam (or Camlann). In this conflict Mordred, as well as thousands of his Saxon allies, was killed and the wounded Arthur was taken away, to the Isle of Avalon, and his crown was handed on to Constantine, the son of the Duke of Cornwall.

Thus ends Geoffrey's account of King Arthur and with it, one feels, his interest in the history of the Britons. The final chapter of the book runs quickly through the events leading up to the Saxon takeover of Britain, lamenting the disunity among the native British that allowed this to happen. It ends with the story of how the Britons, under a king called Cadwallader, had to flee *en masse* across the Channel to avoid a famine and strange pestilence that plagued the land of Britain for ten years. After the plagued ceased, the Saxons were easily able to take over most of the now nearly empty country, with only Wales, Cornwall and parts of the north being retained by the original Britons. According to Geoffrey, Cadwallader retired to Rome, where he died in AD 689. The final paragraph of the book praises the way the Anglo-Saxons (that is, the English), by not quarrelling amongst themselves and instead getting down to the serious business of cultivating fields and building cities, under their king, Athelstan,[6] succeeded in throwing off completely the dominion of the native Britons (that is, the Welsh) and thereby ruling over the whole of Loegres (England).

The question that has always dogged Geoffrey's *History of the Kings of Britain* is: does it contain a substratum of recognizable history or is it all fabulous invention? Was there indeed a king of Britain named Arthur and if so can he be placed in a known dynasty? Born around AD 1100 Geoffrey's real name was Gruffydd ap Arthur and he was well known as the nephew of the Bishop of Llandaff. We know that he had good English connections (he too was later a Bishop of Llandaff) and it is likely that he was ideally placed to have access to genuine historical records, although it is possible that in his account he distorted them. Geoffrey's principal dedicatee was Robert the Consul, Lord of Glamorgan and Earl of Gloucester, the most powerful baron in Britain, which may indicate that he had a political motive in translating the text. England at that time was in turmoil and about to enter a civil war, for following the death of Henry I his daughter Matilda was contesting the right of the new king, Stephen, to the throne. It is possible that Geoffrey was secretly encouraging Robert the Consul to take control of affairs and to seize the throne for himself. In any event, whatever may have been Geoffrey's political motives, *The History of the Kings of Britain* was to have great effect and indeed is still in print today.

In 1190, some fifty years after Geoffrey's translation, William of Malmesbury suggested that the history was a spoof. 'It is quite clear that everything that this man [Geoffrey] wrote about Arthur and his successors, or indeed about his predecessors from Vortigern onwards, was made up, partly by himself and partly by others, either from an inordinate love of lying, or for the sake of pleasing the Britons.'[7]

William was not, however, a dispassionate observer. He hated the Welsh and applauded the expulsion by Athelstan, the English king, of all Welshmen from Exeter to Cornwall, calling them 'polluted vermin'. It is clear that his dismissal of Geoffrey's *History* as pure invention stemmed partly from his adherence to the history of the Venerable Bede, an English monk and historian who also was steeped in anti-Welsh feeling, and partly out of a sense of personal vindictiveness. Following Geoffrey's death, William had been turned down for the post of Bishop of Llandaff, and he seems to have decided out of spite to besmirch not just his memory but the reputation of the whole Welsh race. The story of this is told by the Rev. Theophilus Evans in his book *Drych y Prifoesedd* ('Mirror of the Principal Ages'):

> When Jeffrey ap [son of] Arthur, Lord Bishop of Llandaff [Geoffrey of Monmouth], died, an Englishman of the name Gwilym Bach [little William or William the Less] arrived, of whom I have already spoke, who desired Dafydd ap Owen, Prince of Gwynedd, to make him Bishop in Jeffrey's place about the year 1169 AD. But when it was not in the mind of Dafydd ap Owen to grant him his request the man went home full of hatred and commenced to exercise his mind how best to despise and malign not only the memory of this bishop, who was lying in his grave, but also the whole of the Welsh nation . . . His [William of Malmesbury's] whole book is nothing else than a tissue of barefaced lies against the Welsh . . . Because Jeffrey ap Arthur did nothing but translate the Welsh Chronicles into Latin,[8] so that the educated of the country might read them.[9]

Whatever William of Malmesbury's motives, even today the attitude of academics towards Geoffrey's work is at best ambivalent. The late Dr John Morris, Senior Lecturer in Ancient History at University College, London, for example, writes:

> In the twelfth century, the spoof history of Geoffrey of Monmouth made Arthur a conqueror who subdued not only the Saxons, but most of Europe as well; Geoffrey's Arthur served the ambition of Plantagenet kings, but their subjects welcomed and perpetuated a different Arthur, the hero of the Norman poets, gentle, wise and courteous, whose chivalrous knights, just champions of the afflicted, were all that medieval lords should be but were not.[10]

THE LEGACY

Geoffrey could not have known what he was starting when he translated what he regarded as a simple history of his country. William of

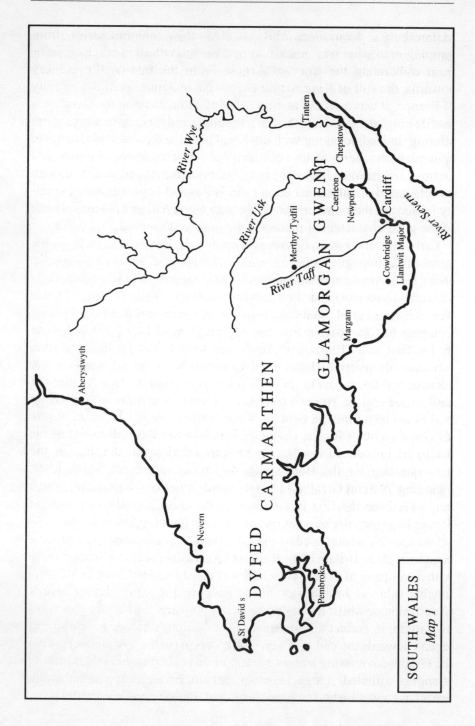

River Wye

River Usk

River Taff

River Severn

Tintern

Chepstow

Caerleon

Newport

Cardiff

Cowbridge

Llantwit Major

Merthyr Tydfil

Margam

GLAMORGAN

GWENT

CARMARTHEN

DYFED

Aberystwyth

Nevern

St David s

Pembroke

SOUTH WALES
Map 1

Malmesbury's accusations did not stop his contemporaries from jumping onto what was quickly to become an Arthurian bandwagon or from elaborating the story of Arthur. From the mid-twelfth century onwards, the cult of King Arthur caught the imagination of the nobility of Europe. It was as if the seeming lack of authentication for Geoffrey's profile only added to King Arthur's mystique and made him all the more alluring. Indeed he, along with his Knights of the Round Table, came to epitomize the very ideals of medieval chivalry. Soon French and German troubadours began to write Arthurian romances, which, though loosely based on tales emanating from Wales and England, were in reality fictions of their own creation. Through them, Arthur's position as one of the great characters of medieval romance was assured.

Early onto the bandwagon was Chrétien de Troyes, a poet from the court of Champagne in northern France. He wrote a series of poems: about King Arthur and his knights 'Érec', 'Cliges', 'Le Chevalier de la Charette' (Lancelot) and 'Le Chevalier au Loin' (Yvain). Most of these were written c. 1164–80 for the benefit of his principal patroness, Marie, Countess of Champagne. She was the daughter of Louis VII of France by his first wife, Eleanor of Aquitaine, who, following their divorce, subsequently married Henry II of England. Since both Louis VII and Eleanor had taken part in the near disastrous Second Crusade, it is not hard to see that de Troyes's romances are as much to do with crusader zeal in his own times as with Dark Age British history. In his *Le Conte du Graal* (written for the Count of Flanders and left unfinished at his death) he introduced another, more spiritual element: the idea of the hero questing for the Holy Grail. According to ancient Welsh texts, including 'Y Seint Greal' ('The Holy Grail') put together in 1106, which may have been the first full account of the Grail legend and which de Troyes in his privileged position at court was possibly aware of, this vessel was a dish or cup used at the Last Supper. It was supposed to have been brought to Britain by St Joseph of Arimathea when he arrived there with a company of exiles. The Grail was considered to be a relic of inestimable value as Joseph was said to have used it, either during Jesus's Crucifixion or whilst his body was being prepared for burial in Joseph's own tomb, to collect a few drops of the Saviour's blood. According to legend, towards the end of King Arthur's reign (in the late sixth century) the Grail went missing and, as a result of this calamity, his kingdom was strangely afflicted. Large areas of Britain became an uninhabitable wasteland and all who ventured there died. In de Troyes's story his hero,

Sir Gawain, has to make a long search – whether it was successful or not we do not know because the story is unfinished – for the mysterious Grail so that King Arthur's kingdom might be restored.

The Grail legend became immensely popular in its own right, Chrétien de Troyes's story containing all the elements of what was destined to become the most important *mysterium* of European literature. In France his unfinished story was added to and elaborated by four other authors with the figure of Perceval taking over from Gawain as the main hero of the quest. This theme was developed further in Robert de Boron's *Perceval* and in the *Perlesvaus* by an unknown writer. Another version of the Grail legend written at the beginning of the twelfth century, and possibly the best of the genre, was called *Perceval le Gallois ou le conte du graal*, known in its English translation as 'The High History of the Holy Grail'. By now the story of King Arthur and his Knights had all but disappeared except to form an almost invisible backdrop to the important business of the Grail Quest, and in this work holy fiction had almost completely displaced fact. The author, whose main concern was to tell a good yarn, shows little interest in the actual history of Britain.

Not only the French were interested in King Arthur and the Grail legend. Another highly influential work was *Parzifal*, a text composed around 1210 by a German knight or *ministeriales* called Wolfram von Eschenbach. In this work the process of divorce between actual history and 'historical narrative' was taken even further than in the French versions. Much, if not most, of the action takes place not in Britain or even Europe but in the Orient – a land made familiar to the nobility of Europe by the Crusades. As was now usual for the genre, von Eschenbach's heroes are not Arthur (called Artus in his text) and his queen, Guinevere (Ginover), though they do appear in supporting roles, but the questing knights: Gawan and Parzifal. In his account the Grail itself, though, as in the earlier stories, still a source of spiritual food and elixir of youth, is now a stone rather than a cup or dish from the Last Supper; and to von Eschenbach the Knights of the Round Table were prototypes of the Templars (a religious-military order of knights) of his own time. He writes:

> The host [a hermit] said: 'It is well-known to me that many a warlike knight lives at Munsalvaesche with the grail. For the sake of adventure they always go on many travels, these same Templars, whether they are looking for care or praise: they endure it for their

sins. There dwells a warlike host. I shall tell you about their food. They live off a stone. Its nature is very pure. If you have not recognized it, it will be named for you here: it is *lapsit excilis*. Through the stone's power the phoenix burns up so that it turns to ashes, but those ashes bring life to it. Therefore the phoenix throws off its molt and gives off a very bright glow afterwards, so that it becomes more beautiful than before. Also, never did such illness overcome a man that if he sees that stone one day he cannot die during the week that comes soonest after it . . . Such power does the stone give to man that his flesh and bone receive youth without delay. The stone is called the grail.'[11]

Why Wolfman should have thought of the Holy Grail as being a stone is not explained but it appears to act as some sort of magical altar. He describes how it hovers in the air whilst a dove, symbolic of the Holy Ghost, flies down from heaven and places a communion host upon it. The words *lapsit excilis* seem to be a corruption of the Latin *lapis excilis*, meaning 'paltry stone'. That such a seemingly valueless object should be the Grail seems to be a reference to Jesus Christ as the 'stone which the builder rejected becoming the chief stone of the corner'.[12] There is, however, another entirely different interpretation, which is that *lapsit excilis* should be read as *lapis ex caelis* – that is, a 'stone which has fallen out of heaven'. Now a stone that falls from heaven is a meteorite. Under this interpretation Wolfram, for whatever reason, seems to be linking a meteorite with the Grail legend.

The Arthurian romances of Chrétien de Troyes and Wolfram von Eschenbach inspired generations of later writers and imitators, in rather the same way that the original adventures of Captain Kirk in *Star Trek* have given birth to a host of imitators today. An important example of the genre was the English prose epic *Le Morte d'Arthur*, by Sir Thomas Malory, written whilst he was in Newgate Prison. Printed by Caxton in 1485, it was based upon a translation of 'Y Seint Greal'. It is Malory's version of the story that is best known to English readers and that has formed the basis of innumerable film and television epics based on the story of King Arthur and his Knights of the Round Table. Today a vast industry based around the legend of Arthur has grown. New books about King Arthur, his times or the Grail legend are being published regularly. The question remains, however: is there any substance to the legend? Was there ever a king of Britain called Arthur and what relationship, if any, did his kingdom have with legends concerning Joseph of Arimathea and the Holy Grail?

THE HISTORICAL ARTHUR

Side by side with the development of Arthur as a figure of literature has been a yearning for more tangible evidence of his life. The starting point for most historians and writers researching into the 'Age of Arthur' is the work of a monk named Gildas, who lived in the sixth century and allegedly wrote a history called *Gildae sapientis de excidio et conquestu Britanniae*, which may or may not be genuine,[13] and which was probably known to Geoffrey of Monmouth. In his short and pungent diatribe, which is more in the character of a sermon than a straightforward history, Gildas vehemently criticizes the Britons for not defending their own homeland following the Roman withdrawal in AD 406. According to Gildas, the Saxons were allowed to settle in eastern Britain ostensibly to fight as mercenaries against Pictish invaders from Scotland (or Albyne as this northern part of Britain was then called). He names Vortigern as the British king responsible for inviting in the Saxons, led by Hengist and Horsa. Realizing the weakness of Vortigern's position, the Saxons soon rose in revolt, causing immense destruction to man and property. This revolt was eventually quashed by a British leader named Ambrosius Aurelianus, but Gildas informs us that a second Saxon war erupted only a couple of generations later. This was a more protracted affair, interrupted by a prolonged interlude of peace after the British victory at the Battle of Badon Hill (or Mount Baedan; the spelling varies). Gildas doesn't name Arthur as the British king responsible for this victory, but he does agree that such a battle was fought. This, in outline, is substantially the same history as recorded by Geoffrey but told in a defeatist as opposed to a triumphalist spirit. Like Geoffrey, Gildas tells of a great famine and disease that for a while rendered the island of Britain virtually uninhabitable and led to a mass migration of the British to the continent. However, he goes to extremes in lambasting the Britons for their slack moral attitudes which caused this to happen. He attributes the catastrophe to God's punishment for the sins of the nation, lamenting, as churchmen are wont to do, that it was loss of faith that brought about the destruction of the nation.

Another more or less accepted authority is a compilation of records, called simply *Historia Britonum*, dated *c*. 800, by a Welshman called Nennius. This book is quite different in tone from Gildas's: it covers much the same ground, providing useful details, but is without Gildas's turgid sermonizing. It is the earliest reference to King Arthur to be found in the generally known and accepted histories of Britain and is widely quoted as the earliest to refer to Arthur by name as the hero of twelve battles, including that at Mount Baedan. Nennius makes the odd remark that at the time of the battle Arthur was not yet a king, which has puzzled many commentators, who have wrongly assumed that this meant that Arthur was either not of royal blood or was still a boy. The facts that other Welsh records show that Arthur's father lived to be a very old man and that at the time of the Battle of Baedan Arthur was still only a viceroy, suggest that Nennius based his history on real events.

Most of what has been written about King Arthur focuses on the mythical Arthur. However, one recent attempt at genuine historicity is *The Age of Arthur* by Dr John Morris of University College, London, who writes in his introduction, 'The interpretation here given of the Arthurian Age can be no more than a preliminary attempt to open up question, and to make it easier for future specialist studies to relate their conclusions to a wider context. The book is therefore published in the confident expectation that many of its conclusions will soon be modified or corrected.'[14]

Not all have shared his open-minded approach and today the true, historical Arthur remains a shadowy figure, partly because many twentieth-century authors have, unfortunately, muddied the waters.

In 1966–70, as Alan Wilson had mentioned, an excavation was carried out in Somerset, at South Cadbury hill fort under the auspices of Leslie Alcock as director and Geoffrey Ashe as secretary of the excavation committee. They concluded that as the hill fort on South Cadbury, which is close to the village of Queen Camel, showed signs of having been refortified during the sixth century – the period of King Arthur – it was 'quite probably Camelot'.[15] In fact the name 'Queen Camel' dates not from the Dark Ages but from 1534. In his *History*, Geoffrey of Monmouth had claimed that Arthur fought against the Romans. In 1532 Henry VIII's court historian Polydore Vergil stated the obvious: that if Arthur had fought against the Romans he would have had to be at least 200 years old when he took on the sixth-century Saxons. This inclined Vergil to favour the argument that Geoffrey's King Arthur was a 'spoof'. But John Leland, Henry VIII's leading antiquarian, was incensed by this.

He was keen to establish both the authenticity of Arthur and that he came from his own county of Somerset. He therefore faked place names around Cadbury Hill in his *King's Itinerary* of 1534, to show that King Arthur's fabled castle of Camelot was originally on this site. In his own book, *Arthur's Britain*, Alcock admits that this was a forgery on Leland's part, but he nevertheless carried on digging the site for seven years as though it really were 'Camelot'. He seemed happy to perpetuate the fiction, referring to South Cadbury castle as 'Cadbury–Camelot' in the index of his book.

Alcock's work, based on Leland's false identification of Somerset with the kingdom of King Arthur, has clouded matters ever since. In particular, it gave rise to the modern notion that King Arthur has no recognizable identity other than as a British leader resisting the Saxon invaders. It also promoted a widely held view that this leader was little more than a local clan-chieftain in a society that had reverted to a semi-savage, pre-Roman past. Today general consensus amongst academics is that though there probably was a Romanized British leader called Arthur living in the sixth century, he was a warlord fighting a rearguard action against the Saxon invasions. In this way the historical if not the literary Arthur was devalued from paramount British king to a nondescript brute ruling over a few hill forts in southern England. Moreover, ignorant of the evidence available concerning his real identity, his would-be biographers have created a plethora of Arthurs from the tip of Cornwall to the Highlands of Scotland. It was against this background that Alan and Baram had taken on the challenge of finding out the truth about the historical King Arthur.

CHAPTER TWO

THE SECRET INHERITANCE OF WALES

When Alan Wilson began his researches into the lost kingdom of Arthur he was aware that Wales figured prominently in the legends. As the Welsh language goes back to long before the coming of the Romans, and its people, who were never conquered by the Saxons, have lived in the same place for at least two and a half thousand years, one would expect to find more evidence preserved in Wales than in England, which has a less continuous cultural past, for the lost semi-legendary kingdom of Arthur. During subsequent conversations Alan told me more about the voluminous writings in Welsh still in existence concerning the history, religious beliefs and traditions of the Khymry,[1] the people from whom the Welsh and indeed to a large part the English – perhaps more than they realize – are descended. It is therefore surprising that he should have found what appeared to be a conspiracy of silence surrounding these important documents. It is almost as though a decision was taken long ago to hide these records of the early history of Britain from ordinary people, the subject being too hot to handle.

What little mention is made in today's history books about Wales in the Dark Ages implies that it was something of a cultural backwater compared with the emergent kingdoms of Northumbria, Wessex and Mercia. Yet Alfred the Great, the Wessex king who ruled over most of England in the late ninth century, sent to Wales for scholars to set up what was later to become Oxford University. His friend and biographer, Asser,[2] was the Bishop of St David's in west Wales long before he met Alfred and it was only with great difficulty that he could be persuaded to move to England and take up an important post in the King's retinue. It is quite clear, once one puts aside national pride and prejudice, that during the Dark Ages Wales was in fact an important centre of learning – as indeed it had been in the times of the Druids. Why, then, is there still today a bias against using Welsh historical records concerning the Dark Age history of Britain?

Part of the answer to this conundrum is hinted at by John Morris, who writes of the difficulty of bringing together the right material for study:

> The evidence must first be collected. Most of the main texts are printed, but many are to be found only in large or specialist libraries. They cannot be studied unless they are assembled for constant reference and comparison.
>
> ... The difficulty of getting at the sources is one of the main reasons why the period is so poorly understood; for any historical study is lame if it can only be undertaken by a few experts, whose judgement their readers cannot easily criticise. If the Arthurian period is to be studied seriously in the future, the first need is to make the sources accessible, no longer the secret lore of the learned.[3]

During my first visit to Cardiff I asked Alan about this, why it was that I, an Englishman, knew so little about Wales or its history. With a shrug of the shoulders he replied that he was not surprised. 'Few people, even in Wales itself,' he said, 'know the true history of Britain in the Dark Ages. Lack of availability of primary source material has undoubtedly been a problem for English researchers and is one of the reasons why so many Arthurian books, such as Leslie Alcock's *Arthur's Britain*, are so wide of the mark, but this is not the whole story.' He explained his view that it is clear to the unbiased researcher that for various reasons – religious as well as political – Welsh historical records have, through the ages, been deliberately suppressed by the English establishment (as he would subsequently explain). It is true that few original manuscripts have survived, one reason being that from 1100 onwards large numbers of these precious documents were transferred to the Tower of London, usually as the personal libraries of Welsh princes held captive there, and these records would probably today be in the library of the British Museum, or some other august institution, were it not that at some time around 1300 a monk named Ysgolan took it upon himself to burn the majority of them.[4] Centuries of chaos, Viking raids, the devastation caused by Henry VIII's closure of the monasteries and plain old neglect also took their toll, causing many records to be lost. Where they have survived they have, unfortunately, been largely ignored as being either unreliable or too late in composition to be relevant. Neither claim is true. Further, whilst it is true that, in common with almost the whole world apart from Egypt, Britain has a climate that is not conducive to the preservation of old manuscripts, this does not mean that all the information contained in old documents has been lost. Important writings, such as histories, genealogies and poems, were copied and recopied by scribes through the ages, preserving their content for future generations. Indeed this was one of the chief duties of pre-Christian bards (and later on medieval monks) who were charged with preserving as much as possible of this national heritage.[5] The accusation that Welsh sources are too late to be relevant because the earliest copies that have come down to us date only from the Middle Ages is both unfair and short-sighted.

Nevertheless we have to be realistic about Welsh sources. If the same criteria for authenticity that are demanded for Welsh documents were applied to Roman and Greek histories, our ancient historians would be so short of source material that they would have to look for other jobs.

Why copies of Latin texts should be considered admissible and Welsh ones not is partly a matter of prejudice, but there have also been problems for modern English-speaking scholars in getting access to reliable translations of this material from the Welsh. This has much to do with politics and the suppression, over the centuries, of the Welsh language and culture, with the result that Welsh is not widely spoken today.

Today when crossing over the Severn Bridge on the M4 motorway, travellers are often amazed to discover that all signs for services, directions, exits and roadworks are written not just in English but also in Welsh, even though only about 20 per cent of the population of Wales speaks Welsh and 100 per cent speaks English. But fortunately, over the last few decades and as a result of local pressure, the enormous cultural value of possibly the oldest language in Europe has slowly become recognized. Today it is taught in most Welsh schools and in many places even the children of English parents have to learn it. As a result, after centuries of decline, the number of Welsh speakers is now on the increase and the language is no longer threatened with extinction. However, the actions of the London government have not always been so benign when dealing with Wales and particularly with Welsh historical records. In the past, positive steps were taken to destroy not only the language but the entire culture of Wales.

The first to make an outright attempt at suppressing the Welsh language was Richard II (1367–1400). Though a cultured and in many ways admirable man – certainly in comparison with his uncouth successor – he attempted to prohibit writing in Wales. This was a punitive measure, as he was anxious to prevent bardic propaganda from urging insurrection and to prevent communication between Welsh princes. After Richard II was deposed by his cousin, Henry Bolingbroke, in 1399, Henry IV (as he became) took his cousin's strategy a stage further. He was faced with the rebellion of Owain Glyndwr, a prince who was backed by the French, rebel Irish and Scots, and, in alliance with Henry Percy (Shakespeare's 'Hotspur') and his brother-in-law Sir Edmund Mortimer, posed a serious threat to Henry's illegal regime. When, after some fourteen years of independence under Owain, Wales was brought back under the control of the English crown, Henry IV had an act of Parliament passed prohibiting the importation of all writing materials and equipment into Wales.

When the printing press was brought to England by William Caxton in 1476,[6] Richard III, who was crowned king in 1483, immediately recognized the danger posed by this new and powerful technology. He was particularly concerned at the way it could be used to spread propaganda in support of his rival, the Welsh pretender Henry Tudor, who was then Earl of Richmond and who was planning an invasion from Brittany. Accordingly, Richard set up prohibitions on the use of printing presses outside London and especially in Wales, where Henry could expect to be well received. On 22 August 1485 Richard III was defeated and killed at the Battle of Bosworth and Henry VII (Tudor) took the throne. However, though he relaxed the laws prohibiting the possession of writing materials in Wales, he maintained controls over printing and publishing. It was not until 1694 that an act of Parliament allowed printing presses to be set up in Wales.

It might have been expected that the Tudors, being of Welsh stock themselves, would be sympathetic to their fellow countrymen and their traditions. This, however, would be to overlook the historic rivalry between north and south Wales, which often overshadowed the dealings of both regions with England. Henry VII, who came from north Wales, was intent not only on establishing himself and his dynasty on the throne of England but on undermining the ancient traditions associated with Glamorgan. His son, Henry VIII, sought to unite the two countries of England and Wales under common laws with one language. An Act of

Union was passed in 1536, which divided Wales into thirteen counties, each of which would thenceforth send two representatives to the parliament in Westminster. In 1542 a further 'Act for certain Ordinances in the King's Majesty's dominion and Principality of Wales' was passed, setting up a court in Wales with powers equivalent to the Star Chamber in England. It also set up courts of justice with the title 'the king's great sessions in Wales' to sit three times a year in every county. All old Welsh laws and customs which were at variance with those in England were abolished, and it was also enacted that all legal procedures in Wales should be conducted in English. This obviously made any legal procedures very difficult for monoglot Welsh speakers, as they now had to use interpreters, and was clearly intended to be a direct attack upon the language. Speaking Welsh meant you were uneducated in English, and so it became a sign of peasant status.

State controls over publishing in Wales remained tight as first the Renaissance and then the Reformation rocked the foundations of the European establishments. During the English Civil War between King and Parliament, the Royalist gentry and priests took advantage of the situation of less than 10 per cent of Welsh yeomanry and peasants being able to understand English by spreading misinformation and propaganda in support of Charles I. After the Battle of St Fagan's, Oliver Cromwell saw to it that an educational programme was quickly put into place in Wales and thereafter Welsh support rapidly switched to the Parliamentary Party. Within months of the King's beheading in 1649, Cromwell exacted his revenge on the established Church by passing through Parliament an 'Act for Better Propagation and Preaching of the Gospel in Wales'. Under this act, a nominated body of seventy commissioners was given virtually unlimited powers to deal with all ecclesiastical matters in Wales. Setting to their task with alacrity, they expelled some 330 out of 520 incumbents in the dioceses of St David's and Llandaff alone; similar measures were taken elsewhere. This high-handed interference in ecclesiastical matters caused an outcry, and a petition, signed by Puritans and high churchmen alike, was presented in Parliament by the Attorney-General for Wales, Colonel Edward Freeman. He declared that by the misguided policy of ejectment and destruction 'the light of the Gospel was almost extinguished in Wales'. Though the act was repealed and, following the restoration of Charles II, those churchmen still alive reinstated, the events left lasting resentment. During this time many more Welsh historical records, which did not fit in with the 'political correctness' of the time, were lost.

The Stuarts and later the Hanoverians traced their lineage back to Scotland and were therefore little interested in Welsh traditions, still less the language. When in 1840 Queen Victoria married Prince Albert, his German origins led to something of a 'Saxon' revival in England, with, for example, the growth of a cult around Alfred, the ninth-century hero-king of Anglo-Saxon England who resisted the incursions of the Vikings. Indeed it was the Victorians who began calling him 'Alfred the Great'. Before then he was best remembered as 'the king who burnt the cakes'. The version of Dark Age history portrayed in *The Anglo-Saxon Chronicle*, which was begun at Alfred's instigation, was therefore taken as true. Naturally, being a Saxon record of events, it has little to say concerning setbacks in the Saxon conquest of Britain and, though it does mention one or two Welsh princes, is silent on the subject of King Arthur. This did not stop Victorian painters and romantics from reworking the legend of Arthur and thoroughly identifying his core kingdom with Cornwall, Devon and Somerset. The knowledge, contained in Welsh histories, that the real personage of this name who fought the Saxons was really a Welsh king with a traceable ancestry became, in time, completely forgotten outside Wales.

Further pressure on the Welsh language and culture came in 1846, when a Parliamentary commission was set up to investigate teaching in Welsh schools. In Wales this event is remembered as the 'Treachery of the Blue Books', as the commissioners made their reports in blue-covered folders. On the strength of the evidence presented in these reports, Parliament passed an act forbidding the teaching of the Welsh language in schools. All children were to be taught only in English and any child speaking so much as a word of Welsh was to be punished. Since the vast majority of children at that time came from families where Welsh was the only language spoken in the home, this was a gross violation of human rights, equivalent to the banning of Kurdish in eastern Turkey today.

First all Welsh teachers were replaced with English ones. To enforce the ban, the 'Welsh knot' was introduced into the classroom. This was a heavy piece of wood strung onto a length of rope, which struck fear into the hearts of the children. Any child who inadvertently uttered the forbidden language had the dreaded 'Welsh knot' placed around his or her neck. The next child to make the same mistake had the feared token passed over to them, and so it went on for the rest of the day. At the end of classes the one unfortunate enough to be wearing the infamous collar was caned as an example to the rest. This system carried on being enforced until modern times: there are still people alive today who are either old enough to remember it themselves or who recall stories about it told to them by their parents and grandparents. Examples of 'Welsh knots' can be seen in museums today. The system was clearly effective and is the main reason why today only about 20 per cent of the population of Wales is able to speak Welsh; these mainly in more remote, rural areas. Unable to read their own language, the Welsh people largely lost confidence in their own historical records, though some of the traditions were kept alive and even as recently as the 1920s a few school books taught that King Arthur was a local king, ruling over south Wales and not Somerset.

To reinforce the position of what was now a German dynasty on the British throne, a concerted effort, led by Bishop Stubbs, was made to rewrite the history of Britain. The teaching of history at Oxford, and therefore throughout the rest of Britain, was changed to fit the contemporary Anglo-Saxonism. Welsh records concerning the early history of Britain before and after the Saxon invasions were disregarded in an attempt to play up the importance of the later Anglo-Saxon kingdoms. The Lloegrian[7] inheritance of England was also ignored, the implication (wrongful, as we have seen) being that since the ancient Britons had been effectively 'ethnically cleansed' to the 'Celtic' fringes of the island by the Anglo-Saxons, their history was of no significance to the English. Unfortunately this historical propaganda put out by Stubbs – and, as we have seen, even earlier under the Hanoverians – persists to this day, with the result that Welsh sources are often overlooked; and with the suppression of the language, when they are sought, few can read them.

THE SCHOLARS SPEAK WITH FORKED TONGUES

In the course of our conversations, Alan also told me how the cause of the Welsh and their venerable history was not helped by the dishonesty of certain of their own scholars. At the time the British Empire (for which, he points out, one might more properly read English Empire) was reaching its zenith, there was a desire amongst many Welsh people to be equal participants in this great 'British' enterprise. The strong and unfortunate bias in nineteenth-century England against accepting Welsh historical records as being authentic was made worse by the gross mistranslation and misrepresentation of Khymric poetry by several eminent Welsh scholars of the day. The first of these was the Rev. Robert Williams, who made a number of appalling translations of Welsh triads.[8] This would not have mattered had his work not been widely circulated. Williams had little knowledge of early British history and seems to have been more interested in making his translations sound poetic English than in being faithful to the original Welsh.[9]

An even worse mistranslator of Welsh texts was Thomas Stephens. Whereas Williams had merely made amateurish mistakes in his translations, Stephens set out consciously to change Welsh history. Keen that Wales should partake fully of the fruits of the British Empire and not be seen as a country apart on the fringes of Europe, he even wrote that in order to persuade the English to respect Welsh history it was necessary for that history to be rewritten. His translations of some important texts were patently absurd and should have been denounced. An example of this is the poem 'Hoianau' by Merddyn Wylt (Martin the Wild) and probably written around 580–600. When properly translated, the first line reads as: 'Listen to the supreme secret of the holy estate and show respect for renewed intelligence.' Stephens translates this as: 'Listen, O little pig, O happy little pig.' How he arrived at this nonsense is itself illuminating. Speculating that Martin the Wild was living in the Forest of Celydon when he wrote the poem, he took this idea a stage further and suggested that his only companion was a pig. He therefore found it credible that Martin should address his poem to the pig.

To the blunderings of Williams and Stephens was added the august weight of a respected professor, J. Gwenogfran Evans. In 1872 a college was founded at Aberystwyth, which in 1889 became Wales's first university since the destructions of the eleventh century. (As all the staff were trained in England, the historical curriculum reflected the attitude of Stubbs and his contemporaries.) Evans was a professor at this new university. He had been schooled in England and knew little about real Welsh history. Being faced with two histories, one based on the narrow records of relatively poor but Tudor-phile north Wales and the other on the much wider heritage of the more populated and prosperous south-east of the country, he sided with the north, which was to be expected, as north Wales was where he came from. He was also prepared to discount all historical records from before 1200. One example of his preposterous reasoning was his labelling of a fifth-century poem, 'Y Goddodin', which concerns a massacre of British lords at a peace conference *c*. 456, as another version of three 1198 poems. Having made this false connection, he then berated its authors for not using the strict twelfth-century Cynhanged poetic style.

In other cases, declaring that he knew so much about poetry that he could tell when words had been added or subtracted through the centuries by incompetent bards, he 'corrected' texts at will. He also claimed to know through intuition when words or the order of verses had been changed and put these 'right'. In his own published work he admits that in one poem of just 6,300 words he made 3,400 word changes, and that even this is not a complete list. Unfortunately, English scholars, who could not be expected to have such subtle insights into Welsh poetry, tended to shy away from the whole subject and accepted his simple pronouncement that there was nothing of value before 1200.

As if all this were not enough, early in the twentieth century Griffith John Williams, another self-styled expert in Welsh poetry who also came from north Wales, set his face against the Khymric inheritance of Glamorgan. Revering the undoubtedly fraudulent work of his teacher, J. G. Evans, he became very popular with the fledgling BBC and spread abroad the idea that there were no reliable Welsh records from before 1200. This was not true. At the turn of the nineteenth century huge numbers of early poems and other hitherto unpublished manuscripts had been gathered together and published by three independent researchers. This was no mean feat as much of this material had never before been printed: the Welsh having, as we have seen, been barred from printing books in their own language until 1694, it was preserved for centuries in handwritten form only. Whereas in England the sixteenth and seventeenth centuries saw an explosion of print and the building of new libraries, such as the Bodleian in Oxford, to house national, literary treasures, most Welsh literature remained in private hands. People were afraid that if they publicized the fact that they had such material in their possession there was a danger, for political or religious reasons, that it would be seized and destroyed. Responsibility for preserving the extraordinary Khymric inheritance, therefore, fell to certain individuals and families. Manuscripts, poems, king lists (that is, lists of successive monarchs) and other archives were handed down from generation to generation without scholars from Oxford or London being any the wiser.

From 1800–6, the three most eminent Khymric scholars of their day,

Owen Jones, William Owen Pughe and Edward Williams (popularly known as Iolo Morganwg and whose name is pronounced 'Yolo' as in 'polo'), worked together to bring these documents out of hiding and to publish them in modern form under the title *Myvyrnian Archaiology*. These documents were mostly drawn from private collections and consisted of historical poetry, Khymric history and triads. In their foreword the scholars write:

> The existence of very ancient Welsh Manuscripts, in prose and verse, has been announced considerably more than two centuries ago: many respectable English writers have expressed a degree of surprise, and even regret, that these valuable remains of antiquity have never been consigned to the press; and so long have their expectations been disappointed, that hints and even assertions, have of late been thrown out, that we have none, or none that are authentic; we will however, advise such as entertain this opinion to suspend their judgement until the completion of this publication . . .
>
> In every other nation of Europe such venerable monuments of ancestral celebrity, in the possession of ancient and opulent families, would have been long ago produced to the world with a degree of exaltation that would have been very laudable; but it has not been so in Wales.[10]

To prove the authenticity of their sources and to avoid accusations of scholastic revision, they published their volume in the original Welsh. This, of course, meant that it was still impenetrable for English speakers, which is perhaps the main reason their work was largely ignored. However, for anyone versed in Welsh and willing, where needed, to transliterate the *Coelbren*[11] script into our modern alphabet, it is readily accessible. For as the editors themselves say: 'they [the writings] contain very few, if any words, either radicals or derivatives, that are not at this day of common use, in one part or other of Wales; nor have many of these words materially changed their acceptation. Our language, as some have imagined, is not altered.'[12] Whether the blame for the suppression of these documents can fairly be laid at the doors of their owners is arguable. Of greater importance is the fact that they have at least survived, for contained in this collection are the poems of Taliesin, the 'Merlin' of later tradition.

Unfortunately, G. J. Williams, of BBC fame, found it necessary to destroy the reputation of his long-dead namesake, Edward Williams, and in the 1930s began a series of scurrilous attacks implying that the latter was a fraudster and a drug-addict – charges which were simply untrue. This cut at the heart of Khymric studies and, given the prestige of G. J. Williams's position and his access to the media, set back the study of Glamorgan history by some fifty years.

Fortunately there is a large amount of other Welsh material in existence verifying the authenticity of the work contained in the *Myvyrnian Archaiology*. Indeed, as a result of the efforts of Alan's friend Brian Davies, more and more original manuscripts whose existence was referred to by Iolo and his friends in the *Myvyrnian Archaiology* are now coming to light. This material, much of it totally unknown to Robert Williams, Thomas Stephens, J. G. Evans and G. J. Williams, has been closely examined by Alan and Baram. It is this inheritance, so long suppressed or discredited, but which Alan and Baram believe is authentic, that forms the research basis of the present work.

CHAPTER THREE

THE LLANDAFF CHARTERS

Central to our story is the issue of whether Arthur was a genuine historical personality. To this end Alan and I made our way to Llandaff, on the outskirts of Cardiff, where stands Wales's most historic cathedral. On our way Alan explained to me the basis of his and Baram's work.

He began by telling me more about Geoffrey of Monmouth, or Gryffyd ap Arthur, as Alan called him, who wrote *The History of the Kings of Britain*. Geoffrey was pilloried, as we have seen, by critics such as William of Malmesbury, who accused him of fraud. In fact Geoffrey, poor man, was only acting on the instructions of his superior, Walter, Archdeacon of Oxford, and translating a book that already existed from Welsh into Latin. This book, known as the *Brut Tysylio* (named after its believed author St Tysylio, a seventh-century Welsh saint), still exists. It was one of the documents published in Welsh as part of the *Myvyrnian Archaiology*, and a new English translation of it was brought out in 1811 by a London bookseller. It is true that Geoffrey added extra colour, extending and elaborating some of the stories contained in the original, but fundamentally his book is a faithful translation of the original. The problems with this original, such as they are, stem from the fact that the author, presumably St Tysylio, was not familiar with ancient British genealogies. Alan and Baram assume that when the book was written, its author did not have available all the references we have today. This is not surprising as he was writing under adverse conditions, at a time when England had been taken over by the Saxons and Scotland by the Scots, and most of the surviving Welsh had fled overseas to Brittany to escape a catastrophic plague that swept the land. Because of this the author made some stupendous mistakes which have unfortunately cast a cloud of suspicion over the rest of his work, much of which is very good. Also, whilst he was keen to play up the achievements of his nation, he had to square these with the political realities of his own day. At that time there was a serious rift between the Apostolic British Church and the Papacy, but little is mentioned about this in the chronicle and what is said tends to favour Roman orthodoxy. We can only assume that either Tysylio himself was being politically cautious in what he said concerning the British Church or, more likely, his manuscript has in part been tampered with by later copyists.

Alan explained that in his and Baram's work, given that such sources were a mixture of reliability and unreliability, they decided that the only sensible way to research the subject of King Arthur was to use the genealogies as their framework (genealogies are family trees in word form, e.g. John son of Adam, son of Paul, etc.). Through them they would be able to correctly interpret the evidence for the Arthurian kingdom that undoubtedly still exists in historic sites.

One such site is Llandaff Cathedral, at which we were now arriving. Though the present building is quite modern, having been rebuilt in the mid nineteenth century and heavily restored after being damaged in the Second World War, it stands on the site of what is reputed to be one of the very first Christian churches in Britain – founded at around AD 150. Surprisingly, the present church lies nestling at the foot of a steep embankment and well below the level of the road leading to it. This detail alone points to the antiquity of the site, for, unlike later churches, which were generally placed on high ground to be seen for miles around, early foundations tend to have been positioned with easy access to water, in this case the nearby River Taff.

I parked the car in the road above and we made our way down a steep staircase to the west door of the cathedral, Alan keeping up a steady commentary as we went. As cathedrals go, though it was nicely proportioned, it was by no means large. Inside, it was light and airy with all the snugness of a parish church and none of the cold, intimidating grandeur of a Durham or Canterbury Cathedral. Though most of the fabric of the building was Victorian, some old and interesting details had been retained. Well above eye height, protruding from one of the walls, was a curious sculpted head. It had three faces, cleverly juxtaposed on three sides in such a way that they shared eyes. There was something very powerful about this head, whose eyes looked in all directions and which clearly represented the Holy Trinity. Alan told me that there were once many of these heads in Welsh churches but, as they were later regarded as pagan and prohibited by Rome, the rest have long since been removed and destroyed. We were lucky this one example has survived to give us some insight into the ways of thinking of the early Christians, whose ideas were clearly influenced by Gnosticism.

As we walked through the cathedral, Alan explained that as a very old foundation, it was extremely important to our quest for the real King Arthur. To understand why, we must look at the history surrounding it. When England was invaded by the Normans in 1066, Wales was independent of England, and the kingdom of Glamorgan, which at that time encompassed the modern counties of Gwent and Brecon as well as what we would know as Glamorgan today, was ruled over by a king called Iestyn ap Gwrgan.[1] According to Welsh histories, the south Welsh might have been allies of the English against the Normans, had they not already fallen out with King Harold Godwinson. As it was, Iestyn was engaged in his own fratricidal conflict with a rival dynasty from west Wales. To aid him in his battles against Rhys ap Tewdwr, the prince of that region, in 1091 he called in Norman mercenaries under the leadership of Sir Robert Fitzhammon. The battle having been won, the mercenaries departed and Iestyn's army stood down. However, the Normans, having taken note of the fertility of the land and well aware of Iestyn's weakness, returned in their ships that same night and seized the castles of the Plain of Glamorgan.

Caught unawares, Iestyn was powerless to resist and fled to Bristol. Sir Robert Fitzhammon was able to inform his liege lord, William Rufus, the son of William the Conqueror, that his conquest of south Wales had been successful. He kept the rights of Iestyn, which included Cardiff Castle, Dindryfan, Dinas Powys, the manors of Boverton and Llantwit Major, the manor of Cowbridge and many other royal estates, for himself. As the new Lord of Glamorgan, he then proceeded to share out other spoils with his retainers. Thus was brought to an end the centuries-old kingdom of Glamorgan.

Later a lady called Nest, the strikingly beautiful daughter of Iestyn, became associated with Henry I, the youngest son of William the Conqueror, who succeeded his brother William Rufus to the throne of England in 1100. They had an illegitimate son called Robert, who married Mabilia, the daughter of Sir Robert Fitzhammon and his sole heiress. Robert was created Earl of Gloucester by his father Henry and

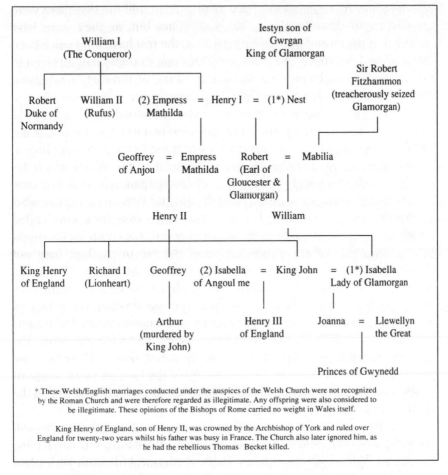

THE NORMANS IN WALES AFTER 1091
Diagram 3

later, on the death of his father-in-law, inherited the title of Lord of Glamorgan.

Earl Robert was a very powerful baron, trusted enough by his father, Henry I, to act as a gaoler to the latter's other brother, Robert, Duke of Normandy. This nobleman, the eldest son of William the Conqueror and a hero of the First Crusade, ought, by the right of primogeniture, to have inherited the throne of England. A combination of bad luck, poor political judgement and defeat at the Battle of Tinchebrai in 1106 meant that he was denied this prize and instead he was incarcerated in Cardiff

43

Castle until his death in 1134. When in 1145 Henry I died, his illegitimate son Robert, Earl of Glamorgan and Gloucester became *ipso facto* the most powerful man in Britain. This is one reason why he was the principal dedicatee of Geoffrey of Monmouth's *History of the Kings of Britain*. He could have made a bid for the throne himself, for although like his grandfather, William the Conqueror, he was illegitimate he was also, through his mother, a direct descendant of the ancient kings of Britain. However, in the civil war that followed Henry I's death and Stephen's accession, Earl Robert settled for the role of king-maker rather than making a bid for the crown himself.

The Norman takeover of the Vale of Glamorgan had another and, from our point of view as historians, fortuitous effect. For as well as taking over properties from Iestyn, the Norman nobles seized lands belonging to the Church. Particularly badly affected was the cathedral of Llandaff, which was shorn of many valuable estates, some of which had been in its possession for centuries. Its loss was exacerbated by the appropri-ation of estates, churches and even whole abbeys by rival dioceses, such as St David's in south-west Wales. This outraged the incumbent bishop, Urban, who decided he had little choice but to marshal his facts and pre-sent them to the Pope, the only authority in the world that could be expected to bring these wayward prelates and nobles alike to heel. Accordingly, in 1108 Urban set his brother Galfrid the task of collating and copying the accumulated records of donations of property to the church of Llandaff into one volume, as part of his appeal first to Pope Honorius II and subsequently to his successor Pope Innocent II. He hoped that the Pope would put pressure on the Normans to return this valuable Church property to the diocese of Llandaff. Urban's pleas did not fall on deaf ears: each Pope in turn subsequently wrote to the King urging him to intervene and instruct the nobles to give back the stolen property.

The volume collated by Galfrid, enlarged with other material such as the lives of various saints and the papal bulls issued in answer to Urban's pleas, is what is known today as the Llandaff Charters. Galfrid's original work, if it still exists, is probably to be found in the Vatican Library. However, copies were made. In the MSS 'Chronicle of the Church of Llandaff', which was written in 1439 and is preserved in the Cottonian Library in the British Museum, the Charters are referred to as the 'Book of St Teilo', the title referring to one of the saints whose lives it contains. Several other old copies of the Charters book are also recorded as having been preserved, including one in the Hengwrt library of Merionethshire and another in the library of Jesus College, Oxford. In 1840 the Llandaff Charters were, for the first time, translated and published in English. In 1980, in order to make this material more widely available, Baram and Alan republished this translation, along with other material and commentaries, under the title *Arthur and the Charters of the Kings*.

Later Alan and Baram were to give me a copy of this book and I was able to read for myself how Pope Innocent II tactfully appealed to Henry I to see to the return of the lost lands:

> Innocent, Bishop, servant of the servants of God, to his most dearly beloved son in Christ, Henry, the illustrious King of England, health and apostolic benediction. It is for the honour of God, and the welfare of the people, that Princes, to whom the rights of a kingdom are committed by God, should love the churches, and defend ecclesiastical persons from injuries. We therefore require thy nobility, and exhort thee in the Lord, that thou therefore support our venerable brother Urban, Bishop of Llandaff, and dost not permit any injury to be inflicted either on him or the church committed to his care – Given at Genoa the 12th day of August [1130].[2]

Pope Honorius II also issued bulls addressing some of the rogues in person (including Walter, son of Richard, Bryan, son of Earl William, Payne, son of John), demanding that restitution be made:

> We are informed through means of report, that contrary to your honour and the salvation of your souls, you have rashly dared to plunder your mother, the Church of Llandaff, and annihilate it. Wherefore having compassion, with paternal affection, on your adverse conduct, we, by means of this present writing, do order and command that ye, without delay, restore whatsoever in the lands, tithes, oblations, sepultres, and other property, you have unjustly taken and retain from the said church, and other churches of the said diocese . . . Given at the Lateran the 19th day of April [1128].[3]

One of Galfrid's principal sources when compiling the material that became the Llandaff Charters was the cathedral's chartulary. During the Dark Ages, rights over a parcel of land, river or other property were often signed over to the Church as atonement for some serious sin, such

45

as murder or adultery. To make such contracts legally and spiritually binding, they were usually written into the margins of the Gospels, thus in effect putting them into Holy Writ. The Bible or New Testament used for this purpose was called a 'chartulary' and was probably the most important legal document possessed by any church. The original chartulary of Llandaff went missing from the cathedral in the late seventeenth century. It turned up again shortly afterwards in Lichfield Cathedral, where it was surreptitiously renamed 'The Book of St Chad'.[4] It is still on show there to this day, but nobody will admit to its having been stolen from Llandaff.

The so-called 'Book of St Chad' has land grants written into the margins around its text. As many of them are in Welsh and concern parcels of land in the south Glamorgan area, it is clear that this is indeed the chartulary. The refusal of the Church of England to return it to Llandaff Cathedral, where it belongs, has caused widespread resentment in Wales. Unfortunately visitors, who come in their thousands to look at the book, for it contains some of the finest examples of early engraving in the world, are still being peddled the lie that it is native to Lichfield. One of the pages sold as a facsimile to tourists is an example proving that this isn't true and that it came from Llandaff Cathedral. Written into its margins are details concerning the accession of one 'Tydfwlch', witnessed by St Teilaw, a Welsh saint, who was a bishop of Llandaff Cathedral. Further, Tydfwlch is an alternative way of spelling Teithfallt, the name of a Glamorgan king, so it is possible that they are one and the same.

Our interest in the Llandaff Charters, which might at first sight seem to have little connection with our quest for King Arthur, stems from the fact that many of the grants listed in it date from the fifth to sixth centuries. During this time the cathedral was rebuilt, in the reign of a king called Meurig (Mauricius in Latin), after it had been destroyed by Saxon raiders. Meurig made some land grants to the church which are important to us because they contain lists of witnesses. To ensure a document's legality and to give the Church the best chance of having its rights respected, the Church authorities sought to have as many witnesses as possible recorded in the chartulary, each with his or her rank and relationship to the person making the donation. Among the entries made during the sixth century are several containing the name of Meurig, his wife Onbrawst and a son called Athrwys, who is clearly identifiable as the King Arthur of legend. As each is named with their exact familial relationship to the donor specified, these documents are invaluable in plotting the family tree of the ruling clan.

Later I was able to check this by referring to the Llandaff Charters themselves and seeing for myself the entries mentioning Athrwys (Welsh for Arthur), the son of King Meurig. For example:

> Be it known to us that Meurig son of Tewdrig, King of Glamorgan, and his wife Onbrawst, daughter of Gwrgan the Great, have given to God and to Oudoceus the Bishop, and to his holy predecessors Teilo and Dubricius, and to all his successors in the church of Llandaff, for their souls and the souls of their parents in perpetual consecration, three modii[5] of land at Cilcinhinn, and six modii at Conouy, that is Langenei, which was heretofore his property, free from every regal service, with all woods, in water and in pastures. Of the laity the witnesses are King Meurig, Queen Onbrawst his wife, his sons Athrwys and Idnerth, Cyndaf, Llyweith, Cadwal, Cadlew, Rhiacad, Cynfryn, Merthyr, Gwrgan; of the clergy, Oudoceus the eminent Bishop, Jacob Abbot of St Cadoc, with his elders, Cadgen, Abbot of St Illdyd, with his family, Eiddigirn, Abbot of Docunni, Cynfran, Cynweon, Cynwar, Mainwg doctor, Gwynfwy master.[6]

From this entry alone we are able to deduce quite a lot. Athrwys, or Arthur, is the son of Meurig and Onbrawst, brother of Idnerth, and grandson of both Tewdrig and Gwrgan the Great.

The power of the bishops of Llandaff, who seem to have been regarded as saints even in their own lifetimes, was extraordinary and at times rivalled that of the kings themselves. This is evidenced in one of the charters, which describes how Oudoceus was able to force King Meurig to do penance for the murder of a rival.

> King Meurig and Cynfeddw met together at Llandaff, in the presence of Bishop Oudoceus, and swore, the relics of the saints being placed before them, that there should be firm peace between them. But although the oath had been taken, after an interval King Meurig, by deceit, killed Cynfeddw; and afterwards Bishop Oudoceus convoked all his clergy from the mouth of Taratyr in Wye to the Towy,[7] and with his three Abbots, Cyngen, Abbot of Carvan valley; Cadgen, Abbot of Illtyd; Sulien, Abbot of Docunni; and in full synod, excommunicated King Meurig on account of the murder committed

by him, and of the agreement made in his presence and upon the altar of St. Peter the apostle, and St. Dubricius, and St. Teilo, being broken, and by laying the crosses on the ground, together with the relics of the saints, he debarred the country from baptism and Christian communion, and cursed the king with his progeny, the synod confirming the same, and saying, 'May his days be few, may his children be orphans, and his wife a widow.' And the king, with the whole of the country, remained for the space of two years and more under excommunication. After these things, the king seeing the perdition of his soul, and the condemnation of his kingdom, could not any longer sustain an excommunication, which had continued so long, and sought pardon from Oudoceus at Llandaff, with shedding of tears and bowing down his head. And before the three Abbots Bishop Oudoceus put on him the yoke of penance suitable to the quality and magnitude of the crime, and recommended him to shew his amendment towards God and the Church of Llandaff in three ways, that is by fasting, prayer and alms-giving. King Meurig accepted the yoke of penance, gave for the redemption of his soul, and for the soul of Cynfeddw, four villages, to the Church of Llandaff, and in the hand of Oudoceus the Bishop, and to all his successors, with all their liberty, free from all service, for ever, and in all commonage throughout the country, to the persons who abode on those lands, in field, and in wood, and in pasture and in water.[8]

It is clear that Llandaff considered itself to be the premier diocese in Wales and, according to the triads, it was also believed to have been the first in Britain to become an archbishopric:

> The three archbishoprics of the Isle of Britain:
> The first, Llandaff; founded by Lleirwg, the son of Coel, the son of Cyllin, who first gave land and national privileges to those who first embraced the faith in Christ.
> The second, Effrawg; founded by the emperor Constantine, who was the first of the Roman emperors who embraced the Christian faith.
> The third, London; founded by the emperor Mascen Wledig [Magnus Maximus].

I knew all about Constantine, but I had not realized that the foundation of Llandaff preceded that at Effrawg – a name usually translated as York

– by some two centuries. The Llandaff Charters also show that the bishops of Llandaff continued to wield considerable power during the time of Meurig's son Athrwys, who, according to a later charter, made a land donation himself, again to St Oudoceus:

It is well known that Bishop Oudoceus acquired land as his own, that is the estate of Cingualan, land indeed of St Dubricius in the country of Gower,[9] which St Oudoceus lost from the time of the mortality, that is the yellow pestilence, until [during?] the time of Athrwys, son of Meurig. And after great contention between Bishop Oudoceus and Bivan, Abbot of Iltyd, who said that the land was his, the aforesaid land was at last, by true judgement, adjudged to St Oudoceus, and the altar of Llandaff, in perpetual inheritance; and the cell of Cynwalan with all its lands, and the cell of Arthfodu, and Ceinwyrig, and Pencreig. And St Oudoceus received the land from the hand of Athrwys, the grandson of Gwrgan the Great, the aforesaid little cells in perpetual consecration, and with all their dignity, and all commonage in field, and in woods, in water and in pastures, and under a perpetual curse against him who should separate the aforesaid churches from the monastery of Llandaff; and whoever will keep them, may the Lord keep him. Amen. Of the clergy, the witnesses are, Oudoceus the Bishop, Cadogen, Bivan with his family; Jacob, Abbot of the altar of St Cadoc; Eiddigirn, Abbot of Docunni; with his clergy. Of the laity, King Meurig on behalf of his son Athrwys, Cynfonog, Gwallonir, Morgeneu, Eithin, Cynfeddw, Gweithgen, the son of Brochwael, Gwyddog, Madog Arthcuman, Ogwyr, Gwrdilig, Gwrwystyl, Arwyredd, Abel, with the presbyters Cynhael, Cynhyfryd, Gweithno. The boundary of Llancynwalan – below the ditches at the sea, following the two ditches at the sea, following the two ditches to the mountain, along it to the ridge of the boundary of Llangenei.[10]

The 'ditches', or dykes, referred to here are probably those still to be seen running along the coast of the Severn Estuary, between Cardiff and Newport. These, like the dykes of Holland, protect a large area of arable land, which, being below sea level, would otherwise be flooded. They probably go back to Roman times and Alan informed me that there are references to their being repaired during the sixth century by monks.

That Athrwys followed his father Meurig as king is evidenced from another grant.

> Be it known to the clergy and people of southern Britain, that Athrwys, King of the region of Gwent, granted to God, and to St Dubricius, and St Teilo, and in the hand of Bishop Comereg, the church of Cynfarch the disciple of St Dubricius, with all its territory, that is, the Manor of Troumur, and Lanndeui, and Lann Junabui, and Lann Guouoe, in the field of Molochu, and the mansion of Mafurn, and Lanncalcuch, and Lann Gerniu, with all their land, without any heir, but according to the will of the Bishops of Llandaff, with all their liberty, and complete commonage in field and in woods, in water and in pastures, for ever. And King Athrwys went round the whole territory in its circuit, with the sprinkling of the dust of the sepulchre of St Cynfarch the disciple of St Dubricius, throughout the whole boundary, the holy cross being carried before, with the sprinkling of consecrated water; and in the presence of Bishop Comereg, with the clergy, and the king alone carried the Gospel on his back, and confirmed forever the alms which had been given for the soul of his father Meurig; and a blessing being given to him and an absolution at the same time pronounced, he commended himself, soul and body, to the present bishop, and his successors in the church of Llandaff.[11]

Included in the list of witnesses for this donation is Athrwys's son Morgan. As the former's successor, Morgan later makes donations of his own, as does his son, Ithael. Thus with the help of the Llandaff Charters, it is easy to draw up a family tree of this King Athrwys, the historical Arthur, his immediate ancestors and descendants. The information contained in the Llandaff Charters matches other records on stones, and in the royal genealogies, histories and poetry.

Having explained the charters as we walked round Llandaff Cathedral, Alan concluded our tour by leading me up to the high altar and showing me several ornate tombs in its vicinity.

'This is the tomb of St Dyfrig, or Dubricius,' he explained in a voice little more than a whisper. 'He was the bishop who, with the support of King Meurig, rebuilt the church in the sixth century AD after it had been destroyed by the Saxons.'

Dyfrig is mentioned both in Nennius's *Historia Britonum* and in

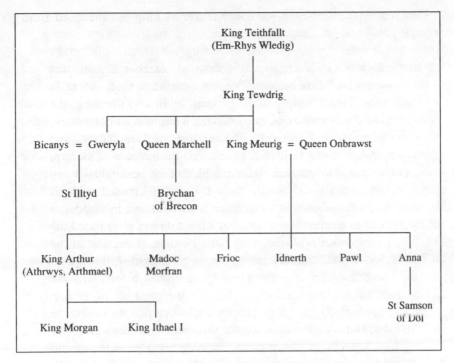

King Teithfallt
(Em-Rhys Wledig)

King Tewdrig

Bicanys = Gweryla   Queen Marchell   King Meurig = Queen Onbrawst

St Illtyd   Brychan
of Brecon

King Arthur   Madoc   Frioc   Idnerth   Pawl   Anna
(Athrwys, Arthmael)   Morfran

St Samson
of Dol

King Morgan   King Ithael I

THE ARTHURIAN DYNASTY
OF SIXTH-CENTURY GLAMORGAN
(as exhibited in the Llandaff Charters)
Diagram 4

Geoffrey's *History* as having been the prelate who crowned King Arthur at Caerleon when he was only fifteen years of age. This is likely, for at first Athrwys was a sort of 'Prince of Wales' to his father King Meurig. St Dyfrig was followed as bishop by St Teilo, and after him came St Docky or Oudoceus, whose tombs Alan also pointed out. These three saints, along with a fourth called Illtyd, were the leading lights of the Welsh church in the era of King Arthur and his immediate forebears.

Llandaff Cathedral fell into dereliction after the reign of Henry VIII. It was rebuilt in the eighteenth century in Italian style, but that building too was torn down by the Victorians and replaced with the present, much more solemn building. Since then pious people have carried on making offerings, including a magnificent set of stained-glass windows, which show that local legends concerning King Arthur and his association with Glamorgan were still very much alive in the early part of this century.

Looking up at the windows I was impressed not so much by their artistry, but by the forthrightness of the imagery. One group of windows showed various saints, including Merthyr Tydfil, patron of my mother's town of birth. She was depicted as an expensively robed lady in the act of being clubbed to death by a group of blond-haired Saxons. Under the window was the self-explanatory caption: 'Saint Tydfil receives the crown of martyrdom.' I couldn't help but wonder what she would have thought of the rather grim mining town that had grown up around the site of her grave. At right-angles to her was the main group of windows. They showed three saintly kings. The first of these was a fresh-faced and youthful-looking Arthur. The second showed an old man, King Tewdrig, who was Arthur's grandfather, whilst the third was of Cadwallader, the last of the British kings recorded in Geoffrey of Monmouth's *History*. Below the main window representing each king was a smaller one showing a major moment in his career. King Arthur was depicted as carrying a cross after the famous Battle of Baedan, the inscription below reading: 'King Arthur returning from the Battle of Mons Badonis.' King Tewdrig, who, evidently holy enough to be considered a saint, had a halo, was shown kneeling before an angelic figure, his inscription reading: 'S. Tewdrig is visited by an angel.' Cadwallader, older than Arthur but a younger man than Tewdrig, was shown marching into battle behind a standard-bearer carrying a flag with a red dragon embroidered on it. The inscription read: 'S. Cadwallader goes forth to battle under the banner of the red dragon.' I asked Alan to explain the symbolism and the historical incidents to which the images referred.

'The Battle of Mount Baedan was the turning-point of Arthur's career, as it put a check on a major invasion into his home territory of south Wales. As Arthur was not at that time paramount king, for his father Meurig had not yet gone into retirement, the window depicts him as a youth. Geoffrey of Monmouth incorrectly confuses Mons Badonis with the city of Bath, which was called Aquae Sulis by the Romans. In fact, "Mons Badonis" or Mynydd Baedan, to give it its Welsh name, is near Bridgend in south Wales. There is no mystery over this: it is marked on all the Ordnance Survey maps of the area.' Alan promised that we would pay the battlefield a visit, where we would be better able to understand how Arthur used the land to his advantage and led the Saxons into a trap.

The significance of the cross he carries in the stained-glass image is that Arthur is said to have carried the True Cross of Christ on his shoulder for three days prior to the battle. Tewdrig, Arthur's grandfather, was a valiant warrior, who, when he reached old age, handed on the crown of Glamorgan to his son Meurig and retired to a life of contemplation at Tintern on the River Wye.

'The story goes that an angel appeared to him and told him he would die in a battle soon to be fought against the Saxons. Sure enough, there was a Saxon attack on Glamorgan and although the British were victorious, the old king was mortally wounded, blocking the ford at Tintern. He was buried by his son Meurig near the well of Mathern and a church was built over his grave in his honour.'

I found this story in the Llandaff Charters:

King Tewdrig when he was in his kingdom, enjoying peace and administering justice with his people, had less regard for temporal than eternal power, and accordingly gave up his kingdom to his son Meurig, and commenced leading a hermitical life among the rocks of Tintern. When he was there resident, the Saxons began to invade his land against his son Meurig, so that unless he individually would afford his assistance, his son would be altogether dispossessed by foreigners. Concerning which, Tewdrig said that while he possessed the kingdom, he was never overcome, but was always victorious; so that when his face was seen in battle, the enemy immediately were turned to flight. And the angel of the Lord said to him on the preceding night, 'Go tomorrow to assist the people of God against the enemies of the church of Christ, and the enemy will turn their face in flight, as far as Pwll Brochwael; and thou, being armed, stand in the battle, and seeing thy face and knowing it, they will, as usual betake themselves to flight and afterwards for the space of thirty years they will not dare, in the time of thy son to invade the country; and the natives and other inhabitants will be in quiet peace; but thou wilt be wounded by a single stroke in the district of Rhyd Tintern, and in three days die in peace.

And rising in the morning, when the army of his son Meurig came, he mounted his horse, and went cheerfully with them, agreeably to the commandment of the angel; and being armed, he stood in the battle on the banks of the Wye, near the ford of Tintern; and on his face being seen, the enemy turned their backs, and betook themselves to flight; but one of them threw a lance, and wounded him therewith, as had been foretold to him; and therefore he rejoiced, as if spoil had been taken on the vanquishing of any enemy. After his son Meurig returned victorious, and with the spoil that had been taken, he requested his father to come with him, who thus said, 'I will not depart hence until my Lord Jesus Christ shall bring me to the place which I have desired, where I shall like to lie after death, that is to the Isle of Echni.' And early in the morning, two stags yoked, and ready with a vehicle, were before the house he lodged, and the man of God, knowing that God had sent them mounted the carriage, and wheresoever they rested, there fountains flowed until they came to a place near a meadow towards the Severn. And when they came there a most clear fountain flowed, and the carriage was completely broken, he then immediately commended his spirit to God, and ordered the stags to depart; and having remained there alone, after a short space of time he expired.

His son Meurig, being informed of the death of his father, built there an oratory and cemetery, which were consecrated by St Oudoceus; and for the soul of his father he granted the whole territory to Bishop Oudoceus and the church of Llandaff, and its pastors, in perpetual consecration, without any payment to any mortal man besides to St Oudoceus, and the church of Llandaff. [What follows is a description of the boundaries of the gifted lands] . . . Whoever will keep these alms, may God keep him; and whoever will separate it from the church of Llandaff, may they be accursed. Amen.[12]

Alan explained that the name 'Mathern', where Tewdrig was said to be buried, is derived either from *marthyr teyrn*, which means 'martyred monarch', or from *ma-teyrn*, meaning 'the place of the monarch'. Tewdrig was regarded as a saint and given the epithet *fendigaid*, which means 'blessed'. His grave was excavated in 1606 and again in 1881, revealing a badly fractured skull, bearing out the truth concerning his death.

Why the last king, Cadwallader, has been included in the windows is a mystery. The significance of his following the banner with the red dragon, which symbolizes Wales, probably relates to a prophecy he received from another angel: that one day, when his bones are brought back from Rome and united with those of other Welsh saints, his kingdom will regain its freedom from the Saxons.

It seemed amazing to me, having now seen the evidence, that so few people realized that Llandaff Cathedral contains such incontrovertible evidence for the existence of an historical King Arthur, linking him, through the Llandaff Charters, to a known dynasty of kings that included such important individuals as Tewdrig, and showing his family to be major benefactors of the cathedral. Since the Llandaff Charters are of such enormous interest it is surprising, too, that these precious documents have been ignored by serious historians of the era. Alan feigned amusement at my innocence as we drove from the cathedral to our next destination. Little did I know that I was about to see even more amazing evidence for the 'lost kingdom' of King Arthur.

CHAPTER FOUR

FORGOTTEN STONES OF HERO KINGS

Leaving Llandaff, Alan and I drove towards Bridgend. It was difficult to visualize Wales as it must have been at the time of Athrwys and before. The busy motorway, like some great snake, cut straight through the surrounding countryside, oblivious of not just the ancient history of the area but even that of the near present. The towns and villages signposted along the way, bearing names such as Aberdare, Abercynon, Pontypridd and Tonypandy, were familiar-sounding not for any ancient connections but for their near contemporary history of mining and trade unionism. Soon we approached Port Talbot. The air became thick with heavy, sulphurous fumes, for here, on what had once been a pleasant and extensive beach, stands Europe's largest steelworks.

Just by the steelworks we turned off the motorway, heading towards the sanctuary of Margam Country Park. Here, just a mile or two up the road but centuries away from the industrial nightmare behind us, was the quiet tranquillity of Margam Abbey. Like Llandaff, and long before it became famous for its now abandoned colliery, Margam was an important centre of Christian learning and a residency of the kings of Glamorgan. Like all the religious houses of England and Wales the Abbey was closed down and ransacked at the time of Henry VIII and today much of the area behind the encircling perimeter wall contains little more than the ruined footings of its previous grand buildings. However, I was gratified to see that the church at least has been restored and is still in use by the local parish. The ruined, twelve-sided chapter house spoke more poignantly about the Abbey's former grandeur.

As is nearly always the case with Welsh churches, as I was soon to see, guidebooks to the area give a totally misleading impression as to the

56

antiquity of the Abbey. They say that it was founded soon after the Norman invasion of 1091, ignoring earlier records to the contrary. The reality is that, like so many other buildings of the ecclesiastical foundations of England and Wales, it had been destroyed many times during earlier troubles and was only rebuilt by the Normans. The Abbey's real foundation, so Alan now informed me, goes back to a prince and bishop called Morgan, who was the uncle of Athrwys. However, it was not the remains of the later Norman abbey which we had come to see but rather some interesting memorial stones, belonging to this earlier dynasty, which lay hidden in a small outbuilding.

Parking next to a tourist coach, we obtained the key from the staff of the nearby café and proceeded to this building, which was little more than a shed. Inside, clustered together like so many tired refugees, was an extraordinary collection of ancient stones and crosses, about eighteen or nineteen in all. They didn't seem to be in any particular order, so as we walked about them I asked Alan to explain their significance and value.

Alan explained that they were very much older than was implied by the faded captions that accompanied some of them. In their own way they were important supporting evidence for the history of the region; in Alan's view they ought to be properly studied and housed in a national museum. They were much neglected, but at least in Margam they were kept in a lockable building and out of the rain. Many other similar stones, of equal antiquity, are still being left outside to weather. Unfortunately people do not recognize how old these stones really are. Archaeologists tend to date artefacts by comparing them with others that they believe to be of the same type.

The problem began in the nineteenth century with a gentleman called W. G. Collingwood, from the north of England. He was really a surveyor, not an archaeologist. In a book entitled *Northumbrian Crosses of the Pre-Norman Age*, he put forward the strange idea that Dark Age monumental carving of religious crosses, memorial stones and similar monuments began around AD 650 in Northumberland (which at that time included Yorkshire, Cleveland and Durham). This was contrary to all the evidence in Wales, Cornwall and elsewhere, but this surveyor had the colossal advantage of total ignorance. He then promulgated the idea that around 700–800 the English spread the new science of stone carving to Ireland; and that the Irish came over to Wales around 800–900 and taught the Welsh how to carve stones. Today the correct datings of Welsh stones, made by Professor McAllister and others, are tossed aside in favour of this 'Northumberland first' theory. The result is that fifth- and sixth-century stones, which clearly name fifth- and sixth-century personages, are now being redated in a campaign of political correctness to absurd dates of around 900–1000.

All this reasoning is at total variance with the real history of Wales, Northumberland and Ireland. Although it is generally believed that Christianity came to Britain with St Augustine in 597, in fact according to triads and other Welsh sources, Christianity in Britain began in Wales in AD 36. From here it was carried to other parts of Britain, including Northumberland, where the local dynasty had close ties with south-east Wales. St Patrick, who is credited with the conversion of Ireland, was himself Welsh. He was born near Cowbridge, which is not much over ten miles from Margam Abbey as the crow flies, and was taken to Ireland as a slave by pirates. It is therefore not unreasonable to suggest that the idea of memorial crosses, particularly wheel crosses, is indigenous to Wales and was exported from Wales to Ireland after that country was converted to Christianity by St Patrick. This should be obvious and would be accepted were it not that the modern Church prefers to draw a veil over the pre-Augustinian Christianity of Britain. It does so because it knows that much of what was taught and believed in Britain at that time was at odds with later Roman Christian traditions. Also, when Augustine came to England in AD 597, the indigenous Welsh bishops refused to accept his authority over them or to acknowledge the supremacy of the Bishop of Rome. In fact, they found this idea laughable and wouldn't cooperate with his mission at all. Later, of course, the native British Church was effectively suppressed as a separate institution from the Roman and, as we have seen, in the eleventh century the Bishop of Llandaff was only too pleased to write pleading letters to the Pope urging him to use his authority to restrain the Normans from plundering the property of his church.

Standing directly ahead of us and drawing the eye was an example of the early Welsh art form Alan had mentioned: a curiously lop-sided wheel cross at least eight feet high. It is, according to Alan, a very important memorial. The design consists of four squares joined to a central fifth and ringed with a halo. Sometimes on crosses such as this the circle is split into twelve, giving the sense of the zodiac or twelve apostles. At the foot of the shaft are three figures, representing the Holy Family of Mary, Joseph and Jesus. The inscription on the back indicates that it was raised by a bishop called Cynvelyn, or Cunobelinus.

According to Alan's and Baram's researches, this bishop was a brother of King Tewdrig and therefore a great-uncle of Athrwys. Families liked to keep appointments to their own kind: one brother would become king, another would be the bishop, another might be a monk and a fourth admiral of the fleet. Unlike the modern concept of religious leaders, if you wanted to be a saint in the Dark Ages you needed to be of the royal lineage or a nobleman, erudite, have held high office and probably founded a few churches yourself. Sometimes bishops, monks or even saints would for a time put aside their pastoral duties and take up arms if there was no one else available to lead the army against pagan invaders.

One such character was the man who had made a small stone cross that was situated on the opposite side of the room. Walking over to it and squatting to read what was written on it, Alan observed that the inscription on this stone had been mistranslated, probably in the seventeenth or eighteenth century, and nobody has challenged it. The naming of the stone as the Stone of Grutne and the translation of the inscription as 'In the name of God most high, The cross of Christ which Grutne prepared for the soul of Ahest', he does not accept. Crosses such as this were put up by kings and major princes and neither 'Grutne' nor 'Ahest' are mentioned anywhere in the histories or genealogies. The cross does, however, have the name 'ThiThELL' inscribed on it. Accordingly, he and Baram think it must be the cross of 'ThiThELL', or Teithfallt.

Teithfallt is a very important figure in the histories. In the *History of the Kings of Britain*, both in its original form and in the translation by Geoffrey of Monmouth, there is an account of events in the fifth century following the treachery of Vortigern, the British king who murdered his predecessor, Constantine the Blessed, and invited over the Saxons. In an attempt to bring to an end the Saxon war which followed and to try to find an amicable solution to what had by then become a pressing problem, a peace conference was held *c*. 466 but during it the Saxons slew the cream of the British nobility. This event, known as the 'Treachery of the Long Knives', cast a long shadow over subsequent Dark Age history and led to a second Saxon war.

Teithfallt had been a monk at the time of the massacre, which is why he wasn't at the peace conference. As virtually the entire royal family had been wiped out, he had to give up the religious life, take up the sword and become King of Glamorgan. In many of the histories Teithfallt – Teithfalch, Tudfwlch, Twdfwlch, his name is spelt in many ways – is listed as the son of Nyniaw or Nennius. Alan's and Baram's researches indicate that this is an error, stemming from the confusion surrounding the Welsh word *ap*, which as well as meaning 'son of' can mean 'successor to'. In reality Teithfallt was the son of Teithrin, as is well attested in the genealogies of the 'Brecon' manuscripts contained in the Harleian 4181 and British Vespasian D. xiv collections. The inscription on this cross seems to be referring to the events surrounding the massacre of the British nobles by the Saxons.

We moved on to another, rather larger and more impressive stone on the wall at the back of the room, 'a bit the worse for wear' as Alan described it. Someone had chopped off the edges of the wheel at its top to make it more oblong-shaped. This sort of vandalism was, Alan explained, unfortunately all too common in centuries past. Good-quality stones, even quite important ones, would be torn out of where they had stood for centuries and be put to use, perhaps as a window-sill, or broken up to reuse as building material. This one was used as a bridge over a small stream. Again, he said, it has been misidentified and the text mistranslated. It is called the Stone of Einnion, even though it says EN-NI-A-CUN; however Alan and Baram think it is the stone of Theoderic, because the inscription, barely legible, also says 'THUORThOREC'. Theoderic is another name for Tewdrig, King Arthur's grandfather, the son of Teithfallt and the king who was mortally wounded in the Battle of Tintern. Since Tewdrig is a well-known figure, that his stone should be misidentified is surprising; but, as Alan said, 'If you don't know the history you aren't going to recognize evidence supporting that history.' According to the rest of the inscription, this cross was put up by Theoderic to celebrate a period of peace.

Another stone, the Bodvoc Stone, carried a much clearer inscription. The lettering was quite crude and the capital As were drawn upside down, but it was readable as: 'BODVOC – HIC IACIT – FILIVS CATOTIGIRNI PRONEPVS ETERNALI VEDOMAV.' This translates as. 'Here is thrown down Bodvoc, the son of Catotigirnus, great-grandson of Eternalus Vedomaus.' There was a Budic, son of Cato, who came to Britain asking for help after he was displaced from his throne in Brittany by his brother. Tewdrig sent one of his generals, Agricola Longhand, over to Brittany with a fleet to have Budic reinstated. A King Budicius of Brittany, who also features in Geoffrey's *History*, is supposed to have raised Aurelius and Uther when they were boys; this would have been in the same epoch. It is quite likely that the 'Bodvoc' of the stone would be either Budic or

Budicius, so physical evidence in the form of a stone provides a link between history and legend.

I walked around examining the rest of the stones. Scattered around the room in higgledy-piggledy fashion were more than a dozen other crosses and stones, many of them, like those of Teithfallt and Tewdrig, inscribed with clumsy Latin scripts. Even I, with my untrained eye, could see that they weren't Norman; and they certainly weren't Saxon as no king of England, Wessex or Mercia ever did more than raid south Wales before 1091. I was certain that these stones of Margam did indeed relate to an earlier, all-but-forgotten Christian kingdom: a kingdom in which the historical King Arthur lived.

THE STONES OF SAMSON

Leaving Margam, we drove back through the Vale of Glamorgan towards Cardiff, stopping off to visit several other sites on our way. Like most Englishmen, my mental picture of south Wales was of a rugged landscape of steep hills and narrow valleys, of mine-workings and slag-heaps. Yet here in the Vale, away from industrial centres like Port Talbot, was a relatively flat landscape which seemed to stretch for miles in all directions. The narrow lines, the pretty villages and lush, green meadows were more like Dorset than the black country of my imaginings. I began to understand why Sir Robert Fitzhammon and the other Normans of 1091 had been keen to settle: this was clearly high-quality agricultural land and would have been a valuable prize.

Soon we arrived at our destination, the village of Llantwit Major, which turned out to be a quaint collection of ancient cottages arranged along several winding lanes, only a mile or so from the sea. At its centre were a number of very old buildings surrounding a small square, including a 700-year-old town hall or 'church loft', said to have been built by Gilbert de Clare, Lord of Glamorgan, who was killed in Scotland at the Battle of Bannockburn in 1314. I parked the car behind the town hall and we made our way through a narrow gate to the precincts of one of the oddest churches I have ever seen.

This building had started life as what must have been a relatively small chapel. As and when more space had been needed, four further sections had been added on to its west end, so that now it stretched back and back like an enormous stone telescope. It would seem that before the dissolution of the monasteries by Henry VIII it was even larger, for beyond its present west face, thrusting out into the present churchyard, there were the ruins of at least one further extension. Judging from the number of memorial stones and several well-preserved effigies inside the church, it was clear that at one time it had had a status much higher than that of a simple parish church. In fact, as I was later to discover, this unpretentious church stood on the site of what is the most venerable Christian settlement in Britain, if not the whole of Europe.

Opening the latch and talking in whispers, we made our way in. As it is the centre of an active parish, it came as no surprise to find that a choir was busy at practice, the lilting Welsh voices adding greatly to the atmosphere. We headed for the back end of the church where, almost hidden from view by piles of tubular chairs and a disconnected organ bench, were several more, very large memorial stones. It was these that Alan had brought me to see, for neglected as they are, they are amongst the most important remnants of Dark Age Britain.

The discovery of one of these stones is itself an interesting story. It was found in 1789 by Edward Williams, the famous Iolo Morganwg who gathered the Welsh manuscripts contained in the *Myvyrnian Archaiology* and who was later abused by his namesake G. J. Williams. A full description of how he found and recovered the stone is contained in a later book, called simply *Iolo MSS*, which was assembled and translated by his son John 'Taliesin' Williams. Iolo writes:

> About forty years ago, a very old man, named Richard Punter, lived at Llanmaes juxta Llantwit: and, though only a shoemaker, was a more intelligent person than most of his class. He had read history more than many; was something of an antiquary; and had stored his memory with a number of interesting traditions. I was then about twelve or fourteen years of age,[1] and, like him, fond of history and antiquities. He, one day, shewed me a spot on the east side of the porch of the old church at Llantwit, where, he said, a large monumental stone lay buried in the ground, with an inscription on it, to the memory of two kings. The tradition of the accident that buried it, he gave as follows:
>
> Long before the memory of the oldest person that ever he knew (and he was then about eighty), for their knowledge of it was only traditional, there was a young man at Llantwit, commonly called Will the Giant. He, at seventeen years of age, was seven feet seven inches

high; but, as is usually the case in premature or preternatural growth, he fell into a decline, of which at that age he died. He had expressed a wish to be buried near the monumental stone which stood near the porch; his wish was complied with and the grave dug, necessarily much larger and longer than usual; so that one end of it extended to the foot of the stone that was fixed in the ground. Just as the corpse had been laid in, the stone gave way, and fell into the grave, filling it up nearly. Some had very narrow escapes for their lives; but as the stone was so large as not to be easily removed, it was left there, and covered over with earth. After I had heard this traditional account, I had a great desire to dig for this stone, and many times endeavoured to engage the attention of several, and their assistance; but my ideas were always treated with ridicule.

In the summer of 1789, I employed a great part of one evening in digging in serch [sic] of this stone, and found it. I then cleared away all the earth about it, and, having obtained assistance, got it out of the ground . . .

It lay on the ground, where it had been raised out of the grave, till August 28th, 1793, when I procured assistance to erect it against the east side of the porch, where it now stands . . .[2]

The dimensions of this stone are – 9 feet high, – 28 inches wide at bottom, – 19 inches wide at top, – and 14^{1}/$_{2}$ inches thick. It is a silicious freestone, of the same kind found in the parishes of Coychurch, Coyty, &c. in this county [Glamorgan]; and is of a durable nature. The workmanship is sufficiently rude, but, at the same time, appears in some degree an imitation of the Roman taste of that age. The letters are promiscuously Roman and Etruscan.[3] The history here given of this monument affords a remarkable instance of the fidelity of tradition.[4]

Iolo goes on to give a description of the inscription on the stone, which reads:

> *in nomine di summi incipit crux salvatoris quae*
> *preparauit samsoni apati pro anima sua et*
> *pro anima iuthahelo rex et artmali tecain.*[5]

Alan explained that Samson (to whom the word '*samsoni*' refers), was of more than passing importance. He was a former Abbot of Llantwit

THE SAMSON STONE

who lived in the sixth century. He was, in fact, the same Samson who later became Bishop of Dol in Brittany and signed the papers of the Second Council of Paris in 556. The stone can therefore be comfortably dated to the sixth century, the period in which Athrwys lived; and Samson was one of Athrwys's nephews. As we stood in front of the stone, Alan pointed out to me how the curious inscription did indeed concern two kings, one of whom was called Artmali and the other Ithael. The first of these names, spelt variously as Artmael, Arthmail or Arthmael, means 'iron-bear' – and was a common appellation of Athrwys, who was indeed a tough nut. Alan and Baram have also been able to identify King Ithael, who would have ruled around the time of Samson, as either a son or grandson of Athrwys. The text on the stone should therefore be properly translated as: 'In the name of God Most High, here begins the cross of the saviour, which Samson the Abbot pre-pared for his own soul and the soul of King Ithael and Iron-bear [Arthur] the Ruler.'

Despite the importance of this stone in the context of the history of the Glamorgan kings, according to Alan we are lucky that these stones are still there at all. In the 1870s the parish council of Llantwit, led by a new minister from England, decided to have them broken up with sledgehammers and removed from the church altogether. It was only the vociferous objections of local people that stopped him from carrying out what Alan believes were probably orders from higher up the hierarchy. As we have already seen, the Church of England doesn't like these old stones, as they draw attention to the fact that Wales was Christian long before the Augustine era. The Church would rather foster the belief that the people of Glamorgan were near barbarians until first the Romans and later the Normans rescued them from their ignorance.

Looking now at this ancient and remarkable stone, which appeared to be the shaft of an even larger memorial cross, I was struck by two things: first how little publicized this extraordinary relic is and second how neglected. The steel-tubed chairs were thrust right up to it and grinding into the face of the delicate inscription. I couldn't help but think that had such a stone been found in Egypt, Assyria, Greece or even England, it would have been treated with much more respect and probably moved into the protective custody of a museum. Miraculously, its burial with 'Will the Giant' had preserved it from some of time's depredations. But now it had to take its chances with vandals or even just people pushing chairs carelessly against it. Inevitably it would not be long before the inscription was completely illegible. On later trips to Wales I was to discover that this is not an isolated case of cultural neglect: I was to see a number of other inscribed stones of equal antiquity, several of which were left totally exposed to the elements, perhaps in the hope that time itself would wash away evidence for a history the Church has chosen to ignore.

Across the aisle from this first stone were several others of equal interest. One of these, though badly worn, was finely sculpted with a complex design. Like the other, it was tapered but this time the shaft was crowned with a by now familiar wheel-cross form. Like the large cross of Cynvelyn at Margam, this seems to represent not so much the Cross of Calvary but rather the sun. Around a central square made out of four interlocking arrows were four similar squares, perhaps representing the cardinal directions or the four seasons. The intervening spaces were mostly filled with loops or knots and the shaft was decorated with a labyrinthine design of interlocking triangles, the whole giving a very pleasing effect. At the base of this ornate cross was again an inscription, this time informing the reader that the cross had been raised in honour of a King Rhys by his son King Howell. Rhys, according to Alan, was a son of the King Ithael mentioned on the Samson stone.

Beside this stone and close to a window was another cross shaft, which, though it had lost most of its decoration, was probably the most important in the collection. It was certainly Alan's favourite: he approached it with a sense of reverence, lowering his voice to almost a whisper as he translated the inscription for me. 'If you look at this inscription,' he said, 'you will see something very curious.' He went on to explain that though it is mostly written in the same primitive Roman letters as the others, these letters are combined with some Coelbren letters. The inscription reveals that it, too, was put up by Samson and it carries the names of other recognizable people of the era, including a saint called Ebissar. According to legend, Ebissar was a Saxon captured in battle, who was given the choice of death or holy orders. Naturally he took the latter course and became a monk. His own stone, with his name clearly inscribed on it, is to be seen in the nearby Coychurch.[6] But the most important name of all to be inscribed on this stone is that of 'Illtu', who can be identified as St Illtutus or Illtyd – 'These people were not strong on spelling,' Alan said – after whom the parish of Llantwit Major is named. He was an important ornament of the Church and is credited with either founding or rebuilding many churches in the area of

Glamorgan, including the one which we were in. However, said Alan, 'Don't be surprised to see this stone, which mentions him by name, languishing amongst the chairs, rather than in a place of honour befitting the founder of the church: the Church in Wales has long since turned its back on its most important saints, preferring instead to elevate the relatively less important David as its patron saint over his contemporaries Illtyd, Teilo, Dyfrig and Oudoceus.'

It seemed to me incredible that there were still such important relics of the Arthurian age as these stones. But as we left Llantwit Major, Alan told me that he and Baram had evidence that Llantwit Major was important for another reason. They believed that Joseph of Arimathea, whom the Welsh identify with another saint called Ilid and who is generally understood to have come with the Holy Grail to Glastonbury in Somerset, in fact came to Llantwit Major, where he founded a Christian college. Nor was our quest for King Arthur to be confined to Athrwys in the sixth century. Athrwys should, Alan and Baram believed, properly be called Arthur II, as he had an earlier ancestor who fought against the Romans in the fourth century and killed one of their emperors. Much of the confusion surrounding the subject of King Arthur stems from the fact that the careers of these two individuals have been merged.

As he saw my jaw dropping with incomprehension, he suggested that before he told me more I should read some historical documents and he gave me the names of a number of sources. Excited by all he had told me and by the prospect of reading them, I left Wales in a state of exultation. The first parts of the puzzle were falling into place and I was beginning to see that there was much that was mysterious about the history of my own country. I was not to know then that I would have to revise my entire view not only of the Dark Ages but also of Roman Britain, for it was then that the Holy Kingdom began.

There was quite a lot of rivalry between David and the other elders of the Welsh Church of his time. When some monks were sent to take a bell fashioned by Gildas, Abbot of Llancarvan Abbey, near Cardiff, to David for his new church in Menevia, now called St David's, they stopped off on the way to visit St Illtyd, who at that time was living as a hermit in a cave. They showed him the bell and he remarked on its quality. When they presented David with the bell, they mentioned that they had visited Illtyd on the way and how he had admired it. David's reply, generally thought to have been a snub, was that if he liked it so much he could have it. Accordingly the bell was taken back to Illtyd and installed in his church at Llantwit. Later, in the tenth century, it was stolen from Llantwit by King Edgar of Wessex on the occasion when the Saxons burnt down the venerable church. He probably took it for his own church at Glastonbury, which was founded around this time by Dunstan. Fortunately Edgar's conscience was troubled by his sacrilegious act and he afterwards returned the bell to its rightful owners. The bell is now housed in Gilbert de Clare's town hall at the centre of Llantwit Major.

CHAPTER FIVE
THE QUEST BEGINS

The phone rang while I was in the bath. Grabbing a dressing gown and leaving a trail of wet footprints behind me, I rushed down the stairs. As I rather expected, it was Alan on the other end of the line. 'Have you got the book yet?' he enquired. He was referring to a thick, musty-smelling tome that had just arrived in the post. Called simply *Iolo MSS*, it was the one Alan and I had talked about a couple of weeks earlier. Most people browsing in a second-hand bookshop, or at least those who didn't know what they were looking for, would have passed it by. But not Alan and his friends. As it is quite a rare book, this the second edition having been published in 1888, I felt especially lucky that they had been able to obtain a copy for me. The title page explained its contents: 'Iolo Manuscripts – A selection of Ancient Welsh Manuscripts, in prose and verse, from the collection made by the late Edward Williams, Iolo Morganwg, for the purpose of forming a continuation of the Myfyrnian Archaiology; and subsequently proposed as materials for a new history of Wales. With English Translation and notes by his son, the late Taliesin Williams (Ab Iolo) of Merthyr Tydfil. First published for The Welsh MSS. Society, in 1848.'

I had been looking forward to having this book in my hands, for having heard about it from Alan I realized it was going to be crucial to our work. I was not to be disappointed. Here, gathered together on its hand-cut, yellowing pages was a vast collection of historical documents which Edward Williams, otherwise known as Iolo, had painstakingly collected. Since his son Taliesin, who like his father before him was a recognized bard, had translated these old manuscripts into English, the collection was in both languages. The book contained ancient histories,

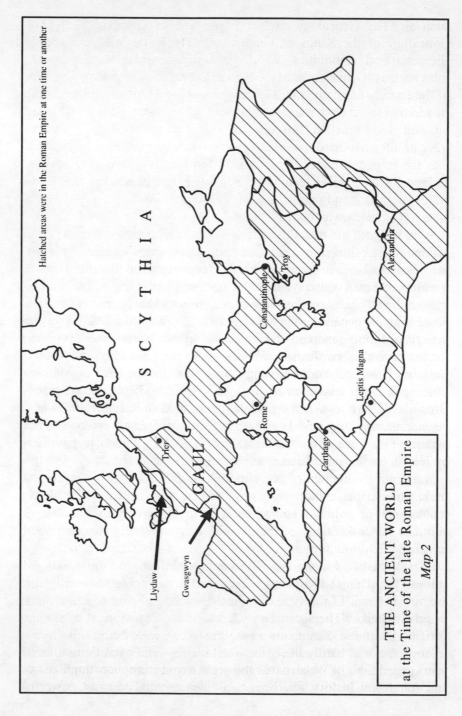

Hatched areas were in the Roman Empire at one time or another

SCYTHIA

Troy

Constantinople

Alexandria

Leptis Magna

Rome

Carthage

Trier

GAUL

Llydaw

Gwasgwyn

THE ANCIENT WORLD
at the Time of the late Roman Empire
Map 2

such as 'The Genealogy of Iestyn the Son of Gwrgan'[1] and 'The Genealogy of the Kings of Glamorgan'. There was a section called 'Ecclesiastical Antiquities' which contained chapters with evocative titles such as 'Genealogies of the British Saints: the Three Holy Families of the Island of Britain' and 'Genealogies of the Families of the Saints'. In addition there were numerous ancient fables, tales, poems and other bits and pieces labelled 'Miscellanies'. All in all the book was a treasure trove of information for people like ourselves who were anxious to delve into the forgotten history of Britain. I felt hugely thankful to the far-sighted Edward Williams and his son for having taken the trouble to collect, translate and publish these manuscripts, which we would otherwise not have known about.

Alan had told me that although he was much criticized after he died, his detractors calling him a forger, a drug addict and giving him all manner of other abuse, Iolo did an immense amount of good work. He was a remarkable man who travelled the length and breadth of Wales, searching out these ancient manuscripts that families had kept secretly in their possession for generations. These he would copy, word for word, for the benefit of future generations. He and his friends were also responsible for the revival of bardism in Wales and for the eisteddfod movement. Certainly not a drug addict (though he may, like most other people of his time, have taken laudanum in proprietary medicines such as Dr Collis Brown's Mixture to ease the pain of rheumatism in later life), he was a vegetarian, and must have been very fit, as he walked everywhere in the pursuit of his trade as well as his hobby. There are 20,000 pages written by Iolo in the National Library of Wales.

Academics – including, as we have seen, G. J. Williams – who find these manuscripts embarrassing, have done their level best to destroy his reputation. For political, social and other reasons they didn't want to admit to the authenticity of these Welsh histories and genealogies and have called Iolo a forger. However, Alan's and Baram's friend Brian Davies, a qualified historian and librarian, has managed to track down some of the original documents Iolo is accused of forging. Some of them are now in Cardiff Library itself, some are in Oxford and others are still in private hands. There can be no question of forgery now as he has verified that these documents were written centuries before Iolo lived. In any case, it is hardly likely that for hundreds and even thousands of years generations of Welsh bards and poets have been concocting a secret and fraudulent history for their own amusement. The most powerful evidence of their authenticity is that all the various histories tie up so well together and fit with other genealogies of monarchs and saints, surviving memorial stones, books such as the Llandaff Charters, place names and a whole plethora of other material. As Alan said, 'All this talk of forgery just doesn't make sense.'

In his view, calling Iolo a forger is an excuse for inertia, giving academics the excuse not to bother with investigating the material he copied. As one archaeologist had confided in him, only in Wales is doing absolutely nothing (with regard to archaeological digging) considered to be progress.

Unfortunately, a different kind of 'progress' has been made. There was uproar in Cardiff a few years ago when, in spite of local objections, the council demolished two fifteenth-century cottages to make way for a roundabout and some council houses. And in the city centre they had no compunction about bulldozing the ruins of the historic Greyfriars Abbey and selling the site so that an insurance company could build a sixteen-storey office-block in its place. Only a year or two ago, in Llantrisant, Alan continued, the house of the historically important Dr Price was demolished. Dr Price's statue, sporting his squirrel-skin, 'Davy Crockett'-style hat, stands in the centre of Llantrisant today. A Victorian gentleman considered eccentric for some of his beliefs, he scandalized his neighbours by cremating his son's body in a nearby field, declaring that ordinary burial was unhygienic. He was taken to court for his actions and, in a landmark case, the judge declared that though there might be Christian objections to cremation it was not against the law. This opened the way for cremation as a standard way of disposing of corpses, something that few people question today. He was a remarkable scholar (he was one of the founding fathers of modern Druidism amongst other things) and one might have thought the Welsh Office would have been keen to preserve his house. But no, they over-ruled local objections and knocked it down anyway. 'That, I am afraid,' concluded Alan, 'sums up the attitude towards our heritage, and I can't see it getting any better. Almost nothing is being done either to investigate important sites or, still worse, to preserve historic buildings from demolition.'

I thought about what he had said and phoned him back later. We continued our conversation. 'The problem,' Alan said, 'is that in England you don't know your own history. Here in Wales we have the best preserved history in Western Europe. Unlike England, France, Germany or even Italy, Wales was not invaded when the Roman Empire collapsed. We have dwelt securely in our own land for over two thousand five hundred years and have not substantially changed our language. We remember where we came from and we remember our history, which is written not only in books but in the names of every hill, field, village and stream in the country. Our ancestors gave names to these places and in most cases they are still called by those same names today. I can show you dozens of tumuli and tell you who is buried there, churches and tell you who founded them, memorial stones and who had them carved. In England you have these same things but you have forgotten who put them there or why. You have important antiquities but for the most part the English have lost connection with them. To fill the vacuum so created, archaeologists have invented a fake history that flies in the face of tradition. We know your history better than you do, but almost nobody from England will listen to the Welsh. Instead you prefer to look with nostalgia at the "glorious" Romans. You forget that these "noble" warriors, who enslaved the nations they conquered and entertained themselves with spectacles of the utmost depravity, were the enemies of our fathers. You write books and make films extolling the virtues of the Romans and their military prowess, forgetting entirely that your own ancestors regarded Rome as a monstrous dragon, which they had to, and indeed did, slay.

'Yet in Wales, in spite of many difficulties, we have preserved the true story – yours as well as ours. The poems and songs written by the bards of old were not like the idle chattering of poets today. Their task was to preserve the knowledge, laws, customs, history and genealogy of the nation. They preserved their heritage and passed on their knowledge to their sons and their sons' sons so that nothing of importance should be forgotten. Later, when things got better, they once more wrote down the histories, keeping their precious heritage in secret from all but a few of the English who could be trusted. It was these written histories, mostly from the Middle Ages, that Iolo copied and his son published.'

These histories show, Alan explained, that the conquest of Britain by the Romans was never as complete as modern historians make out. Julius Caesar himself was twice defeated when he tried to seize Kent and London. 'You should know this,' he said; 'it is your history, yet who has told you of these events? I'll bet you didn't realize either that the City of London existed long before the Romans arrived, when most people think it was founded. Don't worry – your ignorance in this matter is not surprising really, when for centuries academia has denied this very fact.

73

Yet the true history of London is written in its coat of arms, which if but read properly would tell you of this great victory, when the mighty Julius Caesar himself was forced to retreat, losing face and fortune in the process.'

As I listened to Alan, my jaw began to drop again. As an Englishman, albeit that my mother came from Wales, I had indeed never given a second thought to the Roman conquest of Britain. I assumed, like everyone else, that what is written in modern history books is always a factually accurate record of events. Yet as I became aware of Welsh sources such as the *Iolo MSS*, I was beginning to see there was another side to the story, one I had never been told yet somehow I 'knew' from deep within my subconscious. What he was saying was ringing bells, perhaps awakening genetic memories encoded in that long distant past. I had a sense of my world being turned upside-down: suddenly truths that had seemed certain and unassailable no longer appeared to be so. I was beginning to glimpse a different reality: a past which, though still, for me, shrouded in mystery, was somehow familiar as the legends and folktales I had read in childhood. It was a world populated not by people given labels by archaeologists over the last couple of centuries to categorize what they didn't understand, but by real people with real names.

It was also a world where religion mattered, not a little but a great deal. From the ancient Druids with their gnostic religion to the early Christianity of the saints, this was a land that pulsated on a highly charged atmosphere of faith. As Alan and Baram took me round showing me various sites, my eyes were opening to a world of little chapels, hermitages and sacred earth circles. It resonated with the history told not in recent academic works but in far more evocative texts such as the *Mabinogion*[2] and 'Y Seint Greal'. Through them I could almost see and feel the presence of the ancient saints and monks who once made not just Wales but England too a place of spirituality and enlightenment. I could feel them trying so hard to speak to us from the past, lamenting their sadly neglected stones and the way that today they are so misrepresented. Above all I could feel their indignation that the history of Britain and its struggles with Rome during dark days of oppression has now been all but forgotten. With the aid of many books, such as Geoffrey of Monmouth's *History of the Kings of Britain* and the original text from which it is drawn, the *Brut Tysylio*, translations of Gildas's *Gildae sapientis de excidio et conquestu Britanniae* and Nennius's

74

Historia Britonum, plus a huge pile of documents based on Alan's and Baram's own researches, I began the laborious process of self-re-education, starting with the fateful story of Caesar's invasions. I soon discovered that Welsh and indeed English documents reveal a very different pattern of events from what is generally written in history books today, and was able to piece together the story of what really happened.

THE ANCIENT BRITONS

When, in 55 BC, Julius Caesar planned his first attempt at the conquest of Britain, he had little knowledge of what lay ahead of him on the other side of the English Channel, and assumed that all the inhabitants of Britain would be like the Celts of Gaul. Although it is commonplace today to refer to the Welsh as 'Celtic', this description is not correct. Though there may have been a few Celts inhabiting the southern, coastal counties of England and parts of Scotland, the vast majority of Britons were not 'Celtic' in the true sense of the word.

The confusion seems to stem from the identification of the Celts, or Gaels, with all the peoples living throughout what we now call France. Caesar is our earliest authority on the subject and he, in his writings, identifies three groups of tribes living in Gaul prior to his invasion, each with their own language and customs. He writes: 'Gaul comprises three areas, inhabited respectively by the Belgae, the Aquitani, and a people who call themselves Celts, though we call them Gauls. All of these have different languages, customs, and laws.'[3] The Gauls proper, he makes clear, lived in a geographical box bounded by the River Rhone to the east, the River Garonne to the south, the Atlantic Ocean to the west and the territory of the Belgae to the north. The Belgae occupied what is now northern France and Belgium, whilst the Aquitani lived in what we call Gascony, the region bounded by the Garonne to the north and east, the Pyrenees to the south and the Atlantic to the west. By their own accounts, the main body of the ancient Britons were related to the tribes living on the fringes of the English Channel in what is now Brittany and Normandy and to the Aquitani. According to the triads, the Britons always called themselves Khymry. They were not Gauls and never called themselves Celtic, though they may have been related to the Belgae as well as the Aquitani.

75

So who were the Britons, or Khymry, and where did they come from? As we have seen, Welsh legends of origin state with absolute clarity that the Khymry called themselves Britons and believed that they were descended from emigrant Trojans. The historical triads, as recorded in the *Myvyrnian Archaiology*, detail the descent of the paramount kings of Britain from Prydain, which is another name for the legendary Brutus (Brwth).

> There were three names given to the Isle of Britain from the beginning. Before it was inhabited, it was called Clas Merddin [the sea-girt green spot]. After it was inhabited, it was called Y Vel Ynys [the honey isle]. And after the people were formed into a commonwealth by Prydain, the son of Aedd Mawr,[4] it was denominated Ynys Prydain [the isle of Prydain, or Britain].

The story of Brutus is contained in Nennius's history, which confirms the descent of the Britons, or Khymry, from the Trojans. He writes:

> The island of Britain is so called from one Brutus, a Roman consul . . . If anyone wants to know when this island was inhabited after the flood, I find two alternative explanations. The version in the Annals of the Romans is that after the Trojan War Aeneas came to Italy with his son Ascanius, defeated Turnus and married Lavinia, daughter of Latinus, son of Faunus, son of Picus, son of Saturn; and after Lavinia's death, he acquired the kingdom of the Romans and Latins. Aeneas founded Alba, and then married a wife, who bore him a son named Silvius. Silvius married a wife, who became pregnant, and when Aeneas was told that his daughter-in-law was pregnant, he sent word to his son Ascanius, to send a wizard to examine the wife, to discover what she had in the womb, whether it was male or female. The wizard examined the wife and returned, but he was killed by Ascanius because of his prophecy, for he told him that the woman had a male in her womb, who would be a child of death, for he would kill his father and mother, and be hateful to all men. So it happened; for his mother died in his birth, and the boy was reared and named Britto [Brutus]. Much later, according to the wizard's prophecy, when he was playing with others, he killed his father with an arrow shot, not on purpose, but by accident. He was driven from Italy and came to the islands of the Tyrrhene Sea, and was driven from

Greece, because of the killing of Turnus, whom Aeneas had killed, and arrived in Gaul, where he founded the city of Tours, which is called Turnis; and later he came to this island, which is named Brittania from his name, and filled it with his race, and dwelt there. From that day, Britain has been inhabited until the present day.[5]

Elsewhere Nennius gives a slightly different genealogy for Brutus, which he says he derived 'from the books of our elders', presumably meaning Welsh sources. 'The first inhabitants of Britain were the British, from Brutus. Brutus was the son of Hessitio, Hessitio of Alanus. Alanus was the son of Rhea Silvia, daughter of Numa Pompilius, son of Ascanius. Ascanius was the son of Aeneas, son of Anchises, son of Trous, Son of Dardanus, son of Elishah, son of Javan, son of Japheth.[6]

In 'The Genealogy of Iestyn Son of Gwrgan', contained in the *Iolo MSS*, it is claimed that Brutus/Brwth Prydain was the son of Selys (Silvius the Aged), son of Annyn (Aeneas) of Troy, son of Aedd Mawr (Anchises the Great), son of Capys, son of Assaracus.[7] Thus while there is some disagreement about the exact relationship of Brutus and Aeneas, it can be stated with confidence that in antiquity the story of the Trojan migration to Britain was accepted as fact.

Throughout the Middle Ages this was still the consensus of opinion, not just of the Welsh but of the English too. *The Bruts of England* includes the story of the Trojan migration and records that Edward I, who conquered Wales as well as Scotland, wanted his realm to be called 'Troylebaston'. Further references to the Trojan origins of the British are to be found in the works of Shakespeare,[8] Chaucer, Matthew of Paris, Milton, William of Malmesbury, Percy Enderbee, John Hardyng and numerous other English writers. The legends of ancestry were accepted as real history until around the time of the Hanoverian accession in 1714.

The Welsh historical triads indicate that there were several waves of immigrants from the same stock as the Trojan Khymry. As all these peoples had a common ancestry, they were able to live in relative peace and harmony. They describe the tribes thus:

The three social tribes of the Isle of Britain.
The first was the tribe of the Cymry, that came with Hu Gadarn[9] into the Isle of Britain, because he would not possess a country and lands by fighting and persecution, but justly and in peace.
The second was the tribe of the Lloegrians, who came from the land

of Gwasgwyn; and they were descended from the primitive tribe of the Cymry.

The third were the Brython, who came from the land of Llydaw, and who were also descended from the primitive tribe of the Cymry. These were called the three peaceful tribes, because they came, by mutual consent and permission, in peace and tranquillity: and these three tribes had sprung from the primitive race of the Cymry, and the three were of one language and one speech.

Lloegres, or Loegres, is the ancient name for the land that embraced most of southern and central England, as opposed to Cymry (Khymry), which incorporated, besides Wales, northern England, the Scottish borders, much of the west Midlands and Cornwall. Gwasgwyn, where the triads say the Lloegrians came from, was the region of Gaul we now call Gascony; it may also have included the Vendée, the territory of the Veneti. The name is perhaps derived from the same root as the name Loire. Llydaw is the Welsh name for Letavia, which comprised the provinces of Brittany and Normandy. They are called the 'Brython' in the triads because the western part of Llydaw was called Brittany (which means lesser Britain as opposed to Great Britain) at the time of writing.

According to the *Brut Tysylio* and the 'Genealogy of Iestyn the Son of Gwrgan', after the death of Brutus the kingdom of Britain was split between his three sons: Locrinus, Kamber and Albanactus, who gave their names to the territories they controlled. It would seem that from the very earliest times the island of Britain was divided into three sub-kingdoms named after these sons, respectively Lloegres, Cymry and Albyne. It is noteworthy that this division was present in Roman times,[10] and is still evident today (albeit with many border changes in the intervening period) as England, Wales and Scotland. Presumably it was the Lloegrians who settled principally in Lloegres.

Of the history of the next few centuries after the Brutus invasion little can be said.

The triads reveal that the unity of Britain was undermined when invaders from Ireland, Scandinavia, Germany and other places succeeded in settling large areas of the island. It is hard to date when these invasions took place but they seem to have occurred sporadically from *c.* 400 BC to *c.* 60 BC. According to the triads, some of these non-Khymric immigrants came 'without arms' and were allocated land:

> There were three refuge-seeking tribes that came to the Isle of
> Britain; and they came under the peace and permission of the Cymry,
> without arms and without opposition.
> The first was the tribe of the Celyddon [Caledonians] in the north.
> The second was the Gwyddyl tribe, who dwelt in Alban.
> The third were the people of Galedin, who came in naked vessels to
> the Isle of Wight, when their country was drowned, and where they
> had lands granted to them by the Cymry. They had no privilege of
> claim in the Isle of Britain, but they had land and protection assigned
> to them under certain limitations; and it was stated that they should
> not possess the rank of native Cymry until the ninth of their lineal
> descendants.

Other, less welcome immigrants were the Picts and a people called
'Coranians', who were probably related to the later Saxons. The
Gwyddyl Fichti or 'Irish Picts' – Picts who had settled in Ireland and
intermarried with the Irish – settled in Albyne (Scotland) on the shores
of the Irish Sea.

Other immigrants were the later Belgic invaders, not listed in the
triads, who settled the coastal areas of southern England during the
century or so before the arrival of Julius Caesar and also went to Ireland,
where they were known as the Fir Bolg.[11] Some of these Belgic tribes,
such as the Atrebates, had the same tribal names as their continental
counterparts and can easily be identified. Others are harder to identify,
though they left abundant remains of their occupation and conquest in
the form of hill forts.[12]

The capital city of Lloegres was London. In the histories, Brutus himself, the eponymous father of Britain, is credited with founding it on the
north bank of the River Thames. In the *Brut Tysylio* it is said that
London's original name was Troia Newydd, meaning 'New Troy'. In
Geoffrey of Monmouth's Latin translation this becomes Troia Nova,
which he says was later corrupted into Trinovantum or Troynovant.
Nennius too, whose history was written in Latin long before Geoffrey
translated the *Brut Tysylio*, calls London Trinovantum: he says that
Julius Caesar fought a battle against the British 'near the place called
Trinovantum'. Caesar also writes that this battle was fought by the only
ford available on the Thames, at the Island of Thorns, which is now
Westminster – therefore Trinovantum has to have been London.

According to the *Brut Tysylio*, Geoffrey's *History* and other old histories, a king called Llud or Lud is said to have ruled over Britain *c.* 60 BC. He is said to have changed the name of his capital city from 'New Troy' to Caer Llud, which later mutated to Caer Lundein, from which is derived our modern name London.[13]

It would be more than surprising if there were no significant settlement at London prior to the arrival of the Romans, given its strategic location on the Thames. The Romans themselves supply evidence that London was not founded by them. In Tacitus's account of the rebellion in AD 60 led by Boudicca, he writes, 'Suetonius [the Roman procurator] marched through disaffected territory to Londinium. This town did not rank as a Roman settlement, but was an important centre for businessmen and merchandise.' The Boudicca rebellion took place only eighteen years after the Roman invasion by Claudius in AD 43. Archaeological studies assert that a wall around the city of London, eight feet thick at its base, is 'Roman'; and that it was built all at the same time and no later than the first century AD. According to the *Brut Tysylio* and other traditional histories, this wall was not Roman but the work of the same King Llud who gave his name to the city.

According to E. O. Gordon in his book *Prehistoric London*, King Llud began his reign in 72 BC. He quotes Holinshed, the famous historian out of whose work Shakespeare developed many of his plays:

> Llud began his reign in 72 BC, seventeen years before the Romans came. He made a strong wall of lime and stone and fortified it with diverse fair towers, and in the west part of the same wall he erected a strong gate, which he commanded to be called after his name 'Ludgate', and so unto this day it is called Ludgate . . . He caused buildings to be made between London stone and Ludgate and builded for himself not far from the said gate a fair palace, which is the Bishop of London's palace, beside Paules at this day as some think . . .[14]

Gordon also quotes from an ancient Welsh manuscript preserved in Jesus College, Oxford, and translated by Lady Charlotte Guest:

> Llud ruled prosperously and rebuilt the walls of London and encompassed it about with numberless towers. After then he bade the citizens build houses therein, such as no houses in the kingdom could equal. Moreover he was a mighty warrior and generous and liberal in

giving meat and drink to all who sought them, and though he had many castles and cities, this one he loved more than any.[15]

Be this as it may, what is incontrovertible is that the wall enclosed an area of 324 acres. If it was already there before the Boudicca rebellion, which it is likely to have been if it was built by King Llud, it means that London was then probably the largest city not only in Britain but in the whole of western Europe. It is inconceivable that such a large city could have grown up in the short time between the Claudius invasion of AD 43 and the aftermath of the Boudicca rebellion of AD 60. In any case, during this period the Romans themselves concentrated their efforts on building their own cities of Camulodunum (Colchester) and Verulamium (St Albans). There is therefore no real reason to believe that London, or Trinovantum, was not already the leading city of south-east England by the time the Romans arrived and that this is why at that time the local people were known by the name of Trinovantes.

The two branches of the Royal house of Essylwg[16] and the Trinovantum were believed to be descended from Brutus himself and ruled over Cambria (Cymry) and Lloegres respectively. In times of war one or another of their kings would be elected as supreme commander to lead the forces of the entire British nation. To him would be sworn allegiance by all the other minor kings of the different nations of Britain, whether of Khymry or of Lloegres.[17] How effective a high king was in gaining this allegiance and how united the island was in the face of danger depended on the charisma and power of the individual involved. For much of the time the regional kings squabbled amongst themselves, leaving Britain open to outside interference. It was this weakness brought on by internal divisions that the Romans, new arrivals on the coasts of Gaul, were to exploit.

CHAPTER SIX

THE INVASION OF BRITAIN

The next time I went to Wales, for a short holiday, I took the opportunity to discuss the next stage of my researches with Alan. We discussed many issues but the principal subject of the conversation was the Roman invasion of Britain. As a Kentish man myself (I was born at Beckenham, which though it is in the suburbs of London is nevertheless in Kent – west of the River Medway), I was well aware that Julius Caesar had paid our county a visit in 55 BC and again the following year in 54 BC. This now became the subject of our discussions.

He began: 'For some reason, and I can't really understand it myself, there is a strange silence concerning one of the greatest triumphs of British history: the defeat of Julius Caesar. Of course, a fine gloss is put on the accounts of events, recorded in his *De Bello Gallico* (this section being written by one of his lieutenants), but there can be no doubting that his plans for the conquest of Britain were thwarted.'

In a devastatingly successful campaign, lasting only a little over two years, Caesar had become master of Gaul and then, like Napoleon nearly two millennia later, turned his eyes towards Britain. According to Welsh histories, there was an exchange of letters between him and the ruler of the south-eastern part of Britain, who is referred to by Caesar as Cassivellaunus but whom we know as Caswallon.[1] In 55 BC the British army, which was probably composed of levies from all over the island and not just the south-east, met the Romans on the beaches. After a series of bloody encounters, during one of which Caesar lost his own sword in hand-to-hand fighting, the invaders were forced to withdraw.

Archaeological finds at Hengistbury Head in Dorset, especially of wine amphorae, indicate that the Britons traded extensively with the

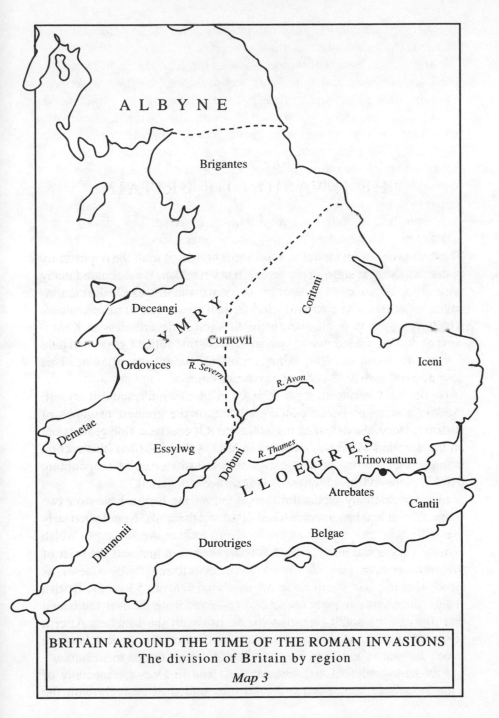

BRITAIN AROUND THE TIME OF THE ROMAN INVASIONS
The division of Britain by region
Map 3

Romans, probably through Gaulish intermediaries, long before Caesar's invasion. Undoubtedly Britain was perceived by Caesar to be a wealthy country, rich in natural resources such as tin, lead and gold as well as wool, leather, corn and flax. Little wonder, then, that he was keen to draw Britain into the Roman Empire to levy taxes on these trade goods as well as a flat-rate tribute. However, in invading Britain, Caesar was exceeding the powers invested in him by the Senate, which extended to Gaul alone. Success would be tolerated and even applauded by both Senate and people; failure, though, was another matter. He therefore had to portray himself as the victor of these operations, even though this was palpably not the case.

A year later Caesar once more landed in Kent. This time he was assisted by a traitor called Afarwy, who was then Duke of Kent, and was able to march without too much difficulty to the Thames. At a ford in the region of what is now Westminster Bridge a major battle was fought with both sides claiming victory. Caesar managed to get his army over to the other side of the river, but it didn't take him long to realize that he was trapped. Running short of supplies, with the days shortening and his fleet at risk of destruction by storms and further attacks by the British, Caesar was once more forced into ignominious retreat. Though in his own account he says that he was given hostages and the promise of trib- ute, this does not seem to have been paid. It also seems likely that Afarwy and his party of traitors went back over the Channel with him: their treachery meant that they could not return home and they therefore had no option but to serve in Caesar's army. Caswallon and his men cel- ebrated their victory with a great banquet in London, where Caesar's sword, captured the previous year, was on view.

It would be nearly a hundred years before the Romans would again cross the Channel to attempt the conquest of Britain. In the meantime peaceful relations had been established, with many Britons visiting Rome. They seem to have been treated well as esteemed guests from what was by now one of the very few free countries of the known world. In AD 43, following the death of a king called Cynvelyn – a name mean- ing 'yellow hair', so presumably he was blond – the Romans returned. This time they were better prepared, whilst the Britons, hearing that the Roman forces were reluctant to embark on their ships, stood down their army. It was a fatal mistake and the Romans were able to land un- opposed. Accordingly, their invading forces, led by the stammering Emperor Claudius, quickly subdued the south-east of the island. He returned home and celebrated with a victory parade; however, his celebrations were premature. The Romans now found themselves drawn into a long and costly war that didn't really end until a peace treaty was signed *c.* 121. It was this treaty, and not the initial conquest, that finally brought Britain as a whole into the Empire.

When I returned home, I started reading about Caesar's invasion to see if the sources bore out Alan's version of events. In the *Brut Tysylio* there is an interesting account of the letters exchanged between the leaders, Caesar and Caswallon, which, though unlikely to be verbatim, is probably faithful to the sentiments expressed on both sides. According to Tysylio, Caesar was well aware of British legends concerning Trojan origins. With a twist of logic that is hard to fathom, he seems to have thought that because Britain had been easily subdued by Brutus, it would be equally easy for him to take the island and make its people subjects of Rome.

At the time Julius Caesar, the Roman emperor, carried on a victorious war against various countries, and having conquered Gaul, and from thence, when he was on the coast of the sea of Ruten [the English Channel], seen Britain, towards the west, he made enquiries as to the opposite country and its inhabitants. And when he received the information as to both; this nation, said he, is of the same origin as we Romans; both are of the Trojan race; for we are derived from Aeneas,[2] who settled in Rome, and whose great-grandson Brutus, settled in Britain. As Brutus subdued the country, I imagine it will not be a hard task for me to make it subject to the Senate of Rome, since they inhabit an island and know nothing of war or arms. Accordingly he then sent a message to Caswallon requiring a peaceable submission of Britain to Rome, and the payment of a tribute, to prevent the shedding of the blood of those who were allied by descents from their common ancestor Priam.

Caswallon, indignant at such a message, peremptorily refused to comply with it, and wished him to know that, as Brutus and his family had from country to country come and settled in Britain to avoid slavery, and found freedom here; so therefore they would now maintain it against all who should attempt to violate it. Caswallon therefore wrote as follows:

'Caswallon to Caesar, the Roman general: Be it known to you, that

> I am astonished in learning that the excessive avarice of the Romans cannot even suffer the inhabitants of an island, remote as this, and surrounded by the perilous sea, to live in peace; but would levy a tribute on us, who have hitherto lived in freedom. Caesar, it is the more disgraceful to yourself, as we acknowledge in Aeneas, a common ancestor. Lay then aside your thoughts of enslaving us. Be assured that, in defence of our freedom and our country, we will maintain the contest till death, rather than suffer you to oppress Britain, if as you announce to us, you should come hither.'[3]

As Alan had said, Caesar's account of the campaign of 55 BC in *De Bello Gallico*, intended for a Roman audience and to enhance rather than diminish his stature, covers up what was clearly a defeat. Arriving on the coast of Kent, with eighty transport ships, two legions of infantry and a number of warships and under constant attack from the indigenous Britons, he was unable to gain much more than a toehold on the beach. Because of a combination of bad weather and high tides, a further eighteen transports carrying cavalry were unable to land a few days later. Without adequate supplies of corn and with many of his remaining ships shattered by the storm, his seventh legion was reduced to scavenging the countryside in search of food.

Caesar's comment, that as the Britons knew nothing of 'war or arms' they would be easy to subdue, probably came from his assumption that technologically they were backward when it came to the manufacture of weapons, such as swords, and that they were ignorant of the modern tactics of legionary warfare that he employed. It must have come as something of a shock to him to discover that they had their own tactics, of which he was ignorant. These were based on the mobility of chariots, as opposed to the plodding power of infantry. The open-order guerilla tactics of Caswallon were not at all what he had been expecting, as he makes clear:

> In chariot fighting the Britons begin by driving all over the field hurling javelins, and generally the terror inspired by the horses and the noise of the wheels are sufficient to throw their opponents' ranks into disorder. Then after making their way between the squadrons of their own cavalry, they jump down from the chariots and engage on foot. In the meantime their charioteers retire a short distance from the battle and place the chariots in such a position that their masters, if

hard pressed by numbers, have an easy means of retreat to their own lines. Thus they combine the mobility of cavalry with the staying power of infantry; and by daily training and practice they attain such proficiency that even on a steep incline they are able to control the horses at full gallop, and to check and turn them in a moment. They can run along the chariot pole, stand on the yoke, and get back in the chariot as quick as lightning.[4]

It is clear from Caesar's description that though he obviously knew about chariots, probably in the context of racing, this was the first time he had seen them used as serious weapons of war. This is not surprising, for chariot warfare had long since disappeared from the battlefields of Europe and the Middle East. The British predilection for chariots can be interpreted as circumstantial evidence for their Trojan origins: Homer's *Iliad* reveals that at the time of the siege of Troy, before the Macedonian kings Philip and Alexander developed techniques of warfare involving the phalanx or infantry square, chariot fighting was the norm. As so often happens on islands, in isolation from the currents of fashion, the Britons preserved the archaic art of charioteering and brought it to great heights.

Though Caesar puts a fine gloss on events, it is clear that his landing party, which may have numbered as many as 12,000 men, was indeed forced to retreat to Gaul. When Caesar returned to make a second attempt at subjugating Britain in the following year, 54 BC, he had a larger army, consisting of five legions (probably about 30,000 men) and 2,000 cavalry. To carry this large force across the Channel he had had 600 flat-bottomed troop-transporters specially built, as well as 28 warships. Once more he landed on the Kent coast, this time on the northern side by Thanet. From here he headed straight for London.

Though he doesn't say so directly, it seems that his reason for heading straight for the capital was that he had made an alliance with a traitor he calls Mandubricius. This was likely to have been the same person as the Afarwy, son of Llud, that Alan had spoken of.[5] In his account of the war Caesar admits that he was using the claims of the young man as a pretext for interfering in the affairs of the Trinovantes – that is, the people who inhabited London and its surrounding area.

Mandubricius, a young prince of this tribe [the Trinovantes], had gone over to the continent to put himself under Caesar's protection, having fled for his life when his father, the king of the Trinovantes, was killed by Cassivellaunus [note: there is no evidence for this other than Caesar's statement]. The envoys promised to surrender and obey Caesar's commands, and asked him to protect Mandubricius from Cassivellaunus and send him home to rule this people as king. Caesar demanded forty hostages and grain for his troops, and then allowed Mandubricius to go. The Trinovantes promptly sent the required number of hostages and the grain.[6]

Caesar's description of an agreement with this prince of the Trinovantes is borne out by British records. In the Welsh triads, Llud's son Afarwy is execrated:

Three men were a disgrace to the Isle of Britain.
One of them was called Afarwy son of Llud son of Beli.
He made an agreement with Julius Caesar and the men of Rome, the first of this island [to do so].
And he offered to pay three thousand pounds of silver every year in tribute from this island if the men of Rome would enter into battle with his uncle Caswallon.

It is perhaps worth mentioning that King Beli – otherwise known as Belin or Belinus – is a key figure in the British histories prior to the Roman invasion. His full title is Beli Mawr and many of the royal genealogies trace back to him as an important patriarch of the dynasty. Like his son Llud he was a builder and is credited with constructing a tower and gateway on the Thames at what is now called Billingsgate:

In the town of Trinovantum Belinus caused to be constructed a gateway of extraordinary workmanship, which in his time the citizens called Billingsgate, from his own name. On the top of it he built a tower which rose to a remarkable height; and down below at its foot he added a water-gate which was convenient for those going on board their ships.[7]

The *Brut Tysylio* agrees with Caesar that following Llud's death Afarwy (here called Androgeus) and his brother Teneufan (Tenuantius) were passed over in favour of Caswallon; but this was, Tysylio says, not because the previous king had been murdered but rather as they were both too young and inexperienced to inherit the throne of Lloegres. This is why it passed to Beli's second son, Caswallon, whilst Afarwy and Teneufan were given the dukedoms of Kent and Cornwall respectively. Tysylio also says that part of Afarwy's secret pact with Caesar was that he would open the gates of London to the Romans in return for being made king. Caesar demanded hostages before he would contemplate a second invasion and thirty of these, including Afarwy's own son (named as Scaeva in other Welsh records), were duly sent over.

Caesar's friendship with the traitor Afarwy possibly explains why in his memoirs he describes the county of Kent as having 'by far the most civilised inhabitants . . . whose way of life differs little from that of the Gauls'. Unfortunately, in the same paragraph he demonizes the rest of the Britons in words that have coloured the opinions of historians ever since. He writes:

> Most of the tribes in the interior do not grow corn but live on milk and meat, and wear skins. All the Britons dye their bodies with woad, which produces a blue colour, and shave the whole of their bodies except the head and the upper lip. Wives are shared between groups of ten or twelve men, especially between brothers and between fathers and sons; but the offspring of these unions are counted as the children of the man with whom a particular woman cohabited first.[8]

These accusations are patently untrue. As Caesar never penetrated very far beyond the north bank of the Thames and therefore had no first-hand knowledge of the rest of Britain, it is likely that he was repeating gossip. That his words give the impression that the Britons were barbarians with shockingly low moral standards, thereby justifying his illegal invasion, could have been part of his public relations exercise intended to win over the home audience at Rome.

Moreover, Caesar's low opinion of the Britons stands in stark contrast to the reports of the Greek geographer Strabo, who was born in 63 BC and died some time after AD 21. It is known that he visited Rome and, as he normally visited the places he described, he almost certainly came to Britain. His unbiased account presents a very different picture from that of the woad-painted savages of popular imagination and is consistent with the Briton's own claims that they, or at least some of them, were the civilized descendants of the Trojans:

He came, not clad in skins like a Scythian, but with a bow in his hand, a quiver hanging on his shoulders, a gilded belt encircling his loins, and trousers reaching from his waist to the soles of his feet. With a plaid wrapped around his body. He was easy in his address, agreeable in his conversation, active in his despatch, and secret in his management of great affairs. Quick in judging of present accuracies, and ready to take his part in any sudden emergency. Provident with-all in guarding against futurity, diligent in his quest for wisdom, fond of friendships trusting very little to fortune, yet having the entire confidence of others, and trusted with everything for his prudence. He spoke Greek with a fluency, that you would have thought he had been bred up in a Lyceum and conversed all his life with the Academy of Athens.[9]

Between Caesar's first and second invasions, the Trinovantes had, as far as possible, repaired their defences and secured the River Thames from seaborn invasion by fencing its banks with sharp stakes. Other, much larger stakes, 'as thick as a man's thigh and shod with iron and lead', were sunk into the river bed, making it impossible for the thin-skinned Roman warships to sail up-stream in support of the legions.[10] Caesar was therefore obliged to march along the south bank of the Thames until he could find a place to ford the river.

Today the flow of the Thames at London is very much confined by the steep walls of the embankments on either side, but in Caesar's time the river was very different. Westminster Abbey stands on what was once known as the Island of Thorns, one of a number of river islands (which included Chelsea and Battersea) in a wide, marshy estuary. These islands have now all disappeared as London has grown, and small streams like the Fleet and Walbrook have been culverted. In Caesar's time, however, the river had a wider flood plain to spread out over. At high tide it would still have been impassable but at low tide and under favourable conditions it was fordable at the Island of Thorns, large boulders having been placed in the water centuries before for this very purpose.[11] It was here that he fought the battle of the ford, which he claims he won:

On learning of the enemy's plan of campaign, Caesar led his army to the Thames in order to enter Cassivellaunus' territory. The river is fordable at one point only, and even there with difficulty. At this place he found large enemy forces drawn up on the opposite bank. The bank was also fenced by sharp stakes fixed along the edge, and he was told by prisoners and deserters that similar ones were concealed in the river-bed. He sent the cavalry across first and then at once ordered the infantry to follow. But the infantry went with such speed and impetuosity, although they had only their heads above the water, that they attacked at the same moment as the cavalry. The enemy was overpowered and fled from the river bank.[12]

Today, at the foot of Westminster Bridge and close to where Caesar's troops would have come ashore, there is a full-size statue of Boudicca driving a chariot. Imagining her chariot multiplied by several thousand gives some idea of what the waiting Britons would have looked like as the Romans waded ashore. As on the beaches of Kent the previous year, Caesar's claimed victory was at best empty. The guerilla tactics of Caswallon had succeeded in stretching Caesar's supply lines, with the result that although he had crossed the Thames safely, he now found himself in the position of being short of food, surrounded by hostile forces; and, because of the wooden stakes, his fleet was unable to sail up the Thames to meet him. His base camp, somewhere near Canterbury, now also came under attack, so he was in real danger of having his fleet destroyed and all retreat cut off. With the days growing ever shorter and Caesar unable to bring in either reinforcements or supplies, Caswallon could afford to take his time. He knew that the Romans could be harried into submission without having to give Caesar the advantage by meeting them in the open field. Caesar would have recognized the danger of such a situation, knowing that this is precisely what had happened to Hannibal when he invaded Italy with an invincible army nearly two centuries before.

Under the circumstances, Caesar found himself with no choice but to retreat or risk losing not only face in Britain but quite possibly his hard-earned gains in Gaul as well.

The implication of Caesar's account has to be that regardless of the outcome of the battle on the Island of Thorns, the gates of London remained closed and in desperation his hungry troops had to go on foraging expeditions further and further afield. Again Caesar puts a fine gloss on events by claiming that his men had succeeded in sacking 'Cassivellaunus' stronghold' during one of these expeditions. Whatever this stronghold was – perhaps St Albans or even Colchester – it certainly wasn't London. It is clear that Afarwy had been unable to keep his side of the bargain, for had Caesar succeeded in taking London and making his protégé king over the Trinovantes, as was his stated war aim, he would have said so. The real situation was that at this point Caswallon felt himself to be sufficiently in control of events to stand down a large part of his army, retaining what he considered to be a sufficient guerilla force to make sure that Caesar's pirates could be contained. Caesar admits as much when he writes the following, though as usual he tries to put a positive spin on events:

> Cassivelaunus [Caswallon] had now given up all hope of fighting a pitched battle. Disbanding the greater part of his troops, he retained only some four thousand charioteers, with whom he watched our line of march. He would retire a short way from the route and hide in dense thickets, driving the inhabitants and cattle from the open country into the woods wherever he knew we intended to pass. If ever our cavalry incautiously ventured too far away in plundering and devastating the country, he would send all his chariots out of the woods by well-known lanes and pathways and deliver very formidable attacks, hoping by this means to make them afraid to go far afield. Caesar was thus compelled to keep the cavalry in touch with the infantry and to let the enemy off with such devastation and burning as could be done under the protection of the legionaries – tired as they often were with marching.[13]

Caswallon had, if needed, many more men in reserve to draw on than the four thousand chariots retained to contain the Roman retreat. This is borne out by modern archaeology, which also reveals that Caesar's statement that Britain was even then a densely populated country is true. The population of the island as a whole was probably at least six million[14] and, as all men between the ages of fourteen and sixty were expected to be available for call-up at any given time, there were plenty of reserves.

According to Welsh records, Caswallon now invited Caesar to dinner, perhaps to demonstrate that, unlike the Romans, he and his men had all the food they needed. They agreed to a truce, by which Caesar and his men would be escorted unmolested out of Britain. Caswallon, who had not started the war, was keen to bring it to an end with as little damage to people, livestock and property as possible. Under these circumstances, letting the Romans conduct an orderly retreat was clearly a sensible move.

In his own account Caesar reports that he agreed to withdraw, provided that he was given hostages and that the Britons agreed to pay an annual tribute. Whether or not he really did secure this promise, there is no evidence that he ever received any payments as a result of this treaty. The 'hostages' referred to were probably Afarwy and his party of traitors, who now entered Caesar's retinue. The reality was that Caesar's army, which had set out in high hopes of conquering Britain and putting a puppet-king on the throne of Lloegres, was now crowded into his remaining ships and headed back for Gaul. That they were in a hurry to go is evidenced by Caesar's own admission that each ship carried three times the number of men it should have. The Welsh triads record that Caswallon and his men celebrated their victory with a great feast for which 120,000 animals were killed. The Romans themselves were probably not really fooled by Caesar's propaganda, as in time they must have heard the terrible truth from the lips of his returning legionnaires. The poet Lucan was to lampoon him with the words: 'In haste he turned and showed his back, To the Britons he had attacked.'

Following Caesar's abortive campaigns, it was, as Alan had said, to be a further ninety-six years before the Roman army, by now the greatest military machine the world had ever seen, returned to Britain. During that time more or less friendly relations were established between the Britons and the Romans. Caswallon was succeeded first by Teneufan, Afarwy's brother, and then Cynvelyn (Cunobelinus),[15] who was also a grandson of Afarwy's grandfather Beli. Cynvelyn visited Rome, where he is said to have been received by the Emperor Augustus, a story borne out when the Lexdon tumulus, believed to be his grave, was opened in 1922–4. In it was found, buried with the king, a remarkable cameo brooch bearing a picture of Augustus. This was almost certainly a present from the Emperor himself when Cynvelyn made his celebrated visit to Rome. For now Britain was safe from Roman predation, and it would remain so until after the death of Augustus and his successors Tiberius and Caligula. Surprisingly, really, it would be left to the non-militaristic Claudius to make the next attempt at the conquest of Britain.

THE INVASION OF CLAUDIUS

Unlike his predecessors, Claudius was something of an intellectual. Unprepossessing in appearance and possibly suffering from cerebral palsy, he had spent a lifetime studying books rather than leading armies, so warfare did not come naturally to him. To be sure of the support of both the army and people, he knew he needed a triumphant victory that they could all celebrate. He needed to add to the accomplishments of Julius Caesar and Augustus, thereby distancing himself from the disastrous Caligula and the decadence that he represented. Realizing this, he turned his attention to Britain, which, in spite of Julius Caesar's claimed victory, still lay outside the Roman Empire. With this in mind Claudius marshalled his forces and in AD 43 some 40,000 troops, led by Aulus Plautius, were ferried over the Channel along with a secret asset: a force of elephants.

This time the British, thinking the Romans weren't coming, were not as well prepared as they had been under Caswallon. In battle the elephants proved to be a formidable weapon, not so much because of what they themselves did but because their unfamiliar noise and smell frightened the horses pulling the British chariots. The Roman army was therefore able to advance on London virtually unhindered. Here it was joined by Claudius himself. Proceeding eastwards, they made their way to the regional city later called Camulodunum (Colchester). Opening a second front, one of Claudius's most able generals, Vespasian, who was later to become Emperor himself, landed with the second legion at Poole on the Dorset coast. Marching inland he seized a line of important hill forts, eventually taking the enormous Maiden Castle on the outskirts of what is now Dorchester. Elsewhere the Romans were able to exploit political divisions between the rulers of different tribes. For example, a Belgic king called Cogidumnus, whose exact relationship with the ruling family is not clear, entered into a tactical alliance with the Romans, much to the fury of his fellow Britons. As a reward, the Romans later built him a sumptuous palace at Fishbourne in Sussex. With moves such as this, the Romans gained a foothold in southern England, with Camulodunum and Verulamium being transformed into Roman *coloniae*. Claudius was able to return home to Rome and award himself a triumph, renaming his young son Britannicus in celebration of his great victory.

However, like Julius Caesar before him, he was being premature.

Though the southern, more Roman-influenced counties of England had more or less acquiesced to Roman authority, this by no means meant that Britain as a whole had been conquered. As they pushed north and west, the Roman legions encountered greater resistance. For whilst the downlands of southern England favoured the Roman infantry and were relatively easy to police, the steep hills and valleys of northern England and of Wales were a different matter. Fortunately for the Romans, the Britons continued to be divided and they were able to deal with individual tribes, such as the Iceni, Brigantes and Ordovices, one at a time. However, the campaign ground to a halt when they tried to enter south Wales. A long war of attrition now got under way against the Khymric tribe resident here, the Essylwg, or 'Silures', as they were called. They turned out to be far more determined to keep their independence from Rome than the tribes of Lloegres and inflicted a series of defeats on the Roman legions sent by Claudius to oppress them. The story of their resistance is recorded by Tacitus in his *Annals of Imperial Rome*: 'Neither sternness nor leniency prevented the Silures from fighting . . . The natural ferocity of the inhabitants was intensified by their belief in the prowess of Caratacus [Caradoc], whose many undefeated battles – and even many victories – had made him pre-eminent among British chieftains.'[16]

Caradoc, or Caratacus, was then the high king of all Britain. He was a son of the previous high king, called Arch,[17] and a direct descendant of Brutus. Tacitus states that Caradoc's successes drew to his ranks recruits from other British tribes. These included some of the

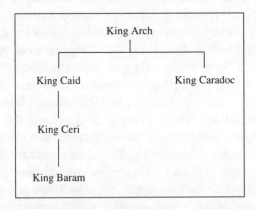

THE HOUSE OF KING ARCH OF GLAMORGAN
Diagram 5

Trinovantes: the Welsh triads record that a retinue from London, led by a prince called Belyn, son of Cynvelyn, joined Caradoc's army to carry on the war with Rome. These volunteers are remembered with particular affection in the Welsh triads for offering their services without pay. Doubtless there were other Lloegrians as well, who, disgusted by the way their own leaders had allowed their personal feuds to enable the Romans to gain a foothold in the south-east of the island, were happy to fight on under the banner of Caradoc.

To try to overcome the Khymry of Essylwg, the Romans now invaded Caradoc's territory in south Wales with a huge army led by their four most able generals: Aulus Plautius, Vespasian, his son Titus, and Geta, the conqueror of Mauretania.[18] To this illustrious company was added the Emperor Claudius himself, who rushed to Britain with the second and fourteenth legions. Brave as he was, Caradoc was up against a formidable foe. However, as long as he stuck to guerilla tactics, as Caswallon had done with Julius Caesar a century before, he was able to compensate for any deficiency in numbers and weaponry and carry on the resistance. Caradoc won a number of battles but eventually a decisive battle was fought which, though the result is open to dispute, effectively put an end to his career as war leader.

Though the outcome of the battle may not have been the great victory for the Romans claimed by Tacitus, for the war between the Khymric Silures and the Romans carried on for another twenty-three years and the latter were not able to enter south Wales until AD 74, it did have important consequences. Following the battle Caradoc journeyed north and appealed to Aregwedd Voeydawg (Cartismandua), queen of the Brigantes,[19] to join his alliance. She, however, had her own preoccupations. Divorced from her husband and unpopular with her own people, she was reliant on Roman support to maintain her throne. She therefore had Caradoc arrested, handing him and his followers to his enemies. Thus it was that in AD 51, as a result of her betrayal, almost the entire family of Caradoc was taken prisoner and shipped back to Rome as hostages. Meanwhile the war in south Wales raged on, the Khymry of Essylwg being led, with considerable success, by Caradoc's nephew, Ceri ap Caid ap Arch, known as 'Longsword'.

It would seem that the Romans had a fascination with Caradoc, who for years had withstood their best efforts and who had come into their hands only as a result of treachery. They turned out by the thousand to see him paraded through the streets of Rome on his way to a trial at the

Senate. The extraordinary events of that day are recorded by Tacitus in his *Annals*:

> The war in Britain was in its ninth year. The reputation of Caratacus had spread beyond the islands and through the neighbouring provinces to Italy itself. These people were curious to see the man who had defied our power for so many years. Even at Rome his name meant something. Besides, the emperor's attempts to glorify himself conferred additional glory on Caratacus in defeat. For the people were summoned as though for a fine spectacle, while the guard stood in arms on the parade ground before their camp. Then there was a march past, with Caratacus' petty vassals, and the decorations and neck-chains and spoils of his foreign wars. Next were displayed his brothers, wife and daughter. Last came the king himself. The others, frightened, degraded themselves by entreaties. But there were no downcast looks or appeals for mercy from Caratacus.[20]

It would have been expected that Caradoc, chained like an animal, would suffer a cruel death and his household be reduced to slavery. Such had been the fate of others, including the brave Gallic leader, Vercingetorix, who had dared to stand up to the might of the burgeoning Roman Empire and had been similarly exhibited at Julius Caesar's triumph in 45 BC, before being executed. But as the Romans had not defeated the Khymry, it was clearly in their interest to come to some sort of accommodation with Caradoc. Claudius must have been mindful of this when Caradoc made his famous speech to the Senate appealing for clemency, the gist of which has fortunately been preserved by Tacitus:

> On reaching the dais he [Caradoc] spoke in these terms. 'Had my lineage and rank been accompanied by only moderate success, I should have come to this city as friend rather than prisoner, and you would not have disdained to ally yourself peacefully with one so nobly born, the ruler of so many nations. As it is, humiliation is my lot, glory yours. I had horses, men, arms, wealth. Are you surprised I am sorry to lose them? If you want to rule the world, does it follow that everyone else welcomes enslavement? If I had surrendered without a blow before being brought before you, neither my downfall nor your triumph would have become famous. If you execute me, they will be forgotten. Spare me, and I shall be an everlasting token of your mercy!'[21]

Amazingly, Claudius did just that, setting free the whole family. This made good political sense, given that, with the war still active in Britain, Claudius couldn't be sure that he might not need Caradoc alive in the future. However, Caradoc was not completely free. Under the terms of the agreement he was effectively a hostage, constrained to stay in Rome for seven years and to take an oath that he would never again bear arms. As befitted their rank, he and his family were given a villa on the Esquiline Hill, known as the Palatium Britannicum, in which to live. As we shall see, this was to turn out to be of great consequence, not just for Caradoc and the Khymry but for the development of the Christian Church.

In AD 60 trouble erupted in the east of Britain. The Iceni, a large tribe occupying most of East Anglia, had voluntarily become allies of the Romans at the time Claudius invaded Britain in AD 43. A minor rebellion by them a few years later had been put down by Ostorius Scapula, the general who later captured Caradoc, and once more they had come to an accommodation with Rome. In AD 60 their king, Prasutagus, died, leaving a will naming his two daughters, along with the Emperor Nero, as his co-heirs; foolishly, he believed that this would preserve the peace and save both his kingdom and family from enslavement. However, it produced the opposite effect, as it gave the Romans the pretext they needed for oppressing the Iceni, the king's family not excepted. With great arrogance the Romans, spurred on by Cicero, who had lent money to Prasutagus, plundered his household as if it were a prize of war. Then, adding injury to insult, they flogged his widow Boudicca and raped their two daughters. Outraged and fearing worse atrocities if they didn't fight back, the Iceni once more rose in rebellion. This time they were joined in a confederation by other tribes, including the Trinovantes. They marched on Camulodunum, which had long been an irritation to the British as it had been taken over by the Romans and turned into a colony for veterans from the legions. The city was razed to the ground and the ninth Roman division, sent to Camulodunum's aid, had its entire infantry force massacred. Only the cavalry units were able to escape and take back bad tidings to Suetonius (Governor of Roman Britain), who was engaged in operations further west. He hastened to London with reinforcements but, realizing that he was outnumbered and fearing defeat, retreated west. The triumphant Iceni carried on their rampage, burning down London and destroying the other Roman city in the area, Verulamium.

Boudicca, who was determined to drive all the Romans and their allies from Britain, now went in pursuit of Suetonius. He was probably stationed at this time in or near the Roman stronghold of Wroxeter, where the fourteenth legion was then stationed. He was joined by elements of the twentieth legion, with the result that altogether, with auxiliaries, he had a force of some ten thousand men under his command and he now felt strong enough to face Boudicca. A decisive battle took place, probably at Gop Paulini in north Wales. Tacitus's boast that the Romans suffered only four hundred casualties compared to the Britons' eighty thousand should be taken with a large pinch of salt. However, what is not in dispute is that Boudicca and her daughters, believing their forces defeated, committed suicide.

The Boudicca rebellion, though unsuccessful, proved to be a decisive moment for the Romans. Catus Decianus, called by Tacitus an 'imperial agent' and the man responsible for the rape of Boudicca's daughters, was forced to withdraw to Gaul in disgrace. Poenius Postumus, the commander of the second legion who had disobeyed orders and not joined forces with Suetonius, committed suicide rather than face a court martial. Even Suetonius, the supposed victor and the proprietor with ultimate responsibility for the safety of the Roman colonies in Britain, did not come out of the affair well. Tacitus, not one to exaggerate setbacks, admits to Roman and provincial deaths of over seventy thousand in the south-east alone. Though not all the dead were soldiers, this huge number was far more than Roman public opinion was willing to sustain for the sake of the conquest of Britain. Even worse, Suetonius had, like his predecessors, proved himself unable to bring to a successful conclusion the war with the Khymry of Essylwg, which by now had been dragging on for nearly twenty years, and his failure in this respect seems to have been the last straw. According to Tacitus, he was demoted and replaced as proprietor after losing some ships and their crews. Though Tacitus doesn't give us any more details, it would be fair to assume that these losses occurred during naval engagements fought against the Khymry, for Ceri 'Longsword', Caradoc's nephew and successor, is recorded as having built up a sizeable navy. The book entitled 'The Genealogy of Iestyn the Son of Gwrgan', contained in the *Iolo MSS*, records: 'Ceri, the son of Caid, was a remarkably wise man, and constructed many ships at the expense of the country and its lords; hence he was called Ceri of the extensive navy, having numerous fleets at sea. He lived at a place called Porth Ceri.'[22]

No emperor, still less an unpopular one such as Nero, could allow such a situation to drag on with no end in sight; at best it could add to his unpopularity and at worst it laid him open to the risk of a military coup. The mailed fist having clearly failed, Nero decided to try a kid-glove approach and sent a former imperial slave, Polyclitus, to talk to the Britons and to see if the war could be brought to an end by negotiation. Suetonius was sacked and the consul Publius Petronius Turpilianus appointed in his place. Tacitus seems not to have approved of this pacifist policy: 'His [Suetonius's] successor, the recent consul Publius Petronius Turpilianus, neither provoking the enemy nor provoked, called this ignoble inactivity peace with honour.'[23] In truth the Romans had shown themselves able to maintain their foothold in Britain only at huge cost and with the active cooperation of the local kings of Britain. This they were now to court with great effect, the British aristocracy becoming 'Romanized' in the process.

CHAPTER SEVEN

THE ROMANS IN BRITAIN

When I joined Alan and Baram in their quest for King Arthur I had not realized how important a knowledge of the history of what is loosely termed Roman Britain is for a proper understanding of what happened subsequently in the fifth and sixth centuries.

Like most people, I suspect, I had always assumed that following the conquest of Claudius Britain was governed by Roman procurators – the equivalents of Pontius Pilate in Judaea – and that native kingship became extinct until its reintroduction following the Romans' departure in AD 406. I was now to discover that this view was false: that throughout the occupation British dynasties continued to rule. This, though omitted from recent history books, is stated openly by Charles II's historian, Percy Enderbee, who, in his *Cambria Triumphans*, explains that the retention of the traditional authority of local kings was a part of Roman policy at that time: 'About that time [AD 87] Arviragus a Briton by birth and education did govern as king in part of the Isle of Britain; the Romans accounting it a point of policy to permit the Britons to be ruled by persons of their own nation.'[1] I was also to discover that inter-marriage between Romans and Britons meant that some of the later Roman emperors were also rightful kings of Britain and some British kings asserted claims over the imperial office. Thus the Romans not only permitted the line of British kings to carry on ruling but eventually laid claim to the throne themselves by virtue not of conquest but of birth, which was to have profound consequences when one of these emperors, Constantine the Great, ultimately turned the whole Roman Empire to Christianity. Learning how all this came about was the next stage of my education into the 'matter of Britain' and was ultimately to lead back to

101

the mysterious cross on the wall. This, however, was still some way off and to understand its significance there was still much I needed to learn about the Romans and what had really happened during the crucial centuries between the invasion of Claudius in AD 43 and the arrival in Britain of Constantius and his son Constantine in AD 305.

In previous conversations with Alan I had asked him a number of questions about his understanding of the Roman occupation of Britain. Not a man to mince words, he repeatedly pointed out how, influenced by Victorian thinking, today we tend not to see things as they really were. He emphasized again that since we are too ready to take the Roman accounts of events, scanty as they are, at face value, and, in fact, ignore British records, which are far more detailed on these matters, we talk of 'Roman Britain'; when really there was no such thing. The Roman influence, though important, was not the only one on the prevailing culture of the time, nor even necessarily the most important.

The Romans' interest in Britain was primarily financial; and they were, Alan said, practical people. Claudius was not intent on destroying British civilization. He had political reasons for invading. Acutely aware that the same forces who had given him the imperium could as easily take it away again, he thought – he hoped – that through the British adventure not only could he be seen to be enlarging the Empire and succeeding where even Julius Caesar himself had failed, he could also, in due course, milk these new territories for tax revenues. What the Romans wanted and needed was not permanent warfare in Britain but to trade profitably with its inhabitants. In fact, Alan pointed out to me, the Roman Empire never was the monolithic entity it is made out to be. It was much more of a trading conglomerate than anything else. Throughout the Empire's history it was in danger of being torn apart as its many components fought and killed one another, with now one emperor or dynasty on top and then another. Throughout all this turmoil the real glue that held the Empire together was not political but economic. As elsewhere in history, the real empire builders were not the legionnaires in their leather skirts but the merchants. Certainly as long as their interests were satisfied, the Empire flourished.

Britain had a particular practical value to the Romans. Later on in the second and third centuries AD the Romans had large standing armies on the Rhine. These needed to be paid, fed, clothed, armed, provided with tents and so on. It was the British who supplied most of these commodities. Huge fleets of ships sailed between Britain and the Rhine ports, carrying corn, meat on the hoof, wool and leather. Britain was also a major exporter of metals, particularly iron, lead and silver but also tin, copper and gold. There are gold mines in Gwynedd that were worked for millennia before Caesar ever set foot in Kent and indeed most of the other metals came from Wales. In south Wales vast lead mines, stretching many miles underground, have been found; and these would have produced prodigious quantities of silver as well. South Wales also had at that time the largest known reserves of iron ore in the whole of Europe before the discovery in recent times of even bigger deposits in northern Sweden; there is much evidence of iron working in the locality in that period. Bearing in mind that Glamorgan was also very rich in coal, with some seams coming right up to the surface or protruding onto cliff faces, it is not hard to see that the ancient Britons had all the minerals needed for an iron and steel industry. Although local archaeologists have done little research on this, the historical records indicate that, although most of the large population would have been employed in agriculture, mining and metal working were also extremely important industries. In the light of this evidence one begins to understand how it was that Caradoc and his successors were able to stand up to the might of Rome. They had the manpower and equipment to do so.

All in all Britain was a rich country and its relationship with Rome was not as subservient as the history books make out. Fighting long and costly wars with Britain was also not in the Romans' interest. They much preferred to do deals with local rulers and work with them than to carry on with conflicts. If you read the histories correctly, this is exactly what happened in Britain. After the supposed Roman victory over the Silures of Wales in AD 74, the war raged on for ten years, after which the Romans backed off, at least from the west: excavations at Wroxeter indicate that they abandoned their fortress there around AD 90 at the latest. They could hardly do anything else. The fourteenth legion was withdrawn from Britain to Germany in AD 69, leaving a total of only some fifteen thousand troops plus auxiliaries to establish garrisons to guard the borders and defend the remaining Roman settlements. Outside these, which were essentially trading stations, the rest of Britain, with a population running into millions, was still governed by its traditional hierarchy of kings, dukes, clan chieftains and so on. In the main it was these people, and not, as Alan put it, 'fictional immigrants from Rome – retired soldiers or whoever', who built and lived in the

'Roman' towns and villas. Between AD 90 and 123 there was no senior Roman governor in Britain.[2] In this way the relationship of the Romans to the Britons'was similar to that of the British to the Indians in the last century.

Whilst the Romans obviously wanted the British to adopt Roman ways, they couldn't impose them. For example, during the persecutions of Diocletian, when thousands of Christians were thrown to the lions in Rome, Gaul and other parts of the Empire, only three Christian martyrs are recorded in Britain. British histories show that by that time the majority of Britons, including the leading families, were all Christians. To try to persecute them for their religion would have been as stupid as the nineteenth-century British trying to suppress Hinduism in India or the French trying to stamp out Islam in north Africa. It would not only not have worked but would have led to a national uprising. Moreover, by the early third century AD the 'Roman' armies in Britain were made up almost entirely of local recruits. They were no longer Roman legions in anything but name but rather British armies whose allegiance to Rome, as events were to prove, was questionable.

Even in the south-east of England, where there was a stronger Roman presence, the Romans were not able to do as they pleased. The rebellion led by Boudicca is one example of British resistance. Later traditions, recorded in Geoffrey of Monmouth's *History*, state that shortly before the arrival of Constantius in AD 305, there was another uprising when the Britons, including the Ordovices of north Wales, sieged London and captured a whole Roman legion. The Ordovices beheaded all of them and threw their heads into the Walbrook stream, a tributary of the Thames. Geoffrey's account was considered to be an exaggeration until the 1860s, when General Pitt-Rivers, the 'father' of modern archaeology, had the bed of the Walbrook excavated and discovered many skulls, with few other bones, dating from the right period. What happened to the headless bodies isn't recorded.

The myth of Roman invincibility, expounded by many academics, is therefore simply not true. Their hold on Britain was tenuous at the best of times, as we shall see. The term 'Roman Britain' is a misnomer; to use it is like talking about 'Russian Poland' or 'American Vietnam'. That the British adopted many Roman ways cannot be disputed but does not undermine the fact that the country was in effect a semi-detached member of the Empire and frequently totally separated.

Alan also made the point that the Romans were to some extent in awe of the Britons, or at least of their leaders. When they married into the Khymric royal families, this was not a matter of a few senators 'going native and having a good time with the local women': to the Romans it was a source of great pride to marry a British princess. As we have seen, the British claimed descent through Brutus, the great-grandson of Aeneas, founder of Rome, to the Trojans. Since the Romans had centuries earlier expelled their own royal family, the Tarquins, for Romans to marry British royalty was to add legitimacy to their own lines, restoring through their descendants their link back to Aeneas and the Trojans.

In the last two centuries scholars have poured scorn on the Trojan traditions of both Britain and Rome, arguing that as there was no such place as Troy, the migration legends were false. But the sceptics failed to revise their opinions after Schliemann discovered Troy and it was shown that the journeys of Aeneas and Brutus were technically possible. Homer's *Iliad* and *Odyssey* well demonstrate that the Greeks and Trojans knew all about navigation as well as chariot warfare; the idea of the surviving Trojans sailing off into the blue yonder to get away as far as they could from the Greeks is not so strange, particularly as it is becoming clearer that the Trojan War took place much more recently than was previously thought.[3] It is only Victorian prejudice, Alan argued, that made this seem impossible. Both the Britons and the Romans believed implicitly not only in Troy itself but also that they were its rightful heirs. From this it followed that in their own eyes the Britons and Romans were relatives. This put the British nobility in a unique and strong position with the Romans.

Further evidence against the argument that the British were defeated and crushed is the prosperity of British aristocrats. 'The lot of the individual peasant might not have been wonderful,' explained Alan, 'but for the aristocracy times were rosy indeed.' The British nobility quickly developed a taste for Roman luxuries. The opening up of export markets for the produce of Britain caused their coffers to overflow, and they were able to commission palaces and country houses for themselves, with all the latest luxuries such as central heating. In a few cases, these buildings were put up for ex-pat Roman governors, merchants and the like, but generally these people retired to Rome or wherever they had come from. In the main these villas were built by and for indigenous British aristocrats who had adopted a Roman lifestyle. Such people learnt Latin and Greek, visited Rome and often took Roman names in addition to those in their own language of Khymric. These people thrived because Romans and Britons, or at least their leaders, recognized that they could do good business together. As long as the Romans respected British traditions, methods of government, religion, laws and ownership, affairs remained peaceable. It was when they forgot this fact that trouble started.

In AD 79 Gnaeus Julius Agricola was made propraetor or governor of Britain. He fought a series of campaigns against the Picts, traditional enemies of the British, and some early campaigns in north Wales. According to Welsh histories, he was eventually driven out of Wales, by a king we call Baram. According to the official Roman histories – based on the not-unbiased accounts of his son-in-law, Tacitus – Agricola was 'recalled' rather than defeated. That something was amiss is suggested by the fact that his retirement was cut short when he was poisoned, probably on the orders of the Emperor Domitian, in AD 93. The man who is believed to have been Agricola's successor to the post of Roman propraetor of Britain, Sallustius Lucullus, was also 'recalled' and met a sticky end in AD 90, again on orders of Domitian, this time, supposedly, for the trivial crime of allowing a new spear to be named after him. It seems more likely that his failure at subjugating Britain was his real crime, for at this point there is an ominous thirty-year silence in the Roman record on the subject of propraetors and it is hard to avoid the conclusion that, as Welsh records testify, Britain had to all intents and purposes regained its independence. Indeed Roman records say that 'Bonassus usurped the Empire in Britain' around this time. It is clear that this 'Bonassus' is to be identified as King Baram, son of Ceri, who in the 'Genealogy of Iestyn the Son of Gwrgan' is indeed said to have 'vanquished the Romans in every engagement'. The destruction of the ninth legion at York at some time between 115 and 120 also shows how little real control the Romans really had, even in the east.

In 117 Hadrian became Emperor and set about putting the Empire on a more sustainable footing. His busts and statues show him as having been physically the very opposite of Julius Caesar, whose chiselled features, smooth chin and beady eyes are indicative of his cold, ruthless personality, while Hadrian's statues, on the other hand, indicate that he was a great bear of a man with curly hair, a beard and a broad chest. He looked like a sort of James Robertson Justice or Brian Blessed and one could well imagine that when not booming orders to quaking subordinates he would be at his happiest drinking with his centurions and

telling jokes. One of history's great pragmatists, he could see how un-
stable was the enormous Empire bequeathed to him by his predecessor
Trajan. He therefore set about pruning it down to a manageable size,
beginning with the territories of Armenia, Assyria and Mesopotamia,
which he prudently judged indefensible in the long term. He contem-
plated doing the same thing in Dacia[4] and was dissuaded from doing so
only on account of the large number of Roman settlers in the area.
Having sorted out those matters, he was then in a position to turn his
attention to Britain.

Returning from the east, Hadrian made his way across the Channel,
arriving on the island in 122. This, however, was not another invasion,
for whilst he was of course keen to include as much as possible of
Britain in the Empire, his policy was one of negotiation rather than co-
ercion. We can guess that he met all the important leaders of the different
tribes of both Lloegres and Cymry and tried to persuade them, rather
like a modern-day European Commissioner, that their own interests
were better served inside a peaceful Empire rather than outside in the
cold. In the main Hadrian's campaign of diplomacy worked and he was
able to negotiate a treaty which brought most of Britain into the Empire.
Alan and Baram believe that his agreement with the kings of Essylwg
was ratified at Cardiff, whose Welsh name Caer-Dydd means 'castle of
the agreement'. Part of the Romans' payment for this new understanding seems to have been the building of Hadrian's Wall, which was
designed to keep out the Britons' enemies, the Picts. This was not the
elaborate wall that we see today which, according to the histories, was
built nearly a century later by Septimius Severus.

With Hadrian's death power passed to Antoninus Pius, his adopted
heir, and thereafter the imperium became once more, for a time, a family affair. When Antoninus died he was succeeded by his adopted son
Marcus Aurelius, first of all in partnership with his brother Verus and
then on his own. Marcus was succeeded in 180 by his mad son
Commodus, called Britannicus, who was assassinated in 192. After a
short period of chaos, he was succeeded by Septimius Severus
(193–211), who supposedly died in York yet left a memorial stone in
Wales. He is recorded in Welsh histories as having been of British
descent. His son Bassianus, 'Caracalla' (211–18), also left a memorial
stone in south Wales.

Alan and Baram believe that from the time of Antoninus Pius onwards
the Emperors of Rome were nearly all of part-British origin. This may

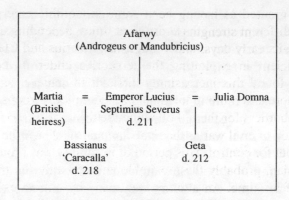

THE DESCENT OF SEPTIMIUS SEVERUS
Diagram 6

seem strange, but is in fact no more so than the fact that prior to the First World War Queen Victoria's grandchildren occupied the thrones of Germany, Russia and many other European countries, some of them Britain's enemies. Regular intermarriage between states means that for every crowned head on a major stem of a family tree, there are always dozens growing on side-shoots – cadet branches ready and waiting for a throne should the opportunity arise.

Alan and Baram are still researching the exact relationship between the royal families of Britain and the imperial lines of the Romans. However, it is clear that, except in extreme circumstances, not just anyone could be elevated to the principate. Claimants needed to have royal blood: either that of the Caesars or better still that of Aeneas. This bloodline was recorded as running through the royal house of Britain and therefore Roman claimants who could show a link with this family tree were in a particularly strong position. This did not mean that either they or their immediate ancestors had to have been born in Britain. By the second century AD there were Britons serving in the legions all over the Empire.[5] Thus a Roman such as Septimus Severus could still be a member of the British royal family even though he was born in Africa.

Once again, after this discussion Alan had left me with a large bundle of notes and assorted family trees, which I took home and added to the huge pile I already had in my possession. I set about, by reading this and other material, to learn more about the period Alan had described. By now I was beginning to realize that the Roman Empire, which I had taken for granted as having been some monolithic enterprise, was in reality of different strengths at different times, depending on who was at the top. In its early days, under Augustus, Tiberius and Claudius, it was fairly efficient in exploiting the territories under its control. Later Emperors found this increasingly difficult to achieve, as the Romans became more and more indolent and relied on local troops and rulers to guard the borders for them. Following the death of Nero in AD 68, there was a period of civil war as the rival claimants Galba, Otho and Vitellius fought it out for control. This period of instability was brought to an end by Vespasian, probably the most able and certainly the most powerful general of his time. An attempt was made by him to establish a new dynasty, for after he died in AD 79 he was succeeded by his two sons: first Titus (AD 79–81) and then Domitian (AD 81–96). The murder of Domitian cleared the way for Nerva (AD 96–8), who had twice before served as consul and was now installed as Emperor by popular demand. His rule was short, but did not end before he had adopted the powerful general Trajan (98–117) as his successor, who in turn adopted Hadrian (117–38), the son of his first cousin Adrianus. Wherever possible, the Emperors of Rome sought to keep the succession in the family.

It was in the last quarter of the first century, under the Emperors Vespasian, Titus and Domitian, that first Agricola and then Sallustius Lucullus were sent to Britain as propraetors. As Alan had said, the latter seems to have been ineffectual and certainly did not conduct any successful campaigns. Percy Enderbee, historian to Charles II, has this to say of him:

> Sallustius Lucullus succeeding Agricola left little memory of himself
> by doing anything here, either for that no occasion was then offered
> to show himself in action, or else for that the fame of so famous a
> predecessor blemished his reputation; for having held the office a
> short time, he was by commandment of Domitian put to death for
> suffering certain spears of a new fashion to be called by his own
> name.[6]

There is indeed no other recorded propraetor after Sallustius, who must have left Britain before AD 90 (the date of his execution), until the arrival of the Emperor Hadrian in AD 123. On balance Hadrian seems to have been a good Emperor. Intelligent, well read and keen to put an end to unnecessary wars, he consolidated the Empire. Wherever he could he tried to bring stability and nowhere was this more necessary than in the matter of imperial succession. This was always one of Rome's greatest problems: how to ensure a smooth transition between generations and provide the Empire with the leadership it needed. Strange as it may seem, his journey to Britain may indeed have been, at least in part, an investigation into the possibility of further linking the destiny of Rome with the British royal line of Brutus. What is certain is that Hadrian was not against the idea of provinces having their own kings. For instance, Spartians, his biographer, records him as allowing the Armenians to have a king of their own and even appointing one for Germany. He would, therefore, have had no problem with the idea of Britain being governed by its own kings, provided the Romans maintained their trading interests and received taxes.

BRITAIN IN THE TIME OF THE ROMANS

As Alan explained, the Romans' main interest in the island of Britain, so far away from the balmy lands of the Mediterranean, was trade and there were indeed rich pickings to be had: gold, silver, tin, corn and leather to name but the most obvious commodities. Contrary to suggestions that prior to the arrival of the vagabond armies of the Caesars the country was a nearly empty wilderness populated by painted savages, Britain was in fact already densely populated with possibly as many as eight million inhabitants. The majority of forest clearance having been achieved centuries earlier, the countryside of southern England probably looked not that much different from today: a patchwork quilt of fields interspersed with small woods, forest and moorland. It was certainly a land of trading opportunities. However, the uprising of Boudicca taught the Romans a sharp lesson: that if they wanted the chance to make money, they needed peace, for which they required the co-operation of the British nobility. They also needed a fairly large standing army with which to police the borders of the areas they controlled and to intimidate any tribes that might be thinking of rebelling.

To administer the territories over which they had nominal control, and for their own safety and security, the Romans built five cities of their own with the status of either *colonia* or *municipia*: Camulodunum (Colchester), Verulamium (St Albans), Lindum (Lincoln), Glevum (Gloucester) and Eburacum (York). Most, if not all, of these cities

Antonine Wall
(Valum Antonia)

VALENTIA

*Oceanus
Germanicus*

Hadrian's Wall

Mona   Monatia
HIBERNIA   Monoedians

MAXIMA
CAESARIENSIS

Brigantes   • EBURACUM

*Oceanus
Hibernicus*

• Mona

ERNE

• DEVA   LINDUM
Cornovii   Coritani

Ordovices   LETOCETUM
• VIROCONIUM   Cenimagni Simeni
BRITANNIA   FLAVIA
SECUNDA   CAESARENSIS   Iceni

GLEVUM   Cotiongiani
Demetae   Essylwg   ISCIA   VERULAMIUM
Dobuni   CAMULODUNUM
*Oceanus
Verginius*   Trinovantes
Atrebates
Sabrina Estuary

BRITANNIA PRIMA   Cantii
Durotriges

Dumnonni

Oceanus Britannicus

This map bears an extraordinary similarity to the later division of Britain in the seventh century:
i.e. Britannia Prima = Wessex and Kent
Britannia Secunda = Wales
Flavia Caesariensis = Mercia   .... 'Roman' roads
Maxima Caesariensis
and Valentia = Northumbria

BRITAIN IN LATER ROMAN TIMES
Map 4

existed in some form before the invasion but were now redeveloped on the Roman model. In a situation similar to that of Hong Kong following the Opium Wars, the cities were islands of alien culture grudgingly accepted by the indigenous population until such time as the outsiders could be expelled completely. In the meantime they provided role models for the British to redevelop their own towns and cities as well as providing outlets for trade.

To maintain their position and to protect the borders of the areas of Britain under their control, the Romans kept three legions on permanent standby: the sixth legion, stationed at York; the twentieth legion, stationed at Deva (Chester); and the second legion, stationed at Isca Silurum (Caerleon). Though at first these legions were composed entirely of non-Britons, drawn from around the Empire, in time, through native recruitment, their composition changed so that they became, in effect, British armies that could and often did intervene in the affairs of Rome itself.

As well as these Roman foundations there were in Britain at that time a large number of essentially British cities that were neither Roman *coloniae* nor *municipiae*. The most important of these were already, prior to the Claudian invasion, the capital cities of the British tribes. They included: Isurium Brigantia (Aldborough), chief city of the Brigantes; Ratae (Leicester), chief city of the Coritani; Viroconium (Wroxeter), chief city of the Cornovii; Corinium (Cirencester), chief city of the Dobuni; Venta Belgarum (Winchester), chief city of the local Belgae; Caleva Atrebatum (Silchester, near Reading), chief city of the Atrebates; Venta Icenorum (Caistor-by-Norwich), chief city of the Iceni; Durovernum Cantiacorum (Canterbury), chief city of the Cantii; and Durnovaria (Dorchester), chief city of the Durotriges. Londinium (London) was, of course, the capital of the Trinovantes as well as being one of the largest cities in the entire western Empire.

Linking the regions was a complex network of roads. Historians regularly refer to these as 'Roman', but some at least may have predated the Roman invasion. The notable feature of the system is that the roads nearly always travel in straight lines, linking the cities of Britain with a spider's web that in its day was the equivalent of our modern motorway network. The idea that the British never built proper roads before the invasion is contrary to the evidence of the written British histories, which state categorically that they did. According to the *Brut Tysylio* and other traditional histories, the road system, as well as the common law, in Britain owed its origins not to the Romans but to the actions of a king called Dyfnwal Moelmud (Moelmutius, or 'Donald the bald'). Tysylio writes:

> He [Dyfnwal Moelmud] also restored the old form of government, and established the laws, known by the name of the laws of Dyfnwall Moelmyd [sic] (which the Saxons still observe); and gave privileges of refuge to the temples and cities, and to the roads leading to the courts of justice . . . He also made many other regulations, which Gildas has written of, but too numerous to treat of here; such as the guardianship of the security of the roads leading to the principal towns, and the granting great roads to the temples and cities to the commonality, so that in his time theft and violence were suppressed.[7]

According to Tysylio, several very important roads were also built by Beli Mawr, father of King Llud.

> At that time there was a contention as to roads, the limits whereof were not ascertained; and he [Beli] therefore assembled all the masons of Britain, and commanded them to make roads of stone and mortar, according to law. One of these passing through the chief cities which lay immediately in the line, went from Penryn in Cornwall, to Penryn Bladon in the North, which is the extent of the Isle of Britain.
>
> The other crossed the island, that is to say, Mynyw [St David's] proceeding along the coast, and to Port-Hamon, that is Northampton. He also commanded two other roads to be made intersecting these, passing as the others did through several cities, and terminating at each end in the angular extremities of the island.
>
> When these roads were completed, he ordered them to be made sacred, and conferred on them a privilege of refuge, so that whoever could escape to any of them was to be free from impediments, whatever wrong he might have done.[8]

These acts by early British kings seem to be the origins of the concept that the 'King's highway' offers special protection to the traveller. The most important roads in Roman times were Ermine Street, running due north from London to York, and Watling Street, which ran north-west from Canterbury and the Kent coast through London to Wroxeter via St

Albans. This road also passed near Lichfield, through the ancient town of Letocetum (Wall).

A few miles down Watling Street, south-east from Letocetum, there was an intersection with the third most important road in the country, the Fosse Way. This road began on the south coast, on the border of Dorset and Devon, at Moridunum (Seaton). From there it ran north-eastwards through Aquae Sulis (Bath), Corinium (Cirencester) to cross Watling Street at Venonae (High Cross), to pass through Ratae (Leicester) and finally link up with Ermine Street at Lindum (Lincoln). A fourth road ran west from London to pass through Calleva Atrebatum (Silchester), Cunetio (Marlborough), Aquae Sulis (Bath) and on to Venta Silurum (Caerwent) and Isca Silurum (Caerleon). Large stretches of these four roads, and the many others that linked up with them, are still used to this day.

Thus it was that Britain entered the Roman Empire already in possession of much of the infrastructure one would associate with a modern, civilized state. Indeed, ruled over by a dynasty of kings, it was not a country of savages but an organized state with cities, religious centres and universities all linked by a functional road network. As trade with the Roman Empire brought increased wealth to the country, so during the second and third centuries all these things were improved and developed; yet regardless of surface changes in the political and economic spheres, the fundamentals of the country remained the same.

For most of the period of their involvement with Britain, the Romans had more pressing problems to contend with in the rest of their sprawling Empire and were content to leave the island alone, which of course suited the British. This period is very shadowy in the histories of Geoffrey of Monmouth and Percy Enderbee, who did not know about the records of south-east Wales. The *Brut Tysylio* affirms that throughout this period, from the end of Gweirydd's reign (*c*. AD 100) to the coming over to Britain of Septimius Severus in AD 208, the kings of Britain kept peace with the Romans, finding common cause against the Picts and gradually adopting Roman ways. He presents the genealogy of Arviragus and his successors in the following manner:

> On the death of Gweyrydd, his son Meurig succeeded to the sovereignty; and in his time Roderic, the king of the Picts, brought a great multitude of them from Scythia[9] to Britain, and seized on Albany [Scotland]. Meurig as soon as he heard this, collected his forces,

attacked and routed them, and in the rout Roderic was slain. To those who survived, Meurig granted a settlement in Albany; but when they had settled, as they had no women there, they came and besought the Britons to give them their daughters in marriage; and having met with a refusal, they married Irish women, and from them have the Scots descended.

When Meurig had brought the island to a state of tranquillity, he granted the Romans a peace, of his own free accord, and made new laws throughout his dominions, and thus rendered the remainder of his life tranquil and happy.

On the death of Meurig, his son Coel succeeded, who having had his education in Rome, and 'been familiarised to the Roman customs and manners,' was attached to the Romans, and fond of their society. Hence, though he had sufficient power to withhold the tribute, he granted it freely during his life 'as he saw the whole world submit to them.'

Coel was succeeded by his son Lles [Lucius], whose disposition resembled that of his father . . .[10]

Lucius is said by Tysylio to have died childless. Following his death there was an uprising of the British, under the leadership of a prince called Julian. Tysylio writes:

Lles having died childless, party tumults arose between the Britons and Romans. As soon as the Roman Senate was informed of the tumults in Britain, it sent Severus, a Roman senator[11] with two legions, who soon after his arrival, subjected the greatest part of the Britons. The rest fled beyond Deira and Bernicia, with Julian at their head, and their frequent encounters so irritated the general, that he directed a dike faced by a stone wall, to be made between Deira and Albania [Northumberland and Scotland], from sea to sea to oppose the Britons. Having so done, he determined to subdue the whole island. Julian feeling the inequality of the contest, went to Scythia [Northern Europe, probably Denmark], from whence the Scots, who had joined Julian, had come to Britain, and from thence brought back with him all the youth of that country, and immediately attacked York. Here he was joined by the greatest part of the Britons, for they forsook Severus as soon as the enterprise of Julian was known. Severus also brought together all his forces, and a severe battle ensued, in which Julian was mortally wounded, and Severus himself was killed and buried at York.[12]

According to Percy Enderbee, Julian, whom he calls 'Fulgentius',[13] was a son of Lles (Lucius) and had a sister called Martia. She, he says, had married the Roman Emperor, Septimius Severus, who was himself of British royal blood, in which case Severus came to Britain to claim not Roman suzerainty *per se* but his own rights to the throne of Lloegres. Enderbee writes:

> *Baronius* with others confess, that *Severus* was descended of most noble parents; *Constat Severum fuisse majorum Claritudine nobilissimum*, and yet not able to describe his Auncestry, doth sufficiently prove him a stranger to those Countries and their Historians, and to make further manifestation herein, although he was born in *Africk* about *Tripolis*, so far from *Brittain*, yet he married a Brittish Lady, as divers of the same authors and others testifie, and had by her *Basianus* his Son, after King of *Brittain*, and Emperor; also some say her name was *Martia*, and the first wife of *Severus*, and sister of *Fulgentius* the *Brittain*, that warred against and slew *Severus* at *York. Fulgentius Matris Basiani Frater.* And this Brittish Lady could not be married to *Severus*, after his coming to into Brittain, but long before, where he then lived in the East Parts of the World. For in *Brittain* he lived but a short time by our modern calculation in their Catalogue of the Kings of *Brittain*, four years . . .
>
> The *Brittains* continuing in variance and contention about a successor to *Lucius* King of this Kingdom, *Severus* the Emperor came hither, some say to quiet the Debates, others affirm, to win honour to himself, he being accounted very greedy and ambitious thereof, and to reduce the Kingdom wholly to the Roman subjection; not willing that any Brittain here born should reign, and therefore as some write they made a decree and law among them, against such Government . . . If there were any such decree of the Romans, it could neither be upon this surmised motive, that the Brittish Kings had been the occasion of any rebellions or seditions against the *Romans*; for it is evident that in the time of the three last Kings, *Merius, Coillus,* and *Lucius*, peace was duely kept with the *Romans*, and their tribute paid unto them, and these Kings descended of *Genuista* a Roman Lady of the Emperors kindred, so well as from

King *Arviragus* the Brittain, did participate both of the Brittish and Roman blood. And these were the onely Kings which were here, after the composition between the Romans and Brittains, in the time of *Claudius* and *Arviragus*, when *Arviragus* marrying the daughter of the Emperour, joining the Brittish and Roman Regal and Imperial lines together, thereby ended all debates between them.[14]

It would seem from this that Severus was at least partly British, being descended from an ex-patriate family which had long since settled in Africa. Pursuing the matter further, Enderbee quotes Hardyng's *Chronicle*, saying that Severus may even have been a direct heir of Androgeus (Afarwy), the son of Llud, who left Britain with Julius Caesar after his failed coup. He writes:

> And the Brittains, except in some municipal places, were governed by their own, and not by the Roman Laws. And for authority, we want not those that write how both our next Kings here, who came from *Rome* after this imagined Decree [a decree from the Roman senate that no-one of British blood could rule in Britain], *Severus* and *Basianus* his son and successor here, were *Brittanici sanguinis* born of Brittish blood, and yet both of them our Kings in Brittain. *Harding* in his Chronicle thus testifieth from antiquity of *Severus*.
>
> Severus thus the worthy Senator,
> Descended down-right heir to Androgeos,
> The eldest son of Lud that was the Emperour,
> Out of Brittain went with Julius;
> Which Senator aforesaid Severus,
> To Brittain came and was inthonisate,
> And with a Crown of Gold was Coronate.
>
> Therefore if *Severus* the Emperour was descended down right heir to *Androgeos* the eldest son of King *Lud*, the words of the Authors so obsolutely and consequently, not without good warrant affirming it, he must needs be descended of the Regal British race, and be also the undoubted next true heir to the Crown of this Kingdom at that time.[15]

As a further twist to what is already becoming a complicated plot, Anderson's *Royal Genealogies*, a book which had royal support and was published around 1800, gives an entirely different descent for both

Septimius Severus and his first wife Martia. According to Anderson, she was his first cousin, being descended on her father's side from his uncle, Geta Lepitanus, and on her mother's from Fulvia Pia, a daughter of Fulvius Pius.

Incidentally, Alan and Baram, realizing that Lucius or Lleirwg is credited with founding many churches in the Cardiff area, were not satisfied that Enderbee had given him the correct descent. They realized that whilst it may be true that Arviragus was succeeded in certain parts of Britain by Marius, Coel and then Lucius, he seemed to be missing something. They investigated other sources of genealogical information, including 'Lives of the Saints' (a book owned by Thomas Hopkin of Coychurch), the royal genealogies of Glamorgan and Gwent, poetic mentions and religious notices. The 'Genealogy of Iestyn the Son of Gwrgan' indicates that around AD 90 King Baram (called Bonassus Rex by the Romans) and the son of Caradoc's nephew Ceri, drove the Romans out of at least western Britain. That as they were based in south Wales pointed to the fact that the Severn rather than the Thames was at that time the principal artery of Britain, or at least that part directly under Royal control.

The 'Tre-Bryn' manuscript, a manuscript copied by Iolo Morganwg, indicates that Lleirwg was descended from Cyllin, a great-grandson of Baram. It states that: 'Lleirwg the son of Coel the son of Cyllin called Lleufer Mawr or the Great Luminary, was a good king . . . He founded a church at Llandaff, and did great service to the Christians, but he resigned the kingdom to his nephew called Meirchon the son of Owain, because he had no children.' This entry is confirmed in the south-east Wales 'Lives of the Saints', which contains the following entry: 'Saint Lucius descended from Bran the Blessed, King of the Island of Britain; who was also called Lleuver, the son of Coel, the son of Cyllin – and Lles [Lucius/Lleirwg] the son of Coel the son of Cyllin. His church was Llandaff, being the first that he erected, and in fact it was the first that was ever built there. Llanlleirwg [St Mellons] in Morganwg is another church dedicated to him.'

The fact that King Lleirwg was descended directly from the kings of Essylwg explains why he built churches in south Wales rather than in the London area. Whilst he seems to have ruled as king of all Britain, Glamorgan was his home territory. However, Alan and Baram discovered that the medieval historians were not entirely wrong in believing that Lleirwg was descended from the House of Beli Mawr, for, as we shall see later, his great-grandfather Bran was descended from Arviragus and his wife Genuissa, on his mother's rather than his father's side. The Glamorgan records also confirm that Lucius or Lleirwg died childless and, notwithstanding the claims of his nephew, Meirchon (called Eirchon in the 'Genealogy of Iestyn'), Septimius Severus came to Britain with claims of his own.

The principal Latin source for the life of Severus is a biography written by Aelius Spartianus (Spartians), now believed to date from the fifth century. Although Spartians's account doesn't confirm Severus's British ancestry, it does not prove that he definitely was not of British blood. It merely says, 'His home town was Leptis Magna, his father was Geta and his ancestors had been Roman knights before citizenship had been given to all.' Clearly, then, his ancestors had been in the Roman army, they were foreign to Leptis and already enjoyed equestrian rank prior to the town being given the status of *colonia* by Trajan. Spartians names Fulvia Pia and Fulvius Pius as Severus's own mother and grand-father respectively, not those of his first wife Martia. If this is so, it is unlikely that Fulvia Pia was Martia's mother, for it would be absurd to think that he married his own sister; however it is not impossible that Martia was also a grandchild of Fulvius Pius and therefore a cousin of Severus. In any event, the names Fulvia and Fulvius are sufficiently similar to Fulgentius to warrant further enquiry, for Martia may have been descended from Fulvius Pius by a different route from Severus, by which her brother, called Geta in Anderson's genealogy, could have been the Fulgentius, otherwise called Julian, who seized northern Britain and died at York whilst fighting Severus. It is perhaps also worth noting that the name Fulvius figures in the family tree of the Roman Emperor Antoninus Pius, who was adopted by Hadrian. His full name was Titus Aurelius Fulvius Antoninus Pius. His father and grandfather, both of whom were consuls, were called respectively Aurelius Fulvius and Titus Aurelius Fulvius.

Severus's links with Afarwy, and hence King Llud, would seem to have come through his father, the consul Marcus Agrippa, and his grandfather, Macer Lepitanus. The second part of this last name is clearly derived from Leptis Magna, one of the most important cities in north Africa and Septimius Severus's birthplace. It is not at all unlikely that at least some of the descendants of Afarwy, who along with his family and retainers had left Britain in 54 BC to enter the retinue of Julius Caesar, should have travelled with the Romans to north Africa and settled there. It is therefore possible that Severus was a descendant of Afarwy, giving him a distant claim of his own on the British throne. The claims to the British throne of his first wife, Martia, would seem to have been stronger than Septimius's: she may indeed have been the daughter of a British king, Lucius or some other.

Whatever his legal rights may have been, Severus was certainly a hard man, a soldier who had seized his chance following the murder of the tyrant Commodus in December 192. With the army behind him, he had made a triumphal entry into Rome in 193 and immediately set about bringing order back into the huge Empire. This he ruled with a rod of iron.

Spartians confirms that Severus's first wife was called Marciana [Martia], though he is somewhat reticent about her true status. He writes: 'At that time [c. 178–9] he [Severus] married Marciana, about whom he was silent in his own account of his life as a private citizen. Subsequently, during his reign, he set up statues to her.' Short though this reference is, it suggests that there was some sort of secret concerning her origins, at least at the time when Spartians was writing. The setting up of statues to her is surprising, since she must have died some time before 187, when Severus married his second wife, Julia Domna, before he became Emperor in 193. There had to be a reason for honouring Martia, long-dead by the time of his reign, in this way. An explanation could be that she had been the daughter of a British king and he wanted to remind the world of his claim, through her, to the throne of Britain.

Severus's son Caracalla (Bassianus) murdered his brother Geta shortly after returning from Britain to Rome. That Julia Domna was not the real mother of both boys is confirmed indirectly by Spartians in his *Life of Caracalla*, where he says: 'When he [Caracalla] saw Geta's mother and other women weeping for his brother's murder he tried to kill the women, but was held back, to prevent him adding to the cruelty of having killed his brother.' Similarly in the *Life of Geta*, Spartians writes: 'Antoninus[16] wanted to kill Geta's mother as well, his stepmother, because she was mourning his brother, and with her the women that he found weeping after his return from the Senate House.' Further confirmation that Caracalla and Geta were only half-brothers is contained in Spartians's *Life of Severus*. Here he repeats what must have been hot gossip of the time: that not only did Caracalla murder Geta but he married his father's widow, Julia Domna: 'What more fortunate for

Severus Septimus, than not to have Bassianus? – who straightaway destroyed his brother . . . who took his stepmother – and what stepmother? rather she was his mother! – to wife, in whose bosom he had killed her son Geta.' The story of the marriage of Caracalla to Julia Domna is contained in the works of other reputable historians of the time, such as Victor, Eutropius and Orosius, so one can only assume that it is true. Julia was too important an heiress to leave both alive and unattached. Leaving base motives aside, Bassianus must have decided that marriage was a safer course than matricide, through which he would have strengthened his own position as sole heir to the Roman Empire. It is, however, inconceivable that he could have got away with this, even in decadent Rome, if she really had been his natural mother. We may therefore safely assume that, as the British histories make clear, Bassianus was really the son of Severus's first wife, Martia (Marciana/Marcia).

We have seen that Martia may indeed have been the daughter of the British King Lucius. She died before 187 and if Julian's (Fulgentius's) claim to the British throne was less direct than that of father to son (he may after all have been a brother, cousin or nephew of the dead king rather than a son), it would indeed have been true, as Tysylio said, that Lucius died without children whilst at the same time having heirs.

Whatever the truth concerning his own ancestry and the rights, if any, of his former wife Martia, Septimius Severus was the fourth Roman Emperor[17] recorded as having visited Britain. After he died, his son Bassianus used Britain as his own springboard to power in Rome – an example followed later by Constantine the Great, as we shall see.

Bassianus went on to carry out massacres in Alexandria and Mesopotamia before finally being assassinated at Carrhae (Harran) in 217. This was done on the orders of the prefect of the guard, Macrinus, who now briefly held the title of Emperor until he was defeated by Elagabalus (Varius Avitus). He, whom many believed to be the illegitimate son of Bassianus,[18] was at first popular but lost support on account of his profligate lifestyle. In 222 he was displaced in favour of his cousin, Alexander Severus, the son of a niece of Julia Domna's who had already been made 'Caesar' – that is to say, deputy to the Emperor. Alexander was only a boy when he inherited, much under the influence of his mother and barely able to control the army. Though he curbed the excesses of his predecessors, celebrations in 233 in honour of his supposed victory over the Persians could not mask the fact that it had been a near-disastrous campaign. His career was cut short when in 235 he went to fight German insurgents and was killed in a mutiny, probably led by Maximinus, who now became Emperor and was the patriarch of a family that figures greatly in the third- and fourth-century history of both Gaul and Britain.[19]

However, closely interwoven with the events of the Roman Empire and the impact of the Romans on Britain is another story. Long before the time of Bassianus another force had made itself felt on the island of Britain: Christianity. How this had come about, and the important role taken by the British King Caradoc and his family in introducing into Britain the new religion, was explained to me by Alan and Baram during subsequent trips to Wales.

CHAPTER EIGHT

THE ROYAL COLLEGE OF THE CHRISTIANS

On a fine day with a gentle breeze and, following weeks of rain, light, wispy clouds flecking the sky, I once again headed across the Severn Bridge into a country I was now beginning to realize is a lot stranger than most people think. Alan was in fine fettle as he greeted me at the door, and soon we were heading west from Cardiff along the M4 towards the heart of the ancient kingdom of Essylwg. Presently we turned off near Pencoed on the upper reaches of the Ewenny River. Threading our way for a couple of miles more along some narrow country lanes, we arrived at our destination: a quiet country church surrounded by a grove of trees.

Standing by the door of the church, Alan began to fill me in on the local history. 'Up there is Mynydd y Gaer or "Fortress Mountain",' he said, pointing at a distant hill. 'It is the site of Caer Caradoc, where the Khymric King Caradoc had his castle and near to where he fought his last battle against the Romans. It is also the site of the St Peter's Church that you read about, where we carried out our archaeological dig. However, that is not what we have come to see today.'

We were at a place called Llanilid, that is to say, the church or holy estate of Ilid. Although the church we could see here today was quite modern, Alan explained that the site on which it stands was one of the oldest ecclesiastical foundations in Britain. He informed me that St Ilid is the Welsh name for Joseph of Arimathea. The name 'Ilid' seems to have been derived from 'Gilead' – that is, the Galilean, and was used as a title or term of affection for him. He was the tutor of a king called Bran the Blessed and just down the road from where we were, not more than a mile or so distant, was Trefran or 'The Manor of Bran'. This, traditionally, was the place where Bran[1] lived, whilst Ilid lived near by. In

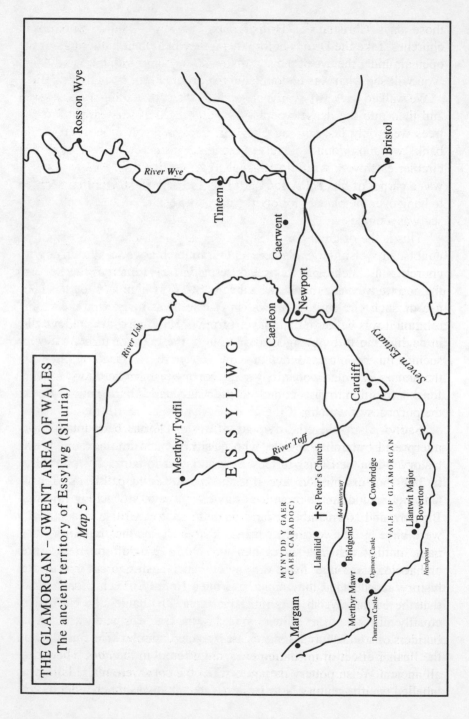

THE GLAMORGAN – GWENT AREA OF WALES
The ancient territory of Essylwg (Siluria)

Map 5

those days Christians – British ones, anyway – didn't worship in churches. Like the Druids before them, they held their gatherings in the open air under the eye of the sun. 'Now if you come with me,' said Alan, 'you will see what was undoubtedly the original *llan* or church of Ilid.'

We walked back fifty yards or so along the path leading to the church and then into the dense woodland behind it. As it was early May, the trees were only just coming into leaf. Crossing over an ancient earth-bank, we soon found ourselves standing inside what was clearly a circular earthwork with the atmosphere of a fairy ring. Below our feet was a carpet of bluebells, adding to the air of enchantment that seemed to hang over the place. I followed Alan to the centre of what I could now see was a circle.

'This is the original *cor* of St Ilid,' he said, in a tone that brooked no doubts. In Welsh, he explained, a *cor* can mean a choir, the choir of a church or a college, but its original meaning is a sacred circle, such as the one we were looking at, which was used for religious meetings. The use of such circles goes back to pre-Christian times. In the Druidic religion it was believed that all ceremonies should be conducted outside in daylight, in full view of God and not furtively in the dark. In circles such as this people used to sing – the Welsh are very fond of singing – the praises of God. Even after the arrival of Christianity, it took a while for this tradition to die out and for people to start building churches for the purposes of worship.

'Sadly,' Alan said, 'the purpose of this circle has been totally mis-interpreted by archaeologists, who have not taken into account Welsh history. When the British armies, under Magnus Maximus, invaded Gaul in 383[2] they established several kingdoms and principalities across the Channel, including the province of Lydaw (Letavia), which we now call Brittany, and Normandy. Several of these ancient British circular *cors* were built by the Welsh in Normandy (which was not known by this name until it was invaded by Norsemen in 852). Unfortunately, when archaeologists found these *cors* in Lydaw they ignored this earlier history and decided they must have been Norman. Then they decided that the earlier, Welsh *cors* must therefore also have been Norman – equally absurdly, for as everyone knows the Normans were great builders of stone churches and castles, not earth circles. The mistake had the further effect of misdating everything found in the *cors*. Thereafter all ancient Welsh pottery dating to when the *cors* were really built was labelled twelfth-century Norman, even though it was much older. It was assumed that following the Roman withdrawal from Britain, the Welsh, uniquely among the nations of Europe, became incapable of making pots until in the late eleventh century the Normans showed them how.'

Wandering round the *cor* I was struck by the logic of what Alan was saying. That this was a religious circle and not a defensive earthwork was clear not only from its location on a plain as opposed to a hilltop but also in the way it was constructed with a ditch inside, as opposed to – had it been a fortress – outside its embankment. Such a construction is not exclusive to Wales and I had seen several such circles in England, not least the outer ditch and bank enclosures of our two foremost Neolithic monuments: Stonehenge and Avebury. Also, take away the trees and the *cor* was strikingly reminiscent in size and construction of one close to my home in Dorset – with one notable difference. That one, known as Knowlton Rings,[3] consists of a similar bank with ditch inside. What distinguishes it from other circles of its type is that in its centre there stands a small ruined church, which is believed to be Norman in construction, and once served a village that was wiped out by the Black Death; today it is a romantic ruin, open to the elements. This is evidence, if any be needed, that the Normans were not content to worship in sacred circles, even where these were already in existence, but preferred to build churches. I had to agree with Alan that it was inconceivable that the Normans would have built the *cor* at Llanilid, though they may have built or replaced the church near by.

Leaving the circle of Ilid we made our way back to the car and onto the motorway. Once more we headed for Llantwit Major, where previously Alan had shown me the stones of Samson. As we drove along he told me more about its history.

THE CONVERSION OF BRITAIN

'As you probably know, Adrian,' he began, 'in AD 597 St Augustine, the emissary of Gregory I, the then Bishop of Rome, arrived in Kent with the mission of converting the pagan English to Christianity.' He was, Alan went on, received cordially by King Aethelbert and was granted leave to preach at Canterbury. Gregory consecrated Augustine as archbishop in 601 and his see of Canterbury became the primary diocese of the English Church. Thus it has remained to this day, the Archbishop of Canterbury being the Church of England's most senior prelate. However,

Augustine's role in converting the English of sixth-century Kent has been greatly exaggerated. In most of Britain, outside the Saxon dominions in eastern England, there already was a Christian church, known to history as the Culdee or Chaldean. This original 'Church of Britain', dating from centuries before the Saxon invasions, claimed to have been founded by the Apostles themselves.

At Llantwit Major there was a college (that is, a small monastery) called the Cor Eurgain, founded by St Ilid at the behest of a princess called Eurgain, perhaps as early as AD 36.[4] How this came about is an extraordinary story, closely connected with the history of Roman involvement in Britain. It is also the beginnings of the Holy Kingdom made famous by the much later King Arthur. King Caradoc and his family are justly famous in the Welsh records not only for their war record but also for welcoming the Apostolic mission into Britain and helping the Culdee church to become established here shortly after the Crucifixion. The Welsh triads, and the equally neglected lists of the 'Lives of the Saints', contain clear and accurate accounts. They describe the arrival in Britain of Christian missionaries, led by St Ilid (Joseph of Arimathea), and how they came at the behest of Caradoc's saintly daughter, Eurgain, who is credited with being the first British convert to the new religion. Accompanying St Ilid, presumably of his twelve, were St Cyndaf and St Mawan. Cyndaf can be identified as meaning 'the first chief, a fisherman', and Mawan may be 'Maw + Anaf', meaning 'what expands + special'.

I was later able to check the veracity of what Alan had said by referring to the 'Genealogy of Iestyn the Son of Gwrgan' contained in the *Iolo MSS*. It did indeed mention that St Ilid had originally come to Britain at the bidding of Eurgain, the daughter of Caradoc, and that he was the chief instructor of the Khymry in the Christian faith. She had established a *cor* of twelve saints, which St Ilid systematized.

> Caradog built a palace, after the manner of the Romans, at Abergwerydwyr, called now Llandunwyd Major, or St Donats. His daughter, Eurgain, married a Roman chieftain, who accompanied her to Cambria. This chieftain had been converted to Christianity, as well as his wife Eurgain, who first introduced the faith among the Cambro-britons, and sent for Ilid (a native of the land of Israel) from Rome to Britain. This Ilid is called, in the service of his commemoration, St Joseph of Arimathea. He became the principal teacher of

Christianity to the Cambro-britons, and introduced good order into the choir of Eurgain, which she had established for twelve saints near the place now called Llantwit; but which was burnt in the time of King Edgar. After this arrangement, Ilid went to Ynys Afallen in Gwlad yr haf ['The Land of Plenty'], where he died and was buried.[5]

It was clear from this that the college, known variously as the Cor Eurgain, Corworgain or Caerworgorn, was indeed the original foundation of the church at Llantwit Major. The tradition, linking St Ilid/Joseph of Arimathea with Wales, is well documented. There are also other traditions saying that he later went from Wales to convert the king of Lloegres (England), as Alan now explained to me.

The king who ruled over Lloegres at the time of the Claudian invasion in AD 43 was called Guiderius, a son of Cynvelyn. The Romans were, as always, keen to interfere in matters of succession in neighbouring states and had used the death of Cynvelyn as a pretext for their invasion. When Guiderius died in battle, he was succeeded by his brother, whom the Welsh call Gweirydd but the English know by his Latin name of Arviragus. Like Caradoc, the high king of all Britain at that time, Gweirydd was to turn out to be, Alan said, 'a very tough nut for the Romans to crack'. Claudius was seeking a quick victory in Britain, so rather than have the war dragging on, after the fall of London and the south-east he deemed it politic to make peace with Gweirydd. Under this arrangement Gweirydd married a daughter of Claudius called Genvissa or Genuissa.[6] She seems to have been Claudius's daughter by adoption rather than consanguinity, for she is not listed amongst his own progeny.

Having set up the Cor Eurgain in Glamorgan, St Ilid is believed to have left Wales and journeyed onwards to the court of this King Gweirydd. There is a trail of St Ilid sites leading north from Llanilid at Trefran in the Vale of Glamorgan, to Llanilid at Gilfach Goch,[7] and then to Capel Ilid in the Brecon area. Ilid seems to have spent some time at this lonely site, for here there are a number of very ancient, tiny chapels, all clustered in a small area; also, several very early inscribed stones have been found there. One of these, the Liwell stone, sold for £10 to the British Museum in London in 1852 by a local farmer, is a most remarkable object. One side of the stone carries a Latin inscription, whilst the other features a series of pictures. At the top there is what looks very like a pyramid, with an animal – presumably representing the great sphinx – drawn crouching on one side. Below the pyramid is shown a crude figure of a man with a crooked staff walking over water. Either side of the man are designs indicating hills. The direction in which he is travelling seems to indicate that he is moving from the Egyptian (represented by the pyramid) end of the Mediterranean towards the west. Below this scene is a further picture of the man, again at sea, and this time he appears to be heading north towards more land. Alan and Baram think that the 'walking man' drawings on this remarkable stone may represent Ilid making his epic journey from the east, perhaps via Egypt and the pyramids, before sailing westwards along the Mediterranean and travelling north to Britain.[8]

Traditions state that when he arrived at the court of King Gweirydd, Ilid was given twelve hides of land at a place called in the Welsh manuscripts and other documents variously Afallach, Aballach, Ynys Wydrin, Ynys Avalon or Glastennen. The proper identification of this place is a matter of great importance, since Ilid/Joseph's arrival there is a central theme of the Arthurian legends and romances, in which he brings with him the Holy Grail; some also say that King Arthur was taken to Afallach or Aballach to recover from wounds he received in battle. Because of the general belief that Glastonbury in Somerset is the site of the first Christian foundation, generations of writers have assumed that Afallach was there. That the Welsh word *afal* means 'apple' and there is a predominance of apple orchards in that area of Somerset has added to this belief; the name Ynys Avalon is believed to mean 'Island of Apples'. As *ynys* can mean 'island', in the sense of a place surrounded by water, and much of the marshy Glastonbury area was under water at that time, it has been assumed that Afallach was an island of land above water there.

However, *ynys* had other meanings too. The present-day village of Ynysbwl, for example, is situated in the hills of Glamorgan on a bend of the River Nant Cludach, a tributary of the River Taff, with the river curving round it; though close to water, the village is not an island in that sense of the word. *Ynys* can also be seen to have a figurative meaning as 'an island of faith'. Therefore, the location of Afallach is not necessarily an island in the sense of a place surrounded entirely by water, and, for reasons that will be explained later, Alan and Baram don't believe that the Afallach in question was in Somerset.

Religious tradition holds that the present giving was not all one way. Like Caradoc, Gweirydd was converted to Christianity, which is why he granted land to the saints. In acknowledgement of his role as supreme battle-sovereign in the struggle against the then pagan Romans, Ilid is said to have given Gweirydd a banner carrying the symbol of a red cross on a white background to act as his standard. This flag was later to become known as the cross of St George (the anglicized form of the name Gweirydd) and is still England's banner to this day.

As an Englishman I was naturally intrigued by this story of how the flag of St George came to be the banner of England. No mention is made of St Ilid, or of Joseph of Arimathea, in the histories of Gildas, Nennius or Geoffrey of Monmouth; however, a variant on the story is contained in the British *Chronicles* of Hardynge, saying that he gave Gweirydd not a flag but arms:

> Joseph converted this King Arviragus [Gweirydd]
> By his preaching to know ye laws divine
> And baptized him as write hath Nennius
> The chronicler in Brytain tongue full fyne
> An to Christian laws made hym inclyne
> And gave him then a shield of silver white
> A cross and long, and overthwart full perfete
> These armes were used throughout all Brytain
> For a common syne, each man to know his nacion
> And thus his armes by Joseph Creacion
> Full longafore Saint George was generate
> Were worshipt here of mykell elder date.[9]

Researching Alan's story further, I learned that if Gildas's statement that Christianity came to Britain in the last years of the reign of Emperor Tiberius is to be believed, at least some members of the Silurian royal family would have been Christians before being taken prisoner by the Romans in AD 51; in the truce that followed, Claudius would have wanted to persuade Gweirydd to enter the Empire peacefully. The marriage of Genuissa to Gweirydd, central to the peace initiative, is recorded in the *Brut Tysylio*:

> ... Gweyrydd, after a bloody engagement was obliged to retreat to
> Winchester. Hither Claudius followed him, hoping to blockade him
> in it. But Gweyrydd, aware of his intention, determined to oppose
> him in the field. This determination, and the resistance he had
> already met with, induced Claudius to send proposals of peace,

which were accepted. A peace was therefore concluded, and to confirm it, Claudius promised to give his daughter to Gweyrydd in marriage. After this arrangement, the Romans, assisted by the Britons, took possession of the Orkney Isles,[10] and others near them, and when the winter was over, the young lady, who was of uncommon beauty, came from Rome, and was married to Gweyrydd.[11]

When Geoffrey of Monmouth translated the *Brut Tysylio* into Latin, he enlarged upon the story in his own 'homely style' to give it more colour:

When Arviragus saw that he was beleaguered, he mustered his troops, threw open the city gates and went forth to do battle. Just as Arviragus was about to lead his men in a charge, Claudius sent envoys to him, asking that they might make peace, for he was afraid of the king's courage and the bravery of the Britons, and he preferred to subdue them by plot and diplomacy rather than incur the hazard of battle. He therefore proposed peace to Arviragus, promising to give him his own daughter, if only he would recognise that the kingdom of Britain was under the sway of Rome. His nobles persuaded Arviragus to abandon his plans for battle and to accept the proposals of Claudius. Their argument was that it could be no disgrace for him to submit to the Romans, since they were the acknowledged overlords of the whole world. Arviragus was swayed by these arguments and by others of a similar nature. He accepted their advice and submitted to Claudius. Claudius soon sent to Rome for his daughter. With the help of Arviragus he subdued the Orkneys and the other islands in the neighbourhood.

At the end of that winter the messengers returned with Claudius' daughter and handed her over to her father. The girl's name was Genuissa.[12] Her beauty was such that everyone who saw her was filled with admiration.[13]

Gweirydd continued to be a thorn in the flesh for the Romans long after Claudius had died, for Juvenal wrote a poem which has been interpreted as being rather sarcastic towards his successor, the Emperor Nero:

Hath our great enemy
Arviragus, the chariot borne British king
dropped from his chariot pole.[14]

Another example of intermarriage between Romans and Britons shows how Christianity spread from Britain to the Roman Empire. According to George Jowett, author of a book called *The Drama of the Lost Disciples*, whose words on this matter reiterate those of eminent historians through the ages, Aulus Plautius, the Roman commander stationed in Britain following the Claudian invasion, married Caradoc's sister Gwladys. Like her niece Eurgain, Caradoc's daughter, Gwladys was a Christian, but in deference to Roman customs, on her marriage she took the name Pomponia. She was a highly gifted and educated lady, who could speak fluent Greek. On account of this she was given the epithet 'Graecina', so her full Roman name became Pomponia Graecina Plautius. Her Christian faith caused waves in Rome: in his *Annals* Tacitus tells the story of how she was tried for 'foreign superstition' – a charge used by writers at that time in Rome specifically to designate Christianity. Fortunately the presiding magistrate was her husband and she was acquitted.[15]

It was probably also during the time of truce that another extra-ordinary connection was made between the families of the Roman Caesars and the Khymric royal family, when the Emperor Claudius adopted as his own Caradoc's youngest daughter, also called Gwladys. This story adds to the evidence showing the spread of Christianity in the early Roman Empire. She changed her name to Claudia and later married a relative of the Emperor called Aulus Rufus Pudens Pudentius. He had earlier served in Britain under Aulus Plautius and they were married at the Palatium Britannicum, the home of Caradoc and his family of exiles whilst they were held hostage in Rome. After Caradoc was set free and allowed to return home to Britain he gave the Palatium Britannicum as a bridal gift to Claudia and her husband Pudens.

At this time there were two Christian congregations in Rome, one Jewish and the other Gentile. The question of whether or not it was necessary to be circumcized in order to become a Christian was a matter of intense debate and it was not until later, when the matter had been resolved, that the two communities merged. Both Claudia, who is said to have been baptized as a child by Joseph of Arimathea himself, and Pudens, who may also have been converted in Britain, were Christians of the Gentile church. Accordingly, their house became one of the most important centres of Christian worship in Rome, which was of course pagan at the time. A frequent house guest of theirs seems to have been St Paul, who sends their greetings at the end of his second Letter to

Timothy – 'Eubulus sends greetings to you as do Pudens and Linus and Claudia and all the brethren'[16] – and sends greeting to 'Rufus [Pudens], eminent in the Lord' in his Letter to the Romans.[17]

The existence of Claudia is disputed, but further confirmation comes from the writings of the Roman poet Martial, who seems to have known her well. In one of his poems, he very positively identifies the Claudia who married Pudens as being foreign:

> Red-haired Claudia who came over, veiled foreign woman of Pudens
> The food having meaning of worshipping the god of marriage thou
> art,
> Such high degrees of beauty are rarely joined together, confusing
> endearments and sweet powers of perception.[18]

He also acknowledges her as having been a Briton:

> Veiled Claudia with eagerness red-haired Briton,
> For what reason published in the Latin tongue blamed in the mind of
> the multitude?
> Of what form of dishonour? The Romans believe in given marriage,
> Women of Italy possess good sense of discernment pertaining to
> exhortation,
> To judge well where sanctity is enrobed.[19]

It would be strange indeed if there were two foreign women with red hair, both called Claudia and eulogized by Martial. As Pudens served in Britain, it would seem obvious that it was from there that he obtained his foreign wife. British histories assert that this Claudia was indeed a daughter of Caradoc.

There is also evidence in Britain for the existence of her husband. A memorial stone set up by Pudens has been found at the newly excavated palace of King Cogidumnus at Fishbourne in Sussex. This Cogidumnus is a shadowy figure, but is believed to have been a king in southern Britain who allied himself with Rome. As a thank-you, the Romans seem to have built him a palace and Pudens, presumably before he moved back to Rome though maybe after he had met Claudia, left a memorial stone there.

The marriage between Gwladys Claudia Rufinus and Aulus Rufus Pudens Pudentius is indisputable and attested voluminously. The objection that the Claudia of Martial's poem could not be the same lady who married the Pudens of St Paul's letters because the poem is too late in composition is not sustainable. For although Martial was writing sixty years after St Paul wrote his letters, he lived to a very great age. This is confirmed by the fact that he was also a personal friend of Silius Italicus, who wrote a volume on the Second Punic War and was a consul at the time Nero committed suicide in AD 68. He could therefore have been writing about an event that happened sixty years before.

What is equally certain is that Linus, also mentioned in the Epistles of St Paul, was Claudia's brother. He was consecrated by Paul and became the first Bishop of Rome. This is confirmed in the *Apostolic Constitutions*, where St Peter is recorded as writing that Linus set up the first church in Rome in AD 58 and: 'Of the church of Rome, Linus, brother of Claudia, was first ordained by Paul, and after Linus's death, Clemens, the second ordained by me Peter.'[20] In his *Epistola ad Corinthios*, Clemens Romanus, the second Bishop of Rome, records 'St Linus, brother of Claudia' and affirms that St Paul did indeed frequently reside at the Palatium Britannicum in Rome. He further attests that this first church in Rome was founded by this British royal family and that St Paul preached 'in the extremity of the West', which has been interpreted as Britain. Iranaeus, the 'Church Father', also recognized that the Linus mentioned in Paul's Letter to Timothy was the 'supervisor' of the first church of Rome: 'The Apostles having founded and built the church at Rome, committed the ministry of its supervision to Linus. This is the Linus mentioned by Paul in his Epistles to Timothy.'[21]

Linus was martyred early on but his sister Claudia returned to Britain with her husband Pudens and died naturally in AD 97. Pudens and Claudia had four children: Pudentiana, Praxades, Novatus and Timotheus. Evidence for this, as well as their birthdays, is recorded in the *Martyrologies of Rome*. In honour of Pudentiana, who was evidently greatly loved and, like her younger sister Praxades, a 'virgin in Christ', the name of the Palatium Britannicum was changed to the Church of St Pudentiana. It would appear that in its grounds the remains of many of the early Christian martyrs, including St Paul, were buried. This church still stands today on the Esquiline Hill and on the wall can be read a Latin inscription which in translation reads:

> In this sacred and most ancient of churches, known as that of Pastor, dedicated by Sanctus Pius Papa, formerly the house of Sanctus

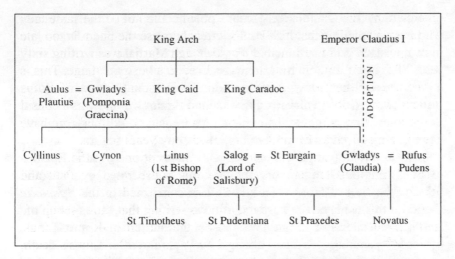

THE FAMILY TREE OF KING CARADOC
AND THE EARLY CHRISTIAN SAINTS
Diagram 7

> Pudens, the senator, and the home of the holy apostles, repose the
> remains of three thousand blessed martyrs which Pudentiana and
> Praxades, virgins of Christ, with their own hands interred.

Near by, a few streets away in the same district, is a church dedicated
to Claudia's other daughter, St Prassede (Praxades). It is strange but perhaps appropriate that these little churches in an unfashionable suburb,
and not the mighty Basilica of St Peter, mark the true origins of Roman
Christianity.

Although dozens of eminent authors down the centuries have detailed
this story of the family of Caradoc, and Jowett had done no more than
to collate this material, his account of the spread of Christianity in the
early Roman Empire was certainly an eye-opener to me. I was, of
course, familiar with the story of how Joseph of Arimathea had brought
the Grail to Britain and I had also read about Caradoc's brave defence in
the Roman forum, but I had not realized that those two stories were connected. Nor had I known how instrumental the Khymric royal family had
been in establishing the new religion not only in Britain but also in
Rome. It also indicated something else: that the early Roman church did
not consist solely of slaves, as I was brought up to understand, but had
connections at the very highest levels of society.

However, Ilid was not solely responsible for the spread of Christianity. Alan now explained that his was not the only mission sent to Britain and that the island had been visited by other saints. At the same time as St Ilid, St Cyndaf and St Mawan were busy establishing themselves in Glamorgan, before moving on to the court of King Gweirydd, another missionary arrived in Britain. He was an old man: in the Welsh records he is called Arwystli Hen – a name that is translated as 'Aristobulus the Aged'. He concentrated most of his efforts on converting the Britons of Lloegres, that is southern England, presumably leaving the Khymry to St Ilid. Religious scholars identify Aristobulus as having been a brother of the Apostle St Barnabas and the father-in-law of St Peter. He is also believed to have been the husband of a woman who was the subject of a miracle recorded in St Matthew's Gospel and he is listed as one of the seventy elected by Jesus, although he was not one of the twelve Apostles. He is said to have been consecrated as a bishop late in life by St Paul, who sent him to Britain. Like Joseph of Arimathea, Aristobulus is one of the peripheral characters mentioned in the New Testament: in his Letters to the Romans and to Timothy, St Paul sends his greeting 'to the household of Aristobulus'. Arwystli Hen, as he was known in Britain, is also prominently named in the Welsh 'Lives of the Saints', which confirms him as having been in Britain in Apostolic times.

St Paul himself may also have visited Britain. There is certainly a tradition in London that he stood and preached at the site of what is now St Paul's cathedral by Ludgate. There is documentary evidence that St Paul made at least one visit to Britain: medieval copies of a series of letters stated to have been exchanged between him and Seneca, the Roman philosopher, exist in the Bodleian Library, Oxford, and fourteen other great libraries spread all across Europe, and the Oxford versions contain passages thought to allude to Wales. There is also another tradition in Wales that Paul preached on the outcrop of rock just above the St Peter's Church on Caer Caradoc.

Alan subsequently sent me confirmation of what he said about Paul, documentary evidence that he preached not only in Britain but in Spain too. This is contained in Chapter 29 of the Acts of the Apostles, which is not included in the Bible as it was lost until rediscovered in the archives of the Greek Orthodox Church in Istanbul. It was translated by C. S. Sonnini, who later presented it to Sultan Abdul Achmet. Verses 4–7 read:

And no man hindered Paul; for he testified boldly of Jesus before the tribunes and among the people; and he took with him certain of the brethren which abode with him at Rome, and they took shipping to Ostium [a port at the mouth of the River Tiber], and having the winds fair were brought safely into a haven of Spain.

And much people were gathered together from the towns and villages, and the hill country: for they had heard of the conversion of the apostle, and many miracles which he had wrought.

And Paul preached mightily in Spain, and great multitudes believed and were converted, for they perceived he was an apostle sent from God.

And they departed out of Spain, and Paul and his company finding ship in Armorica [Brittany] sailing unto Britain, they were therein, and passing along the south coast they reached a port called Raphinus.[22]

Reading Jowett's *Drama of the Lost Disciples*, I found further references, confirming what Alan had said, concerning the mission of Aristobulus to Britain. As a scholar, Jowett had examined in depth the *Martyrologies of the Greek Church*, which, he says, state that

Aristobulus was one of the seventy disciples and a follower of St Paul the Apostle, along with whom he preached the Gospel to the whole world, and, ministered to them. He was chosen by St Paul to be the missionary bishop to the land of Britain. He was there martyred after he had built churches and ordained deacons and priests on the island.[23]

According to Jowett, Aristobulus was the first martyr in Britain, killed at Verulamium not by the Romans but by Britons who were not ready for conversion. According to tradition, this was not before he had prepared the way for St Paul himself to visit London and preach on the site where his cathedral now stands.

An early Roman stone naming a man called Aristobulus has been found in Dorset at St George's, Fordington. It carries a Latin inscription which translates as: 'Gaius Aristobulus, a Roman citizen, aged [indecipherable] years; Rufinus and Marina and Avca, his children, and Romana his wife.' Though there is no way of knowing if this was the same Aristobulus or why his stone should be in Dorset, it is possible that

Aristobulus visited Dorset and founded a church there. As we have seen, there is what looks to have been a *cor* or sacred circle at a place now called Knowlton Rings. A few miles to the north of this is another place of great interest called Woodyates. Today this is just a small village on the Dorset–Hampshire borders but in Roman times it was the city of Vindogladia. Situated at a crossroads on the main road from Dorchester to London, this was an important centre. It is therefore tempting to think, although we can only conjecture, that during the course of his missionary work, Aristobulus visited Vindogladia and caused a church to be built in the pre-existent *cor* at Knowlton.

Haleca, Bishop of Augusta, also mentions Aristobulus: 'The memory of many martyrs is celebrated by the Britons, especially that of St Aristobulus, one of the seventy disciples.' Further evidence for the role of Aristobulus is contained in the *Adonis Martyrologies* which lists: 'March 15 Natal day of St Aristobulus, Bishop of Britain, brother of St Barnabas the Apostle, by whom he was ordained bishop. He was sent to Britain where, after preaching the faith of Christ and forming a church, he received martyrdom.' Thus records emanating from the Greek and Latin churches give an independent corroboration of British historical traditions that the native church was established in the Apostolic era.

Further confirmation of the story comes from Dorotheus, Bishop of Tyre. Writing in 303 in his *Synopsis de Apostol*, he says: 'Aristobulus who is mentioned by the apostle in his Epistle to the Romans, was made Bishop in Britain.' He also states that the disciple St Simon Zelotes, one of Jesus's twelve Apostles, was killed in Britain soon after arriving in AD 60, at the height of the savagery of the Boudiccan rebellion. Simon was the second martyr in Britain and was put to death at Caistor by crucifixion, on the orders of the Roman imperial agent Catus Decianus.

We have seen that as a result of the Apostolic missions, it would seem that not only the royal families but a large part of the population became Christians very early on. The edicts against Christians of such Emperors as Nero and Diocletian, which led to thousands of deaths in the arenas of Rome, were not heeded at all in Britain outside of the garrison towns and were applied only to Roman citizens, which is why there were very few Christian martyrs in Britain during the Roman occupation. One to whom the edicts did apply was a Roman soldier called Alban, who was beheaded at Verulamium. The city was later renamed St Albans in his honour and a cathedral built to house his shrine.

A third mission to Britain seems to have arrived at around 167, after King Lleirwg (Lucius) sent an embassy to discuss religious matters with Eleutherius, the then Bishop of Rome. This event is recorded by the Venerable Bede around 720. Tysylio, Geoffrey of Monmouth, Urban and John of Teignmouth also all mention this mission. The Welsh triads reinforce the evidence and the event is also recorded in the Llandaff Charters. According to these sources, the British ambassador was Elfan, a brother of King Lleirwg, who was accompanied by Medwy and two other teachers, called Dyfan and Fagan, who had studied at St Ilid's foundation of Aballach.

Lleirwg, or Luke, is a key figure in the genealogies of Britain. Significantly, Lleirwg founded his own church of Llan-Lleirwg (now called St Mellons) on the east side of Cardiff. This church, as I discovered when I went there later with Alan, contains some ancient features, not generally found in Norman churches, that are indicative of its great antiquity. St Fagan, St Dyfan, St Medwy and St Elfan all founded churches in Cardiff and its environs too. Lleirwg is also credited with founding a church of St Peter's Cornhill, which, given his activity and that of the saints associated with him in the south Wales area, is likely to have been the church of St Peter's-super-Montem, which lies just twenty-two miles from Cardiff. All this, well recorded and still evident today, indicates the spiritual importance of south Wales as the place of origin of Christianity in Britain. Learning how Wales's role as spiritual custodian of Britain developed in later centuries was to be the next stage of my journey.

CHAPTER NINE

THE CROSS OF CHRIST

When on my first trip to Wales Alan and Baram had shown me their video of a sculpted cross on a wall, and told me that they were convinced that the wall on which it was carved fronted a sealed cave inside which was hidden the Holy Cross of Christ, it sent shivers down my spine. The implications of their claim were astounding, for it suggested the possibility that the True Cross of Christ could be concealed in Britain, a matter of great interest to Christians of all denominations.

Pressure from other commitments meant it was some time before I was able to follow up on this at first sight improbable story, but at last I found time and persuaded Alan to take me along to see the cross for myself. I stayed overnight at Alan's house so that we could make an early start in the morning, yet I hardly got a wink of sleep, so exciting was the prospect of where we were to go the following day. On the evening before we set out, Alan and Baram once more explained the significance of the site we were to visit.

'One of the most significant events of the early centuries of the Christian era concerns the Empress Helen and the True Cross of Christ. You may not have heard about this because in modern Britain the story is not mentioned in schools and is therefore unknown to the vast majority of people. But in medieval times and earlier it was a well-known tale and one that was frequently represented in religious art.

The Empress Helen is said to have been born in *c.* 265, dying in 336 at the age of seventy-one. She was a British queen and was the mother of Constantine the Great, who became ruler over the whole Roman Empire in 324. She became Empress and for a long time ruled the Empire in partnership with her son. Though it was he who made

Christianity the official religion of the Empire, there can be little doubt that he did so largely because of her influence; she was certainly a force to be reckoned with.'

The story goes, Alan told me, that whilst her son was building his new imperial city of Constantinople – now called Istanbul – Empress Helen went on a pilgrimage to Jerusalem and Sinai. Accompanied by a formidable bodyguard, she entered the Holy City and demanded that its leaders hand over to her the True Cross on which Christ had been crucified. After an exchange of threats and excuses, three pieces of timber were eventually brought out for her inspection. She was told that one of them was the Cross she was looking for, the other two being those of the thieves crucified either side of Jesus. This posed a dilemma as to which was the right one, but apparently the problem was solved when a sick woman was miraculously cured after touching one of the pieces of wood.

As well as the Cross itself, Helen was presented with what were supposedly the very nails used in the Crucifixion. Realizing that her son Constantine would have to be made aware of events, she had these made into a bridle bit for his horse and had it sent to him. Meanwhile she employed goldsmiths to cover the Cross with gold, silver and jewels before having it encased in a silver casket. She then took ship, taking the Cross with her. Though details vary, this is in outline the story as recorded in a multitude of ancient sources. The question then arises: what happened to this precious relic? Surprising as it may seem, the evidence is that Helen, who was of course a British queen, brought the Cross to Britain, more specifically to Wales.

All over Wales there are ancient roads which are called the Sarn Helen – 'the causeways of Helen'. Of course Helen didn't build these roads, but she is somehow connected. What seems to have happened is that Helen paraded the Cross around the country on a grand tour, before depositing it in its final resting place for safekeeping. The route that she followed then became a sort of 'pilgrim's way'. It is significant that you can today go along these roads following a route marked by Cross names. There is 'the Pass of the Cross', 'the Mountain of the Cross', 'the Valley of the Cross', 'the Ford of the Cross', 'the Vale of the Cross', 'the Fields of the Cross' and so on. The final destination of the Cross is recorded in the king lists drawn up for the wedding of Owen, the son of Hywell Dda (Howell the Good) of Dyfed – part of the Harleian 3859 collection of manuscripts. This collection is a most important corpus of texts concerning Wales and the Dark Ages. The king lists are contained in the famous 'Black Book of Carmarthen', and were drawn up to demonstrate his descent from a number of intermarried royal houses. Surprising as it may seem, it states clearly that at the time of writing, around 920, the Cross was in Dyfed in south-west Wales. Though the earliest surviving copy of these manuscripts has not, to Alan's and Baram's knowledge, been radiocarbon dated, it is believed to date from no later than 1100. As there is no record of the Cross having been moved since, Alan and Baram have every reason to believe that it is still in Dyfed. The question is: where is it hidden?

Just as all over Wales there are places associated with the Empress Helen's journey to put the Cross in its resting place in western Dyfed, there is, too, a collection of villages named after places associated with Helen's pilgrimage to the East. These are Gethsemane, Bethlehem, Dinas Cross (City of the Cross), Jericho and Constantinople. After bringing the Cross back to Britain, the Empress Helen is believed to have spent her last ten years in Constantinople but, as Alan pointed out, one has to ask which Constantinople she retired to: was it the imperial capital of the eastern Empire or the place in Dyfed called by the same name? Given that Hywell Dda, who was a king of this area, refers in his king lists to her residing in Constantinople, this is not as stupid a question as it might first appear.

The place where Helen hid the Cross must by definition have been considered both holy and royal. Now there can be no argument that, prior to the building of St David's in the sixth century, the most celebrated holy place in the whole of the Dyfed area was a church at a place called Nevern. Alan explained that he and Baram have done a great deal of research into the archaeology of this area and have found evidence for Nevern having been considered a very special place long, long before the coming of Christianity to Britain. They are not yet able to reveal much about this, as it is still a subject of ongoing research; but from that research they have discovered that the choice of Nevern was no accident. Laid out on the ground around there is a sort of star-map, composed of cromlechs and other monuments, a bit like the layout of pyramids representing the constellation of Orion that I wrote about in *The Orion Mystery* (which is why they contacted me). The whole plan is detailed and maps out many constellations, of which the one most relevant to Nevern is Cygnus the Swan. This has the alternative name of the Northern Cross and in older Egyptian zodiacs is often shown as a

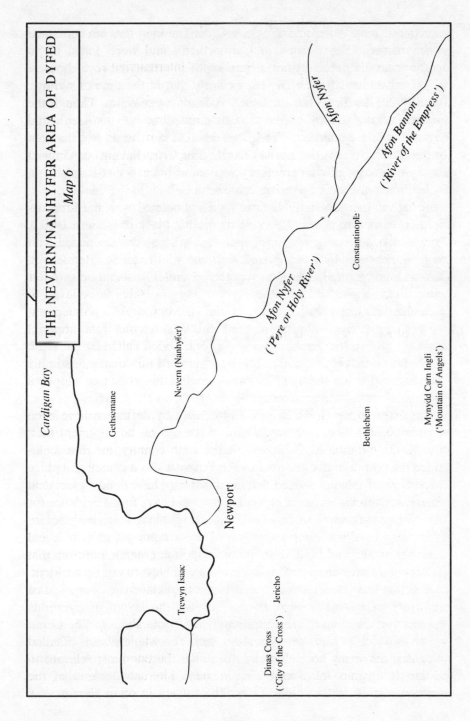

THE NEVERN/NANHYFER AREA OF DYFED

Map 6

Cardigan Bay

Afon Nyfer

Afon Nyfer
('Pere or Holy River')

Afon Bannon
('River of the Empress')

Constantinople

Gethsemane

Nevern (Nanhyfer)

Bethlehem

Mynydd Carn Ingli
('Mountain of Angels')

Newport

Trewyn Isaac

Jericho

Dinas Cross
('City of the Cross')

sacrificial lamb instead of a cross, which has obvious Christian connotations.

The constellation of Cygnus is to be found marked out on the ground by sacred stones. The star Deneb, the 'tail' of the swan, is marked by a dolmen at Trelyffant, the 'Place of the Toads'. The outstretched wings are the Coetan Arthur dolmen and a cup-marked rock at Cwmgloyne, the 'Valley of the Butterflies'. The head is a dolmen at Pentreifan. The central star of Cygnus, Gamma or *sadr*, falls over Nevern. In terms of sacred astrology, this is therefore the natural place for concealing the Holy Cross. Anyone who doubts that the people living in this area were interested in the stars in the Bronze Age and before has only to remember that it was from near Nevern that the Prescelly bluestones used at Stonehenge were dragged. So the idea makes sense that the people who built Stonehenge, long recognized as being some sort of astronomical observatory, might also have been active in building astrally significant cairns in the region of Nevern.

At the time when King Arthur's father Meurig reigned in Glamorgan, the resident bishop at Nevern, then called Nanhyfer, was Meurig's brother Cuhylyn – an important posting for an important man. The name Nanhyfer is derived from Nant Hyfer, which is an alternative name for the stream flowing through the village, called the Afon Nyfer – *nant* meaning 'stream' and *afon* meaning 'river'. In an 1848 dictionary, *nyfer* means 'pure or holy', whilst in a 1648 dictionary *nyf* means 'heaven', from which Alan and Baram conclude that the name Afon Nyfer means 'the Holy or Heavenly river'. Running into it is another small stream called the Afon Bannon or 'river of the Empress'. This stream passes by the village of Constantinople, which is but a couple of miles from the village of Nevern/Nanhyfer. The church at Nevern, though the present building is of fairly recent construction, is, like that at Llantwit Major, in possession of ancient stones. Two of these belonged to pendragons dating from the fifth and sixth centuries, indicating its importance in Arthurian times. Because of all these associations, Alan and Baram concluded that it is near this church that Helen concealed the Cross. That is where we were to go the next day.

Later I checked up on the Empress Helen. Though she was described in an encyclopaedia as probably the daughter of an 'Illyrian [Yugoslavian] inn-keeper', this did not fit with either the Welsh records or the strong European traditions that placed her in Trèves, the west German town now known as Trier. The true position of the Cross is

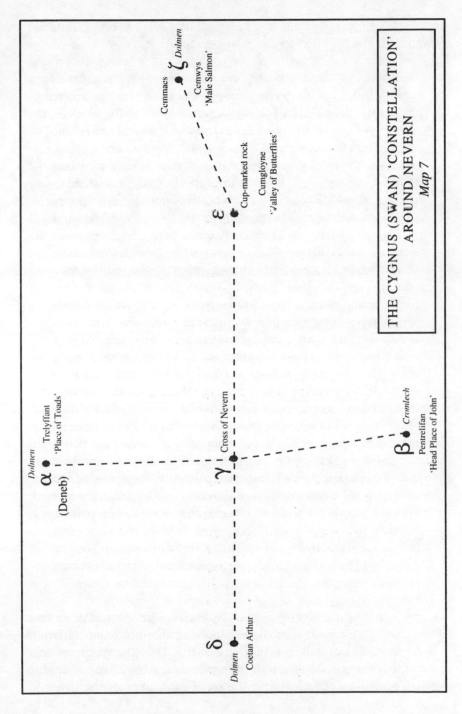

THE CYGNUS (SWAN) 'CONSTELLATION'
AROUND NEVERN
Map 7

α (Deneb) *Dolmen*
Trelyffant
'Place of Toads'

ζ *Dolmen*
Cemmaes
Cemwys
'Male Salmon'

ε
Cup-marked rock
Cumgloyne
'Valley of Butterflies'

γ Cross of Nevern

β *Cromlech*
Pentrelifan
'Head Place of John'

δ *Dolmen*
Coetan Arthur

discussed in great detail by Percy Enderbee in his *Cambrians Triumphans* and his arguments are worth repeating.

> Nicephorus and some later after him would have her [Helena] to be born in Bithinia at Drepanum, and the Daughter of an Innkeeper there, with whom Constantius passing that way to the Persians, fell in love, but this is made unpossible, by that is said before, of the being of both Constantius and Helena in Brittain, so remote from any part of Bithinia at that time, and neither of them coming to or near Drepanum or any part of Bithinia, at or after this time, but when she was an holy widow, many years after Constantius' death, passed by Greece on her way to Hierusalem, as is evident in all kind of Antiquaries, and will most manifestly appear in its due place. Others there be which do term this renowned Empress by the name Concubina, as Marianus and Florentius Wigorniensis, as they have been lately published; and Regino, without speaking anything of her parentage and country; and Martinus Polonus, who confesseth she was Daughter to the King of Brittain; . . . This I have written here to answer these frivolous cavils against that blessed woman, and with John Capgrove, call their allegations no better than dreams, and to speak still in his words, that opinion doth not only blemish the fame of so holy a woman, but maketh that most Noble Constantine to be a Bastard begot out of marriage, and so disableth him to have been heir of Constantius either King or Emperor, when all men know he came to the imperial dignity by right of inheritance . . .
>
> . . . it is a pagan report, and first raised by Zosimus that most malicious ethnick, and rayler against Constantine, for professing and advancing of Christian Religion and renouncing idolotry: and this is evident by the best learned authors themselves which in any sense called St Helena by that name, for they do plainly confess, as namely Marianus, that St Helen was the true wife of Constantius, and he forced by Maximian the Emperor to put her away and take Theodora his wife's daughter.[1]

As the implication of this slur, if it were true, would be that Helen's son Constantine was illegitimate and that his posterity would also be illegitimate, it is not hard to see that Helen's reputation was, for political reasons, deliberately smeared some years after his death. I was later to discover that one of the chief rumour-mongers, if not its architect, seems to have been St Ambrose, a late fourth-century Bishop of Milan.[2]

The next day we once more headed west along the M4, this time carrying on until the motorway came to an end. It was a bright June day with thick cumulus clouds skittering across the sky. For a time we followed the old road west. Turning north at Haverfordwest, we skirted our way past the Prescelly mountains, to the port of Fishguard. The final leg of this scenic jaunt saw us doubling back eastwards, following the coastroad towards Cardigan before turning off for our eventual destination: Nevern. After lunch in the local pub, we drove through the village, a picturesque collection of old stone cottages, over an ancient stone bridge that spanned the Nanhyfer, and parked in front of the church.

At long last I was, I believed, in the sacred precinct of the Holy Cross and I could barely contain my excitement as, entering through a small gate, we made our way through the churchyard. On either side, the path was flanked by ancient yew trees rising to thirty or forty feet. The cult of the yew, a traditional symbol of eternal life and therefore frequently found planted in graveyards, predates Christianity in Britain. As some at least of these great trees were planted long before ever the church was built, it seemed likely that this was already a holy site in pre-Christian times.

Walking over to one of the yews, Alan beckoned to me. 'Come and have a look at this, Adrian. It's got nothing to do with why we're here but I think you'll find it rather interesting.' He was pointing to the stump of a branch, a wound from which sap was bleeding and trickling onto some stones, staining them red.

'There is a legend that a man hanged himself from this tree and, in an attempt to wipe out the memory of the horrible event, the villagers cut off the branch from which he swung. The wound inflicted on the tree, where the branch was cut, has never healed and it has been bleeding ever since. People used to place handkerchiefs under it to catch the dripping sap, which would be clear at first before staining the material a blood-red colour, giving the impression that the tree was bleeding.

'It's been like this as long as I can remember, and that's a long time. As a child, during the war, I was evacuated from Cardiff to stay with relatives on a farm near Fishguard. That's when I learned Welsh, as they still speak it round here. I was first brought to Nevern to see this tree by my aunt when I was eleven. She told me that when she was a girl she was taken here by her grandmother, who remarked it had been bleeding as long as she too could remember. So we're talking about a good 150 years at least that the tree has been in this condition. Of course there must be a scientific reason why the tree never heals and the sap is red. It has been suggested that the soil beneath the tree is rich in iron oxide, but that doesn't explain why the tree has been bleeding like this for at least 150 years. Remarkable, isn't it? Certainly beats the Glastonbury Thorn for interest.' The bleeding tree was certainly a strange phenomenon but it seemed an appropriate manifestation of the strangely magical atmosphere that still hung over the graveyard. Having no handkerchief, I dabbed the sap with my finger and then wished I hadn't as the sticky residue proved hard to wipe off. However, there was no time for further reflection on this natural wonder. We had other things to see.

Proceeding round a corner we came to a very tall stone cross. This was decorated with 'Celtic' knotwork and was clearly very old. 'This cross was erected by "Higuel Rex", the famous Hywell Dda, who died in 948,' Alan continued, pointing out an inscription that gave his name. Since it was his king lists that gave Dyfed as the Cross's hiding place, the fact that Hywell Dda's own cross was here suggested, Alan and Baram believed, that the church was important.

Moving back to the front of the church, Alan pointed out another, even more venerable stone, standing near to the entrance and carrying an inscription in runes as well as one in Latin. 'This,' Alan said, 'is the Vitaliani Emerito stone. We think he was the Utherpendragon Gwythelyn, who is also known as Vortimer, the son of Vortigern. He is credited in the *Kentish Chronicles* of Nennius and other histories with driving the Saxon invaders Hengist and Horsa out of Kent around 456. Following his death – he is said to have been poisoned by his stepmother Rhonwen, the daughter of Hengist – Vortigern was able to regain the throne and the Saxons came back to England. That such an important stone as this was placed in Nevern again indicates the sanctity of the site.'

Once more I was struck by the carelessness with which such ancient relics are treated. Why was such an ancient stone, one that carried inscriptions that were now barely legible, being left out in the frost and rain? It surely merited having at least a little shelter raised around it; better still, it should be brought indoors, like the stones of Llantwit. It seemed that nobody in authority cared what happened to either it or the cross of Hywell Dda. It would be left for future generations to weep that such carelessness in our time robbed them of so much of their heritage.

Leaving the stone of Vortimer, we made our way inside the church and over to one of the windows. Here there was evidence of recycling, for one of the sills, which bore the inscription 'MAGLOCVNI FILI CLVTORI', was made out of what had clearly started life as a memorial stone. It was this that Alan now wanted me to see. 'As you can see the Latin inscription is repeated in Ogham letters [an ancient Irish alphabet] down the side. This reads "MAGLOCUNAS MAQI CLUTOR". Duplicating inscriptions in Ogham was quite commonly done in this area, where there was a sizeable Irish population. This stone has been remarked on by numerous scholars, including Professor McAllister, and though the grammar is not perfect, the consensus of opinion is that the ''MAGLOCUNUS'' in question is King Maelgwn.' Alan went on to explain that with this stone there is the usual problem of identification, as there were two important sixth-century Maelgwns. One was Maelgwn of Llandaff, who was a brother of King Meurig and therefore King Arthur's uncle; the other was Maelgwn of Gwynedd, or Maelgwn the Troublesome, for whom it is believed it is more likely this stone was made. He was elected 'Dragon of the Island' (commander of the army of all Britons) in 580, following the death of King Arthur. He is called 'Maglo' in Geoffrey of Monmouth's *History* and is also recorded in the 'Life of Saint Cadoc'. He was a son of Caswallon Lawhir, whose real name was Clutorius, or 'Clutor' as it says on the stone. Caswallon means 'Ruler of the Separated State', or Viceroy. Lawhir means 'Long-hand', implying a big man. This must have been a family trait, for Maelgwn Gwynedd is said to have been the biggest man in Wales. He was also ruthless, for, according to Gildas, he murdered his first wife, his uncle and his nephew, in order to marry the latter's young widow himself. It was he who started a civil war in Wales that raged on and off for centuries and that eventually led to the country's eclipse. The fact that his stone is in Dyfed and not in Gwynedd, his home kingdom in north Wales, again indicates the importance of Nevern historically.

Thus three prominent kings all left stones in this church: first Vortimer, at around 456; then Maelgwn or Maglo, who was elected to rule Gwynedd, Powys and this area, Dyfed, in 580; and finally Hywell Dda, who died in 948.

Having paid our respects to Maelgwn's stone and examined another curious window sill alongside, which featured a strange knot-work cross in the shape of a female figure, we left the church. A short drive up a very steep and winding road took us to a gateway leading into a grassy enclosure. On the gate was a sign put up, helpfully, by the Welsh Tourist Board informing us that we were now entering Castell Nanhyfer. As this was certainly the highest position in the vicinity, commanding the valley of the Nanhyfer, it was the obvious place for the local lord to build his castle. Though there was little to show for it today, earthen banks made it clear that this had indeed once been a castle.

Alan continued his lecture, explaining that Castell Nanhyfer meant 'Castle of the Sanctuary'. Giraldus Cambrensis, who in spite of his name was really three-quarters Norman and, according to Alan, 'quite a fanatic', records how when a political marriage was arranged between a minor Welsh princess and a young Norman nobleman, this castle was demanded as a dowry. The local Welsh prince flatly refused and was prepared to risk all-out war before he would surrender it. The Normans were bemused and could not understand why he was so intransigent, so they let the matter go. It seems obvious from this story that there was some sort of secret involved, to which the Normans were not going to be made privy. Giraldus and his fellow traveller, the Norman Archbishop of Canterbury, who were at the time acting as spies under the cover of recruiting soldiers to fight in the Crusades, were not informed either and passed by in ignorance of what was hidden here – something considered so precious that the prince would rather die than give it up to the Normans.

'Below the castle,' Alan said, 'is the cliff face on which is sculpted the Pilgrim's Cross, which you saw on the video and which we are going to look at next.' He explained his and Baram's reasoning. 'Given all the evidence, albeit circumstantial, linking Helen's journey with the Cross to this area, we believe that this is the place the Empress Helen brought the Holy Cross on returning from her pilgrimage to Jerusalem. This is the great secret that the prince kept from the Normans. And, what's more, it is not impossible that Helen herself used this castle.'

We split up and I walked around the perimeter of the grassy enclosure of what had once been an important castle. It was all curiously 'Arthurian' in atmosphere, like a Pre-Raphaelite painting. I could imagine knights courting fair ladies in the shade of the trees. It was just the sort of place to go and search for a missing Grail or to joust with a passing green knight. Here, on this westernmost tip of Wales, the problems of the twentieth century, of pollution, overpopulation and unemployment, seemed a million miles away.

Leaving the castle we drove back down the hill and parked near to the church again. We made our way across the road and on to a path that ran along the flank of a cliff. The path was shaded by a canopy of oak trees, whose fresh leaves cast their shadows on the vibrant green ferns that grew in great bunches at the foot of the cliff. In places, where piled-up earth and clinging bracken permitted, the cliff face itself could be seen: greystone rock that contrasted pleasingly with the lichens growing on its face. This was not a man-made environment. Whatever geological process or event had been responsible for the creation of this cliff was clearly so long ago that even nature herself had all but forgotten it. All that remained of the past was this grey cliff face, a silent reminder of earth-changes that probably occurred when dinosaurs walked planet Earth. After walking a little more than a hundred yards along the path we reached our destination and Alan pointed triumphantly to what I had so long been waiting to see: a sculpted cross on the cliff face.

'This is the Pilgrim's Cross of Nevern,' he said, touching it with his finger. 'At first sight it looks as though someone has, for some religious reason, simply carved a cross on the cliff face. Yet closer inspection reveals that this is not the case. Whilst the upper part of the cross is cut out of the natural rock, the lower portion is sculpted out of loose stones which have been slotted into place. In fact, if you study the whole area carefully, you will see that what we are looking at in the lower portion of the cross is a wall cunningly disguised to look like part of the cliff. Over here is where it starts' – he pointed to an obvious margin marking the division between natural cliff and a man-made wall composed of smaller stones – 'and it skirts all the way around here, through the lower arm of the cross and down to the left. In all this wall is about nine feet wide and the same in height.

'Now you have to ask yourself,' he went on, 'why would anybody go to the trouble of building an artificial wall such as this on a cliff face in western Wales? And why then carve a cross here in such a way that it overlaps the natural and artificial face of the cliff?' A clue, he said, was in its name: the Pilgrim's Cross. Pointing to a sort of ledge, just a foot or so above ground level, he explained that at one time pilgrims used to come here in their thousands to kneel on the ledge and pray for a vision: not just any vision – of the Saviour, the Virgin Mary or whatever – but specifically a vision of the Cross of Christ. That pilgrims prayed in such a way here suggests that the Cross was strongly associated with this place.

Alan and Baram surmise that the cross on the front of the wall is acting like sealing wax on a parcel: disturb the wall and a seal will be broken. There were no burglar alarms or security devices in those days and, though Constantine turned the Roman Empire to Christianity, there was no certainty that it would stay Christian after his death, which is why Helen, who clearly wanted to safeguard the precious Cross, brought it to Britain, where the Christian religion was more deeply rooted. A sensible thing to do would have been to place the Cross in a cave for safekeeping and then to seal up its mouth in such a way that it would be obvious if it had been disturbed. Alan and Baram believe the Pilgrim's Cross not only marks the right spot, guiding later generations to the cave behind it containing the Cross, but acts as such a security device, making it very difficult for anyone to break into the cave to steal the Cross without the fact being detected.

After taking some pictures, kneeling on the ledge and making a close examination of the cliff face, we left the Cross and made our way back to the car. I asked Alan what he and Baram had done about alerting the world to their findings. If it is true that the Holy Cross is buried here in west Wales, it would be such a startling discovery that it would shake the Christian world. There is also no telling what else might be buried alongside the Cross – perhaps a time capsule of writings, pictures and other mementoes from the fourth century. Given the potential controversy I was not surprised to hear that they had met with opposition.

'Naturally we wanted to see the investigation taken further,' Alan said in a matter-of-fact way, 'and in November 1994 we alerted the *Western Telegraph* to our findings, who published an article about it. This produced a vitriolic response in their letters column, especially from certain members of the clergy who clearly knew little, if anything, about the history of the British Church before the coming of St Augustine in 597, and who seemed to consider this line of research an outrage, as though it was an insult to the people of Dyfed that we should even have raised the subject of Helen and the Cross. We couldn't understand this attitude, as everyone we had spoken to was supportive of our work and keen to see it continue.'

He explained that their further researches indicate that an understanding that the Holy Cross was in Wales appears to have been common knowledge at one time. King Arthur himself is said to have carried it at the Battle of Baedan, as can be seen in the stained-glass window depicting him at Llandaff Cathedral. Similarly, the Llandaff Charters say when he was regranting lands after the catastrophe of 562–9, the Holy Cross was carried in front of him in procession. Much later, when Edward I finally overcame Gwynedd after murdering Llewellyn the Last, he demanded the Cross as part of his booty. He was given a piece of timber and held a great tournament to celebrate. There is some dispute as to whether this tournament was held at Neven in Gwynedd or at Nevern in Dyfed. Alan and Baram think it was in Dyfed, as the name of a field near by indicates that a tournament was held here at some time. It is doubtful, however, that Edward I was given the real thing, for the Cross he subsequently sent to Westminster Abbey is never described as having been ornamented with jewels or kept in a silver casket. Anyway, his son and successor Edward II gave this trophy and other treasures to his friend Piers Gaveston, who was a Templar knight and subsequently took the treasure with him to France to an 'Amery', who is probably the same person as a Grand Master of the Templars called Amery. It is possible that it was to get hold of this Cross and other treasures that later the French King Philip 'the Good' (le Bel) and the Pope (Clement) conspired to suppress the Order of the Templars in 1307. If that was their aim and they had succeeded in it, they would have been sorely disappointed, given that the trophy, which many people believe is still hidden somewhere in a sealed cave in southern France, was not the True Cross.

'In any case,' Alan continued, 'whether people are sympathetic or not the genie is now well and truly out of the bottle as far as the Cross is concerned. As a result, though we notified the authorities and had the Pilgrim's Cross registered as a scheduled monument, others are impatient to see what lies concealed in the cave behind. In 1994 an American acquaintance of ours, despite being warned that it is illegal in Britain to tamper with any ancient monument unless proper consents have first been granted, removed a brick from the face of the wall. I want to make it clear that although Baram and I are keen that a proper archaeological investigation be carried out on the site, we in no way condone what he did.

'His vandalism did, however, have one positive outcome, in that he claims to have discovered that there is indeed a cave. It would seem that behind the outer wall there is a second wall of better chiselled stones. In the centre of this wall there is a gap or passageway leading into the cave itself. It should therefore be possible, without too much difficulty, to pass a fibre optic cable through a crack or small hole drilled in the outer wall, and to push it along this passageway and into the depths of the cave itself. This would confirm whether or not there really is a cross, a tomb or anything else of value inside the cave.

'It wouldn't cost very much to do and I am sure that there are any number of sponsors, including television companies, who would be willing to carry out the work if only permission were granted. However, unless the public demand that action is taken, this is unlikely. CADW (the Welsh Ancient Monuments Commission) has, over the years, consistently opposed our work. Even though it has registered the Pilgrim's Cross under the Archaeological Areas Act of 1979, CADW appears to be in no hurry to investigate what may or may not lie behind it. They would certainly not sanction work that might lead to the destruction of the cliff wall; but as I have said, we would not support such work and it is not what we are proposing. Even so, it will take considerable lobbying of the appropriate authorities to have an investigation take place, but we are hopeful that one day the True Cross will again be revealed.'

To me Alan's words had a certain *déjà vu* quality to them. In 1993, in the course of carrying out remedial work to improve ventilation of Egypt's Great Pyramid, a German engineer called Rudolf Gantenbrink stumbled upon what appeared to be a little door leading to a possible hidden chamber at the end of a long narrow shaft and accessible only with the aid of a remote robot. At the time I was working on *The Orion Mystery* with Robert Bauval, and our work brought us into contact with Gantenbrink. The 'secret door' appeared to be relevant to Bauval's idea, presented in our book, that the pyramids of Giza were laid out to represent the Belt of Orion. The discovery provoked great excitement internationally and it was hoped that within a few months, even if it weren't possible to open it, at the very least a fibre optic cable might be pushed through a narrow gap at one corner and an investigation made of what lay behind it.

This, however, was to underestimate the serious political difficulties in the way of such a – on the face of it – simple procedure. By announcing his findings to the press without going through official channels, Gantenbrink greatly upset the Egyptians, who were in any case hesitant about carrying out any sort of investigation that might encourage 'New Age' speculation concerning the origins and purpose of the pyramids. Now, over four years later, the 'door' in the pyramid remains closed and, despite rumours to the contrary, there is no sign that the Egyptians plan to open it.

Alan and Baram, whose work, challenging traditional views, had antagonized the authorities, faced a similar situation. In Britain things are getting tighter where the discovery of precious artefacts is concerned. Rightly, new laws governing buried treasure, intended to control the activities of 'night-hawks',[3] have recently been put onto the statute books. As most archaeological departments, strapped for cash, are stretched by having to carry out rescue digs on sites discovered in the course of new building activity, they have little incentive to explore a site such as the Pilgrim's Cross, and what may or may not lie behind it.

I was therefore not surprised by the negative reaction Alan and Baram had received but I couldn't help but think about the story of Perceval and the Grail Castle. He, having spent years searching for the Holy Grail, suddenly stumbles upon the ruins of a castle. There he is served a sumptuous banquet and even sees the sacred vessel itself, but in his excitement he forgets to ask the vital question: who does the Grail serve? If our society resists the pursuit of genuine historical research, could we all be guilty of the same negligence where the Holy Cross is concerned? Time will be the judge of this. In the meantime I had much work to do piecing together the story of Helen, Constantine and why Britain was so important in the third and fourth centuries.

CHAPTER TEN

THE PIRATE KINGDOM AND THE
CONSTANTINE SUCCESSION

With the sun shining and spring in the air, I had spent a busy day with
Alan and Baram visiting sites in south Wales and now, late in the afternoon, we turned up a small country lane to Caermead, not far from
Llantwit Major. On either side of the road, flanked by hedges, were
grassy fields. Other than a few cows which interrupted their feeding to
eye us curiously as we went past, there was no one to be seen. Before
entering one of the fields, we made our way to the farmhouse to request
permission to walk on the land. A dog barked and presently the farmer,
a young man in his thirties, opened the door. Unphased by our request,
he pointed in the direction of what we were seeking and left us to our
own devices. Presently we were standing on top of what were clearly
very significant remains, which for some reason reminded me of
Knossos in Crete. Though little was visible under a thick mantle of turf,
both the height and extent of this grassy mound indicated the scale of
the ruins it concealed, which seemed to be more in the nature of a
domestic residence than a fortified castle. With dimming light and
lengthening shadows, I took a few photographs of ditches and dressed
stones, whilst Alan explained the significance of what we were
exploring.

This site, which, as he said, you could easily drive by without giving
a second thought, is mentioned in guidebooks to the area as being the
remains of a Roman villa. The villa, with its outbuildings – stables,
barns and the like – stretched over an area of some eight acres. It is
therefore one of the most important Romano-British sites in Wales, if
not in the whole of Britain, on a par with the palace of Cogidumnus at
Fishbourne. This alone indicates that it was a royal residence of some

sort, as no one but a king would have had the resources to build on that sort of scale at that time. Alan and Baram therefore believe it is the site not of a Roman villa as such but of an ancient palace of the kings of Glamorgan. It is they, after all, who are said to have endowed Llantwit Major, the original foundation of the old Cor Eurgain, so it would not be surprising if they built themselves a palace near by.

Experts have established that the main building, which is by no means all of the site, extends over some two acres and probably dates from before the middle of the second century AD. A small dig was done, secretly, a few years ago – not, Alan made clear, by him and Baram – which revealed that there are still intact murals and mosaics underneath the earth. Yet these ruins lie entirely neglected and the question of just who built the palace is still unanswered.

Alan and Baram, having given this a lot of thought over the years, believe they know the answer. 'The Genealogy of Iestyn the Son of Gwrgan' records that King Caradoc built a palace at Llantwit Major, considered to be one of the chief royal residences of the country. As Llantwit is less than a mile away and these are clearly the ruins of what must once have been the most important building in the area, it seems logical that this could be the site of that palace (c. AD 40–290). Alternatively, it is also recorded that a king called Meurig, who lived in the second century, built a palace at Boverton. As Boverton is only a couple of miles south-east of this site, this palace could be Meurig's, or maybe Meurig rebuilt the older palace of Caradoc and the two palaces are one and the same. Nobody knows for sure, as a proper excavation of the ruins has not yet been carried out, but Alan and Baram think the latter solution is the more likely.

An exploratory dig in the 1880s revealed that the principal building was burnt down. The archaeologists think this happened in the fourth century; however, Alan and Baram believe that this must have taken place earlier, in 293 to be precise, when King Carawn, or 'Crair' – the Carausius of the Roman records – was murdered by Allectus, although again this can't be proved until the site is properly excavated. Once again, Alan lamented the fact that nobody has yet done anything about this site.

Alan referred me to Professor McAllister's book, *Glamorgan: History and Topography*, where I was able to read more about Caermead. The book, which was very enlightening, did indeed indicate that Glamorgan was much more important in Roman times than is generally thought.

About Caermead Professor McAllister had this to say:

> One mile north north-west of the town [Llantwit], adjoining a quiet lane, is a field known as Caermead, wherein is the site of a *Roman Villa*. It is, however, fruitless to visit the spot as no remains are exposed; the site was only partially excavated in 1888, and was afterwards earthed over and turfed. The *villa* covered a considerable area, about eight acres big enclosed within its defences, the buildings alone occupying two acres, and comprising 20 rooms, one of them being 60 feet by 51 feet, the remaining walls of which rose to a height of nine feet. A smaller room, 39 feet by 27 feet preserved a floor covered with coloured mosaic pavement of rich design, and the plastered walls exhibited vestiges of beautiful paintwork. In this room were discovered 43 human skeletons and bones of three horses, and that and the evidence of burned masonry seem to indicate that the villa was attacked by Irish raiders[1] about the beginning of the 4th century, and the occupants massacred. It is one of the few Roman civil sites in Wales and *was probably built before the middle of the 2nd century* [my italics] . . . It is to be hoped that this wonderful relic of Roman–British civilisation (unique in Glamorgan) will not be allowed to remain buried indefinitely; it is a treasure that should be enjoyed.[2]

We ambled round the site taking pictures for half an hour or so longer before the sun sank below the horizon. Later, over a pint in one of the Llantwit pubs, I asked Alan to tell me a bit more about King Carausius and where he fits into the Arthurian story.

Happy to oblige, he explained that Carausius is one of the most important figures in early British history. In the Welsh records he is treated as a hero, but in books based on Roman history he is invariably referred to as a 'usurper'. Nennius, Alan said, who 'should have known better', calls Carausius a tyrant and accuses him of killing Severus, who was Emperor at that time. This is clearly untrue as Severus died in 211 – nearly eighty years earlier – and though Carausius drove out the Romans, there is no suggestion in other records that his rule was tyrannical. On the contrary, he was a Christian.

Geoffrey of Monmouth is little better in this respect for in his *History* he falsely claims that Carausius fought and killed Bassianus, the eldest son of Severus, who was actually murdered at the

Mesopotamian city of Carrhae in 217. Alan and Baram suspect that these histories have, over the centuries, been doctored by the 'Romano-philic' monks, who copied them as part of a general policy of putting the ancient Britons in a bad light. Modern historians claim that Carausius was a Gaul from the Menapii tribe of Belgium, which again is not true: in fact he came from Menevia, the region of Wales we now call St David's, or Dyfed. At first Diocletian and Maximian, the other Roman Emperors of the time, recognized his imperium in Britain and northern Gaul, the three of them forming a triumvirate. Later, as they were not so friendly, Carausius operated fleets from Milford Haven and Boulogne that swept the Channel, thereby keeping the Romans at bay. For this reason he is often called 'Carausius the Admiral'. Proof of his Welsh credentials is that he is listed in a number of venerable manuscripts, including the 'The Genealogy of Iestyn the Son of Gwrgan', as Caron the son of the King Meurig who built the palace at Boverton, from which we know he was a Glamorgan king as well as being overall Emperor of Britain.

The Empire of Carausius, which officially lasted for only seven years, from 286 to 293, was but one chapter in a process that was ultimately to lead to the Christianization of the whole Roman Empire: the result of the influence of Empress Helen, the mother of Constantine the Great, whose recovery of the Cross of Christ was described in the previous chapter. To understand this process, Alan said, it is necessary to learn how the Roman Empire of the third century was not at all a stable affair and indeed very nearly disintegrated altogether. And the event that had a direct bearing on this was the formation of the so-called 'Gallic Empire'.

From 260 to 274 Gaul, Germany, Spain for a time and Britain separated entirely from Rome and formed their own Empire, with its capital at Trier, or Trèves, in what is today Germany. It is a curious fact, seldom remarked upon, that some of the most impressive Roman ruins in Europe are to be found not in Rome but on the River Mosel, on the site of Trier. This is because from the late third century onwards Trier was nearly as politically important as Rome itself, which later lost further status to Constantinople after its foundation by Constantine in 328. Though this Empire was only shortlived, it was to have a profound effect on the whole history of western Europe, and on the Holy Kingdom.

Heeding Alan's words, I therefore set off to look into this story.

THE GALLIC EMPIRE

Among the notes given to me by Alan were a number of family trees of the ruling Roman dynasties of the third and fourth centuries. What was amazing about these charts, with their many branches and cross-connections, was the way that the leading Roman figures who contended for power were nearly all related. It quickly became apparent that close study of these family relationships is crucial for an understanding of what happened as the Roman Empire gradually broke down and the countries of western Europe emerged.

Not surprisingly, the central figure in all this was Constantine the Great. Through his father Constantius Chlorus he had a legitimate claim on the Roman Empire;[3] more importantly, he was able to enlist the help of British legions in pressing forward his claims first as Augustus of the West and later as undisputed Emperor, mainly because he was the son of Helen – this connection to the indigenous royal family gave him both legitimacy and a power base. Once he had secured the rest of the western territories – Gaul, Germany and Spain – his success was virtually assured. However, closer inspection of the histories reveals that Constantine's meteoric rise really owed much to earlier events in 260 when, as Alan had said, almost the entire western Empire revolted against Roman rule and for fourteen years a breakaway territory, consisting of Gaul, Germany, Britain and Spain, had a totally independent existence.

This 'Gallic Empire' was ruled over by a dynasty of five western emperors: Postumus (260–9); Laelianus (269); Marius (269); Victorinus (269–71) and Tetricus (271–4). The exact familial relationship between these Emperors isn't known, though it could perhaps be researched.[4] Perhaps significantly, tombstones which seem to be those of three of these western 'Gallic' Emperors have been found near mounds in south Wales.

Ruling from Rome at the same time were: Valerian (253–60);[5] Gallienus (253–68); Claudius II (268–70);[6] Quintillus (270) and Aurelian (270–75). To add to Rome's problems, from 267 to 272 it lost control over most of the East, including Egypt for a short time, to Zenobia, Queen of Palmyra. Suppressing the revolt of Zenobia occupied the attentions of the Emperor Aurelian and his generals from 270 to 272, when the city of Palmyra was destroyed and its queen brought back in chains to Rome. The experimental Gallic Empire was brought to an end in 274 when Aurelian defeated the forces of Tetricus and his son (also called Tetricus) at Châlons-sur-Marne. Though Aurelian had recaptured lost territory in the East, driving out the Goths from Moesia as well as destroying the breakaway kingdom of Palmyra, in the West a precedent had been set and the hold of the restored Roman Empire on these provinces, already at times tenuous, had been fatally weakened. Aurelian's victory over Tetricus gave him nominal control over the western Empire but it seems that Britain and northern France were still, to all intents and purposes, independent of Roman control.

In 284 Diocletian was elected Emperor by the troops at Chalcedon. His rule (284–305) brought some semblance of order to Rome and he began reforming the Empire. In 285 he elevated Marcus Aurelius Valerius Maximianus (Maximian) to the title of Caesar; then the following year he appointed him Co-emperor, with the title of Augustus of the West. It was probably this appointment that jolted Carausius, who had actually been in control of Britain and northern Gaul since 276, into declaring independence from Rome. Though Maximian was able to suppress a peasant uprising in central Gaul, he was for the time being unable to bring Britain and the coastal areas of Gaul back into the Empire.

The British royals regarded themselves as having rights over at least Britain and the northern parts of Gaul. The basis of these claims are complex and have to do both with their ancestral landholdings in Gaul prior to the arrival of Julius Caesar and with the various intermarriages between Britons and Romans that took place subsequently. The secession of Carausius was a major upheaval. Although in today's history books he is dismissed as a usurper, it is clear that as far as the British themselves were concerned he was a legitimate king. In fact both he and his father Meurig are mentioned in 'The Genealogy of Iestyn Son of Gwrgan' in glowing terms:

> Meyrig, the son of Meirchon, was a brave far-famed king. In his time the Irish-Picts came to Cambria: he however marched against them, drove them away and slew them; but was killed by an Irishman concealed in a wood, since called Ystrad Meyrig. He built a palace at a place called Boverton, which has ever since been considered one of the chief royal residences of the country.
>
> Crair [Carausius], the son of Meyrig; a very religious, wise and merciful prince, who was slain by the unconverted.[7]

Following Carausius's secession, an uneasy *modus vivendi* ensued. To show his good intentions – that he was not planning on expanding his fiefdom – he had coins minted with three Emperors' heads upon them: Diocletian's, Maximian's and his own. Large hoards of these coins have been found and examples can be viewed in the Museum of London. A stone with the inscription 'HIC IACET CARAUSIUS' is today to be found in Camarthen Museum.

However, Britain was too important in trade terms to be allowed to secede totally for ever and once Diocletian felt strong enough, steps were taken to bring both it and northern Gaul back into the Empire. In March 293 Flavius Valerius Constantius (Constantius Chlorus), a great-nephew of Claudius II, was adopted by Maximian and given the title Caesar of the West. At the same time, Diocletian adopted Galerius Valerius Maximianus (Galerius) as Caesar of the East. Thus both Emperors, Diocletian and Maximian, now had adoptive heirs and the Roman Empire had four joint rulers. In 293 Constantius Chlorus, who now ruled from Trier and whose designated territories as Caesar included Gaul and Britain, captured Boulogne. Whilst he was making preparations to sail to Britain, Carausius was killed by a kinsman called Eleath or Allectus, who, though he may have originally been sent over by the Romans, was by this time Carausius's own prefect of the guards. Allectus made himself king and reigned for four years but his treachery, which no doubt he thought would please the Romans, didn't avail him. According to the *Brut Tysylio*, the British, led by a Duke of Cornwall called Asclepiodotus, rose in rebellion. Allectus was defeated and killed outside London; the remains of his army fled into the city for protection. Tysylio writes:

> When the Roman Senate heard that Caron [Carausius] was elected king, and that he withheld the tribute, it was greatly irritated, and despatched Allectus with three legions to Britain; who coming to an engagement with Caron, overpowered him by numbers. The death of Caron in the battle, which was hard fought, exposed the Britons to great severities, and they were oppressed and slaughtered without mercy.
>
> By this means Allectus became king, but such was his cruelty, that the Britons, unable to support it, chose Alysgapitulus [Asclepiodotus], Earl of Cornwall for their king, and under his command marched to London. Allectus, who when they approached the town, was sacrificing to his national gods, broke off the ceremony, and sallied out to attack them; but his troops after a severe

162

engagement were routed, and himself with many thousands were slain. Hereupon Livius Gallus shut the gates of the city, and endeavoured to keep it, but Asclepiodotus and the Britons invested it, and sent advice to the several chieftains of the island, and solicited their aid. This summons brought thither the men of North and South Wales, and those of Deira and Bernicia. The city was taken by storm, and the Romans now subject to the sword, sent to the king to intreat that their lives might be spared; but whilst this was under consideration, the North Wales men fell upon them in their station, which was on a declivity over river, and left none alive. This place is called in Welsh Gallgwn, in English Wallbrook.[8]

As usual, Geoffrey of Monmouth's translation enlarges upon the original text of Tysylio, adding that the Venodoti (the men of north Wales) decapitated the captured Romans.[9] The description of Asclepiodotus as 'Earl of Cornwall' is almost certainly an error. Matthew of Paris describes him as 'Asclepiodotus dux Cornubiae'. Now the Cornubiae or Cornovii were a very powerful Midlands tribe whose territory embraced the city of Wroxeter or Viroconium Cornoviorum. It seems far more likely that Asclepiodotus was the local ruler of this city and its surrounding areas than of Cornwall, which at that time was part of Dumnonia. This also explains the presence of north Welsh troops amongst his supporters: the Venodoti would have been neighbours of the Cornovii and very likely they would have joined his insurrection.

Asclepiodotus was soon replaced as king of Lloegres by King Coel, known as Godebog, or 'Hairy Trousers', to distinguish him from the earlier Coel Hen, 'Coel the Aged'. This Coel, after whom it is said that Camulodunum was renamed as Colchester, came to an accommodation with the Romans whereby they would leave him alone, provided he paid the usual tribute. He seems to have ruled until 303.

In King List 10 of the King Lists of Owen, the son of Howell Dda, Coel Hen Guotepauc is listed with an ancestry tracing back to King Beli. In the *Brut Tysylio* he is described as the 'Earl of Gloucester', which may mean that he belonged to one of the branches of the Lloegrian royal family, split off from before the time of Septimius Severus. What is not in doubt is that all the British histories state categorically that he was the father of the Empress Helen, who is thought to have been born c. 265. Though she was a British princess, she is said to have been schooled in Trier, which at that time was not only the capital of the independent

Gallic Empire but was a famous centre of Christian learning. There is a local tradition that Helen lived in a palace on the site of what is now the cathedral, and it is possible that this royal home, like the Palatium Britannicum in Rome, served as a sanctuary in times of religious persecution. She did not forget her friends in Trier after her son Constantine became emperor: she is revered for presenting the city with *der heilige Rock* or the 'Holy Robe', supposedly the seamless garment once worn by Christ. This is still one of the treasures of Trier cathedral and must have been one of the relics she recovered from Jerusalem during her pilgrimage.

It is probable that it was whilst Helen was a girl living at Trier that she met Constantius: they may even have met in Britain. Certainly they must have been married by 287 for Constantine to have been born in 288. Constantius's marriage to Helen would have meant that he had every reason to support the claims of his father-in-law Coel to the throne of Lloegres, with the expectation that on his death he and Helen, and later their son Constantine, would inherit the title. Unfortunately, to complicate matters further, part of the price that Constantius paid in order to become Caesar under Maximian was to divorce Helen and marry the Emperor's stepdaughter Theodora. This marriage was clearly political and Constantius seems to have been blackmailed into it. The hold that Maximian had over Constantius was that his son Constantine, putative heir to the Empire of Coel, was being held a virtual prisoner by Galerius in the East. With his son's life at stake, the offer of the Emperor's stepdaughter in marriage was one that Constantius could not refuse, even though this meant divorcing Helen.

In 303, at Galerius's instigation, Diocletian carried out the persecution of Christians for which he is famous. Thousands died in continental Europe but Constantius either couldn't or wouldn't execute the Emperor's orders in the territories that he controlled. Then, in 305, Diocletian and Maximian both abdicated in favour of their junior partners, Galerius and Constantius respectively. In their place Maximinus Galerius (Galerius's son-in-law) and Valerius Severus were raised to the rank of Caesar. Constantius immediately demanded the return of his eldest son, Constantine, who rode non-stop across Europe to be at his father's side. There is a legend that, knowing the danger he was in and in order to prevent his enemies from catching up with him, at each station he changed horses and had all but his own put to death.

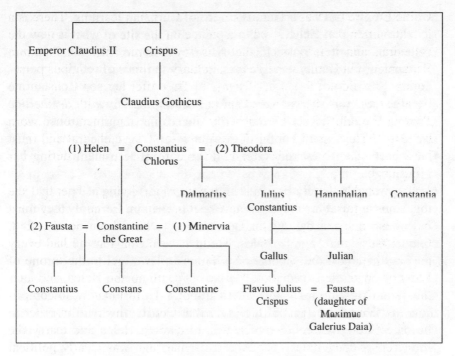

THE IMPERIAL CLAN OF CONSTANTIUS CHLORUS
Diagram 8

Constantine, now a young man of seventeen or eighteen years of age, joined Constantius just as the latter was about to sail to Britain to deal with an invasion of Picts and Scots and to assert his rights of succession to the throne of Coel. Then in 306, in a sequence of events remarkably reminiscent of those nearly a hundred years earlier when Septimius Severus and his son Bassianus had been in a similar situation, Constantius died and his son Constantine was elected Augustus by the British 'Roman' legions. At first he refused the title and wrote to Galerius asking to be recognized only as Caesar. However, in October of the same year Maxentius, the son of Maximian, who had been left out of the new division of the Empire, rebelled at Rome. Bringing his father out of retirement, he captured and killed Valerius Severus and repelled an invasion of Italy by Galerius. To bolster their position the rebels turned to Constantine, who was now recognized as Augustus of the West. Constantine joined forces with Maxentius, he and Maximian now becoming joint consuls of Rome. Galerius and Diocletian, who had by now also come out of retirement, tried to overturn these decisions but were unsuccessful. Thus it was that in 324, after a number of other battles and intrigues, in which he outwitted all his remaining opponents, Constantine eventually emerged as undisputed master of the entire Empire.

His success was to have a profound effect on the future of the Roman Empire. Though divorced from her husband Constantius, Helen continued to have a strong influence on her son. As the daughter of a Christian king she naturally promoted the new religion and it is almost inconceivable, though he may have kept this a secret, that Constantine himself was not already baptized long before he became Emperor. The story told by Eusebius in his *Life of Constantine* that, prior to marching on Rome, he saw a flaming cross in the sky with the legend 'By this conquer' is probably apocryphal. He may well, however, have been carrying the cross of St George on a banner, as had Gweirydd centuries earlier. Constantine's edict of Milan of 313 further confirms his Christian affiliation for it secured tolerance for Christianity, at least in the West. With the defeat of his last rival, Licinius, he was able to make Christianity the state religion of the Empire and to call a council of the Church at Nicaea. It was at this council that the so-called Nicene or Apostle's Creed was formulated. The Holy Kingdom had become a Holy Empire.

Having defeated Licinius, Constantine was free to travel east and establish a new capital at Byzantium, which he renamed Constantinople. His reason for moving the centre of gravity of Roman civilization to the East was its position on important trade routes. He also wanted to give the Empire a fresh start, untainted by its pagan past. His new capital was free from the ghosts of Rome and the influence of powerful factions who were still very unhappy about Christianity supplanting ancient religious traditions. In addition, there was also a sense that Constantine was refounding Troy. He is said to have visited its site but decided it was unsuitable for his purposes. That he was symbolically if not actually refounding Troy may well have been in the front of his mind: as a British king as well as an Emperor of Rome, he would have known all about the Aeneas and Brutus legends regarding Trojan migrations, and would therefore have seen himself as bringing history round full circle. Whether or not this is the case, the wisdom of Constantine's policy was to be borne out by events, for when, a century later, most of Europe fell to barbarians, his new city of Constantinople was to survive virtually unchanged for a further thousand years until its eventual capture by the Turks in 1453.

Unfortunately not all Constantine's decisions were either as wise or far-sighted. In 306, to cement his political alliance with the Augustus of Rome, he divorced his first wife, Minervia, and married Maximianus's daughter, Fausta. By rights Minervia's son Crispus, his first-born, should have inherited the Empire on Constantine's death. However, Fausta, anxious that her own sons should be preferred and perhaps mindful of how Constantine's own half-brothers by his father's second wife had been passed over, plotted against Crispus. In 326, the very year the capital was moved to Byzantium, she persuaded Constantine to banish Crispus and his wife, also called Fausta, to Pola. Shortly afterwards, again at her instigation, they were put to death. By the time Constantine discovered that they were innocent of all charges, it was too late. His only consolation was in having his evil wife Fausta herself executed. This might have been the end of the matter had it not been, as is well recorded, that Crispus had had a son. This grandson of Constantine, in whom flowed the blood of not only the imperial family of Rome but the senior house of Britain, was to turn out to be of profound significance to the Arthurian legends.

THE CONSTANTINE SUCCESSION

Constantine the Great died on 27 May 337, leaving behind him an Empire with at least two capitals, Rome and Constantinople. By this time Britain was already once more independent, having revolted again in 312[10] under a leader called King Euddav (Octavius). He seems to have been a grandson of Victorinus, the last but one Emperor of the breakaway Brittano-Gallic Empire who had died in 271. To further legitimize his claims on the throne, he married the daughter of Carausius. Euddav defeated Trahearn, the general sent by Constantine with three legions to oppose him, and once more drove the Romans out of Britain,[11] his brother Casnar Wledig storming the fortress of Caerleon. Thus by 322 Britain was once more an independent kingdom. At this time Gaul and Spain were ruled over by Maxentius, the son of Maximian, to be followed by his son Magnus Maxentius (Magnentius), who ruled until 353. Thus though in theory Constantine ruled the whole Empire, in practice it was far from being the unified colossus that is imagined, the by now usual split between east and west being very much in evidence.

Constantine was succeeded by his three sons by his second wife Fausta: Constantine, Constans and Constantius, who had already been made Caesars by their father. It was a predictably unhappy situation and one that was to have serious results. To ensure the succession, immediately after Constantine's death his generals carried out a wholesale massacre of other male members of the family, leaving Julian and Gallus, the young sons of his half-brother Julius Constantius, as the only living male cousins. The three remaining sons of Constantine met at Pannonia and agreed to split the Empire between them according to their father's will. The twenty-year-old Constantine II was awarded the West (the usual grouping of Britain, Gaul and Spain), his twin brother Constantius was given the East (Thrace, Macedonia, Greece, Asia and Egypt), whilst fourteen-year-old Constans was left with Italy, Illyricum (Yugoslavia) and Africa west of Egypt. Given the temperaments of the individuals involved and the fact that the western Empire was in reality beyond their control, it was a recipe for disaster.

By virtue of his seniority, Constantine II asserted his authority over his brothers, particularly the young Constans. In particular he demanded the cession of Africa and equal authority in Italy. When this was refused he invaded Italy, only to be killed near Aquileia. This left just two brothers to contend for control over the Empire: Constantius and Constans. In 350 the latter rashly marched against Magnentius, intent on bringing the western Empire back under his control, but in the Pyrenees he too was defeated and killed. In 351, taking advantage of a temporary lull in his ongoing wars with the Persians, Constantius also switched his attention west and defeated Magnentius at Mursa on the river Drava. It was a pyrrhic victory, for the Gallic troops of Magnentius refused to surrender, with the result that both sides suffered huge casualties.[12] Magnentius himself was not killed, and the breakaway Gallic Empire was not finally brought back under Roman control until two years later in 353.

By now cousin Julian had grown to manhood. As his elder half-brother Gallus was executed in 354,[13] Julian was the last known heir to the crown of Constantine. Constantius now bestowed on him the title of Caesar, along with the hand of his sister, Helena. Julian set about the task of defending the frontiers of the western Empire against the incursions of the Alemanni and other German tribes. When in 360 Constantius recalled a large part of the Gallic army to aid him in a new campaign against the Persians, the legionnaires, who had no interest in the eastern Empire, refused to go. Instead, they proclaimed Julian Emperor. Constantius's untimely death at Tarsus in 361 saved the Empire from another costly showdown and, except in Britain, Julian was accepted by both East and West as undisputed Emperor.

The fratricidal wars of Constantine's successors had taken their toll in what was already an Empire in crisis. The Alemanni and other barbarian tribes were pressing hard on the frontiers of not just Gaul but also Illyria and Thrace. In the east the Persians, under one of their greatest kings, Sharpur II, were a constant menace. Now, making things worse, Julian, known as 'the Apostate', tried to reintroduce paganism to what was now a Christian Empire. These matters came to a head when Julian took his army into Persia in 362. Though he managed to advance as far as Ctesiphon, the Persian capital, the Romans were eventually forced into an ignominious retreat through the desert under a blinding sun. During one of the many skirmishes that followed, Julian was mortally wounded and died in his tent, some say at the hand of a Christian assassin, on 26 June 363.

In the crisis that followed, Jovian, till then an unspectacular staff officer, was declared Emperor by the demoralized army. He now led them back west, concluding a humiliating peace treaty with the Persians that surrendered Mesopotamia and Armenia to their control. Jovian never made it back home to Constantinople for he too died in his bed under suspicious circumstances near Ankara. In his place Valentinian, a senior military man, was elected Emperor and he immediately appointed his brother Valens as Co-emperor.

Valentinian's connection with the royal family is a little hard to trace but it would seem that his father was Gratian Farrovian, who had married Faustina, the widow of Constantius. Valentinian and his brother Valens would appear to have been Gratian Farrovian's children by an earlier marriage. Valentinian's father's name was passed on to his own son, who was called Flavius Gratianus (Gratian). In 367 he too, having come of age, was promoted to the position of joint Emperor by his father. Around this time Theodosius, a senior general of Valentinian's, was sent over to Britain, ostensibly to deal with incursions by Saxons, Picts and other barbarians. Though the account of Theodosius's campaign contained in the works of Ammianus Marcellinus presents a rosy picture of the Romans arriving, like the cavalry in a western, to save south-east Britain from the predations of barbarians, this isn't how the Britons viewed his intervention. It is also more than likely that it was the

Romans themselves who encouraged the Saxons, Irish and others to go to Britain, partly to take the pressure off Gaul but also to destabilize what was by now a country used to being entirely outside the Empire. General Theodosius didn't stay long in Britain, however, and was put to death in 376. Valentinian had already died in a fit of apoplexy in 375 and his brother Valens died not long after in 378. This left just Gratian, who appointed his younger brother, Valentinian II, as co-Augustus in the West and Theodosius, the son of the former general, as Augustus of the East. The stage was now set for the events that were to seal the fate of the western Empire and to plunge Europe into the Dark Ages: the fall of the Roman Empire.

THE ADVENT OF MAGNUS MAXIMUS

The historical drama which was now to take place would have made a good subject for a Shakespearean tragedy. Gratian was an able soldier but little else. His only other recorded interest lay in hunting: like the mad Emperor Commodus, son of Marcus Aurelius, before him, he would enter himself into the Roman arena to kill wild animals. On his accession all around him was social and economic ruin. It was clear that the Empire was crumbling. In the East, long wars against Persia had taken a heavy toll; in 376 the Huns had swept south to attack Antioch; and pressure from Germanic tribes on the Danube border was intense. Theodosius had the difficult task of securing the now tottering eastern Empire, in which he was successful, but at the expense of the West. For generations the Romans had been forced to recruit soldiers from the Germanic tribes which pressed along the northern borders of the Empire, to prevent other Germans from invading. Some tribes had even been admitted into the Empire itself *en masse* to farm its fertile lands and to bolster up its dwindling population. In 379 two of the strongest tribes, the Franks and Vandals, crossed the Rhine, but Gratian, with the help of soldiers mainly drawn from the tribe of the Alans, managed to throw them back. This, however, did not end the Empire's troubles.

In 383, alarmed at the situation on the Continent, the British, under their own Emperor, a king called Magnus Maximus, decided to intervene. Though, like Carausius, he is dismissed in modern history books as a foreign adventurer and usurper, this labelling is not accurate. Detailed investigations reveal that Magnus Maximus, or Mascen

Wlendig, to give him his Welsh name, was not a nobody. According to Tysylio and other sources, he became king of Britain by virtue of a marriage to Helen, the daughter of King Euddav. This would not have been possible had he not been of noble ancestry but nevertheless a question mark hangs over his origins. Just who was this Maximus and why, if he was not of noble ancestry, had he been so readily accepted by King Euddav, who had, after all, seen off the generals sent by Constantine and was therefore a powerful king? This was a question I asked Alan at one of our meetings. From his answer I learned that Magnus Maximus was not only historically interesting but also central to our search for the origins of the King Arthur story as recorded by Geoffrey of Monmouth.

Contemporary historians are vague about Magnus's origins, Alan explained; they merely say that he was a native of Spain, without going into any further details. But this does not mean that he was necessarily Spanish any more than, as we saw, Severus was African. It only means that Spain is where he grew up. In *The Anglo-Saxon Chronicle*, where Magnus Maximus gets a mention, it is stated that he was born in Britain. Geoffrey of Monmouth takes this line a stage further, stating that he was the son of Ioelinus (Llewellyn), a brother of King Coel. Unfortunately this is impossible, as it would make him a cousin of the Empress Helen. Since she was seventy-one when she died in 336, had he been roughly the same age he would have been about 123 when he died in 388. Even if he were a lot younger than her, say thirty years, he would have died as a very old man of ninety-three. It is difficult to see how such an ancient would have found the energy to invade Europe, as we know he did, in 383.

Alan and Baram have discovered that in 326, the same year that Crispus and Fausta, Constantine the Great's son and daughter-in-law, were put to death on the machinations of his evil second wife, they already had a baby son. This child was put into the care of a Christian Spaniard called Severus Aelius. They believe, and they showed me research documents to back up their claims, that Magnus Maximus was this child, the grandson of Constantine the Great by his eldest son Crispus. This appears to be the basis of his claims first of all to the throne of Britain but subsequently to the whole Roman Empire. Also, his full name, Magnus Flavius Clemens Maximus, indicates an inherited claim from his mother's side of the family, she having been the daughter of Maximinus Galerius (Galerius Valerius Maximinus d. 317), granddaughter of Maximus Galerius (Gaius Galerius Valerius Maximinius d.

311) and great-granddaughter of the Emperor Maximian (Marcus Aurelius Valerius Maximian d. 308).

It would appear that, prior to their deaths, Crispus and his wife Fausta arranged for the child to be sent away to Spain so that he would be as far away as possible from the rest of the family and the threat presented by Constantine's second wife. It looks as though this was kept a closely guarded secret and, in view of what happened to most of his cousins following the death of Constantine, this was probably wise. Magnus Maximus seems to have continued to keep his origins secret from the Romans until such time as he was ready to make his bid for the western Empire. However, he was in Persia with his uncle, Julian the Apostate, who may have planned to put him in charge of the western Empire. In Britain, there was no need to keep his origins secret: as the great-grandson (on his father's side) of Queen Helen, who was deeply revered, he was treated with respect and allowed to marry into the leading families – first to Ceindrech, the daughter of a Khymric king called Rheiden, and later to Helen, the daughter of King Euddav.

'If we are correct in our assumptions,' Alan concluded, 'as Constantine's grandson by his eldest son Crispus, Magnus Maximus was no usurper. He had every right to the succession of the Empire, especially now that his uncles, Constantine II, Constantius and Constans were dead and the claims of Gratian and Valentinian II were legitimate only by virtue of their mother having once been married to Constantius. Also, if Magnus Maximus had indeed been born in 325, then his age is right. In 388 he would still only have been sixty-three – a suitable age to have been active himself whilst having grown-up sons to lead his armies.'

I was impressed by what Alan said and found that this claim was supported not only by his evidence but also indirectly by Jowett, who in his book *The Drama of the Lost Disciples* quotes Hewin's *Royal Saints of Britain*: 'The Emperor Maximus Magnus or Maxen Wledig was a Roman-Spaniard related to the Emperor Theodosius, and of the family of Constantine the Great, and of British Royal descent on his mother's side.'[14]

The last clause could be true only if Maximus was a direct descendant of Constantine, whose mother was the British Empress Helen. The statement that he was a Roman-Spaniard, which neither Constantine nor his first wife were, is understandable in the context of Maximus being brought up in the family of Severus Aelius. The connection with

THE PIRATE KINGDOM AND CONSTANTINE SUCCESSION

Theodosius is harder to understand, for he was to turn out to be
Magnus's nemesis.

In 383 Maximus crossed into Gaul with two of his sons, Andragathius
and Victor, at the head of a large army. He was well received by the
Gauls, who recognized that such a force was badly needed if they were
to be saved from any further encroachment by the barbarians of Europe.
After five days of desultory skirmishing with an army brought to oppose
him by Gratian, Paris fell and Maximus was able to make its queen,
Genevieve, a prisoner. His eldest son, Andragathius, now pursued
Gratian to Lyons, where he slew him. After this the rest of the old Gallic
Empire – Gaul, Germany, Spain and Africa – rallied to the cause. Statues
of Maximus were erected in his honour in public places and even in
Egypt mobs roamed the streets of Alexandria shouting out their support
for him. Maximus appointed Victor, then only about sixteen years of
age, as Augustus of Gaul, whilst his brother Andragathius became
known as King of Greece.

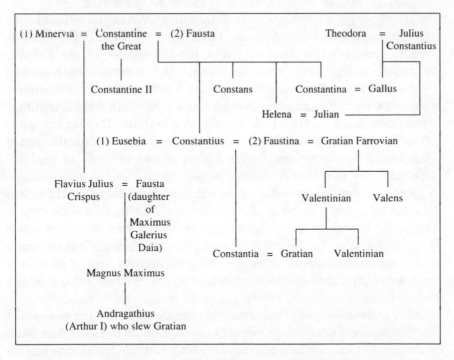

THE IMPERIAL CLAN OF CONSTANTINE THE GREAT
Diagram 9

To ratify the situation on the ground, Maximus now sent an embassy to Theodosius (who was Gratian's Augustus of the East) in Constantinople, who had little choice but to accept the status quo and agree to acknowledge Maximus as Emperor of the West. There remained the question of Italy and the fate of the young Valentinian II, brother of the deceased Gratian, who was under the control of Bishop Ambrose of Milan. Had Maximus invaded Italy immediately and deposed Valentinian he would probably have clinched the situation, but unfortunately he hesitated. Following a policy of procrastination, Ambrose spun out negotiations and it was not until 385–6 that he eventually made the journey to Trier, now Maximus's capital, to discuss the issue. By this time Ambrose and Valentinian had had time to prepare a strategy and to secure the support of Theodosius, who, meanwhile, had also not been idle. Realizing the seriousness of his own situation, should Maximus succeed in consolidating his power in Italy, he opened his treasury and recruited barbarians from all quarters to his standard; there were promises of further largesse to come once the western Empire was brought back under his control. The chance to ransack Italy, Gaul and the West brought soldiers of fortune flocking in from the Taurus to the Danube, from the Nile to the Caucasus, including warriors from some of the most feared barbaric tribes: the Goths, the Huns and the Franks. Little wonder, then, that many Italians wanted to be included in the western Empire with Maximus and invited him in. When he and his armies eventually crossed the Alps in 387 he knew it was bound to lead to all-out war with Theodosius and his mercenaries. As at the time of Constantine, the winner would take all.

Theodosius's hordes moved steadily westwards to be confronted in Yugoslavia by a smaller army commanded by Andragathius. Overwhelmed by superior numbers, the British lost two battles, at Sisica and Poetovio. Maximus was trapped and beheaded by Theodosius at Aquileia and, according to one Roman account, Andragathius is alleged to have committed suicide by jumping from a boat. This, however, is far from certain and other evidence indicates that he succeeded in escaping back to Britain. All that is known is that he was found to be no longer present on the boat when it docked. The most senior of Theodosius's generals, the Frankish king Arbogast, now invaded Gaul, where he defeated and killed Victor, Maximus's eldest son by his second marriage, who had been appointed Augustus by his father.

History had not repeated itself: Maximus's attempt to seize the

Empire, unlike Constantine's, had ultimately been unsuccessful. This now left Theodosius in control of both Constantinople and Rome, with Arbogast the Frank as master of Gaul. The unfortunate Valentinian II, who only now woke up to the seriousness of his situation, was left with little room for manoeuvre. Naively he went to Gaul to dismiss Arbogast and in the hope of taking over the running of the western Empire, but this was not to be. The Frankish general laughed at him, tearing up the letter of dismissal and throwing the pieces in the Emperor's face. To emphasize the point he butchered Harmonius, the Emperor's chief minister. Fearing for his own life, Valentinian sent for his mentor, Bishop Ambrose. However he, too, was powerless to intervene and on 15 May 394 Valentinian was found strangled in his bed. Theodosius died the following year, but not before he had achieved what had been his overriding ambition: to ensure the succession of his own two sons, Arcadius and Honorius.

In reality the situation was no cause for delight as far as the Empire was concerned. Arcadius, titular Emperor of the East, was firmly under the wing of Ruffinus the Goth, whilst Honorius, Emperor of the West, was completely under the control of a Vandal general called Stilicho. Though Constantinople would in time recover its strength to shine on for a further thousand years, it was effectively the end of the road for the Roman Empire of the West.

However, as I was now to learn from Alan and Baram, the real situation was even more complicated than this, for Magnus Maximus, the legitimate heir of Constantine the Great, had also left behind several sons, including Andragathius, the slayer of Gratian. What this all meant and how both he and his father Magnus Maximus fitted into the Arthurian dynasty was to be a further revelation.

CHAPTER ELEVEN

THE GLASTONBURY HOAX

I was keen to bring my discussions with Alan and Baram back to the core issue of King Arthur and their discovery that he was buried not at Glastonbury, Somerset, but at a site in the Midlands. One sunny day in early June I crossed the Severn Bridge once more to meet them, and Baram explained what had led them to this conviction.

'One of the first tasks confronting us,' he began, 'was the thorny subject of King Arthur's supposed burial at Glastonbury, proudly promoted in that Somerset town. When we set out on this quest we soon discovered that there is a curious inertia in British academic circles concerning the real identity of King Arthur, his ancestry, his personal place of residence and of course his grave. Most historians have opted for the easy way out by simply stating that Arthur never existed, thereby excusing themselves from having to trace him. A minority accept that there must have been a leader of the Dark Age Britons, living during the sixth century, who, for want of a better name, we can call "Arthur", but in many ways these people have only added academic respectability to completely false ideas.'

Both schools of thought, Baram explained, take little or no account of, or treat as inadmissible evidence, the vast number of documents in Britain referring to a King Athrwys, not as some faceless leader but as an identifiable king of Glamorgan in Wales. Likewise, many books inform the general reader that remains from the Arthurian period are scant; but in reality there is a considerable amount of physical evidence – in the form of inscriptions, place names and so on. From both the written and physical evidence, Alan and Baram knew a lot about this sixth-century King Arthur – his ancestry, the site of his major battles,

'Three faces in one' – a Gnostic-influenced image of
God. Architectural detail from Llandaff Cathedral.

Twentieth-century stained-glass windows from Llandaff Cathedral depicting kings from the
Arthurian dynasty of Glamorgan. ABOVE: King Arthur II (Athrwys), his grandfather, King Tewdrig,
and Cadwallader, last of the 'Battle Sovereigns'.

King Arthur II carrying the Holy Cross
after his most famous battle at Mount Baedan
in Glamorgan.

King Tewdrig's vision before the
Battle of Tintern.

The tomb of St Dyfrig (Dubricius) in Llandaff Cathedral. King Arthur II was crowned by St Dyfrig at Caerleon.

The fifth- or sixth-century stone of Bishop Cynvelyn, a great-uncle of King Arthur II, Margam Abbey.

Stone of King Tewdrig (Theoderic), grandfather of King Arthur II, Margam Abbey.

Stone of Bodvoc (Budicius), a King from
Brittany allied to Tewdrig, Margam Abbey.

The 'cross on the wall', behind which, in a
secret cave, may be concealed the True Cross
of Christ.

Stone of King Hywell Dda (*d.* AD 948) in
Nevern Church. Hywell Dda's King Lists,
compiled for the wedding of his son Owain,
are key evidence in the identification
of the two King Arthurs.

The Empress Helen (mother of Constantine the Great) with the Holy Cross, symbolized by the constellation of Cygnus. (Taken from *Atlas Coelestis seu Harmonia Macrocosmica*, by Andreas Cellarius, 1660).

Julius Caesar, who attempted to invade Britain in 55 BC and again in 54 BC.

Hadrian, who visited Britain in AD 123 and made peace with its kings.

Septimius Severus, Emperor of British descent, who died at York in AD 211.

Constantine the Great, who eventually converted the Roman Empire to Christianity.

Romano-British ruins at Wall, Old Lichfield, or *Loytcoyt*, near which is to be found the original Christian foundation of Glastennen (Glastonbury).

Engraving by Edward Burne-Jones of a Grail Knight. (Taken from an old edition of *The High History of the Holy Grail*.)

Alan and Baram at Old Bury, close to the site where they found the memorial stone of King Arthur I, son of Magnus Maximus.

Five-fold embankments at Castle Ditches hill fort on Cannock Chase, the probable headquarters of King Arthur I near Old Lichfield.

Remains of the bath house at Viroćonium (Wroxeter), capital city of the kings of Britain throughout most of the Roman period.

Alan and Baram on the hill fort of Caerleon, reused by King Arthur II, and the centre of a network of lesser forts guarding Gwent.

The church at Llantwit Major, refounded by Saint Illtyd in the sixth century on the presumed site of the first church of St Joseph of Arimathea, the Cor Eurgain.

Maescadlawr on Mynydd Baedan in Glamorgan, where King Arthur II fought his most famous battle and thereby preserved his kingdom from conquest by the Saxons.

The site of the Palace of Caermead, probable residence of the Rhymric kings in early Roman times and of the Emperor Carausius (King Carawn).

The dingle at Nash Point, which fits the description given in the 'Perlesvaux' of the place where a company of French knights landed, on pilgrimage, to visit the grave of King Arthur.

ABOVE AND BELOW: the estuary leading to the Ogmore and Ewenny Rivers, along which the body of the dead King Arthur II was brought for burial.

The confluence of the Ogmore and Ewenny Rivers, where Arthur II gathered his forces before the Battle of Baedan.

Ogmore Castle, protective of the Ogmore-Ewenny River system, but one of those seized by the Normans in 1091.

The Ogmore stone, which records land donations by 'Arthmail' ('Iron-Bear'), King Arthur II.

Artist's representation of the first burial of King Arthur II in a cave.

Alan Wilson outside the cave of St Illtyd in the Coed y Mwstyr ('Forest of Mystery'), the probable site of King Arthur II's first burial.

The 'anvil stone', which used to point towards the Church of St Peter's, Mynydd y Gaer, where King Arthur II was commemorated with a memorial stone.

Sword mark on the 'anvil stone', reminiscent of the legend of King Arthur and the Sword in the Stone.

ABOVE AND BELOW: the ruined Church of St Peter's, probably founded by
King Lleirwg (Lucius) *c.* AD 160, and rebuilt many times.

The 1990 excavation of St Peter's, under the direction of Dr Eric Talbot, which yielded significant
Arthurian remains.

Alan Wilson (*left*) with the stone of Arthur II, found in the dig at the Church of St Peter's. The stone carries the legend 'REX ARTORIVS FILI MAVRICIVS'. Baram Blackett (*right*) stands behind the stone of Arthur I, found near Atherstone in Warwickshire. The fragments on Arthur I's stone read: 'ARTORIV... IACIT IN ... MACI ...'

The coat of arms of London, which features the Pendragon helmet of King Arthur II, red crosses of St George (King Gweirydd) and the Mors Crocca, or 'Red Death' – the sword captured from Julius Caesar by Nennius, brother of Caswallon.

A grille-protected fragment of the London Stone, the body of which lies buried in Cannon Street, and which was probably originally placed as the foundation stone of Trinovantum, 'New Troy', by Brutus, patriarch of Britain and great-grandson of Aeneas.

The Liwell stone from Breconshire, which shows a figure, possibly Joseph of Arimathea, travelling to Britain via Egypt (symbolized by a pyramid).

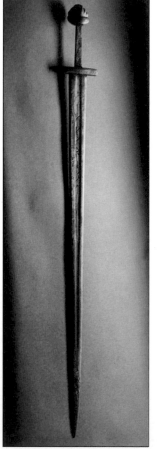

An ancient sword, recently discovered in America, which is quite possibly the original Sword of Constantine, or even Arthur's Excalibur.

even the location of his fabled castle of Camelot – and were very sure that he was buried in Glamorgan. However, it was also abundantly clear that the tradition that Arthur was buried in Glastonbury had to be based on something, even though the historical records had been distorted out of all recognition. They realized that if they wanted to resolve this contradiction they would need to look again, without prejudice, into the whole 'matter of Britain'.

At this point Baram interrupted his narrative to show me a photograph. It was a picture of a broken memorial or accession stone, with a Latin inscription in a style somewhat similar to that of the Bodvoc stone we had seen at Margam. It read: 'ARTORIU . . . IACIT IN . . . MACI.' 'This,' said Baram, flourishing the photograph, 'is a picture of a stone found at the site of the real "Glastennen", which is nowhere near Glastonbury in Somerset. It belonged to a son of Magnus Maximus, whose abortive attempt at seizing control over the Roman Empire so nearly succeeded.'

Maximus's claim to be rightful Emperor in succession to his grandfather Constantine the Great would have been one of the things he discussed in his negotiations with Bishop Ambrose of Milan. That this same Ambrose was the patron of first Gratian and then Valentinian II is, Baram explained, clearly of importance when we consider the story which seems to have first been put into circulation around this time, to the effect that Helen, the first wife of Constantius Chlorus, was a common barmaid from Illyria (as I had read when researching Helen). To discredit this marriage, and thereby cast doubt on the legitimacy of Constantine the Great himself, was the only legal defence available to the real usurpers: Gratian, Valentinian and Theodosius. To his great discredit Ambrose went along with this deception; indeed his animosity to Maximus was such that it was probably he who started the rumour in the first place.

Looking further into the family records of Maximus and his heirs Alan and Baram found more surprises. Consulting the Harleian 3859 collection of manuscripts, they discovered something very interesting in List 4 of the King Lists of Owain, the son of Hywell Dda. This particular list traces the descent of a Welsh prince called Iudgual (Idwal), who they think lived around 800. It was the origins or base of this particular ancestral tree, which attracted their attention. It reads:

Eidinet ap
Arthun ap
Maxim Gulc
tic qui occidit
Gratian cum regum
Romanorum.

This translates as: 'Eidinet the son of Arthun the son of Maxim the legate who killed Gratian the king of the Romans.' Now, we have seen that it was not Maximus who killed Gratian but his son. The inference is clear: Andragathius, which was the Roman name for Maximus's son, was in Britain called Arthun – that is, Arthur.

This statement identifying Arthur, son of Magnus Maximus, as the general who killed Gratian of Rome is supported by further records in no less than three other, equally authentic, ancient British sources known as the 'Brecon' Manuscripts. A thousand years old, these are contained in the British Museum Vespasian A. XIV and the Harleian 4181 collections. They are invaluable records, much quoted and referred to but, according to Alan and Baram, never actually read by those who quote them. Three times the statement is made, in Welsh as well as Latin, that Arthun the Black, known as the 'King of Greece', was a son of Mascen Wledig – Magnus Maximus.

Moreover, his descendants are listed each time, beginning with his son, Tathall, followed by Teithrin, Teithfallt, Tewdrig and then a queen called Marchell. She was a daughter of Tewdrig and the mother of Brychan of Brecon. From the Llandaff Charters we already knew that there was a 'King Arthur' or Athrwys who was a son of Meurig and grandson of Tewdrig who fought against the Saxons. Marchell was clearly the aunt and Brychan of Brecon the cousin of this Athrwys.

This had to be the answer to Polydore Virgil's riddle: how could King Arthur have fought both the Romans and the Saxons? The 'Arthur' of legend was not one mythical, superhuman king who lived for two hundred years but two different people separated by several generations. The first of these Arthurs had indeed, as Geoffrey wrote in his confused way, slain an Emperor of Rome: Arthur I is identifiable as the killer of Gratian in 383 and as the 'King of Greece' who traversed Italy before crossing over to Greece and moving north to fight Theodosius of Constantinople at Poetovio and Sisica. The second, Arthur II, who was his direct lineal descendant of the sixth generation, was the hero who fought against the Saxons at the Battle of Baedan in the sixth century.

Geoffrey, or rather Tysylio, whose work he translated, confused the careers of these two very different individuals. Because he didn't realize he was dealing with not one but two Arthurs, he made the mistake of duplicating the battle fought in Gaul between the forces loyal to Magnus Maximus and those of Gratian. In the first account he correctly states that Maximus caused the Emperor Gratian to be killed and established himself as western Emperor at Trier. Later he gives a fictitious account of how 'King Arthur' invaded Gaul and fought a terrible battle against the Romans at a place called Sassy. It became obvious to us that this 'Sassy' was in fact Soissons, an important city close to Paris, and that this was the same battle fought by the forces of Magnus Maximus and led by his son Arthun, not yet a king, which led to the seizure of Genevieve of Paris. As he did not realize that he was dealing with two different Arthurs, he perhaps didn't know about Andragathius's later career, which would explain why Geoffrey does not report that Andragathius/Arthur's victory over Gratian at the Battle of Sassy was later followed by disaster at Sisica.

Further confirmation that there was an Arthur living around the period of the late fourth century can be gleaned from the story of his slaying an Irish chieftain called Reueth (alias 'King Ryons' or 'Rhitta Gawr') in 367 on the slopes of Mount Snowdon. The grave of Reueth is still there to be seen. In the story 'King Arthur' was still a youth when he took on this giant of a man. The King Arthur in question couldn't have been Arthur II – Athrwys son of Meurig – as the date is far too early, but would have been Arthur I, son of Magnus Maximus.

This story also helps to provide a date for Arthur I's probable birth. The invasion of Reueth or King Ryons took place about 367. At that time Magnus Maximus would have been about forty-three or forty-four years of age, at which time it is likely that his eldest son, Andragathius (Arthur), was in his early twenties. This means Arthur I was probably born around 345. He therefore would have been in his forties at the time Magnus made his bid for the Empire.

Baram said that this discovery that there were not one but two Arthurs gave their researches a fresh impetus. They also surmised that the legend of King Arthur's burial at Glastennen or Ynys Wydrin probably referred to Arthur I and not Arthur II, whom they knew was buried in Glamorgan. With this in mind they took a fresh look at the legends of Arthur's burial at Glastonbury. What soon became apparent was the 'Glastonbury' in question was not the small market town in Somerset but somewhere else entirely.

Alan now took over the narrative, filling in the details of what was an extraordinary story of deception going back a thousand years. I was all ears as he began to explain. 'This was the situation which confronted us when we began searching for the grave of King Arthur, a quest, incidentally, which quickly bore results. However, as we soon found out, before we could convince anyone else of the seriousness of what we had found, we had first to slay what might be appropriately called the "Glastonbury dragon". This is a mythical beast of gargantuan appetite which has long since swallowed up the Arthurian legend and turned it into a profitable tourist trade. It stands, barring the way, in front of any serious searcher after the truth about King Arthur. Yet if you ask the right questions eventually it shrivels up and disappears, for in reality it is a legend based on a pack of lies.'

He went back to the beginning of the story. In 1191 the Benedictine monks of Glastonbury Abbey in Somerset carried out an archaeological dig. Their monastery had recently been burnt to the ground in a terrible conflagration and they were sorely in need of funds to rebuild it. At the time, as we have seen, stories concerning King Arthur were all the rage in the courts of Europe and nowhere more so than in Wales. Hearing from a Welsh bard that Arthur was said to have been buried at a place called Glastennen, Henry II passed on the information to his cousin the Abbot of Glastonbury. Equating 'Glastennen'[1] with their own Glastonbury, the monks set about looking for Arthur's tomb in the vicinity of their abbey. In the course of a dig that they conducted in the graveyard they turned up some curiously large bones, which they had no scruples in identifying as those of King Arthur and Queen Guinevere, immediately informing Henry II of the success of the operation.

Actually, the monks were not acting totally in the dark. They had in their possession other legends stating that Arthur had been taken to a place called Afallach or Aballach to recover from the wounds he received in his last battle. It was assumed that this must be the same place as 'Avalon', another name by which the Glastonbury area was known in the Middle Ages. Other documents spoke of a place called Ynys Wydrin as being the place of refuge where Joseph of Arimathea had been granted lands by King Gweirydd (Arviragus). As they knew that *ynys* can mean 'island' in Welsh and it was assumed that *wydrin* meant 'glassy', as in 'vitreous', Ynys Wydrin was translated as 'Glassy Island', which they took to mean Glastonbury. Thus the monks were happy to believe, and to tell anyone who asked them, that their monastery of Glastonbury was built on the same 'Glassy Island' on which Joseph of Arimathea had established his first community. This same story is repeated in innumerable guidebooks to this day.

That during the first century AD the area of Somerset around Glastonbury was a marshy wilderness with little to recommend it and therefore unlikely to have been gifted by a friendly king to a dignitary of Joseph's standing was not allowed to block the way of a good story of origins. Nor were the myth-makers, foremost among whom must be counted William of Malmesbury, anxious to probe too deeply into Welsh records that contradicted it. He, like so many academics today, was not a Welsh speaker and was in fact virulently anti-Welsh. He was only too happy to twist the evidence to give the Somerset Avalon an antique history it didn't merit.

The discovery in 1191 of such holy relics as the 'bones of Arthur' turned Glastonbury Abbey, which as a religious house had until then been relatively unimportant, into a centre of pilgrimage. This greatly aided the monks in their task of acquiring the necessary funds for rebuilding the Abbey after the fire. It also fitted in with the policy of the king, who wanted to anglicize the Arthurian legend, which until then had been closely identified with Wales.

There is a corollary to the story of the Glastonbury hoax, for in the next century Edward I used the pretext of Arthur's having been king not only of England but also of Scotland and Wales to argue that he, as Arthur's successor in England, had every right to subjugate these independent kingdoms. His main opponent in Wales was a king called Llewellyn Fawr – that is, Llewellyn the Great. He was in alliance with Simon de Montfort, the Earl of Leicester, who had a beautiful daughter named Eleanor with whom Llewellyn was besotted. To cement their alliance, Simon promised her hand in marriage to the Welsh king and in 1277 she was duly despatched by ship to be taken to join her fiancée. However, Edward, if not totally against this match, was determined that it should happen only on his terms. He sent three warships to intercept the bride-to-be in the Severn Estuary and she was taken back to England as a hostage. Llewellyn was beside himself with anguish but Edward declared that she would be released only if Llewellyn came in person to meet him at Glastonbury. Here Edward had the collection of 'Arthur' bones brought out and exhibited for the benefit of his guest. It is said that Llewellyn burst out laughing when he saw them and invited Edward to place his hand on the skull, thus demonstrating that, as his palm fitted comfortably between its eyes, the bones were not those of a giant but of an ox. The wedding between Llewellyn and Eleanor took place in Westminster Abbey in 1278.

Thereafter the myth that Glastonbury was the final resting place of Arthur fell into some disrepute, though it was not until the dissolution of the monasteries by Henry VIII in 1539 that the elaborate tomb housing these 'bovine' remains was eventually demolished. This might have been the end of the matter but for a mysterious leaden cross said also to have been discovered by the monks in 1191 at the time they excavated 'Arthur's' tomb. On this cross was inscribed: 'HIC IACET SEPULTUS INCLITUS REX ARTURIUS IN INSULA AVALONIA' – 'Here lies buried the famous King Arthur in the Isle of Avalon.' The leaden cross was probably once visible on the outside of the tomb built by the monks to house the remains of the great king. For a while it was on display in nearby Wells Cathedral but it has long since gone missing. However, a drawing was made of it by the historian William Camden at some time prior to 1607, and though most people who have looked into the matter agree that it was a forgery – the lettering, for instance, is not considered to be contemporaneous with the age of Arthur – it continues to cast a long shadow over Arthurian affairs.

Around this time, 1607, a local innkeeper, presumably anxious to increase trade, which of course had fallen off dramatically following the closure of the Abbey, started off another 'legend' about Joseph of Arimathea. According to this, the saint had planted his staff, symbolic of his family tree, on Wirral Hill on the outskirts of Glastonbury, where it had taken root to become a tree that was named the Glastonbury Thorn. The tree was cut down soon after by a Puritan fanatic at the time of Oliver Cromwell but cuttings were taken and new trees grown. Today one stands in the Abbey grounds and another in the yard of the parish church of St John. Much is made of the fact that the thorn flowers around Christmas but this, Alan asserted, means nothing. For one thing, Christmas was not celebrated at the time Joseph came to Britain and, even when it was, it displaced the older feast of Christ's Baptism on 6 January, not 25 December. The thorn itself is of a genus common in the Levant and the staff from which it sprang was probably brought back by a pilgrim not long before 1600. Thus the story that Joseph came to Glastonbury and there planted his staff is unfortunately nothing more than a colourful myth designed to attract pilgrims.

I felt very uncomfortable about what Alan was telling me. Glastonbury is a place I know very well and to which I have a strong emotional attachment. For me the majestic Abbey ruins, the isolated church tower of St Michael perched on the Tor and the tranquil Chalice Well gardens had long been places of refuge from the hurly-burly of life; my wife Dee and I had even been married there in 1984 in the Church of St Mary – an expression of our feelings for the place and for what it represents. To hear now that its associations were all a myth, when all the guidebooks and local traditions said otherwise, was not a message I either liked or wanted to hear.

Yet in my dealings with these two over the preceding year I had learnt to suspend disbelief. I had come to realize that they were quite exceptional researchers. Under Alan's sometimes gruff exterior lay a mind of exceptional brilliance. He had an extraordinary memory for detail and an unparalleled knowledge of British Dark Age history. Like a bard of old he could rattle out the genealogies of the Dark Age kings of Britain going back for twenty or more generations. Baram, his loyal and trusted associate, had put Alan's multifarious researches into order so that they were able to publish their findings in the form of books. That these had been published at their own expense, costing both of them very dear, was strong evidence that they were not playing with ideas simply for the sake of originality or to earn a fast buck. They had been on a quest to find the truth, leaving few stones unturned. In the light of this, being asked to be open-minded enough to consider their message seemed a not unreasonable request, even if it meant abandoning preconceived notions concerning Glastonbury.

A little detective work of my own revealed that the real founding of Glastonbury Abbey was rather different from that described by the legends and had nothing whatever to do with either King Arthur or Joseph of Arimathea. Instead it concerned the much later Saxon kings Alfred and Edgar.[2] In 878 Alfred defeated a Viking leader called Gudrum at the Battle of Edington, after which they signed a peace treaty at Wedmore, a few miles to the north-west of Glastonbury. As a thanksgiving to God for this providential victory, Alfred founded a monastery on Athelney Island, where he had spent the winter before planning his campaign and no doubt praying for divine help. The site of this monastery, which soon closed down for lack of recruits, lies about ten miles to the south-west of Glastonbury. Though there may have been a small, Christian community at Glastonbury (which may not even have been known as either Avalon or Glastonbury in Alfred's time), it is clear that in Alfred's day this settlement was not viewed as important: had it been, the treaty between Alfred and Gudrum, which involved the latter's baptism with Alfred acting as godfather, would have been signed at Glastonbury rather than in neighbouring Wedmore.

In fact, as Alan had said, until the Middle Ages the whole area around Glastonbury was a marshy fen, punctuated by a few small islands. Far from the paradisaical fantasies of Romantic poets, it would have been a very unpleasant place in which to live – cold and wet in winter, plagued by mosquitoes in summer. The excavation of the first-century Lake Village at Mere, one mile from Glastonbury (where no comparable remains of this period of any significance have yet been found), indicate the primitive nature of life in this marshland. At Mere people lived in huts built on stilts and rowed around in dug-out canoes. Whilst they may have had a few apple trees, in the main they were subsistence farmers relying on the good fishing to support themselves and their families. All in all these lake-dwellers lived lives not too dissimilar from their remote ancestors in the Stone Age. Given these considerations, the suggestion that King Gweirydd would have invited his mentor, Joseph of Arimathea, to settle in this inhospitable region was unlikely to say the least.

It seems that the first person to have linked this story with Glastonbury was St Dunstan, who was born at West Pennard, a few miles from Glastonbury, in 909, thirty-one years after the Battle of Edington. Of noble birth, he entered the household of King Athelstan, the most colourful of Alfred's grandsons and probably the most brilliant of all the Wessex kings. However, Dunstan's interest in strange books (and possibly magic) excited the distrust of his contemporaries and he was obliged to leave court. He returned home to the Glastonbury area until recalled to court in 942 to be awarded the title of Abbot of Glastonbury by Athelstan's successor, Edmund, who had founded the Abbey in 941. Thereafter Dunstan's career underwent one or two more twists and turns, reflecting the political turmoil of the time, until 959, by which time he was Bishop of Worcester. That year Edmund's younger son, Edgar, became undisputed king and Dunstan was given the see of London, and in the same year became Archbishop of Canterbury.

Needless to say, a certain amount of confusion surrounds Dunstan's career at Glastonbury. Well read as he undoubtedly was, he seems to have known at least something about the legends concerning Joseph of Arimathea and his foundation at Ynys Wydrin of Afallach and linked them – as we have seen, falsely – to the Somerset area. Almost certainly it was the library that he founded which William of Malmesbury consulted when employed *c*. 1125 to collect all the evidence and write a definitive history of Glastonbury[3] The monastery of which he became abbot in 942 seems to have been a refounding of Alfred's at Athelney. At the time Dunstan was resident there was no monastery building: its first really substantive building was a chapel of rest built as a memorial for King Edgar after he died in 975. It was this structure, and its associated monastic buildings, which burnt down in 1184, prompting the monks to search for the grave of King Arthur.

During the Middle Ages the great abbeys of Shaftesbury[4] and Glastonbury received large donations of land and, by carefully husbanding their resources, they became extremely wealthy. The success of Shaftesbury in attracting pilgrims, and therefore extra donations, by virtue of being in possession of the shrine of St Edward the Martyr, probably encouraged the monks of Glastonbury to build a similar shrine of their own in which to house the supposed bones of King Arthur. That the ploy was successful cannot be denied. From being a rather poor relation of older, genuine shrines such as St Albans, Glastonbury quickly rose in both wealth and status. This wealth was, however, to be its downfall, as it attracted the attentions of the spendthrift Henry VIII. He, as the descendant of a long line of Welsh kings and therefore in possession of a family tree going back to Roman times and before, was well aware that Glastonbury's supposed Arthurian connections were bogus. When in 1539, nearly six hundred years after its founding, Henry VIII seized the Abbey, along with every other religious house in England and Wales, Richard Whiting, the last Abbot, was hanged, drawn and quartered on Glastonbury Tor and the abbey was plundered of its treasure. The buildings, or what was left of them, passed into private hands until they were bought back by the diocese of Bath and Wells in 1907.

Between 1908 and 1919 a curious individual named Frederick Bligh Bond held the post of Diocesan Architect and Director of Excavations for the Somerset Archaeological Society. He carried out an extensive series of digs at Glastonbury, searching for evidence both of its full extent (by then not apparent from surface examination) and of the history of its building. Bligh Bond was also a keen member of the Society for Psychical Research – spiritualism at that time undergoing one of its periodic revivals. To aid him in the process of excavating the ruins he made use of the psychic talents of a friend named John Alleyne, who, by means of 'automatic writing', was able to receive messages from a group of spirits identifying themselves as 'the Company of Avalon'. These 'spirits', it seems mostly of former monks, passed messages through the pen of John Alleyne, telling him where to dig and what he would find. Needless to say, Bligh Bond kept these spiritual sources of information secret from the Church commissioners who had given him permission to do this work in the first place. When a report on his findings was published under the title *An Architectural Handbook of Glastonbury Abbey*, no mention was made of spirit writing or of a community of deceased monks; however, in 1918, he published the truth about his sources, which caused such a scandal that he was forced to quit his post with the Church of England and died in penury not many years later.

By common consent, long before Bligh Bond's dig, the Chapel of St Mary was considered to be the oldest extant building on the Glastonbury site. It stands at the western end of the surviving part of the Great Church and is believed by many (this is repeated endlessly in popular books on Glastonbury) to have been put up in 1184 on the site of what had previously been known as the *vetusta ecclesia*, or Old Church, which was believed to have been built on the orders of King Ina of Wessex (688–726) and to have enclosed an even earlier building of wattle and daub that was supposedly built by Joseph of Arimathea. The principal documentary evidence for the existence of these earlier buildings lies in William of Malmesbury's history of Glastonbury. He writes that 'annals of good authority' (unspecified) 'inform us that a little wattle church, dedicated to the Virgin Mary, had been built at Glastonbury by missionaries sent by Eleutherius at the request of King Lucius in 166'. Later this account was elaborated by other authors to the effect that these missionaries were not the builders but merely the restorers of a church originally built by Joseph of Arimathea or even by Jesus himself.[5]

If Bligh Bond and his team had been hopeful of finding any remains of either the *vetusta ecclesia* or the wattle hut, they were to be sorely disappointed. The vast majority of the Abbey ruins were shown, as was to be expected, to date only from the twelfth to the sixteenth centuries and careful excavation revealed nothing earlier than the tenth century. Of the so-called *vetusta ecclesia* absolutely nothing remained, if it had ever existed in the first place. The oldest structure discovered was that termed by Bond 'St Dunstan's Chapel' and evidently dedicated to St John the Baptist. This building lay a few yards to the west of the main church and was not even connected to the Chapel of St Mary. Bligh Bond looked for traces of earlier structures but found no evidence whatsoever for the existence of any church preceding this one, which was probably built on the orders of King Edmund in 941.

Though Bligh Bond found no traces of the *vetusta ecclesia*, still less of Joseph of Arimathea's original wattle hut, ironically his work has coloured people's appreciation of Glastonbury ever since. The excitement caused first by his excavations and then by the disclosure of his spiritualist interests brought people flocking from all over the country. Suddenly Glastonbury became a mecca for a fashionable in-crowd of poets, artists, writers and mystics. With the development of 'New Age' consciousness in the swinging sixties, and the town's further associations with rock music through the Glastonbury festivals, it was almost inevitable that it became the hippy capital of Europe. Meanwhile Bligh Bond has become a sort of patron saint of the unorthodox, his psychic involvements only making him more appealing to later generations of channelers and researchers.

Today Glastonbury High Street is lined with trinket and gift shops and in summer, in a way that would have brought tears to the eyes of its old innkeepers, it is thronging with pilgrims anxious to partake of its bogus spirituality. Unfortunately, few of its visitors realize that, as we have seen, almost everything about Glastonbury is suspect. Like a hall of mirrors, today's Glastonbury reflects back to the viewer a distorted picture of his own thoughts, views and opinions. The only religious relic of any real consequence, the Benedictine Abbey founded by St Dunstan, tends to be disregarded by those more anxious to tune into a fanciful pagan past. More's the shame, for the Abbey was a very fine building with an interesting history. The discoveries by Bligh Bond have greatly increased our knowledge concerning this once magnificent edifice and his work deserves careful scrutiny.

The evidence is clear for those with the eyes to see it. Glastonbury Abbey owes its foundation to Dunstan under the patronage of King Edgar. It was never the home of Joseph of Arimathea and neither was it the final resting place of King Arthur. Why then was it so elevated? Again the answer seems to be tied up with the career of Alfred the Great, the grandfather of Edgar and one of the great Saxon heroes. As a warrior-king who fought against pagan Vikings in the name of Christ, he had a cult of his own, not unlike that attending the legendary King Arthur, and in time his achievements seem to have been merged with those of Arthur. As a result the Glastonbury area, which was really a Saxon foundation and had indeed been the secret retreat of Alfred after a defeat at Chippenham, became associated with the mythology of Arthur, and so came to be known as the magic Island of Avalon to which the broken body of King Arthur had been spirited away following the Battle of Camlam. This misidentification suited such Plantagenet kings as Henry II and Edward I. They wished to be seen as Arthur's heirs, whilst at the same time playing down his Welsh associations; they also, as Normans, had a vested interest in reducing the stature of such Saxon heroes as Alfred. Falsifying the legends surrounding Glastonbury, thereby building up the reputation of Arthur, helped them achieve these aims.

All this, however, begs another question: if Glastonbury is neither the Ynys Wydrin of Joseph of Arimathea nor the real burial place of King Arthur, then where is?

CHAPTER TWELVE

THE SEARCH FOR ARTHUR I

'Today,' said Baram with a twinkle in his eye, 'we are going to visit the real Glastennen – which isn't where most people think it is.' I was in the mood for an adventure and to record the event I brought with me a video camera as well as an ordinary one for taking slides, as I was anxious to build up an archive of images. On the way to our mystery destination Alan, who usually did most of the talking, fell silent and let the younger man take over, explaining that tracing Arthur I had mostly been his project. Baram, who usually sat back listening, explained how they had come to find his grave.

'It all began,' he started in his gravelly, Newcastle accent, 'when I started looking closely into the royal dynasties of Wales and their connections with the ruling families of England. Northumberland, where I come from, was once closely linked with Wales. In exploring the family trees of the Dark Age kings of Northumberland I was surprised to see a reference to a marriage between a princess of the region and a king from Glamorgan. Curiously enough it was while I was researching this link between the north-east of England and Glamorgan that I first met Alan.'

In the family trees or King Lists of Owain, the son of Hywell Dda, King List 25 appears to list kings of the West Midlands, the majority of whom have names beginning with 'M'. The first of these is someone called Mormayl, who comes from a place called Glastunum. By it there is a side-note explaining where Glastunum is to be found. It reads as follows:

> *Mormayl Glastunum*
> *Sunt Glastunum qui ex uenerunt*
> *qui vocatur Loytcoyt.*

What it is saying is that the people of Glastunum, or Glastennen – that is, Glastonbury – are those who come from a place called Loytcoyt. In Welsh *llwydcoed* means grey or hoary woods, probably meaning that there are lichens growing on the trees which give them a grey colour. This is also a direct translation of the Latin name Letocetum.[1] This was an ancient Romano-British town, now a village called Wall, the ruins of which Baram and Alan were taking me to see. When this town was abandoned, a new city was built on fields about three miles to the north, rather as in Wiltshire 'Old Sarum' was relocated in the Middle Ages to its present site of 'New Sarum' or Salisbury. The new town of Letocetum was and is called Lichfield, the name retaining the meaning of the first half of the old town – *leto* means 'lichen' – and suffixing it with 'field'. By thus identifying Loytcoyt (*llwydcoed*), described by the 'Black Book of Carmarthen' as the place where the people of Glastonbury came from, as Letocetum – and, since the 'Black Book' is a tenth-century source, it must be the first Letocetum – Baram and Alan had identified the true location of Glastennen as at or close to the present-day village of Wall, which lies on the old Watling Street to the north of Lichfield in the West Midlands. Later research and a mass of additional facts support this conclusion.

Arriving at our destination, I pulled up in a small car park just off the A5 at the village of Wall. Unfortunately the remains of the old Romano-British town were closed for the winter but it was possible to walk along the edge of a neighbouring field and peer across the boundary hedge to see the excavated trenches. These showed the sort of typical red-brick footings that one associates with 'Roman' sites. The land rose steeply from the area that had been excavated to what was clearly the centre of the present village of Wall. Standing on the crest of the hill was a church, probably marking the site of some older building. It was easy to see the attractions of such a strategic site, the hilltop probably originally crowned with lichen-covered trees. If, as seemed likely, the old town had stretched all the way from the present-day village to the excavated area, then it would have been quite a sizeable township. The map showed that it lay on the crossroads of two major highways: Watling Street, which runs from London to Wroxeter, and the Fosse Way, which comes up from the Devon coast, through Bath and Cirencester and all the way to Yorkshire, suggesting that this town would have been the ancient equivalent of modern-day Birmingham. Its location gave it great importance both strategically and in terms of trade.

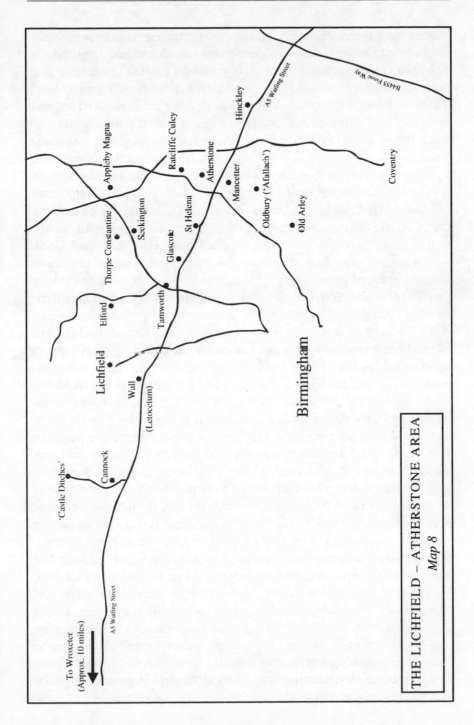

THE LICHFIELD – ATHERSTONE AREA
Map 8

Resuming our conversation, Baram began telling me about an earth-work called Castle Ditches on the nearby Cannock Chase. This he and Alan had identified with Arthurian traditions. They found a reference to what they believe to be Arthur I in the 'Hanes of Gruffyd ap Cynan'. This says that King Arthur – and they believe this to mean Arthur I, son of Maximus – fortified the Lichfield area. Just to the west of Wall, or Loytcoyt, Watling Street has a branch road running north through Cannock Chase, terminating at Castle Ditches. This is the major castle in the area and they believe it is where Arthur I gathered his forces prior to marching into north Wales to defeat the Irish chieftain Reueth.

Leaving Wall, we got back into the car and headed in the direction of Cannock and after a few false turns found ourselves at our destination. Before us was one of the most impressive hill forts I have ever seen – and living in Dorset I have visited a fair few over the years. Much of it was now covered in trees, tidy ranks of Forestry Commission evergreens that obscured the view. But as the fort stood on the highest ground in the area, one could imagine that at the time it was occupied it would have had a commanding view over the entire region. The earthbanks sur-rounding the central area were extremely deep and again one could imagine that as they would have had palisades on top they would have presented a formidable barrier to anyone attempting to storm the fortress. At the far end, where the land sloped away steeply anyway, there were only two of these defensive ditch-and-bank barriers. However, on the near side, where the approach was easier, we counted no less than five of these concentric fortifications. As even major Dorset hill forts such as Badbury Rings, Hambledon Hill, Maiden Castle and Rawleston have only three sets of such ditch-and-bank defences, this was extremely unusual to say the least and was evidence that the fortress was of major, even royal, importance. At the far end of the enclosed area was circum-stantial evidence linking the castle with the Arthurian dynasty rather than earlier periods, for here were the footings of a major building. This must have been quite substantial judging from the lower courses, con-sisting of large, dressed blocks of stone which were still visible. This 'keep', if such we may call it, was rectangular in shape and, as it stood at the highest point of the hill, would not have needed to be particularly tall to have allowed perfect visibility over the earthbanks towards the surrounding countryside on all sides.

To my, admittedly untrained, eye, Castle Ditches looked too large and imposing to have been merely a 'refuge for local farmers', as was suggested by English Heritage on their noticeboard at the entrance to the site. It fitted the idea of a Dark Age military barracks and I could see why Baram was of the opinion that this fortress could have been what was being referred to by King Gruffyd ap Cynan when he said that Arthur had fortified the Lichfield area. The dating of the fort to a period of 1000 years ranging from 500 BC to AD 500 also tied in with the period of Khymric domination of Britain from the arrival of Brutus to the Saxon rebellion shortly before the time of Arthur II. It was not hard to see that Arthur I could have made use of such a powerful castle as a gathering place for his army and it seems not unreasonable to suppose that it may indeed have been refortified with a stone keep around 350.

Returning to the car, Baram continued with his story. 'Having ascertained that this was the right area in which to look for the real burial place of Arthur I, I decided to move to the Midlands. I bought a house in Coventry, which is only a few miles from here, and began not only to explore the area physically but to examine local myths and legends. I was amazed to discover that there was a local hero, known as "Guy of Warwick", whose mythical career closely parallels that of the legendary King Arthur.'

According to the legends, Baram continued, Guy of Warwick invaded Europe at the head of a military retinue and fought against the Emperor of Constantinople. Of course this war was fictional but that it was supposed to have happened at the time of Arthur I seemed too much of a coincidence to be accidental. Baram and Alan worked out that it was a distant memory of the exploits of Arthur, son of Maximus, that had been recorded as the exploits of Guy.

Later Baram and Alan were both surprised and delighted to discover that they were not the first to have made the connection between King Arthur and Guy of Warwick. Whilst looking through the itinerary of Edward Llwyd,[2] they found a reference stating that in his opinion Guy of Warwick and King Arthur were one and the same. That this statement, which had been published around 1700, had never before been remarked on by the legions of Arthurian researchers who have come after Llwyd was puzzling. However, it gave them the confidence to believe that they were at least looking in the right area by turning their attention to the West Midlands in their search for King Arthur.

Having made this discovery, they took another look at the writings of William of Malmesbury. Although his history of Glastonbury Abbey is frequently quoted in support of the Abbey having been founded on the site of Joseph of Arimathea's Old Church, by referring to his original Latin text, which seems to have been derived from earlier sources, it became clear to Baram and Alan that in fact he says nothing of the sort. His actual words are: '... *Glasteing. Hic est ille Glasteing, qui Mediterraneos Angles, secus villam, quae dicitur Escebtione, scrofam suam usque ad Wellis, et a Wellis per inviam et aquosam, quae Sugewege, id est Scrofae via dictur ...*' The mention of '*Mediterraneos Angles*', meaning either 'Mediterranean' or 'Midlands Angles', shows that William's Glasteing, or Glastennen couldn't have been in Somerset as this county isn't in the Midlands of England and was never settled by the Angles. The passage seems to be talking about an important road, which skirted past Glasteing and along which pigs were driven. Since there was no such road in the Somerset area at that time, '*Wellis*' cannot mean the city of Wells, which is eight miles from Glastonbury; instead it could mean Wales. In ancient Latin texts Wales is not usually called Cambria, as you might think, but is called *Wallis* or *Wellis* (indeed names such as 'Wallis' or 'Wallace' mean 'Welsh' and William Wallace, champion of Scotland's independence, was actually more Welsh than Scottish, being a descendant of Llewellyn the Great's daughter Helen). In the text the road in question could well be Watling Street, which ran, as we have seen, from London through Letocetum to the regional capital of Wroxeter and on into north Wales. When this region of the West Midlands was subjugated by the Mercians, they called Glasteing by the name of Glastonbiri.

William of Malmesbury next tells us, Baram continued, that the Glasteing area was called 'Avalloniae' (Avalon) and that it was a place of apples. He himself seems to have been seriously misled on this score. This word Avalon or Afallach is derived not from *afal* meaning 'apple' but from the Welsh word *afallach*, which Alan and Baram think means 'land given up for another use', for example, to the church. This would explain the naming of the lands granted to St Ilid/Joseph of Arimathea by King Gweirydd as Aballach or Afallach.

The false identification of Afallach/Glastein/Avalon as Somerset goes back a long way. One piece of evidence for it was a forged document claiming that King Ina of the West Saxons made land bequests to Glastonbury Abbey. This famous bequest of Ina's, which also supposedly gave tax-free status to certain lands possessed by the Abbey, though acknowledged in the Domesday Book, was never accepted as genuine by the Bishops of Bath and Wells. The real bequests were made by a British king called Ivor, who ruled in the West Midlands area before it was taken over by the Mercians.

A much-quoted medieval manuscript attributed to Maelgwyn of Llandaff states that King Gweirydd granted twelve hides of land to the first Christian mission led by Joseph. Although it was assumed that this land was at Glastonbury, in fact this could not have been so. With one hide being 160 acres, this land grant would therefore have been of 1,920 acres. Traditionally one acre was the amount of land an ox could plough in one day but today[3] it is more accurately defined as 4,840 square yards; this means that the total grant of twelve hides would have come to 2 3/4 square miles – a considerable estate. It is difficult to see how such a grant could have been made at Glastonbury in Somerset, as at the time there would not have been that much land above water. The story of the twelve hides of land was evidently well known in 1086 when William the Conqueror had his Domesday Book compiled as it is entered into the accounts for Glastonbury Abbey. The mistake, though, and the misappropriation of the legend, had been made long before this, probably when Dunstan became Abbot of the Abbey in 942.

After reading as much as they could, Baram and Alan began looking at detailed maps of the Lichfield area to see whether Glastonbury might indeed have been located close by. They were amazed to discover that there is indeed a village called Glascote[4] just a few miles to the southeast of Wall and very near Tamworth, an important town on what is now the A5 and was formerly Watling Street. Tamworth itself features prominently in *The Anglo-Saxon Chronicles* of 912, which state that 'Aethelflaed, lady of the Mercians' went there and built a borough, or fortified town, on the site. It was an important and strategic place, as it lies on the River Anker, a tributary of the Thames, which would have been navigable to small craft. Almost certainly there was a British palace or other important residence, long before the days of Aethelflaed, on the site where Tamworth Castle presently stands.

Further confirmation that this West Midlands area was the right place to search for the real Glastonbury is contained in the 'Life of St Collen of Llangollen', which tells how Collen was once the Abbot of 'Glastenic' and how later he returned to Llangollen in his old age. One glance at the map will show you that whilst Llangollen is only up the road (the A5) from the Tamworth/Lichfield area, it is literally hundreds of miles from Glastonbury in Somerset; Collen is unlikely to have travelled so far.

When they began looking a little further south-east along Watling

Street they found a number of place names that seemed to relate to the land grants made to Glastonbury Abbey. They are mostly meaningless in English, being clearly derived from Welsh and connecting with the idea of 'lands being given over for other use'. Immediately north-west of Lichfield is the village of Maesvyn Ridware, whose name seems to derive from *maes* – 'field', *ffynnu* – 'to prosper', *rhydd* – 'free', *gwared* – 'released, delivered, redeemed', suggesting a royal land grant with tax-free status. Likewise, the name of another village, Ratcliffe Culey, seems to be derived from the Welsh *raddu cyllid*, which means 'free grazing for lambs'.

Next to the church in this village is a large earthwork circle or *cor*. As these earthworks were used for Christian worship before the building of churches, it suggests that the village of Ratcliffe Culey had once, like Llanilid in Wales, been home to an early Christian community. A little further to the north-east you come to Appleby Magna and Appleby Parva, two villages with obvious 'apple' connections. These are just a few of the things Baram and Alan found – there are, they say, many other place names in the area relating to a long-forgotten history and con-necting it to the Arthurian period.

Alan and Baram had not only been able to link the area generally with Glastonbury but had also been able to ascertain the very site. Now they were going to take me to the original Ynys Wydrin or Glastonbury, near the site of the ancient Romano-British town of Mancetter, now called Atherstone, and where they have proof that Arthur I was buried.

At Atherstone, we turned off the A5 and proceeded along a non-descript residential street, aptly named Old Bury Road. After driving a couple of miles along a country lane we arrived at the Hartshill Nature Reserve, which the local council has recently turned into a birdwatch-ers' paradise. Here we parked the car and proceeded over to the entrance to what was quite dense woodland.

'Now, look over here, Adrian, and tell me what you see,' Baram said, pointing to a large, overgrown mound.

Without hesitation I replied, 'Well, it looks to me very much like a tumulus.'

'Now, come over here,' he said, leading me a short distance to another lower but longer mound. 'What do you make of that?'

Again I had to reply that it looked as though it could have been a burial mound, though not as impressive as the first.

'Now, remember what William of Malmesbury had to say about the way the grave of Arthur had been neglected.' The quotation he was referring to is contained in his history of Glastonbury, which like others has often been misquoted: 'The neglect of Arthur, renowned King of the British in the cemetery of the monks between two pyramids, with his wife's tumulus where multitudes of the eminent British are buried.'

We made our way through a narrow entrance onto a new path. All around us was thick forest, the floor covered with leaf-litter which in summer would be hidden by dense patches of bracken. In other places where there were rocks, moss was growing abundantly. In one place I noticed some deer droppings, indicative perhaps of the park's other name of Hart's Hill.[5] The silence was eerie, broken only by the song of the odd robin, most of the other birds having migrated for the winter.

'This is Old Bury,' Baram continued, 'and it is a very ancient graveyard belonging to what we believe was the original monastery of Glastenic/Glastons/Glastonbury. Now, we know that *glastons* in Breton and Cornish is said to mean "oak trees", and *glastennen* in Welsh means "the scarlet oak tree" – possibly a tree of sacrifice or religious celebration. What do you see all around you? Not like Glastonbury in Somerset, is it?'

I had to agree. Unlike the open treeless fens of the Somerset Levels, here the forest was thick with deciduous trees. Many of them were oaks, though there were also stools of hazel for coppicing, and growing on them were lichens.

Baram explained that it is perhaps not so surprising that the true location of Arthur I's tomb was remembered and recorded: he was, after all, one of the greatest of all British warrior kings. What is more, the location of his burial site is described very accurately, around 1156, by Caradoc of Llancarfan. The abbey of Llancarfan lay just nine miles from Cardiff and, being one of the most senior in Wales, would have had a library in which important documents were kept. It would not have been difficult for readers of William of Malmesbury's history to check such records.

Baram pointed out that around the park there were not just two grave mounds but many, all over the place. Some were simple earth mounds but others were marked by great heaps of stones. 'We have seen the same kind of thing in south Wales,' he said, 'which is how we are so sure that this graveyard goes back to the pre-Saxon era. It was probably used during Roman times.'

We carried on walking, penetrating deeply into the woods. Now that my eyes were tuned in I could see what he meant. Everywhere there were small or large eminences, some of earth only, others of carefully placed stones. It was, as he had said, undoubtedly a graveyard. I couldn't remember seeing a single grave-mound at Glastonbury in Somerset – something that had always puzzled me since Arthur was supposed to have been buried there – yet here they were in an abundance that would have been spooky were it not so exciting.

Pausing near a long, flat tumulus Baram beckoned me over, pointing to a spot on the ground. For security reasons he and Alan do not want me to reveal the actual location. 'It was just here,' he said 'that we found what was for us the clinching factor convincing us that this was the right place: a part of what could have been an accession stone or even memorial stone to Arthur I.' This was the stone of which they had previously shown me a picture. It was only a fragment of what must have been a larger stone but fortunately enough of its inscription had been preserved to give a good idea of its significance. The preserved words read in Latin: 'ARTORIU . . . IACIT IN . . . MACI . . .'. The first word was nearly complete: Artorius. *Iacit* means 'cast down' – the same word used on the Bodvoc stone at Margam Abbey. *Maci* could be part of his father's name, 'Mascen' or 'Maximus', with whatever spelling, as it was common to enter such information on stones. It was a shame that the stone was broken and that there was only a fragment, but all in all it was clearly a very significant find.

It seems likely that after his father's failure to take over the Roman Empire Arthur I returned from the Balkans to his home in the west Midlands, his exploits being made famous in the later legends concerning Guy of Warwick, and when he eventually died, maybe around 400, he was buried here in the cemetery.

'We are confident that the stone is genuine,' Baram said, 'and we would like it examined by unbiased experts, preferably abroad. We would also like people to know about it. The sword-shaped stone of Arthur II, which we found in the Church of St Peter's, was on public display for ten days in the tourist board offices at 34 Piccadilly, London, but no one took much notice. We don't intend this to happen with this stone pertaining to Arthur I.

'We have little confidence in the authorities. It seems that what can't be explained in terms of the current orthodoxy is either destroyed or locked away so that the public remains none the wiser. Instead of preserving what should be one of the most important British archaeological sites in the country, they have turned it into a nature reserve. As you can see, already some of the tombs have been disturbed, probably by night-hawks.

'On 30 April 1980 we presented our findings concerning Arthur I to the Lord Mayor of Coventry. At the time we hadn't yet discovered Arthur's stone but we prepared a selected array of charts and other historical data to get across the main points of our arguments concerning the history of the area. The Lord Mayor was polite and most attentive, realizing the cultural significance of such a find. He put us onto the local authority at Atherstone and we made another appointment to go and visit them. The gentleman we spoke to there was again very friendly and supportive towards the project, which he recognized was greatly in the interest of Atherstone. Unfortunately he was too good at his job and shortly afterwards was promoted to a more senior position in a different district. His replacement was a young man with little interest in the subject and still less common sense. He effectively told us to get lost. It was the usual story, depressingly familiar to us, of significant discoveries being disregarded by officialdom.

'From then we encountered a wall of obstruction and trying to break it was a real problem. It seemed that every time we got someone half-interested in our ideas, they would phone up some academic "authority" who instead of analysing the work objectively would take great pleasure in repudiating it. We did, however, make one small breakthrough in the Midlands when we had an article published in a local newspaper: the *Nuneaton and North Warwickshire Recorder*. It was a piece of spoof reporting, an account of Arthur I's campaign in Europe as it might have been reported locally had they had newspapers in his day. The headline read: "WARWICKSHIRE'S ARTHUR VICTORIOUS. TYRANT SLAIN AND GREAT VICTORIES IN FRANCE." It wasn't very much but it gave us a chuckle and at least alerted some of the local people to what lay on their own doorsteps.'

Baram added that the fact that this area of England continued to be closely connected with the royal houses of Britain after the death of Arthur I is evidenced by some other place names. Just a few miles to the north-east of Tamworth is the village of Thorpe Constantine. There was a King Constantine, the nephew of Arthur I, who was murdered by Vortigern, the king who invited the Saxons into Britain. Half a mile from Thorpe Constantine is Seckington, which in Welsh would be Sychnant, meaning 'dry place'; there, to the west of the church, is a very large burial mound. It seems likely that this is the grave of this Constantine. South-east of Atherstone – a name which Alan and Baram are now tempted to think is derived from 'Arthur's Stone', though it may also come from the Welsh *Arthur twyn*, meaning 'Arthur's gravemound' – is Hinckley. This was an important town with a castle, whose name they believe is derived from *hynaf-llys*, meaning 'the Ancient Court'. South of Old Bury is Anley (*anllys* – 'without the court') and Arley (*arllys* – 'plough land of the court').

Leaving Atherstone we visited one further site before heading for home. This was a small village named Elford to the north of Tamworth. Here, on top of a hill and sitting in the crook of a busy road overlooking the River Tame, was the strangest tumulus I have ever seen. Much larger than those we had been climbing at Old Bury, it had clearly been raised in honour of an important individual. Growing from its crown was a mighty oak tree that gave it an ancient presence that somehow was not at odds with the modern hay-barn behind. Though we had no obvious proof other than its name, it seemed not unreasonable to believe that buried here was Elfan, the brother of King Lleirwg, who was sent on an important mission to Rome around 167 and later sent to revitalize 'Glastonbury'. If so, this grave was not pagan but another tangible link with those days of early Christianity that seem to have been inextricably bound up with the history of the Midlands. It was a salutary reminder of how much we have forgotten in England that, even where place names provide the clues, we are ignorant about so much of what we see.

That Arthur, son of Magnus Maximus, was active in the Midlands was remembered in medieval times. Baram sent me a photocopy of a little-known volume of medieval poems from the Warwickshire, Derby and Shropshire area, entitled *The Awentures of Arthure* and containing four ancient poems about King Arthur. In these *Awentures* Arthur leads his army into Europe, defeats a Roman Emperor and later besieges Milan. Though the tales are undoubtedly elaborated, they are not fictional: they refer to real events that took place in the fourth century. There can be little doubt that Arthur's centre of operations is located in the Midlands area though he ranges up as far as Carlisle. Thus local traditions about King Arthur in north Wales, the Midlands and Scotland clearly concern Arthur I and not Athrwys, Arthur II, his sixth-century descendant. Once it is realized that the 'Arthure' in question is Andragathius, or Arthur, I son of Magnus Maximus, and not the later Arthur II, then it all fits into place.

THE LEGACY OF THEODOSIUS

On the way home Alan told me that the history of what happened after the death of Magnus Maximus and his son Arthun is confusing, not least because around this time there were a number of kings all called Constantine or Constans. Roman records show that in 391 a 'Eugeneus' once more 'usurped' the western Empire by invading Gaul. He must have been a powerful figure because it seems it was he who had instructed Arbogast to have Valentinian II killed. Almost certainly this 'Eugeneus' is to be identified with Owain Vinddu,[6] who is listed in the genealogies and would have been a brother of Arthur I. He is, Alan and Baram believe, the Sir Gawain of the medieval legends. He was clearly carrying on the family tradition by asserting his rights in Gaul and the

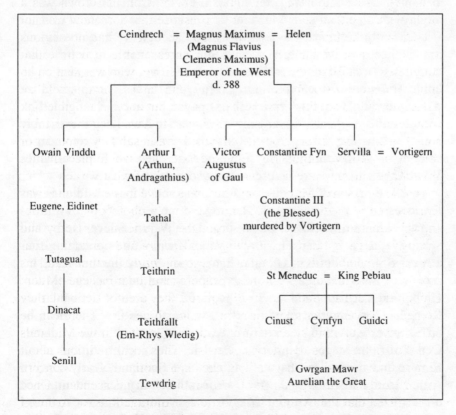

THE DESCENDANTS OF MAGNUS MAXIMUS
Diagram 10

other western provinces. Although Owain doesn't seem to have stayed in Gaul for very long, the British principalities established there by Magnus Maximus were still intact as a federation. Owain seems to have returned to Britain to drive off another Irish invasion of north Wales and to have died as a very old man in 434.

In 406 a vast confederation of barbarian tribes crossed the Rhine into Gaul, under the leadership of a Vandal king called Gunderic. Roman duplicity, which had sought to play off the barbarians against each other, having clearly failed, Gaul was once more vulnerable to their aggression. In the face of this threat the British once more mobilized and made one final attempt at saving the western Empire from total collapse. By now another Constantine, perhaps the Cystennyn 'Gorneu' or 'Coronog' (crowned) mentioned in some of the king lists, had become ruler of Britain. He seems to have been a cousin of Arthur I. This Constantine, along with a general called Geraint or Gerontius, now crossed over the Channel into Gaul with a large army and succeeded in defeating the massed hordes of Vandals, Alans and Sueves. However, these tribes had come west because they were under pressure from the even more frightening Huns and therefore couldn't return home. As Geraint held the passes leading to Spain, the barbarians were effectively penned in, unable either to press forwards or to go back where they came from. Honorius, the titular Emperor of Rome, did nothing to help and refused to even try. Accordingly, Constantine declared himself Emperor of the West whilst, to protect Gaul, especially the northern provinces which were close allies of Britain, Geraint opened the passes through the Pyrenees.

The barbarian horde therefore surged south, the Sueves and Alans seizing large parts of Spain with the Vandals carrying on south, eventually crossing the Straits of Gibraltar into Africa. There they seized all the province of North Africa west of Egypt, including the important cities of Hippo and Carthage, and set up a powerful kingdom of their own. As Rome had for centuries relied on Africa to supply it with grain, it was in an even worse situation than before. Accordingly, Geraint was eager for Constantine to depose Honorius so as to take control of the whole Empire and also ensure that Italy as well as Britain and Gaul would be spared from barbarian domination. Unfortunately Constantine dithered, unsure whether to stay put at Trier or to move on to Rome. Honorius, like Valentinian before him, bought time for himself by keeping up the pretence that he was prepared to share the Empire with Constantine. In the end Geraint lost patience with his king and revolted against him, in favour of another called Constantius 'Lydaw' (from Brittany). This Constantius (or Constantine) was a younger half-brother of Arthur, a son of Magnus Maximus by his second wife, who probably settled in Brittany at the time of Magnus's invasion. The first Constantine had by this time invaded Italy, but without Geraint's support he was defeated by the generals of Honorius and executed.

Rome was, however, still in a weak position because of its dependence on Africa for its food supplies, while Britain was in a powerful position relative to the rest of the Continent. As an island it was well able to look after itself and, as we have seen, frequently sent armies to intervene in the political scene of the rest of the western Empire. Academics, including such eminent figures as Dr John Morris, refer to a letter from Honorius, *c*. 410–11, said to be warning Britain that, as he was over-stretched, it would have to look to itself for its defence against the barbarians. In fact, it is clear from the Sixth Book of Zosimus that the letter was addressed not to Britain but to the citizens of Rhegium in Brittium, the Roman province in the toe of Italy. Honorius had no reason to write to Britain, which in any case had long since gone its own way politically, economically and militarily. That it was Italy not Britain that was threatened was proved in 410 when on 24 August Alaric the Goth entered Rome and plundered its treasures. Well might the citizens of Brittium quake as this tidal wave of humanity, threatening all that they treasured, approached them too.

Following the invasion of Magnus Maximus, the British presence in Brittany and Normandy, which had always been strong, had been extended further south to include a league of seven cities centred on Soissons. This league proved to be a relatively stable entity in a fast-changing world. In the late fifth century it was ruled over by one Afranius Syagrius Aegidius, who was so well thought of that for eight years he was also the elected king of the Franks. He is Geoffrey's 'Aganypus' or 'Agitus', to whom the British wrote an important letter in 474, requesting help against the Saxons. As he was a close ally, there is nothing surprising in this.

However, the addressee of this letter is frequently misquoted. Though Gildas's Latin text, the source of this story, says it was addressed to 'Agitus', clearly meaning Aegidius, in translation the name is twisted to 'Aetius' – a Roman consul living around 442. It would seem, Alan said, that scholars and writers, from Gibbon onwards, perpetuate mistaken translation because they want to believe that the Britons were incapable either of governing themselves effectively or of meeting the threat of Saxon invasion. In fact, as we shall see later, both these suppositions were untrue.

As we drove back late to Cardiff, it was a clear night and the sky was bright with stars. Looking north I could see the Great Bear, also known popularly as 'Arthur's Wain', visible over the rooftops. That *Un-Arth* means 'the bear' in Welsh shows an obvious connection between Arthun and the Great Bear constellation, but there is another. In Britain, as in all northern countries, the Great Bear constellation is circumpolar: in a very real sense it forever wanders around the Pole Star, which is like the tip of a long stake driven into the ground to which the circling constellations are tethered. In this sense it is like a dancing bear, forever pacing round and round its tether, free to move but only in a circle. It was another reminder of the connection between Arthur I and the county of Warwickshire, whose symbol is a bear tethered to a stake.

How Warwickshire came by this symbol of the dancing bear is a mystery. Perhaps it was the emblem of the Dobuni tribe, to whose territory it once belonged. Yet I can't help believing that there is here an almost forgotten link to Arthur I, the 'bear' son of Magnus Maximus, who lives on in legend as 'Guy of Warwick'. Later Baram pointed out that the centre of Britain was always believed to be at Meridien in the Warwickshire–Midlands area. Perhaps, therefore, it seemed apposite to Warwickshire to adopt a symbol that connected it to Arthur, guardian of Britain, and to the Bear constellation, from which his name derives and which protects the still point of the sky.

CHAPTER THIRTEEN

THE CHURCH ON THE HILL

On another visit to Glamorgan I looked once more at the strange slab of stone with its inscription 'REX ARTORIUS FILI MAURICIUS' which Alan and Baram had shown me on my first trip. I reminded Alan of his promise that he would take me to see the church where it was found and soon we were again driving along country lanes. We turned off at the small village of Brynna, where the road rose steeply, fast turning into a heavily pot-holed dirt track. To save the suspension, I parked the car and we began walking. We carried on up the steep lane until we came to a large, pointed boulder in a field to our right. Alan beckoned me over, indicating that this was of some importance.

'If you look at the shape of this rock, you will see that it has been carefully cut to resemble an anvil. Here's the pointy bit and there it broadens out.' He explained that until quite recently it was turned over with the left face on the ground. The face now on the bottom was then on the right of the boulder and carved on it, he said, was the impression of a sword blade. He believes that the anvil shape and the sword mark may refer to the Arthurian legend of the sword in the stone. Though not suggesting that this was that very stone, he thinks that someone, at some time – probably in the Middle Ages – wanted to draw attention to the Arthurian connections of this area. The stone was also orientated in such a way that the sharp end was pointing towards the Church of St Peter's. Since it gets very foggy up there in the winter, he believes that this stone was intended to be a marker for pilgrims in search of the church. Today the local landowners are not keen on tourists coming up here, so someone had taken the trouble to turn the stone over so that the sword mark was no longer visible. Fortunately he and Baram have pictures of it.

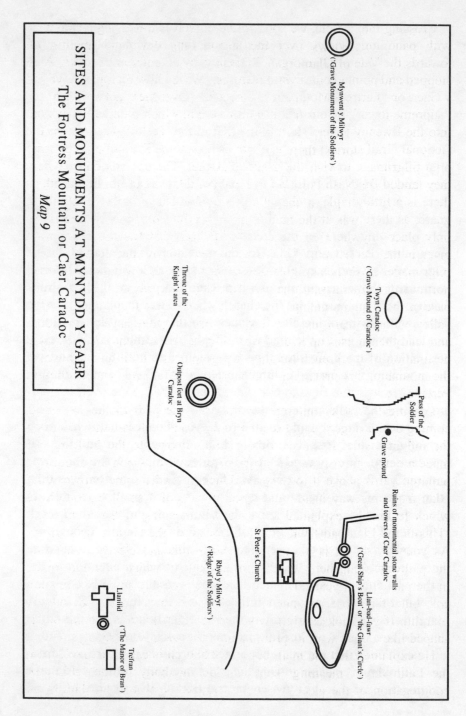

SITES AND MONUMENTS AT MYNYDD Y GAER
The Fortress Mountain or Caer Caradoc
Map 9

Mynwent y Milwyr
('Grave Monument of the Soldiers')

Twyn Caradoc
('Grave Mound of Caradoc')

Throne of the
Knight's area

Outpost fort at Bryn
Caradoc

Pass of the
Soldier

Grave mound

Ruins of monumental stone walls
and towers of Caer Caradoc

St Peter's Church

Rhyd y Milwyr
('Ridge of the Soldiers')

Llan-bad-fawr
('Great Ship's Boat' or 'the Giant's Circle')

Llanilid
('The Manor of Bran')

Trefran
('The Manor of Bran')

Crossing into a field, we soon found ourselves traversing a ridgeway with panoramic views over the surrounding downland leading on towards the Vale of Glamorgan. Presently, by an outcrop of rocks, Alan stopped and pointed out several features. 'We are now on top of Mynydd y Gaer, or "Fortress Mountain",' he began. 'Over there is Portref, or the "supreme town"; by our feet is a little stream which eventually runs out into the Ewenny River.' He told me that in the 'Perlesvaux' (one of the fictional Grail stories) there is a tale of how some French knights came on a pilgrimage to visit the grave of Arthur. The description of where they landed fits Nash Point on the coast of Glamorgan, for at that place there is a little dingle, a chapel and a double-banked hill fort standing guard, as there was at the landing place in the story; indeed this is the only place anywhere on the coast of Britain that fits the description given in the 'Perlesvaux'. This account seems to have been based on real pilgrimages by French knights. From Nash Point they would have ridden northwards to Llantrisant, then west along a 'long wooded valley' to the base of the 'long mountain' (Mynydd y Gaer). Here they ascend a little valley, with a stream just like this, so steep that they have to dismount and lead their horses up it. Just west of it lies the old church: the stated destination of the French knights. Geographically it all fits: the wood, the mountain, this stream and the church are all exactly as described in Perlesvaux.

Leaving the rocky outcrop we followed the path to the west and, coming over a ridge, I could see the ruins of a church standing proud on the mountainside. However, before walking over to the building we made a detour to visit an earthwork of some size, which lay about one hundred yards above it to the east. Ducking under some barbed wire, Alan made his way inside and stood on top of a small barrow, from which lectern he explained the symbolic meaning of the monument. 'This is the Llan-bad-fawr, or "Holy Estate of the Great Ship's Boat". As you can see, it is a very large earthwork and clearly older than the pathway along here which cuts through it, which was only made in the past fifteen years. This earthwork is probably an early Christian *cor*, but of a more advanced type than the one you saw at nearby Llanilid. If you look carefully you can see that it is not circular but is shaped like a boat, with its prow facing east towards the rising sun.'

He explained that the main body of a church is called its nave, from the Latin *navis*, meaning 'ship'. Inside the body of the 'ship' the congregation of the elect are kept safe, like Noah and his family on board the ark. Alan explained that where he was standing was a burial mound, towards the 'stern' of the ship in what is called the 'helmsman's position', which implies that whoever was buried there was important. In numerous histories it is stated that 'Utherpendragon' (who according to Geoffrey and Tysylio was Arthur's father) was buried in the 'Giant's Circle' at Caer Caradoc. The problem for Arthurian researchers has always been to find the correct location of this fortress, misidentified by Geoffrey as Salisbury. Immediately to the west of the Llan-bad-fawr at a place called Por-Tref, 'the supreme place', lies a ruined castle. Little remains of it except the foundations of circular turrets and thick walls. Adjacent to these ruins is a tumulus called Twyn Caradoc: 'the grave mound of Caradoc'. Some two miles further west along the mountain is the circular Mynwent-y-Milwyr, 'the grave-monument of the soldiers'. Such a monument is recorded as having been raised at Caer Caradoc by Ambrosius (Em-Rhys Wledig) over the graves of the victims of the Peace Conference. All evidence would seem, therefore, to suggest that this mountain, Mynydd y Gaer, is the real Caer Caradoc, and this impression is further strengthened by the identification of St Peter's Church – super-Montem with that founded by King Lleirwg in c. AD160 on the 'Corne Hill'. This being the case the Llan-bad-fawr, albeit boat-shaped, can be identified as the real 'Giant's Circle', and it seems likely that the 'helmsman' guiding the holy ship is none other than the Uthyr Pendragon Meurig, the father of Arthur II.

Leaving the earthwork with its eternal helmsman, we carried on walking back down the hill until we reached the boundary wall of what was once the yard of the old Church of St Peter's. It was surrounded by a six-foot high, wire-mesh fence, such as one might find round a tennis court. Rusty in places and with a damaged gate, this seemed to be mainly of symbolic importance. Alan walked over to it and gave it a shake. 'As you know, we had a dig here in 1990 and we put up this fence after that. We hoped it would deter vandals but it hasn't really been of much use. There used to be a number of old gravestones – not particularly old but obviously of value – and these have all disappeared now. One company took some of them for bench surfaces in a food-processing plant, others have been taken for use in patios or whatever. There were also some nice stone roofing tiles which have gone. Even the walls of the building itself are noticeably lower than they were. We suspect local farmers of taking stones from the walls of the building to fill in deep wet spots at field gates. At this rate in a few years' time there will be nothing left of the building. Now you know why we didn't dare leave the Arthur stone. Come inside and I'll show you where we found it.'

Alan and Baram bought these ruins of St Peter's-super-Montem from the Church in Wales because they were certain not only that it was highly important from the Arthurian point of view, but also that it was founded by King Lleirwg or Lucius (whom researches in the genealogies of Wales reveal to have been a descendant of Bran the Blessed) at some time around 160. As we have explained, he is well recorded in the histories as the founder of Llandaff Cathedral as well as Llanlleirwg – now the Church of St Mellons and also in Cardiff. The ambassadors that he sent to visit the Bishop of Rome c. 160 – St Fagan, St Dyfan, St Elford and St Medwy – all founded churches in the Cardiff area. It therefore followed that where the histories said that King Lleirwg also founded a Church of St Peter's on the 'Corne Hill', this was very likely the same foundation as the St Peter's-super-Montem where we were now standing.

Alan had told me when we first met that there had been much opposition to their opinions. He believes that this opposition – in effect an attempt to undermine their entire work on Arthur – has more to do with local politics and economics than with history, as he now explained.

During the 1980s almost the entire Welsh coal mining industry was closed down – there is now only one deep mine left in Wales, the Tower Colliery – not because there is no longer any coal left in Wales, but because it is considered uneconomic to mine it in the traditional fashion. Now new opencast collieries are taking the place of the old deep mines. Privatized mining companies, using strip mining, dynamite and JCBs instead of having to pay the wages of a legion of miners, are able to make vast profits.

These opencast mines cause a lot of pollution and people object violently to what is happening to their environment, even though they do create a handful of jobs in very depressed areas. Alan and Baram have noticed that a number of the local farms on this hill have changed hands in recent years and that, although on the outside everything seems to be the same, with sheep grazing in the fields and so on, the old farmhouses are now deserted and left to fall to ruin. Mynydd y Gaer lies on the edge of the Rhondda drift, traditionally the most important mining district in Wales, since it is well established that there is a vast amount of coal lying under it. Alan and Baram believe that there are powerful mining interests that would like to strip-mine the mountain. In fact, plans were published in *The Western Mail* a few years back showing a prospective opencast development, 25 miles long by 1 mile wide and 350 feet deep, right through the Vale of Glamorgan. It would wreck for ever some of the most beautiful countryside in Britain. Needless to say there was a public outcry.

Alan and Baram feel that Mynydd y Gaer should be a scheduled monument. However, they believe that the Taffia's political interests are such that they do not want it proved that the whole area of the Vale of Glamorgan and its surrounding hills is of great historical importance. Although the potential revenue for south Wales from tourism once the real Arthurian connection of the area is revealed would in time far outstrip the 'dirty dollars of strip-mining a beautiful area', as Alan put it, and would also create more jobs, unfortunately big business doesn't think like that, wanting the most money for the least effort in the shortest time.

To make it harder for the authorities to issue a compulsory purchase order on the church at some time in the future, Alan and Baram issued share certificates. So St Peter's now has a couple of hundred owners worldwide, each one of whom would have to be tracked down and paid out. It was the best way they could think of to preserve this important piece of Welsh heritage for future generations.

When they had the church excavated in order to prove its antiquity, an appeal was launched and they received backing from an organization in England. To carry out the work they employed archaeologists from outside the area. In charge of the dig was Dr Eric Talbot, for twenty-two years senior lecturer in archaeology at Glasgow university. Assisting him was Alan Wishart, who has an MA in archaeology from the same university. Even though CADW, the Welsh Ancient Monuments Commission, tried to make the dig impossible for them by delaying permission for it throughout the summer, in the four weeks in the middle of September in which they were finally allowed to investigate the church ruins, the dig turned out to be more successful than they could possibly have hoped.

Not only were they able to show conclusively that a whole series of churches had been built on the site prior to the Norman church,[1] but they also found a number of interesting artefacts. Among these were a dagger, a small iron axe such as might have been used for cutting inscriptions on wood or stone and a little cross made out of electrum. This cross was cast from a mould and carried a Latin inscription: *Pro anima Artorius* – 'For the soul of Arthur'. North of the altar – the most prestigious site for burials – they found the flat stone carrying both Arthur's and his father's names. Though neither the cross nor the stone proves that Arthur II was buried here, they do mean that someone at some time connected an Arthur with this church. Near the altar there were six piles of four skulls, each with paired 'cross-bones', indicating a Templar interest, as the skull and cross-bones was a Templar device long before it was adopted by pirates. In the nave was the skeleton of a very tall man, though we know this was not Arthur II.

The floor of the first church built here was found buried several feet below the present building and measured about 35 feet long by 16. Alan and Baram think this was King Lleirwg's church, which ancient historical records say he built *c*. AD 150. The archaeological evidence was that this first church had been burnt down. At first they thought this was evidence that the Saxons had destroyed the church at the time of the massacre at the Peace Conference *c*. 466. However, the fire was so intense that human bones had been melted onto the stones. They now think this was the result of a later, natural catastrophe that was cosmic in its origins. (This will be explained in greater detail later.)

To the east of this first church was found the remains of a beehive-shaped 'hermitage', which was dated to between 400 and 600. It seems likely that this building was erected, perhaps as a temporary measure, after the original building burnt down, they think in 562. A third church was built and destroyed by, they believe, the Mercians *c*. 800. This church enclosed the ground area originally covered by the previous two buildings. Then between 1200 and 1300 a fourth church was constructed. Again, this was bigger than its predecessors, extending back further east. Later still a chancel was tacked onto the east end and a porch onto the south. The final modifications took place in the seventeenth century, when sixteen feet of the church were removed from its western end and a new west wall was built. This foreshortened church cannot have been in use for very long for when the antiquarian Edward Llwyd visited it in 1697 it had already been abandoned. It was later brought back into use, but was again abandoned in 1838 and left to fall into ruin.

The histories show that this was once one of the prime churches of the British Isles. In the triads it is recorded that there were three churches in

Britain where prayers were said for twenty-four hours a day. Triad 80 of Series 1, for instance, mentions:

> The three diligent harmonies of the Isle of Britain, one was the Isle of Afallach, the second was Caer Caradoc, and the third was the Bangor. In every one of these three there were 2400 men worshipping and of these 100 exchanging every hour of the 24 in the day and night in courtesy and service to God in endless continuation.

Triad 84 of Series 3 confirms this:

> The three chief harmonies of the Isle of Britain, the Bangor of Illtyd the Knight in Caer Worgorn, the Choir of Emrys in Caer Caradoc, and Bangor Wydrin in the Isle of Affalen, and in every one of these three Bangors there were four and twenty hundred of Saints, that is there were a hundred for every hour of the day and night in their circle in joining praise of service to God without reward without ceasing.

Caer Worgorn is Llantwit Major, which Alan and Baram believe would be the *bangor*, or religious college, referred to in Triad 80. The bangor Wydrin in the Isle of Affalen, or Afallach is, as we have seen, Glastonbury, which was not in Somerset but in the Lichfield area. Since St Peter's is the only church at Caer Caradoc, it makes sense that the Choir of Emrys would have operated here in St Peter's.

We have seen that traditionally the first two *bangors* are closely associated with St Ilid or Joseph of Arimathea: the bangor at Llantwit was founded for him by Eurgain, the daughter of Caradoc, and the one at Affallach as a result of the donation to him by Arviragus. It is quite likely, then, that the Choir of Emrys also has a connection with royalty and Ilid. Caradoc is buried in a tumulus to the west of St Peter's. The remains of his castle are to the north. Llanilid, where we saw the large wooded *cor*, lies in the vale to the south-west of Mynydd y Gaer, whilst a second place also called Llanilid lies about a mile to the north-east of St Peter's. There is also a stream called the Nant Ilid which has its source just fifty yards to the west of the church. Alan and Baram believe this is no coincidence; evidence suggests that St Peter's was probably associated with Ilid.

The hill top continued to be important centuries later. Somewhere near here was held the Peace Conference of *c*. 466 between the British under their King, Vortigern, and the Saxons led by Hengist. Everyone was supposed to be unarmed but Hengist ordered his followers to bring along concealed weapons. They waited until their opposite numbers were sufficiently drunk to offer little resistance and then, on a signal, slew them. Three hundred and sixty-three British nobles were killed and Vortigern was taken prisoner. Fortunately not everyone was present at the feast. A prince entitled Em-Rhys Wledig ('Wledig' is a title meaning 'the legate'; Em-Rhys means 'Jewelled' or 'Crowned' Prince) was able to lead a counter-attack and eventually Hengist was defeated and beheaded near York. The histories say that Em-Rhys, returning south, had the victims of the massacre properly buried and a monument erected in their honour.

This Em-Rhys, whom we know as Teithfallt, is the king who is referred to as 'Aurelius Ambrosius' by Geoffrey of Monmouth. Unfortunately Geoffrey confused two characters as one: Aurelius and Em-Rhys. In actual fact Aurelius was a king called Gwrgan Mawr in the genealogies. He was a great-grandson of Magnus Maximus. Aurelius's 'brother', Utherpendragon, was really Teithfallt or Theodosius, a great-grandson of Arthur I and therefore a great-great-grandson of Maximus but by his first wife Ceindrich. Teithfallt and Gwrgan were contemporaries, the one being a Glamorgan king, the other coming from the north Gwent, Evas and Erging area. Both this Teithfallt and Gwrgan Mawr had stronger claims to the throne than Vortigern, but they were only boys at the time of his usurpation.

Tysylio and Geoffrey wrongly identify the site of the peace conference with Old Sarum in Wiltshire, probably because the nearby town of Amesbury sounds like 'Emrys-bury'. They suggest that the monument erected by Em-Rhys is none other than Stonehenge. In fact Stonehenge, whatever its function and purpose, is now known to have been built in stages from *c*. 2500 BC onwards and was therefore very ancient by then. There is also a mythical tale that on Ambrosius's orders Merlin flew over stones from Ireland with which to build Stonehenge. The real monument erected by Em-Rhys – Emrys Wledig – to bury his fellow countrymen is to the west of where we were standing, at St Peter's. 'Over there past the windmills,' Alan said, pointing to where a forest of modern wind-turbines turned gracefully in the breeze. 'It's called the Mynwent y Milwyr – the "Grave Monument of the Soldiers". It is marked on old Ordnance Survey maps of the area, but has been dropped from recent editions.'

Leaving the Church of St Peter's, we wandered back to the car, visiting first the site of Caradoc's castle on top of the hill. There was not much in the way of earthbanks to be seen, perhaps indicating that this was more in the nature of a palace than a hill fort such as Caerleon. There were, however, impressions in the ground that could have marked the course of some now vanished building. Whatever the truth of the matter, it clearly merited proper archaeological investigation and, if possible, a dig.

THE TREACHERY OF THE PEACE CONFERENCE

It was clear that the story of the Peace Conference was not as simple as it first appears – that like Afallach the real site had been misplaced. As this event was crucial to our story, I decided to look more closely into Alan's story about Vortigern. I also wanted to know more about Hengist, who he was and where he fitted in with the Saxon invasions. Fortunately there is quite a bit of information concerning Vortigern, Hengist and the Peace Conference to be found in many of the ancient histories of Britain, including Geoffrey of Monmouth, Nennius, Gildas and *The Anglo-Saxon Chronicle*. All tell basically the same story of deceit, betrayal and eventually the loss of England to the Saxons. The fullest account is contained in the *Brut Tysylio*, the original version of Geoffrey's history, and begins with the story of how Vortigern manipulated events to usurp the throne.

> The death of Constantine [the son of Magnus Maximus] gave rise to a contention between the chiefs as to a successor, some of them wishing to elect Uther and others one of their own kindred. At length, as there appeared but little hopes of their agreement, Vortigern, sirnamed Gwrthenau, 'lord of Erging and Euas',[2] one of the council, and whose opinion was of the highest authority, asserted that no other than one of the sons of Constantine had a right to it. Constans the eldest was at this time a monk, and the other two[3] were under age. Vortigern therefore went to the monk, and enquired of him what honours he might expect, if he made him king. The monk answered, that Vortigern should have the whole conduct of the state. Vortigern therefore, notwithstanding the opposition of the Abbot, took Constans [the grandson of Magnus

214

Maximus] out of the monastery, and made him king.

Vortigern himself set the crown on his head, and in return was made superintendent of the whole island. This was exactly to the wish of the weak mind of Constans, and moreover what he had learned in the cloister was not how to govern a kingdom.

When some time had elapsed, Vortigern conceived the design of making himself king by treasonable means, and having laid down his plan, he informed the king that a foreign fleet, whose destination was unknown, was at sea, and that it would therefore be necessary to garrison the castles, and stock them with provisions. The king desired him to do what he thought best, as he had given him the superintendence of everything. Vortigern, thus answered, inspected every fort personally, and placed confidential friends of his own in them, and provided them for three years. He then appointed a guard of fourscore Picts of the best families, and most approved courage, to ride out with the king, under the pretext that in case of war, they might be detained as hostages. At the same time by gifts, and the ease of their service he attached them to himself. And these Picts, in their drunken revels, sung songs, in which Constans was represented as contemptible, and Vortigern as the only one fit to reign.

In this train the plan had proceeded for some time, when one night, the king having retired to his bed, Vortigern complained to the Picts of his inability to be of essential service to them, and added that, had he the power, they should enjoy the highest honours he could confer. To this they retorted, why not? was not he the king? to which he replied, that he was not king, he had only the small territory of Erging and Euas. Having said so he immediately retired to rest. When he had gone they went to the king's chamber, cut off his head and brought it to Vortigern, saying, take this, and now, if you will, be king. Vortigern shed some dissembling tears, and committed the murderers to prison. And when the council was informed of the king's death, they met in London, condemned the fourscore Picts to be hanged, and committed the care of the state to Vortigern, until the rightful king should be established. The archbishop Chyelin [Cuhelyn], when he heard of the death of the king, became apprehensive of treachery to his wards [the other two sons of Constantine] and fled with them to Emyr king of Armorica, by whom they were joyfully received. The Picts also, when they found that their friends were hanged, began a war against Vortigern, whilst he, thinking that he had now no opposition to dread, assumed the sovereignty without the consent of the chieftains.[4]

The impression given by Tysylio is that Vortigern had absolutely no right to the throne. However, in the Jesus College Manuscript 20 he is listed with an ancestry tracing him back to someone called Gloyw Gwalltir. The first four entries in this king list are:

1. Gloyw Gwalltir
2. Gwdoloeu
3. Gwidawl
4. Gwrtheyrn Gwrthenau [Vortigern]

There is a reference by the name Gloyw Gwalltir saying: 'this man here made on the border of the Severn a town and his name he truly concealed in "Castle of Gloyw (Claudius)".' This is clearly referring to the foundation of Gloucester: Vortigern's province of Erging was near Gloucester. It is therefore a fair assumption to assume that Gloyw Gwalltir is the Emperor Claudius II who died in 270. Another list shows Vortigern's descent from Beli Mawr, the famous king who was the father of Llud. This goes as follows:

1. Belil Mawr [Llud]
2. Avlech
3. Avallach
4. Endolau
5. Ennos
6. Ennydd
7. Aurdeyrn
8. Eiddigant
9. Deheufraint
10. Rhydeyrn
11. Gwrtheyrn Gwrthenau [Vortigern]

Rhydeyrn was the father of Ceindrich, who was the first wife of Magnus Maximus and the mother of Arthur I. As this king list is different from that going back to Gloyw Gwalltir, which seems to be the paternal line, it follows that there is a generation missing. Rhydeyrn should be the grandfather of Vortigern, which would make him a first cousin of Arthur I.

216

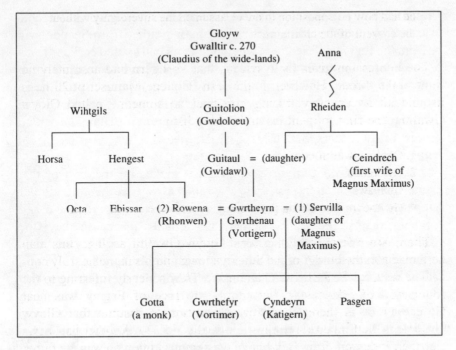

THE DESCENT OF VORTIGERN
Diagram 11

Vortigern was not directly related to the sons of Magnus Maximus by his second wife, Helen, but by marrying Servilla, Constantine's sister, he became Constantine's brother-in-law. With nearly all the sons of Magnus Maximus – Victor, Arthur, Owain and Constantine – dead, Vortigern was in a strong position as the young king Constans's guardian. It was a relatively simple matter for him to arrange for the death of Constantine and then to put himself forward as the best man to take his place.

Throughout the era of the late Roman Empire the main military command in the south of Britain was what the Romans called the 'Saxon shore'. This was a string of fortresses, such as Burgh Castle in Norfolk, stretching along the coast from Portsmouth to the Wash as a sort of 'Maginot Line'. Like all such military schemes it probably worked well so long as rulers and people had, and were willing to invest, the necessary resources and manpower for its upkeep. However, by the late fourth and early fifth centuries these were not as forthcoming as they had been. The invasions of Gaul by first Magnus Maximus and then Constantine depleted resources, particularly the availability of young fighting men.

217

Under these circumstances, the coastline of England became vulnerable to attack by Pictish raiding parties, emanating either from Scandinavia or from the regions of Scotland where the Picts had settled earlier. It was ostensibly to counteract these raiders that, as we have seen, the Roman general Theodosius (father of the later Emperor) was sent to Britain around 370 by Valentinian I. It seems that, in line with Roman policy in Gaul, far from keeping all barbarians out of southern Britain, he settled groups of mercenary Saxons in East Anglia; in a sense, wolves were being employed as sheep dogs.

The Anglo-Saxon Chronicle, although it makes no mention of that event, includes an entry for the year 446 that says something similar happened then: 'The British sent men over the sea to Rome, and asked for help against the Picts, but they never had it, because they [the Romans] were on expedition against king Attila the Hun. They sent then to the Angles and the Anglian athelings, with the same request.'[5]

The person who made this invitation was Vortigern. Not content with usurping the kingdom, or perhaps for his own protection now that he had upset the Picts as well as the British, he invited a party of Saxon warriors to settle in Kent, who in return would act as mercenaries, fighting on his behalf. *The Anglo-Saxon Chronicle* was begun in the late ninth century on the orders of King Alfred the Great. Though it is probably accurate for events subsequent to that date, its compilers were reliant on earlier histories, such as that of Gildas, for the history of Britain prior to the Saxon invasions. Gildas's hoary story of the British begging the Romans for help against the Picts seems to have been included as some sort of justification for the subsequent full-scale invasion of the English. In the beginning of the story of Hengist and his brother Horsa, in the entry for the year 449, Gildas presents a picture of an easy conquest of a land ripe for the picking.

Martianus and Valentinian[6] received the kingdom and reigned for seven years. In their days the Angles were invited here by King Vortigern, and they then came to Britain in three longships, landing at Ebbesfleet.[7] King Vortigern gave them territory in the southeast of this land, on the condition that they fight the Picts. This they did, and had victory wherever they went. They then sent to Angel, commanded more aid, and commanded that they should be told of the Britons' worthlessness and the choice nature of the land. They soon sent hither a greater host to help the others. Then came the men of three Germanic tribes: Old Saxons, Angles and Jutes. Of the Jutes came the people of Kent and the Isle of Wight; that is the tribe which now lives on Wight, and that race among the West-Saxons which men even now call Jutish. Of the Old Saxons came the East Saxons, South Saxons and West Saxons. Of the Angles – the country they left has since stood empty between the Jutes and Saxons – come the East Anglians, Middle Anglians, Mercians and all the Northumbrians. Their war leaders were two brothers, Hengest and Horsa, who were Wihtgils' sons. First of all they killed and drove away the king's enemies; then later they turned on the British, destroying through fire and the sword's edge.

Since *The Anglo-Saxon Chronicle* was primarily intended to bolster up the image of the Saxon royal house of Wessex, it makes no mention of any major setbacks to the invasion. A fuller and rather more balanced account of the arrival of Hengist is presented by Nennius, who was writing around 850 and who gives the date of 447 for the arrival of the Saxons. He writes:

Vortigern then reigned in Britain. In his time, the natives had cause of dread, not only from the inroads of the Scots and Picts, but also from the Romans, and their apprehensions of Ambrosius.[8]

In the meantime, three vessels, exiled from Germany, arrived in Britain. They were commanded by Horsa and Hengist, brothers, and sons of Wightgils ... Vortigern received them as friends, and delivered up to them the island which is in their language called Thanet,[9] and by the Britons, Ruym.[10] Gratianus Æquantius at that time reigned in Rome. The Saxons were received by Vortigern, four hundred and forty-seven years after the passion of Christ, and according to the tradition of our ancestors, from the period of their first arrival in Britain, to the first year of the reign of King Edmund, five hundred and forty-two years . . .[11]

This statement gives a date for the arrival of the Saxons long before the coming of Hengist. Edmund ruled from 940 to 945, so 542 years before his reign we can fix this date as *c.* 398, exactly the right time for Theodosius. These immigrants were mostly from the tribe of the Alemanni, led by a king called Fraomar, and they were settled in the region of the Roman cities of East Anglia and Yorkshire. It was therefore a second wave of Saxons who arrived with Hengist at the time of Vortigern.

These Saxons made a deal with him.

> After the Saxons had continued some time in the island of Thanet,
> Vortigern promised to supply them with clothing and provision, on
> condition they would engage to fight against the enemies of his
> country. But the barbarians having greatly increased in number, the
> Britons became incapable of fulfilling their engagement; and when
> the Saxons, according to the promise they had received, claimed a
> supply of provisions and clothing, the Britons replied, 'Your number
> is increased; your assistance is now unnecessary; you may therefore
> return home, for we can no longer support you;' and hereupon they
> began to devise means of breaking the peace between them.[12]

Hengist and his fellow Saxons were not going to be dismissed so easily,
particularly by a king who was dependent upon them militarily. Hengist
therefore replied:

> 'We are, indeed, few in number; but if you will give us leave, we will
> send to our country for an additional number of forces, with whom
> we will fight for you and your subjects.' Vortigern assenting to this
> proposal, messengers were sent to Scythia, where selecting a number
> of warlike troops, they returned with sixteen vessels, bringing with
> them the beautiful daughter of Hengist.[13]

This daughter of Hengist, Rhonwen or Rowena, was greatly to complicate matters. Like Delilah, she stole the heart of the king and was later
to prove instrumental in his downfall.

> And now the Saxon chief prepared an entertainment, to which he
> invited the king, his officers, and Ceretic, his interpreter, having
> previously enjoined his daughter to serve them so profusely with
> wine and ale, that they might soon become intoxicated. This plan
> succeeded; and Vortigern, at the instigation of the devil, and en-
> amoured with the beauty of the damsel, demanding her, through the
> medium of his interpreter, of the father, promising to give for her
> whatever he should ask. Then Hengist, who had already consulted
> with the elders who attended him of the Oghgul race, demanded for

his daughter the province, called in English, Centland, in British, Ceint . . . Thus the maid was delivered up to the king, who slept with her, and loved her exceedingly.[14]

Having now extended his domain from the island of Thanet to the whole of Kent, Hengist set about bringing over more and more of his kinsmen, including his sons Octa and Ebissa. According to Nennius, so many people came and joined Hengist that many of the islands of Frisia, from which they came, were now left empty of people. Vortigern's marriage to the pagan Rhonwen did not please most of the Britons, least of all his sons by his first wife. His gift of Kent to the newcomers was an outrage to its inhabitants, who hadn't even been consulted concerning such a drastic measure. Accordingly he was deposed and his eldest son Vortimer, whose stone we saw at Nevern, was put on the throne in his place. He fought a series of battles with the Saxons, driving them back over the Channel. Unfortunately for the British, Rhonwen was not amongst them and in 460 she succeeded in having Vortimer poisoned. With the whole country in uproar, Vortigern took his chance and once more seized the throne.

Again Vortigern turned to the Saxons, realizing that he needed them as allies against rival claimants to the throne. Hengist and his followers returned in strength, but rather than fight they proposed that a peace conference should be held where a treaty between the warring parties should be negotiated. Nennius's version of events supports Alan's description of the Peace Conference:

> Hengist, under pretence of ratifying the treaty, prepared an enter-
> tainment, to which he invited the king, the nobles, and military
> officers, in number about three hundred; speciously concealing his
> wicked intentions, he ordered three hundred Saxons to conceal each
> a knife under his feet, and to mix with the Britons; 'and when', said
> he, 'they are sufficiently inebriated, and I cry out *Nimed eure Saxes*,
> then let each draw out his knife, and kill his man; but spare the king,
> on account of his marriage with my daughter, for it is better that he
> should be ransomed than killed.[15]

In this way nearly everyone but Vortigern, who was now a virtual prisoner, was killed. In one day nearly the entire nobility of Britain was wiped out. The cost of Vortigern's freedom was Lloegres, which fell to the Saxons, and Vortigern was banished to Wales.

In a curious aside to the main story,[16] Vortigern is said to have built a fort in north Wales[17] to flee to in case of further difficulty with either his fellow Britons or the Saxons. Unfortunately the castle kept sinking without trace. Consulting his magicians, he learned that for the enterprise to succeed, it would be necessary to sacrifice a boy without a father and to sprinkle his blood upon the ground where the castle was built. Vortigern sent messengers throughout the kingdom and they eventually found a boy fitting this description, either at Caervyrddin – Carmarthen (Tysylio), Kaermerdin (Geoffrey of Monmouth) – or at 'the field of Ælecti, in the district of Glevesing' (Nennius). The boy was brought back but before being sacrificed he questioned the magicians and revealed their ignorance about what really lay below the site of the castle. With his prophetic eye he was able to see that below a pavement there was a pool and at the bottom of this a chest containing two fighting dragons, one white and the other red. He prophesied that though the white, symbolizing the Saxons, would at first conquer the red, symbolizing the Welsh, eventually the latter would drive out the former.

In the *Brut Tysylio* the boy is called Merddin, his mother, a nun, being the daughter of the king of Demetia (Dyfed). In Geoffrey of Monmouth's *History* his name is Merlin, though he is also called Ambrosius; his mother lives in St Peter's Church with a group of other nuns. Nennius has nothing of this but states that the boy's name is simply Ambrosius or Embresguletic (Em-Rhys Wledig) in British and that his father was a Roman consul. Vortigern, impressed by his prophetic powers, assigned him a city along with all the western provinces of Britain – that is, Wales.

The importance of all this is that in the Tysylio version of the Hengist story it is stated plainly that the Peace Conference took place 'on a large plain in Cymry near Ambresbury'. Since Cymry is Wales, the plain must be the Vale of Glamorgan rather than Salisbury Plain, which is in England or Lloegres. It follows that Ambresbury is not Amesbury but rather 'Emrys-bury', or Mynydd y Gaer, where the cor Emrys, the great boat-shaped 'circle', stands near the Church of St Peter.

Geoffrey enlarged his *History* by adding a Latin translation of an entirely different book, 'The Prophecies of Merlin', to the original text of Tysylio. This text complicates things greatly and the identity of Merddin, whose real name Geoffrey says is Ambrosius, becomes confused between Teithfallt, who is known as the Em-Rhys Wledig or 'diademned-prince the legate', and Amloyd Wledig. The Merddin or

Merlin in question would appear to be Teithfallt, who was a boy at the time.[18]

Teithfallt, as we saw earlier, was a monk before becoming King of Glamorgan, and crossed over from Brittany to avenge the slaughter of the Peace Conference. Em-Rhys or Teithfallt was responsible for the rebuilding of churches, as is clear from his entry in 'The Genealogy of Iestyn the Son of Gwrgan'. This stresses both his military and ecclesiastical exploits:

> Teithfallt, the son of Nyniaw,[19] called also Teithfalch in some books, was a beneficent and religious – a wise and heroic monarch. He fought powerfully with the Saxons, and vanquished them; and he passed a law that made it imperative on all to contribute a portion of their wealth towards supporting religion, the clergy, learning and the repairs of churches. Many of the Saxons and Picts came to Cambria in his time, and slew great numbers of the natives; burning also churches and choirs. He retired in his latter days, to a life of sanctity, transferring the government on his son Tewdric.'[20]

Alan told me that in the margins of the Chartulary from Llandaff Cathedral, now renamed the 'Book of St Chad' and held since it was stolen from Llandaff at Lichfield Cathedral, there is mention of benefactions by 'Tydfwlch' – another spelling of Teithfallt or Teithfalch. About a mile to the north of the Mynwent y Milwyr, the monument described by Alan as marking the grave of the soldiers massacred at the Peace Conference, erected by Teithfallt, is the Church of Llandyfodwg. On the floor of this ancient church is a memorial stone showing St Tyfodwg, believed to have come from Brittany and to have built the church. Given the location of the church so near the monument and the fact that churches were routinely built as a result of royal benefactions, it seems almost certain that the 'Tyfodwg' who founded this church is really Tydfwlch – Teithfallt.[21] It all fits and it seems likely that he lies buried here beneath the memorial stone showing his donation. If this is so, Llandyfodwg Church, and not Stonehenge as some believe, is the final resting place of Em-Rhys Wledig, the 'diademned prince' who avenged the tragedy of the Peace Conference and gave the British another chance in their long struggle against Saxon domination. It would be left to his descendants to carry on the fight and to keep intact what remained of the Holy Kingdom.

CHAPTER FOURTEEN

ARTHUR II, KING OF GLAMORGAN

One of the strengths of Alan and Baram's approach is their ability to link legends and written histories to archaeological sites. Some of these relate to battles, like Mount Baedan and Camlann, others are connected with famous religious establishments such as Llantwit Major and Glastonbury; a third category are castles, the most important of which are linked with Athrwys, that is Arthur II. Critical to their researches in the early days had been finding the true location of Arthur II's principal castle of Caerleon, which is spoken of in many early manuscripts. Eventually we managed to pay it a visit, and Baram explained to me the significance of the site.

Various amateur attempts had been made to locate the court or courts of King Arthur, he said, including the extensive archaeological dig at South Cadbury in Somerset. These attempts had failed because they were founded on romantic hope rather than careful analysis. In order to locate the king and his courts it is necessary to strip back the accretions of medieval mythologizing and examine the real practice and customs of the sixth-century British kings. Once this is done it is possible to pinpoint the precise locations of King Arthur's courts.

The most obvious place to begin looking for the court of Arthur II, missed by those who are preoccupied with all things Roman, is at Caerleon, which is named in numerous histories, triads, poems and Mabinogi[1] tales as having been the site where he was most often resident. At Caerleon lie the ruins of the Roman city of Isca. Its fortress had been abandoned long before the time of Arthur and lay in ruins when he became king. Even so, because these extensive ruins, which stretch to over forty-eight acres, are now called Caerleon, people tend to think this is where Arthur held his courts. In fact Welsh kings such as Arthur II did not occupy huge, stone fortresses set out on flat, indefensible plains: rather they used the techniques of their forefathers and reoccupied forts on hilltops. Significantly, the ideal spot for the defence of central Gwent is a very steep hill which stands just half a mile to the north of the ruins of the Roman city of Isca. This hill fort here dominates the tidal reaches of the River Usk as it flows down to the Severn Estuary and guards the entrance to the valleys of the upper reaches of the Usk and Ebbw rivers as they lead into central Gwent. This, Baram and Alan believe, is the real Caerleon, where Arthur held his courts. All the hill forts are part of a gigantic system arranged in 'wheels' of interlocked circles with royal or central forts at their hubs. Caerleon is at the centre of one of these hubs.

We drove through the town of Caerleon, avoiding the 'heritage centre' which has been made out of the Roman ruins of Isca, and then along some narrow residential streets that threaded their way up a steep hill. We parked at the top of the hill and made our way past an evangelical Christian centre to reach an area of wooded parkland. As it was wintertime the trees and other vegetation were dormant; even so there were thick areas of brambles and bracken all but obscuring the paths and contours of what was clearly another hill fort.

'We are now on Lodge Hill, a name which we think is derived from the Welsh word *llys*, meaning "court". This is undoubtedly the ancient fortress of Caerleon,' said Alan triumphantly, as, pushing back the undergrowth, he led us through into a clearing. The idea that the name is Roman, a corruption of *caer legionis* or 'fortress of the legions', is wrong, he explained. The Romans never called their town by that name. Their fortress on the site of the present town of Caerleon was called Isca Augusta, or Isca for short. The town of Isca was a major trading centre for the area, for it stands on a bend of the river Usk. The river is tidal, well up to this point and beyond, and ships could sail up from what is now Newport to load and unload cargoes, and as usual, once they had made peace with the Khymry of Essylwg, the Romans were interested in trade.

The castle of Caerleon, where we were standing, is much older than this Roman settlement and was reoccupied at the time of King Arthur. Alan and Baram believe that it gets its name from a king called Lleon, who, according to the histories, dates from the pre-Brutus era, probably around 550. The histories record that the principal court of King Arthur was here at Caerleon. There can be no doubting that this was the place. One medieval story tells of how Arthur II watched people arriving at his

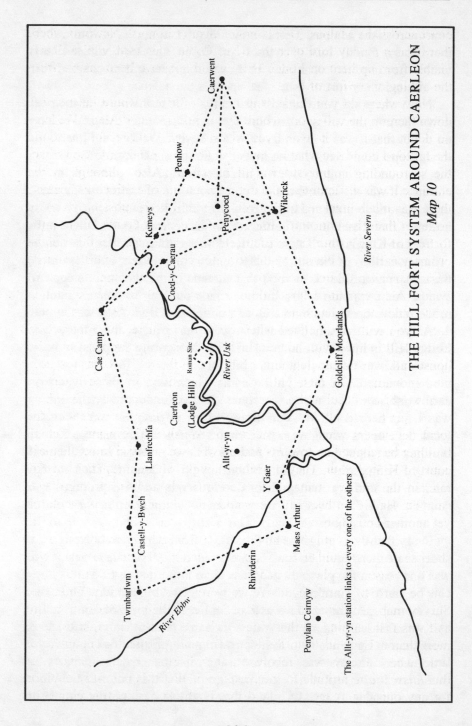

Caerwent

Penhow

Penycoed

Wilcrick

Kemeys

Coed-y-Caerau

River Severn

Cae Camp

Goldcliff Moorlands

Roman Site

River Usk

Caerleon
(Lodge Hill)

Llanfrechfa

Allt-yr-yn

Y Gaer

Castell-y-Bwch

Maes Arthur

Rhiwderin

Twmbarlwm

River Ebbw

Penylan Ceirmyw

The Allt-yr-yn station links to every one of the others

THE HILL FORT SYSTEM AROUND CAERLEON
Map 10

court across the Malpas. This is now a district in north Newport where there was a muddy ford over the River Ebbw. This ford, whilst clearly visible from up here on Lodge Hill, would not have been visible from the old legionary fort of Isca.

'Now where do you think King Arthur's fortress would have stood: down there in the valley or up here on the hilltop?' said Alan. 'We have no doubt that it was here and you will see why.' Walking further round the hilltop I could see what he meant: it afforded panoramic views over the surrounding countryside in all directions. Also, although at the entrance it was difficult to make out the contours of earthworks because there was much bracken, further round the hill it was possible to count no fewer than five concentric lines of defence. As at Castle Ditches, the fortress of King Arthur I near Lichfield, these indicated that this was no ordinary earthwork but a major castle. Returning to one of his favourite themes, academic and municipal indifference to the real history of Wales, Alan explained how Lodge Hill would have fallen victim to modern developers had not he and Baram stirred up interest in the site.

'As you will have noticed when we drove up here, the approach to Lodge Hill is lined with houses. In 1981 there was a proposal to build houses all over this ancient site, even though the hill fort was a scheduled monument. In fact, until we drew attention to these extensive earthworks, the local authorities seem to have been unaware that there was a fort here at all. You can imagine how popular we were with the local developers when we wrote to the Welsh Office asking that all building be stopped up towards and on what we believed to be the main court of King Arthur. They probably thought we were lunatics. At any rate, in the end we managed to alert officials and the proposal was stopped. Had it not been, all we would be looking at up here would be yet another housing estate.'

To say that I was impressed by Lodge Hill was an understatement. For sheer scale there could be few forts to touch it in all Britain. Perhaps this was one reason the planners had missed its importance: a fort this large can be hard to comprehend. Yet it is marked on modern Ordnance Survey maps, so they had no excuse for not realizing its existence. But as I was fast learning, in the Wales of the get-rich-quick eighties, even more than in England, historic sites and planning regulations counted for little when money was involved. The disastrous consequences of this *laissez-faire* attitude to the heritage of Wales is painfully obvious for any outsider to see. In a land that ought to be boasting about the achievements of the remarkable Glamorgan dynasty, scarcely a word is mentioned about King Arthur, and that usually in derision. Today, when the coal mines, steelworks and docks – the nineteenth-century heritage of south Wales – have all but disappeared to be replaced by a few car plants and light engineering, it is understandable that those who have witnessed the great changes wrought on Wales over the last fifty years should want to preserve for posterity the memory of how it once was. Instead of developing the undoubted tourist potential of world-class sites such as this one outside Caerleon, CADW seems to spend more time and money on industrial archaeology than on anything pertaining to Arthurian Wales. Worthy though this may be, when all around the remains of Britain's most famous king, Arthur, lie unexcavated and undervalued, this concern smacks not so much of carelessness but of stupidity.

THE CASTLE OF THE KNIGHTS

Caerleon, impressive as it is, was only one of Arthur's courts. The real centre of his activity was in the Cardiff area and now Alan and Baram took me to Castle Field, a grassy hill fort, now part of Craig Llwyn – 'Greystones' – Farm, just a few miles from the centre of Cardiff. The farmer's wife, Mrs Lewis, was an old friend of Alan's and allowed us to park our car in her driveway before we headed across a muddy field, past a fine but frisky young chestnut stallion who came bounding up from nowhere to check on what we were doing in his field.

'This, believe it or not, was once the centre of King Arthur's kingdom, the site of his fabled castle of Camelot,' said Alan. Its real name, he went on, is Caer Melyn, the 'Yellow Fortress', on account of the yellow sulphur pits near by, which coloured the water of the springs. *Mellitus* means honey in Latin, which is of course yellow-coloured, so it is easy to see how in the French legends the Welsh Caer Melyn could be corrupted to Caer Mellitus and this shortened to Camelot.

British – and that includes English as well as Welsh – kings generally had more than one place of residence where they held court. They were in the habit of touring round these various courts, which were administered by stewards in their absence, rather as assize judges do today. The king would spend a period of time at each court and then move on to the next. In this way the burden of supporting the large retinue which travelled with him would be spread out and they would not exhaust the supplies of any one region. Although all we could see now were some low, grassy banks, as late as the fifteenth century there was a castle standing here. When it fell derelict it was, as usual, quarried for stone by the local farmers and now there is not much to see. However, were archaeologists to dig here there is no knowing what they might find. It's ironic, Alan pointed out, that this fortress can be seen from Cardiff University, yet it has so far been ignored by the archaeological faculty which spent hundreds of thousands of pounds on fruitlessly excavating South Cadbury Hill in Somerset. Craig Llwyn is only a quarter of a mile away from the university.

The area dominated by this castle was known in ancient times as part of the Commote of Cibbor – also spelt Kibor, Kibbor and Cybwr. Alan and Baram think it comes from the joining together of two Welsh words: *cy* and *bwr*. *Cy* means 'a mutual action' or 'something done together'; *bwr* seems to be related to the word *bwrdd*, which means 'table'. Thus *Cybwr*, combining these two words, would seem to mean something like 'the mutually together table' – a good description of King Arthur's famous Round Table where traditionally the knights ate together and held their meetings. The men of the Commote of Cybwr used to enjoy special privileges under the law, which were upheld even after the Norman invasion of Wales of 1091. Among these privileges were rights regarding freedom from taxation. Usually such rights were conferred in gratitude for acts of conspicuous bravery during war. It is therefore tempting to think that these rights originated as recognition of the exploits of the Knights of the Round Table.

The importance of Cybwr was well recognized until quite recently. Both Rice Merrick (Rhys Meurig), writing in 1578, and John Leland in *c*. 1534 refer to the 'Hundred' or Commote of 'Kybor' or 'Kibworth'. We know that it is the same place for they accurately describe it as lying between the River Taff to the west, the River Rumney to the east and bounded by the Cefn-On ridge to the north. Merrick records that even after the Normans arrived the statutory privileges of Cybwr were preserved: 'Most of this Hundred in the old times was called Kybor, which was endued with liberties and privileges above the rest as before I have remembered, and therefore termed in Welsh, Comod Bryniol.'

He further states that Cardiff lies within the 'Hundred' of Cybwr and not vice versa. This is confirmed by Leland, who writes: 'If Cardiff be not a Commote in itself, it seemeth to be in Kibworth.' There can

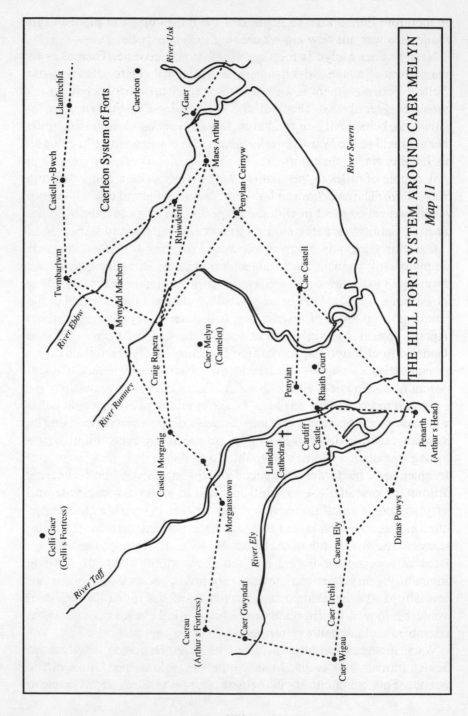

THE HILL FORT SYSTEM AROUND CAER MELYN
Map 11

Caerleon System of Forts

River Usk

Caerleon

Llanfrechfa

Castell-y-Bwch

Y-Gaer

Maes Arthur

River Severn

Penylan Ceirnyw

Twmbarlwm

Rhiwderin

River Ebbw

Mynydd Machen

Cae Castell

Craig Rupera

Caer Melyn
(Camelot)

River Rumney

Penylan

Rhaith Court

Castell Morgraig

Gelli Gaer
(Gelli's Fortress)

Llandaff
Cathedral

Cardiff
Castle

Penarth
(Arthur's Head)

Morganstown

River Taff

River Ely

Caerau Ely

Dinas Powys

Caerau
(Arthur's Fortress)

Caer Gwyndaf

Caer Trehil

Caer Wigau

be therefore little reason to doubt that the most important place in this whole area was this now almost entirely vanished castle.

Next to Caer Melyn is the Cardiff suburb of Lisvane. This takes its name from *llys-faen*, which means 'stone court'. Here, close to our 'Yellow Fortress', there is an old road called Pen-yr-heol-felyn, which translates literally as 'Head of the Yellow Road'. Further over in Rhiwbina, behind All Saints Church, is a field called Cae Meich, which means 'Field of the War Horses'. Perhaps this is where King Arthur and his knights grazed their horses.

A couple of miles to the south of Lisvane is Roath, a name deriving from *rhaith*. The *rhaith* was a law court, a form of grand council or jury which was called to sit in with the king. So Roath would have been the place in Cardiff where the king sat in council with his ministers.

Camelot, then, was no great city with walls and battlements; it was simply one of the main manor house courts of the Glamorgan kings. As it was close to the law courts at Roath, it was the obvious gathering place for Arthur's knights. The fortress was built because this site lies at the centre of a vast web of interlinking fortresses. A cryptic reference to 'Adras, son of Meyrig' yet another name for Arthur – in the 'Genealogy of Iestyn the Son of Gwrgan', says that he established both an equestrian class, that is, a company of knights, and 'an efficient system of communications, with regard to hostilities and legislation'.

Central to this system was his network of hill forts. To understand this it is necessary to consider the way British hill forts were used. Unlike Norman castles, which were basically a means of controlling an un-willing population from whom they were alienated, they were not designed to be held statically against a besieging enemy. For the ancient Britons the essential use of a hill fort was to act as a watchtower and relay station. A small garrison with horses would keep watch over the surrounding countryside and relay messages to their neighbours using beacons, mirrors or riders. At night the hill fort, with its high banks, acted as a corral for horses and cattle, preventing them from being driven off by a swift-moving invader. Should an enemy appear, codes of necessity demanded that he be met in the field. Women and children would be moved to the relative safety of a hill fort, whilst the men assembled and did battle in the open.

Wars, though often bloody, tended to be quick affairs to safeguard fields, animals and crops. In this type of warfare speed was of the essence. Fast communications between hill forts and a rapid reaction

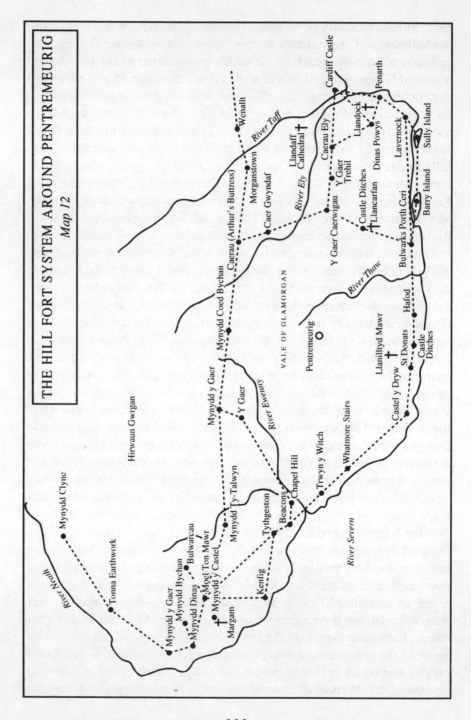

THE HILL FORT SYSTEM AROUND PENTREMEURIG

Map 12

force of heavy cavalry to intercept trouble almost before it arrived were the hallmarks of the military system developed by Arthur II. This was certainly not a new idea, but one which he exploited to the full. As the region of Glamorgan and Gwent was his core kingdom, this is where the system was most developed at this time; however similar systems of hill forts, reused at the time of Arthur, exist throughout Britain. Caer Melyn itself stands at the centre of a 'wheel' of forts guarding the Glamorgan coast around Cardiff. Some of these hill forts were later developed into fully fledged stone castles. One such is Castell Morgraig, which stands north-west of Caer Melyn, midway between the Rivers Taff and Rumney. It is a very large Welsh castle, which even the establishment is now admitting is pre-Norman. Of course, Alan observed, as it isn't Roman or Norman, no money is being spent on preserving it.

There is a second system to the west, around Pentremeurig, guarding the Vale of Glamorgan. To the east, in Gwent, lay another 'wheel' around the most powerful fortress of all: Caerleon, which we had already seen. Taken together these forts and way stations made the kingdom of Glamorgan virtually impregnable. Though it was raided from time to time by the Saxons, invariably they were driven out again and it was not until 1091, when the Normans used stealth to seize the low-lying castles guarding the Vale of Glamorgan, that this part of Wales was successfully invaded. Before the last century, when mass immigration into South Wales from Ireland, England and Scotland took place, nearly everyone spoke Welsh. This was sufficiently recent for Welsh names not to have changed out of recognition, that so much is still preserved here, not just in the way of artefacts but also as place names. As Alan said, 'You don't need a degree in archaeo-geography to pin down exactly where events recorded in our history actually took place. It's all written in the land-scape.'

What Alan said struck a chord with me. Living in Dorset, I was sur-rounded by a similar network of hill forts and had already come to the same conclusion: that most of these were relay stations and look-out posts, not static castles. The ancient Britons, as Julius Caesar admitted, relied on mobility. At the time of the Roman invasions they used war chariots, enabling their archers and spear-throwers to operate at a dis-tance. Later on they switched to horseback and mounted cavalry replaced the charioteers. During the later Roman era, British and Gallic cavalry served all over the Empire, the legions of foot-sloggers having given way to cohorts of armoured knights. In these companies of cavalry

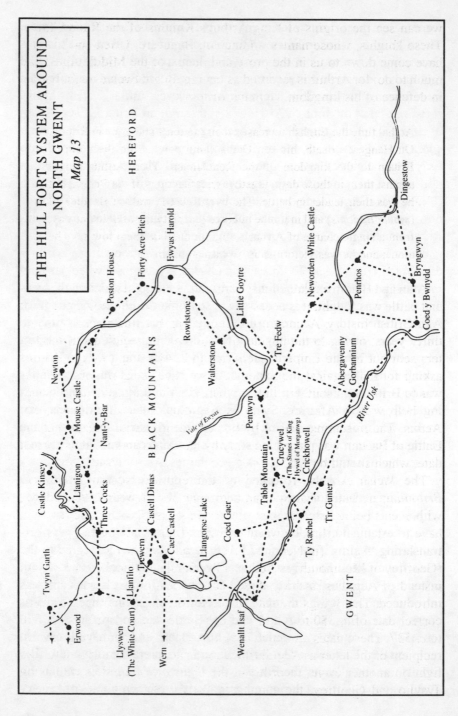

THE HILL FORT SYSTEM AROUND
NORTH GWENT
Map 13

we can see the origins of King Arthur's Knights of the Round Table. These knights, whose names – Lancelot, Bedevere, Urien and so on – have come down to us in the prose and poetry of the Middle Ages, had much to do, for Arthur is recorded as having fought twelve major battles in defence of his kingdom. Nennius writes:

> At that time the English increased their numbers and grew in Britain. On Hengest's death, his son Octha came down from the north of Britain to the kingdom of the Kentishmen. Then Arthur fought against them in those days, together with the kings of the British; but he was their leader in battle. The twelfth battle was on Badon Hill (*monte Badonis*) and in it nine hundred and sixty men fell in one day, from a single charge of Arthur's, and no one laid them low save he alone; and he was victorious in all his campaigns.[1]

Alan and Baram explained that to reach the proper date when this crucial battle was fought, it is necessary to put right the chronology of Dark Age British history. According to them it has been displaced by some thirty years, owing to the misidentification of the recipients of the letters sent out by the Emperor Honorius in *c.* 410 – and by the Britons asking for help against the Saxons. As we have seen, Honorius's letter was to Brittium in southern Italy, not Britain; the Britons' letter requesting help was to Afranius Syagrius Aegidius, ruler of Soissons, not Aetius. The misdating caused by this misidentification meant that the Battle of Baedan was placed too early by historians and not at its correct date, which should be *c.* 550.

The Welsh Annals, recorded at the end of Nennius's *Historia Britonum*, are listed year by year, beginning Year 1, Year 2, Year 3, etc., with events being listed against successive years. To use these lists you have to establish a link between Year 1 and its AD equivalent. By mistranslating 'Agitus' (in Nennius), 'Acanypus' (Tysylio) and 'Aganypus' (Geoffrey of Monmouth) as Aetius, a Roman general and consul in 444, instead of Aegidius, a thirty-three-year dislocation in the records was introduced. This brings the date of the Battle of Baedan back from its correct date of *c.* 550 to *c.* 517 and the Battle of Camlann from *c.* 570 to *c.* 537. These dates are much too early. However, identifying the real recipient of the letter as Aegidius, we get an accurate date. It also throws light on another event, recorded in the *Bruts of England* as well as by Tysylio and Geoffrey: the coming to Britain of the 'King of Africa', against whose forces the Battle of Baedan was fought.

The Battle of Baedan or Badon was the decisive victory that confirmed Arthur's control over Britain. It is even mentioned by Gildas, though unlike Nennius he doesn't name the victor as Arthur. Much to my surprise, Alan and Baram were now able to show me the very site where this epic battle had taken place: not in England, as many suppose, but in Wales.

THE BATTLE OF BAEDAN

Whilst historians, past and present, are agreed that the battle which more than any other established King Arthur's reputation was fought at a place called Mount Baedan (for which the spellings vary), just where this place was is a matter of contention. Prime contenders are Badbury Hill in Dorset,[2] And Solsbury Hill near Bath. Both these sites, linguistically attractive in their own ways, are within thirty miles of South Cadbury, the site favoured by academics as King Arthur's Camelot ever since Alcock's fruitless dig in the 1960s. Yet nothing whatsoever has ever been found on these sites to suggest, still less prove, that they really were battlefields in the sixth century. As King Arthur seems to have been defending his home turf from invaders, the fact that he came from Glamorgan in south Wales makes these English sites even more unlikely.

Alan and Baram showed me on a map exactly where these battles, and others, took place. Once shown it seemed so obvious I couldn't help but wonder why no one had seen this before. Before we set out to visit Mount Baedan, Alan explained how they had rediscovered the location, which has been woefully neglected by popular authors such as Leslie Alcock, Geoffrey Ashe and John Morris, none of them appreciating the importance of Arthur's Welsh connection.

Alan explained that by using old Ordnance Survey maps and guided by ancient Welsh records, such as the 'Songs of the Graves', it is possible to locate the real sites where crucial events of Dark Age British history took place. Thus he and Baram are able to say with certainty that the Battle of Baedan, since historically it is said to have taken place 'close to the banks of the river Severn', could not possibly, as many commentators have suggested, have been fought at Badbury Rings in Dorset; nor was it the 'Battle of Bath', as John Morris suggests in his book *The Age of Arthur*. Bath was not even called by that name in the sixth century: the Romans knew it as Aquae Sulis, which probably means 'the waters of the Sun', a clear reference to the fact that the springs were hot. The similarity between the Welsh and English word *baedan* and the German *baden* meaning 'to bathe' is no more than a co-incidence. However, in Welsh *baedd* means either 'boar' or 'challenge', both of which translations make sense in terms of a battle with the Saxons, who were certainly a challenge and for whom the boar was a favourite emblem; thus the site of Baedan is likely to have a Welsh connection.

In the Mabinogi stories, King Arthur is said to have fought the Battle of Baedan just a few miles from the River Severn. Taking this clue seriously, Baram and Alan explored all the Ordnance Survey maps covering the Severn, inch by inch, looking for likely sites. It didn't take them very long to find Mynydd Baedan, and having found it they wondered why the site had ever been disputed; in fact it is still marked on modern OS maps. It lies above the Maesteg Valley, just six miles from the River Severn, not in England but in Wales. Moreover, the large, north-eastern slopes of the mountain are still called Maescadlawr in Welsh, which translates as 'Field of the Battle Area'. Here there are grave mounds in which, after the battle, the large numbers of war dead were entombed. The road leading to the top of Maescadlawr is also still known as Ffordd y Gyfraith or 'Road to the Tumult' and near by is a field where the army must have pitched camp, for it is called the 'Field of the White Tents'.

Once more we headed westwards along the M4, turning off towards Maesteg. The road became steadily steeper as we followed it up the Llynfi Valley. At the foot of the hill we saw a signpost giving directions to 'Mynydd Baedan 4 miles', before coming to a turning marked by another signpost which read 'Ffordd y Gyfraith $1^1/2$'. The day before I would have passed this without a second thought, but now that I knew that it meant 'Road to the Tumult' it was rather exciting. Going beyond this we came to a smaller turning near a shop selling farm produce, with a brightly painted sign reading 'MAESCADLAWR FARMSHOP FRESH FRUIT – VEG HAY AND STRAW'. Again this would have meant nothing to me had I not been told that Maescadlawr translates into English as 'Field of the Battle Area'.

But though they would have meant nothing to me, since I do not speak Welsh, I couldn't help but wonder why Welsh speakers had not taken any notice of these clues relating to an important battle; given that we were in the heart of King Arthur's kingdom of Glamorgan, could this be referring to any other battle than Baedan?

We turned off here and made our way up a steep winding track. Alan, who was by now becoming more and more excited, explained that in fact some local people had taken notice. When they first came here in the early eighties and asked the owner, a middle-aged lady, for directions, she had no difficulty at all in pointing the way. 'Oh,' she said, 'you'll be wanting the battle site. It's straight up that road. It was a big battle, fought just after the time of the Romans.' They realized that they were not the first to put two and two together: clearly the locals knew all about it. Later they discovered that there were local historians who had taken the trouble to map out the entire area, working out the progress of the battle from still extant ditches, banks and other features; a book had even been published on the subject. Some of the features described have disappeared over the course of the last twenty years, and conifers have been planted, but there is still enough visible to get a general impression.

As we drove up the hill the road became narrower and narrower with high banks on either side. Coming to a clearing we found a gateway, beyond which I was able to park. The view was spectacular over the whole Maesteg Valley, an area of outstanding natural beauty. With the sun shining down from a southerly direction but, as it was still early March, not too high in the sky, it was possible to see how the side of the hill was pockmarked with tumuli. To the left of the road and behind a modern fence, sheep were grazing contentedly on what had been the site of the Field of the White Tents, where there were the remains of some very large tumuli, though it looked as though they had been dug into at some time in the perhaps not-too-distant past. Fringing the road were embankments, several feet high, immediately recognizable as ancient fortifications.

Alan explained that all ancient battlefields have at least two large grave mounds – war cemeteries for the dead of each side, which is what the tumuli in the Field of the White Tents were. All along the top of the hill, and skirting right around over the brow, were earthworks. The maps compiled in the last century by local historians plotting out the entire course of the battle confirm that these earthworks are nothing to do with the modern road, which makes use of the path cut by the ancients between the old earthworks, and indeed in places we would see that they skirted away from the course taken by the road.

Opposite us, across the valley, was Brynllywarch, which is possibly

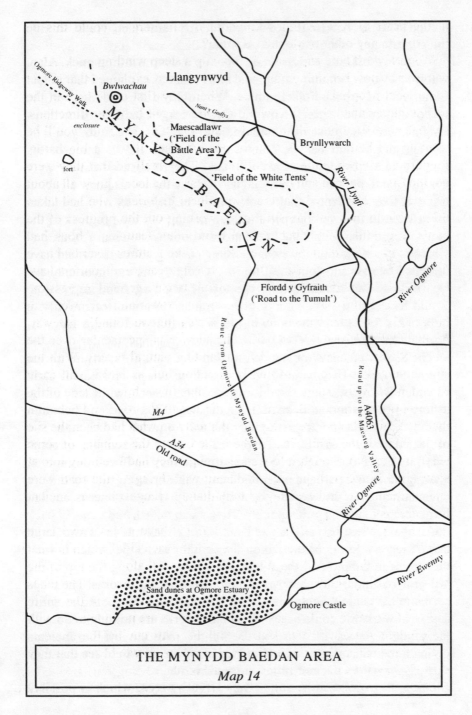

Ogmore Ridgeway Walk

Bwlwachau

Llangynwyd

MYNYDD

enclosure

Nant y Gadlys

fort

Maescadlawr
('Field of the
Battle Area')

Brynllywarch

River Llynfi

BAEDAN

'Field of the White Tents'

Ffordd y Gyfraith
('Road to the Tumult')

River Ogmore

Route from Ogmore to Mynydd Baedan

Road up to the Maesteg Valley

A4063

M4

A34
Old road

River Ogmore

River Ewenny

Sand dunes at Ogmore Estuary

Ogmore Castle

THE MYNYDD BAEDAN AREA
Map 14

named after one of Arthur's knights called Llywarch Hen. He is listed in the genealogies as a great-great-grandson of Tewdrig and was therefore a young kinsman of Arthur. Near by was a stream called the Nant y Gadlys – the 'Stream of the Battle-court'; and the village of Llangynwydd, whose little church we could see reflecting the sunlight, is possibly named after Cynwydd-Cynwyddion, another of Arthur's knights, who was presumably buried there.[3]

Alan and Baram believe that Athrwys, or Arthur II, gathered his forces together by Ogmore Castle, on the fields by the confluence of the Ewenny and Ogmore Rivers. (The little streams around Mynydd Baedan, like the Nant y Gadlys, flow into the Ogmore.) Arthur and his army are said to have marched for three hours from nine o'clock in the morning and then fought the battle around noon, which makes Ogmore, which is about six miles away, a plausible starting point. He would have marched overland to join the Ffordd-y-Gyfraith, which links onto the Ogwr Ridgeway running along the top of Mynydd Baedan. Here he would have had a commanding position and been able to conceal the bulk of his forces over the brow of the hill, leading the enemy to underestimate his strength.

The Saxons, meanwhile, landed further along on the coast near what is now Swansea. They would have beached their boats on an area called Crymlyn Burrows, where there is a wide open beach – ideal for putting ashore in flat-bottomed boats. Here they would have been very hard to dislodge, as there are dunes all along the way in which to hide. It is also protected from the east by the River Neath, very fast flowing and recognized as being one of the most dangerous rivers in Britain. However, although they were able to assemble here with impunity, they would not have had much in the way of food with them and would have needed to bring things to a head quite quickly. They swung north and then cut back down again. Place names such as Pant y Sais ('Dell of the Saxons') and Cefn-Saeson ('Ridge of the Saxons') mark the route they took on their way to meet Arthur at Mynydd Baedan.

Local traditions say that Arthur split his force into three parts. He seems to have lured the Saxons into a trap and then cut off their retreat. The earthworks we could see were where his infantry would have stood. He would have wanted to stand on higher ground than his opponent, giving him an advantage, and would have used his cavalry on the wings, as was normal in ancient times: he had to avoid being outflanked. In addition, he had the protection of the earthworks, which terminated in a complex network of ditches and banks, making it more difficult for the enemy to come up from the side.

Alan pointed out that the battle area was extremely large and there must have been quite considerable forces marshalled on both sides. It was clearly an all-or-nothing situation: had Arthur lost, his entire kingdom would have been wide open. As it was, the Saxons were trapped. Perhaps, he suggested, the stragglers who tried to escape were cut down in the 'Valley of Retribution'. It is unlikely that they bothered taking many prisoners; they wouldn't have known what to do with them and they didn't trust the Saxons after the 'Treachery of the Long Knives' at the Peace Conference.

Returning to the car, we drove back to Cardiff, where I was able to take another look at the maps and discuss the matter with Baram. 'Now what do you think?' asked Baram rhetorically. 'Why do modern historians ignore or misrepresent all this real evidence of a real battle? Why do today's "Arthurian" authors carry on deceiving themselves and the public? Is it because if they admit that Mount Baedan is in Wales, then they also have to accept that King Arthur was south-Welsh? I rather think so. For some reason, which I have to confess I don't really understand, as I'm English myself, these English writers would rather live with lies than admit that King Arthur was a Welshman. Time and again we have been attacked and vilified for stating what we think is obvious. Yet surely what matters in the whole Arthurian quest is getting to the truth? Only by placing the two King Arthurs in their true context – Arthur I in the Midlands and Arthur II in Glamorgan and Gwent – can we begin to understand their achievements.'

This denial of the evidence, he continued, extends to other sites. For example, it is often suggested that the two great battles of Llongborth and Camlann, which were fought by King Arthur against his treacherous nephew Mordred, took place at Portsmouth in Hampshire and Camelford in Cornwall respectively. Yet Baram and Alan believe it is clear that the Battle of Llongborth was fought at a place still called Llongborth on Cardigan Bay, where a mass of place names are indicative of this dire event. A prince named Geraint was killed during this battle and his *marwnad* or 'grave elegy' is quoted by most Arthurian authors, but they fail to mention that Bedd Geraint Farm is near Llongborth and on it is a tumulus known as Bedd Geraint – the grave of Geraint. Alan and Baram have been to this battle site and established that it fits the descriptions given in the histories.

The Battle of Camlann, they believe, was fought at a place still called Camlann, just inland from Llongborth. Camlann means 'Crooked Glen' in Welsh, which is a precise description of the Camlann Valley, just ten miles south of Dolgellau. The scatter of grave mounds attests that this was the scene of another great battle and indeed this is known by local people. What happened was that Arthur and his army were in Brittany at the time when his nephew Mordred attempted to seize the kingdom. Mordred had roots from the other side of his family in Northumberland and as he and his Saxon allies marched south, Arthur landed at Llongborth to cut eastwards into the Midlands. Mordred had no choice but to meet him on the beach and try to prevent the landing. When this failed, the rebels were driven up the Camlann Valley, both sides suffering many casualties. There is no equivalent 'crooked glen' to be seen at Camelford, or at Queen's Camel in Somerset, another favourite siting; nor are there large tumuli at either of those sites attesting to a field of battle.

Looking at the map, I had to agree with all Baram had explained and shared his sentiments lamenting the resistance of researchers to the truth. Arthur II's main battles had been fought to preserve the freedom of Britain in trying to hold back the Anglo-Saxon tide. South Wales was his core kingdom, his home, the place where he would hang his hat, and the Battle of Baedan, fought near the River Severn, prevented Saxon expansion into south Wales. Llongborth and Camlann, in the far west of Wales, were civil war battles. All this made sense militarily and historically.

I was now to discover, though, that the Saxons were only the beginning of Arthur II's problems. He had to defend his kingdom not only against their depredations but also, strange as it might seem, against an invasion by the 'King of Africa', as Alan had hinted, as well as a disaster of apocalyptic proportions. It seems that these events – and we have evidence for them – which most investigators would be happy to dismiss as a crazy fantasy, were recorded by the Welsh and duly misunderstood by Geoffrey of Monmouth when incorporated into his own history. Unravelling the true story behind the King of Africa was to be our next adventure.

CHAPTER FIFTEEN

THE COMING OF THE KING OF AFRICA

To date our work had focused mainly upon the origins of the British, that is to say Welsh, during the time of the Roman Empire. I realized now that to understand the story of the Saxons and their invasion of England I needed to know more about the origins of the Anglo-Saxons, that is to say the English. I was to discover that the Saxons' successful conquest of the island of Britain was not entirely due to their own prowess. Certain factors, such as the chaos ensuing from the collapse of the western Roman Empire, and the ensuing conflicts between British and Roman Emperors for control of Gaul, worked in their favour. Without these preconditions it is doubtful that the Saxons could have obtained a toehold in Britain, still less have taken over the best part of the island.

Alan was keen that I should get a view of the larger picture in all of this and see the Saxon invasions in context.

The fall of the Roman Empire, he reminded me, was in large part due to the machinations of the Emperor of Constantinople, Theodosius. For centuries there had been a struggle between various branches of the imperial royal family for control of western Europe. Faced with the near certainty of his own fall at the hands of Magnus Maximus, Theodosius recruited into the Roman army of the East a huge contingent of barbarian mercenaries. The Battles of Sisica and Poetovio in 388 sealed the fate of the western Empire, for with the defeat of Maximus and his sons there was no means of securing the Rhineland borders from the hordes of Franks, Sueves, Alemanni, Vandals and others that had long been anxious to break into the fertile lands of Gaul.

One of Theodosius's first acts following the defeat and death of Magnus's son Victor, the Augustus of Gaul, was to cross over to Britain.

243

This was ostensibly to deal with invading Picts but his real reason seems to have been to give land to some of his Saxon allies. The idea, mooted by some, of Theodosius crossing over to Britain with an invincible legion of highly trained and motivated Romans is a myth. What he had at his disposal was a rabble host of mercenaries intent on finding themselves new homes away from the approaching Huns. Following the invasion of Gaul in 406 by the British Emperor, Constantine Coronog, in order to protect Britain from further penetration by German tribes, the Alans and Sueves settled in Spain; the Vandals, the senior tribe, at first settled in southern Spain, bequeathing their name to the province of Andalusia, and then crossed over to Africa, where they established an Empire with its capital at Carthage. They were eventually driven out of here by the Byzantines in 548 and departed in a great fleet, never to be heard of again.

Alan and Baram believe that these 'Africans', led by their king Gormund, are the same people whom Tysylio, Geoffrey and the *Bruts of England* accuse of wreaking destruction in Ireland and Britain. The coming of the King of Africa was a real event, closely linked with the story of King Arthur's battle at Baedan. They date the arrival of the King of Africa in Britain to around 548, during the reign of Arthur II, not of Ceredig, as is said by Geoffrey.

Curiously, the coming of the King of Africa or Great Boar is the real event recorded symbolically in the Mabinogi story, 'Culhwch and Olwen'. The folk tales recorded in the Mabinogi are allegories. In 'Culhwch and Olwen' King Arthur and his men have to hunt a ferocious wild boar called Twrch Trwyth. On the surface it concerns a great boar hunt, masterminded by none other than King Arthur himself. In reality it is the story of one of his greatest wars against an enemy that came near to destroying his kingdom completely, for the Vandal King Gormund is Twrch Trwyth, the Great Boar, and his nine 'piglets' are his major commanders.

Still somewhat sceptical about 'Africans' having landed in Britain, I returned home and dug out the appropriate sections of the notes they had sent me. I also consulted the *Encyclopaedia Britannica* for corroboration of the basic Vandal story and found that it was exactly as they had said. For the best part of a hundred years there had indeed been a Vandal Empire ruling the Mediterranean from a base in Carthage. What was even more fascinating was that this piece of history was well documented by Roman historians, so the family tree of the Vandal kings is known. 'Gormund', the African king of the *Bruts*, would appear to be the 'Guerdmund' in the genealogy of the kings of Mercia as given by Nennius.

The extraordinary story of the Vandals, which has all the adventure of a Hollywood epic, is as follows. In 401 a combined horde of Vandals, led by their king Godigisel, in alliance with the Sueves and the Alans, poured west in an orgy of mayhem and destruction. At this time the Roman army was under the control of barbarian mercenaries and a Vandal general called Stilicho was guardian to the boy Emperor, Honorius. Stilicho seems to have arranged with the Emperor for his fellow kinsmen to be granted lands in Noricum and Vindelicia, a territory roughly corresponding to southern Germany, Austria and Switzerland. Here they were no doubt expected, in the time-honoured way, to form a buffer state against the approach of other barbarians, most notably the Huns. For a time they honoured their agreement and in 402 they joined the Romans and Alans to fight against Alaric the Goth. However, the Vandals' allegiance to the Roman cause was only temporary, as three years later a leader called Radagasius led a combined force of Ostrogoths, Vandals, Alans and Quadi in an invasion of Italy itself. That this invasion was halted by a 'Roman' army under the joint command of Stilicho the Vandal, Sarus the Goth and Uldin the Hun speaks volumes about the security of what was left of the western Empire following Theodosius's victory over Magnus Maximus.

Having failed to gain access to Italy, in 406 the German Vandal tribes turned west and entered Gaul. In another orgy of destruction they ravaged one city after another: Mainz, Trier, Rheims, Tournai, Terouenre, Arass and Amiens. It was this trail of devastation and woe that motivated the British Emperor, Constantine Coronog, to cross over to Gaul with as many men as he could muster. They were immediately attacked by Stilicho and his 'Roman' army, who feared that were Constantine to enter Italy his own position and that of his puppet Emperor Honorius would be threatened. Eventually, by uniting with the Franks, the Britons were successful in driving the duplicitous Stilicho and his forces out of Gaul. The united forces of the Franks and Britons now took on the Vandal horde in what was to turn out to be a decisive battle. Godigisel was defeated and the Vandals were penned into southern Gaul. Later his son Gunderic was allowed to lead the remaining Vandals and their allies from Gaul into Spain. Here they remained for the next twenty-two years, causing all sorts of mayhem, whilst the Alans and Sueves settled permanently in northern Spain.

In 428 Gunderic's son Gaiseric, who was born around 400 and was therefore a boy at the time of the great Spanish migration, became king. The following year he led the Vandal horde, which, not counting the women, numbered 80,000, into Africa. They arrived at an opportune time when the whole province was in religious turmoil and were easily able to overrun most of its cities. Ten years later, in 439, having already taken control of the rest of the province, they seized Carthage. To secure his new kingdom, Gaiseric immediately set about refortifying the port and building a new fleet. This he put to good effect by blockading Rome and effectively starving it into submission. A peace treaty was signed whereby the Emperor recognized the autonomy of the Vandal state, ceding most of north-west Africa in the process.

All remained reasonably peaceable until in 455 the Emperor Valentinian III murdered his most able general, Aetius, the man who at Châlons-sur-Marne had defeated the forces of Attila the Hun. Outraged, Aetius's lieutenants retaliated by killing Valentinian. A new Emperor, Maximus, who had in fact been implicated in both murders, now married Eudoxia, Valentinian III's widow. She, however, was not happy with the situation and appealed to Gaiseric the Vandal for help, thus giving him the excuse he needed to sack Rome. The Vandals took the city without difficulty and proceeded to loot it systematically, even stripping the roofs of the temples and palaces. They also took away the treasures of Jerusalem, which had been brought to Rome by Vespasian following the temple's destruction in AD 70. The Empress Eudoxia, along with her daughters, was taken back alive to Carthage.

The power of the Vandal Empire was now approaching its zenith. In 460 a new Emperor, Marjorian, who had successfully driven the Vandals out of southern Italy, was unable to return to Italy from Gibraltar when Gaiseric attacked his fleet while it was lying at anchor. The Vandals seized most of the ships, leaving the Emperor helpless, on the wrong side of the Straits, with a massive army and few supplies. Consequently Marjorian was deposed and a new Emperor, Livius Severus, appointed. He, and a new eastern Emperor called Leo, sent embassies to Gaiseric and secured the release of Eudoxia and her daughter Placida in return for Valentinian's treasures. Eudoxia's other daughter, also called Eudoxia, was kept as a pawn by the Vandal king, to be married off in due course to his son Huneric. After further battles with both Rome and Constantinople, Gaiseric died in 477.

The Vandals' naval Empire, inherited by the next king, Huneric, was now quite large. It embraced all of north Africa, the Balearic Islands, Corsica, Sardinia and many other small islands. At first the new king was weak in the face of outside demands. He returned Valentinian's treasures to Eudoxia and allowed the appointment of a new bishop to the see of Carthage. Faced by a revolt of the Moors, he was forced to fight and this seems to have transformed his personality from one of mildness to one of cruelty. In a reign of terror, he murdered most of his own family as well as friends and nobles, all in the cause of securing the succession for his son Hilderic. However, the Germanic code dictated that rulership was not hereditary but that kings be elected from suitable candidates. So when Huneric died in 484 he was succeeded not by his son but by the latter's cousin, Gunthramund. He in turn was succeeded by his brother Thrasamund. It was not until he also died, in 523, that Hilderic finally gained the throne. He turned out to be a disastrous choice and in 530 was deposed in favour of Gelimer, a great-grandson of Gaiseric.

By this time the tide had firmly turned on the Vandal Empire and after their many setbacks the Romans were determined to bring it to an end. In 532 Justinian I, who was probably the greatest of the Byzantine Emperors (that is, the Emperors of the eastern part of the Roman Empire, which survived the western part), made peace with the Persians, freeing his forces and therefore enabling him to send his most gifted general, Belisarius, to deal with the Vandals, who were by now a menace to shipping in the eastern Mediterranean as well as the west. Belisarius brought with him 30,000 infantry and 5,000 knights, but even this large force would not have been enough had he not also had the good fortune to arrive at a time when the main Vandal army was away in Sardinia. Consequently he was easily able to take Carthage.

The Vandal fleet returned to find themselves locked out of their main cities. In an attempt to dislodge the Byzantines, they wrecked what was left of the province, destroying the irrigation systems on which its agriculture depended. Though King Gelimer was eventually captured and taken back to Constantinople, this was by no means the end of the war, which rumbled on until 548. Then, realizing that staying in Africa was pointless, as the country was devastated, the remaining Vandals boarded their ships and left.

Procopius, the war correspondent sent with General Belisarius by the

Emperor Justinian, details the fifteen-year war between the Byzantines and Vandals and how the former strove to drive the latter out of Africa. Several times he refers to their king as the 'King of Africa', the same name used by British historians such as Geoffrey to describe King Gormund. The exact relationship of Gormund to Gelimer isn't known. He may have been a son but could have been a brother or cousin. What is stated by Procopius is that the entire Vandal nation took ship and sailed away from north Africa. As Vandal fleets of over 500 ships were not uncommon, the idea of a massive fleet able to evacuate the entire nation of some 160,000 people should not be discounted, as has been the academic practice. It seems strange that until now no one seems to have traced where they went. The disappearance of a 'King of Africa' from Africa and the appearance at around the same date of a 'King of Africa' in Ireland and Britain seems more than coincidental.

According to the *Bruts*, Gormund and his army laid waste a large part of Britain, destroying towns and cities. He and his men also burnt down churches, forcing the archbishops of London and York to flee to Wales with their precious collections of holy relics. In a lament, to be echoed in the work of Gildas, Tysylio blames the disunity of the Britons for this calamity which finally lost them control of England. Unfortunately Gormund and his host are not mentioned in *The Anglo-Saxon Chronicle*, and as a result this crucial event in English as well as Welsh history is never discussed in modern history books.

THE INVASION OF THE PIGS

As Alan and Baram had suggested, I read the Mabinogi story, 'Culhwch and Olwen', the tale concerning the hunt for a ferocious wild boar called Twrch Trwyth. This was a fairy tale with hidden meaning, for in reality Twrch Trwyth 'was a king, but because of his sins God turned him into a pig'.[1] King Arthur's task (really one of a series of impossible 'labours' set for his kinsman Culhwch by the giant father of the latter's would-be bride, Olwen) was to obtain a 'comb and shears' that lay between the ears of the boar. This was clearly not going to be easy, for in one passage the spokesman of the pigs (the king's commanders who had been turned into pigs) says: 'For the sake of Him who put this form upon us, we will neither say nor do anything for Arthur. God did us injury enough, making pigs out of us, without your coming to fight us . . . Tomorrow we will start out for Arthur's country, and once there we will do the greatest possible damage.' The great boar hunt begins in Ireland but then Twrch Trwyth and his 'piglets' swim across to Wales. In a series of battles, fought all along the way through south Wales, one after another of Arthur's valiant knights is killed and still the boar remains undefeated. He crosses the River Severn and ravages Cornwall before Arthur eventually obtains the comb and the boar disappears across the sea.

In the story King Arthur goes to Ireland to do battle with Twrch Trwyth – whose name means 'the hog which lies' – along with his nine piglets. The Saxons and the Vandals venerated the boar. It was considered sacred to their gods, and they often had helmets made with boar crests. A well known example of such a 'boar' helmet is the 'Benty Grange Helmet', which is dated to the mid to late seventh century; and several others of these helmets have been found, including the recently discovered 'Pioneer Helmet', found in April 1997 in a quarry in Northamptonshire, which is dated to the late sixth and early seventh centuries – just the time in question. 'Obtaining the comb', which Arthur was charged to achieve, refers to the practice of tonsuring defeated enemies and forcing them to choose between death or becoming monks.

When the Vandals disappeared from the Mediterranean area in 548, as far as the Romans were concerned it was a case of good riddance. Their historians don't have anything else to add to the matter. But there is strong evidence that the Vandals boarded their ships and made a beeline for Ireland. This was not a stupid thing to do. The Vandals desperately needed a new homeland and Ireland was sufficiently out of the way for them to be well clear of Byzantine interference. They had, however, reckoned without King Arthur.

Alan explained to me (with a warning that it was complicated) that the reason Arthur would have involved himself in this was that he had relatives in Ireland. In the Welsh records there are many references to a character called Brychan, or Brychan of Brecon. Actually there were three Brychans, living at different times, and their careers have become mixed up. This is why in various manuscripts Brychan is listed as having had twenty-four sons and twelve daughters. The second of the three Brychans was first cousin to Arthur II. His mother, called Marchell, was the sister of Arthur's father Meurig. She married a king named Enllech Coronog, who, though he was descended from Cuneda Wledig ('Lord of the Restoration'), had a principality in Ireland. (Recently, he added, the Irish have announced the discovery of a 'Roman' fortress near Dublin.

Perhaps when this is properly examined, it will be found to have been British of this era.)

Brychan II, the son of Enllech Coronog, ruled over a principality centred on Brecon and is a very important figure in our history as the progenitor of saints. He married his first cousin, Arthur's sister Eurbrawst, and was the father of a daughter called Tydfil (Theodora), amongst others.[2] Through his connections with Brychan, therefore, Arthur II had family business in Ireland and would not have been prepared to allow the Vandals to take over without a fight. Accordingly he assembled his fleet and sailed over the Irish Sea to confront Gormund. However, no sooner had he arrived than the Vandals climbed back into their ships and set sail for Wales, landing at Milford Haven on the coast of Pembroke. Arthur II had to follow them and it was then that the pursuit – described in the Mabinogi story as of the 'hog' and his nine piglets – took place, right across Wales to the banks of the River Severn. Eventually the Vandals crossed over into England to settle in the East Midlands area. According to the *Bruts*, once he had pillaged Britain, Gormund handed England to the Saxons, for it was they who had invited him over in the first place. It is from this time that the name 'Lloegres' for this part of the island was changed to 'England'. This too is recorded in the *Bruts of England*.[3] However, the *Bruts*'s statement that Gormund then crossed the Channel to plunder Gaul is not supported by Frankish records of the time. Alan and Baram believe that after Gormund's battles with Arthur, his people settled in the East Midlands of England and became known as the Mercians. (They have documented this in their books, *Artorius Rex Discovered* and *King Arthur, King of Gwent and Glamorgan.*) This is neither discussed nor understood by historians who ignore the Welsh stories.

In *The Anglo-Saxon Chronicle*, the best known record of the invasion and conquest of England by the Saxons, there is complete silence concerning the formation and foundation of the kingdom of Mercia, for long the most powerful of the Anglo-Saxon principalities. It is not until a king called Penda 'inherits the kingdom' in 626 that a Mercian king is mentioned at all. This is not surprising, given that *The Anglo-Saxon Chronicle* was compiled to celebrate the ascendancy of the House of Wessex.[4] Yet Mercia, the kingdom that ruled over the Midlands of England and which dominated England throughout the seventh century, was in fact already a powerful state before the rise of Wessex. Fortunately the gaps in the records of Wessex are covered by the history

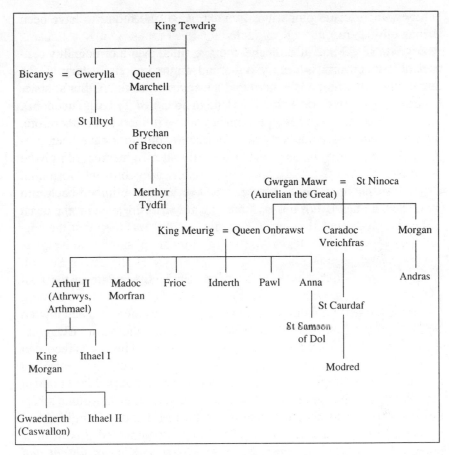

THE FAMILY TREE OF ARTHUR II (ATHRWYS)
Diagram 12

of Nennius, which gives king lists for Mercia as well as the other Saxon successor-states of England. In each case these go back to a common ancestor named as 'Woden' or 'Voden'. By comparing the king list of Mercia with the known descent of the Vandal kings, Alan and Baram have been able to show that they were one and the same.

With Alan's explanations, supported by the notes he and Baram gave me, and my own reading, the story of the Germanic invasion of Britain was becoming very clear. Throughout the Roman period, the region of Germany north and east of their own provinces as well as most of Holland, Denmark and probably southern Sweden was called Scythia.

There were a number of tribes, who may be collectively described as Saxon, living in this region, including the Franks, Goths, Alemanni, Burgundiones, Marcomanni and the Quadi. Other Saxon tribes there would have been the Jutes, who under Hengist and Horsa migrated to Kent from Jutland and Friesia, and of course the Vandals, who came to Britain via Spain, Africa and Ireland. Though these invasions appear on the surface to have been piecemeal events, in fact, as centuries later when the Vikings made a similar concerted attempt at the seizure of England, they were all part and parcel of a large migration of related tribes.

Had Arthur II simply had to deal with invasions by Saxons he would have had his hands full but, as Alan and Baram were now to explain to me, even God seemed to be against him.

CHAPTER SIXTEEN

THE LOST CITY

On one of our journeys Alan and I travelled again to the Midlands of England, this time to visit the Romano-British city of Wroxeter. The ruins of this city, once linked to London by the old Watling Street, are in Shropshire on the borders between Wales and England. Long abandoned, the city was only rediscovered when a mosaic was found there in the eighteenth century. Since then it has been the subject of several excavations revealing impressive ruins. It is now generally recognized that during Roman times it was the fourth largest city in Britain, larger than Bath, Caerleon or Gloucester. Even this estimate may have to be revised upwards, for recent work involving aerial photography and ground-penetrating radar has revealed that at one time Wroxeter spread far out into the surrounding fields, so whilst it was probably always smaller than London, it may at one time have been larger than York and Colchester too. That such a large city should have disappeared without trace is one of the great mysteries of history. Even more so is the fact that it doesn't seem to be mentioned anywhere in Roman records.

Arriving at Wroxeter, we got out of the car and made our way onto the site. Most of the city, particularly its residential quarters, is still un-excavated, but even so there was enough on view to get an impression of what it must have been like. The most striking feature was a large section of red-brick wall, part of the complex associated with an exercise hall and public baths. These had evidently been elaborate affairs with under-floor heating, steam baths, saunas and plunge pools. The gym itself had been an enormous hall – as big as a cathedral – with colonnades and porticoes supporting its roof. One could easily imagine soldiers practising their martial arts within its cavernous interior, though it could as well have been used by citizens for the ancient equivalent of aerobics. Either way, it was curious that this temple of the body was the best pre-served part of the city and it gave a perhaps unbalanced idea that whoever had built the city was fitness mad.

Alan had a different perspective on all this, as he explained to me the significance of the ruins. 'The importance of this city,' he began, 'has been greatly underestimated, even by our Romano-centric academia, but this is perhaps changing now that in the last year or two it has been realized just how extensive the ruins of this city really are. Perhaps others will come to share our belief that for much of the period in question it was not just an urban sprawl but a royal capital.'

The history of Wroxeter seems to have begun with the establishment of a temporary fortress for the fourteenth Roman legion at some time around AD 58. This time-frame corresponds with the chronology of events that saw the Romans, under Suetonius, carrying out operations in north Wales. It was he who led a force across the Mona Straits into Anglesey, where they massacred the inhabitants and cut down groves of oak trees, sacred to the Druids. It is presumed that he used Wroxeter as some sort of base camp during these operations. However, this fortress can't have been in use very long, for in AD 60 Suetonius had to deal with the Boudicca rebellion in the London area, the fourteenth legion being withdrawn from north Wales for this campaign and never returning. Although historians assume that the fortress was subsequently re-used by the twentieth legion prior to Agricola's removal of it to Scotland c. AD 80, there is no evidence for this and, said Alan, such a scenario flies in the face of events as written in the Welsh records.

The evidence of archaeology shows that Wroxeter grew in wealth and prestige through ensuing centuries. The heated Roman baths and gym-nasium must be amongst the most elaborate of such structures not just in Britain but in all of Europe. Recent surveys with ground-penetrating radar have also revealed the outlines of a large building believed to have been a church, proving that the city was Christian from an early date. This evidence convinces Alan and Baram that Wroxeter was actually the royal capital of Britain in Roman times.

They also believe that it was the city called Caer Effrawg in Welsh, a name that is generally translated as 'York' but really means 'Castle of the Hebrews'; and that Wroxeter is therefore the original 'York'. This might seem ludicrous at first, but there is evidence to support it. In the histories we are told that two Emperors died at a place called York: first of all Septimius Severus in 211 and then Constantius, the father of Constantine, in 306. Since, as Alan put it, 'They didn't have refrigerated transport to take their bodies back to Rome, even if that is what they would have wanted,' we would therefore expect that they would have had tombs or at least cenotaphs in Britain. These are not to be found at present-day York, or anywhere else in the east of England for that matter. However, there are two Constantine mounds in Wales, just to the west of Shrewsbury, one of which may be that of Constantius. Just to the south-east of Wroxeter is the village of Eaton Constantine, where there are the remains of large marching camps. A stone with the inscription 'SEVERINI FILI SEVERI' is documented by Samuel Lewis in his 1883 *Topical Dictionary of Wales* as being at Abernant in south Wales. According to local legends this Severini was a Roman general who died in battle near there. It is difficult to see how this could be anyone other than Septimius Severus, whose father was called Marcus Didius Salvius Julianus Severus. Nobody has been able to account for these monuments or why they should be where they are. That both are much nearer to Wroxeter than York adds weight to the idea that this city was the original York and that it, not the present-day York, which anyway was called Eboracum by the Romans, was the real capital of the kings of Britain. This makes sense, for unlike York, which is on the eastern periphery of England, Wroxeter was near the centre of the island, midway between the garrison towns of Chester and Caerleon. From here forces could be sent to repel Irish invasions from the west and Scottish invasions from the north. Watling Street meant that the kings also had a direct link to London and the south-east, should trouble arise from that direction. The religious centre of Glastennen, near to old Loytcoyt or Letocetum, was also just a few miles down the road. The large number of tumuli at nearby Oldbury, where Alan and Baram found the gravestone of Arthur I, son of Magnus Maximus, indicate that this was an area where many British nobles chose to be buried.

All this would be uncontested had Wroxeter, like York, survived to become an important city in the Middle Ages. Unfortunately, a combination of human and natural catastrophes that affected Britain in the fifth and sixth centuries led to its being abandoned. Whereas other places, perhaps equally badly affected, were rebuilt by the Saxons, Vikings, Normans or whoever, this city disappeared from view as completely as if it had been in the jungles of Central America. In time it was completely forgotten and all references to it were assumed to be about York.

'This is what we think,' said Alan. 'You look around and make up your own mind.' We walked around in silence for an hour or so, admiring the cemented bricks which had survived for nearly two millennia and taking pictures of the gymnasium and other obvious structures, before making our way back to the car via the tourist bureau where we had come in. At the office I purchased a small guidebook which I later studied in depth. This provided a great deal of useful information concerning both what had been found on the site and its dates, interpreted with a strongly Roman slant. However, reading the archaeology in the context of British history as presented by Nennius, Tysylio, Geoffrey of Monmouth, Percy Enderbee and other sources, a completely different picture of the city's significance emerged.

By AD 70 Britain, part of it controlled by its native kings, who were Christian, though ostensibly under Roman rule, was as yet very far from being a Roman province. Indeed the conquest was never as complete or as deep as most modern historians would have us believe. Even though Caradoc and his family were taken off to Rome, war raged on in the west and north of Britain for another generation. In AD 70 the Roman general Agricola with his twentieth legion was stationed in Deva (Chester). He returned to Rome three years later to be made a consul and take on the governorship of Aquitaine. Then in AD 79 he returned to Britain, this time fighting wars in Scotland. He is credited with defeating the Caledonians but more importantly he seems to have succeeded in per-suading the British to build cities after the Roman manner. One such was Wroxeter, which, as we have seen, grew in the second and third centuries to become possibly the second largest city in Britain.

The pamphlet agreed that the fortress had been used as a military depot of some sort from about AD 58 to 90. After that, or so the archae-ological evidence implied, it 'was handed over to the civil authorities'. The fortress was then demolished and a brand new city, on the Roman model, built in its place. As we have seen, British traditional histories state that subsequent to the death of his brother Guiderius, Gweirydd (Arviragus) became the leader of Lloegrian resistance to Roman occupation. London and the south-east having been lost, he was most likely to have been active in this part of England on the borders of Wales, in alliance with the Khymry of south Wales. Following the first rebellion of the Iceni in AD 47 and the capture of Caradoc in AD 51, he seems to have made some sort of peace treaty with the Romans, involving a marriage between himself and a daughter of Claudius. When the Iceni revolted again under Boudicca in AD 60, he seems to once more have gone to war with the Romans. Finally, following her death, he again found a *modus vivendi* with the Romans, probably based on trade agreements, thus freeing Agricola to take his twentieth legion into Scotland to fight a common enemy, the Caledonian Picts. Part of this agreement seems to have been the building of Wroxeter in suitably advanced style for a capital city and in accordance with Agricola's policy, which was to persuade the Britons, especially their leaders, to adopt Roman ways.

I found supporting evidence for a linguistic connection between Arviragus and Wroxeter. Wroxeter is a shortened form of Wrox-chester or Wroc-castra, 'the fortress of Wroc'. However, in Roman times it was called not this but Viroconium Cornoviorum. The second part of the name derives from that of the local tribe, the Cornovii, but academic opinion is divided concerning the origins of the word Viroconium. In the course of a long article contained in a book entitled *The Place Names of Britain*, the authors, Rivet and Smith, put forward a case for believing it was derived from someone's proper name.

It could be . . . we have in Viroconium[1] a personal name plus suffix. The place-name Viroconium might therefore more properly be Viriconium to be analysed in British terms as **Uirico-* with suffixes *-on-io-* as in CANONIUM, etc.; a meaning 'town of *Uirico-' is likely, and is one of the possibilities admitted by Jackson in his study of the name in *Britannia*, I (1970), 81. The name presumably applied originally to the hill-fort on the Wrekin, and was transferred to the Roman fortress and town which grew from it.[2]

If this is the case, the likelihood is that the city was named after Gweirydd, for the probable pronunciation of his name would have been 'Wiridd'. A place called Uiri-conium and pronounced 'Wiri-conium', losing the Welsh 'dd' sound, is not out of the question. It could also be, of course, that the name Viroconium is derived from the name Arviragus. Either way, the scenario that emerges is of a British king making peace with the Romans and then employing Roman builders to turn his hill-fort stronghold into a regional capital. This would agree with the story told in the *Brut Tysylio* about the founding of a city on the River Severn following the marriage of Arviragus to Genuissa, the daughter of Claudius: 'Claudius also built a city on the Severn, which from his name was called Claudii castra on the boundary between Wales and England.'[3]

The story is enlarged upon by Geoffrey of Monmouth in his *History*, where he identifies the city with Gloucester:

> At the end of that winter the messengers returned with Claudius' daughter and handed her over to her father. The girl's name was Genvissa. Her beauty was such that everyone who saw her was filled with admiration. Once she had been united to him in lawful marriage, she inflamed the king with such burning passion that he preferred her company to anything else in the world. As a result of this Arviragus made up his mind to give some special mark of distinction to the place where he had married her. He suggested to Claudius that the two of them should found there a city which should perpetuate in times to come so happy a marriage. Claudius agreed and ordered a town to be built which should be called Kaerglou or Gloucester.[4]

Now as we have seen, according to Welsh records Gloucester was founded in the third century by Gloyw Gwalltir or Gloyw wlad lydan ('Claudius of the Extensive Country'), who is probably to be identified with the Emperor Claudius II *c.* 260. Geoffrey is therefore wrong in believing that Claudius I, who died in AD 54, could have had anything to do with the foundation of Gloucester. On the other hand, Viroconium is on both the River Severn and the borders of England and Wales; furthermore it is in what was then a highly strategic location, as it overlooks a ford on the River Severn at the point where it meets with Watling Street – the route that would have been taken by Ostorius Scapula when he invaded north Wales in AD 48. The neighbouring British hill fort would have been important at the time. It is therefore tempting to think that it was at Wroxeter, not Gloucester, that Arviragus entertained his new wife and invited Claudius, in her honour, to build him a new city in the Roman manner. The archaeological evidence supports the suggestion that Claudius I was responsible for the building of the first Roman fort at Wroxeter, quite possibly during the period of peace that all the annals say ensued upon the marriage of his daughter to Arviragus in AD 52. It was Claudius himself who brought the fourteenth legion to Britain and it was this force that was subsequently stationed at Wroxeter until AD 60 and the revolt of Boudicca. Later on other kings and Emperors, notably Hadrian, added to the grandeur of Wroxeter, steadily enlarging the city throughout the second and third centuries. Further, since the church is believed to be one of the oldest in Britain, it is not impossible that it dates from the time of Arviragus and may even have been founded by St Ilid himself.

On looking deeper into the matter I discovered that Alan's suggestion that the medievals confused York with Wroxeter or Viroconium Cornoviorum was also not at all unlikely. There is no doubting that York too was an important city, serving as a port of supply for northern Britain. However, its modern name of York is derived not from the Roman Eboracum but from the Viking name for it: Yarvik. It is very easy to see how medieval monks could confuse written historical references to a city called Viroconium or Uiroconium (possibly shortened to Uiroco and pronounced 'Yuroco') with the city they knew as York, particularly as all traces of ancient Wroxeter had disappeared by that time and there was no evidence then of how large a city Wroxeter once was.

THE COMING OF THE DRAGON

There is still, however, the perplexing question of how it was that Wroxeter experienced such a devastating collapse. What was it that caused this thriving metropolis, which by rights should have grown by now to be a Birmingham or Manchester, to be abandoned? This too was a subject to which Alan and Baram had given much thought and on our way back down the M5 Alan explained their theories and how these tied up with what is written in the histories.

'Around the period of the mid sixth century, arguably the most awesome event in the whole of British recorded and remembered history took place. As far as can be gleaned and calculated from the many surviving records, it was a tremendous catastrophe which befell the British nation. Although this is detailed in a number of authentic records, conventional history books written either for schools or for the public at large never mention a single word about it. It is as though in a few centuries' time the Jews were to forget all about the Holocaust or the Irish the potato famine.

'Unmentioned and unremarked by modern archaeologists there are, beneath the sea at Cardiff, the remains of the great stone port of the

Welsh monarchs. This seems to have been submerged around this time. Likewise, on the other side of the Channel and in the Scilly Isles, areas sank beneath the waves, giving rise to stories about the lost land of Lyonesse. It would also seem that the sinking or inundation of Heligoland, an area of submerged land that has been explored by divers off the coast of Denmark, was a result of this same catastrophe. Both here and around the Scillies there are submerged walls as evidence that fields at one time stretched out under what is now sea. Mainland Britain was also affected, areas of Cardigan Bay and the Conway Estuary sinking beneath the waves.

'Of course the people witnessing these events didn't use modern scientific language to describe what was clearly a natural disaster. It was viewed, at least by the monks who wrote about it, as God's punishment of Britain for the sins of its people. The agent of this punishment was a comet, pictured as an awesome dragon. Strange as it may seem, what probably happened is that Britain was hit by a scatter of meteorites. Detailed analysis of the histories reveals that prior to this event a giant comet was seen in the skies, which approached close to our planet Earth. Whether it was this comet that showered Britain with debris as it passed by or another is not quite clear. What is recorded is that Britain was hit by something and most of the island was devastated by the enormous blast of this collision. Vast tracts were laid into total ruin. Nearly all the animals died, domesticated and wild, as did the birds, fish and reptiles. Even plants would not grow. Mud slithered everywhere, and clouds of gas enveloped the land with a poisonous mist. Winter descended suddenly and stayed for years, so that absolutely nothing could live in the wide sweep of stricken areas. It was like the aftermath of a nuclear assault.

'All across Britain walls were shaken to their very foundations and roofs slithered down in a rush of debris. Cities, towns, country villas and farms – the legacy of pre-Saxon Britain – tottered into ruin. The city of Wroxeter fell into ruin, never again to be inhabited or rebuilt. Survivors stumbled around the ruins of their homes under darkened skies full of poisonous clouds, droplets from which brought death to those who were unfortunate enough to be soaked by them. In one disastrous moment, a great and powerful state had been brought to its knees by what was interpreted as an act of God. Thus it was that the wasteland sung about by medieval troubadours and written of by Arthurian poets came into being. All this is detailed in sixth-century records.

It was to restore the kingdom, to find a cure for the sick land, that the Knights of the Round Table were sent in search of the Holy Grail. Only this most important relic, it was felt, had the power to effect such a cure and it was believed that its loss was what had so angered God that he had sent this terrible punishment. As the tale was told and retold, the reason for the quest was gradually forgotten, with the result that in the later romances of the Middle Ages there is only passing reference to the wasteland, and still less to what caused it. Yet that, on one level, is what the Grail story is all about – the search for an antidote.'

What Alan said about the destruction of Arthur's kingdom, though extraordinary, was not entirely unexpected. I had spent many years studying and reading about the Grail legend and was well aware that it had cosmic dimensions. For one thing the Grail itself is, as we have seen, at times referred to as a *lapis excilis*, believed to be a corruption of *lapis ex caelis* – 'stone from heaven'. The connection between this name and the idea of a falling meteorite was one I had considered before, but I had not connected the name with a comet or considered the consequences of a celestial body of any great size striking Britain. As I was still more than slightly sceptical about the scale of such a disaster, I decided to research the matter for myself and to check Alan's references. They seemed to bear out what he was saying. Gildas, for instance, had written that the island of Britain was set on fire from end to end, a level of destruction that could not be attributed to marauding Saxons alone.

The dragon-like quality of a comet that appeared around this time is something that needs closer scrutiny. In his *Brut*, Tysylio claims that the dragon-comet was first seen just prior to the reign of Arthur II's father, Utherpendragon, auguring both his own elevation and the birth of his hero son:

> At that time a star of amazing size appeared. It had one beam, and on the head of the beam was a ball of fire resembling a dragon; and from the jaws of the dragon two beams ascended, the one towards the extremity of France, and the other towards Ireland, subdividing itself into seven small beams.
>
> Uthyr and all around him, alarmed by such an appearance, enquired of the learned men what it might portend. Merddyn bursting into tears, exclaimed, 'Sons of Britain, ye have suffered an irrecoverable loss, ye are widowed of Emrys the Great.[5] But still ye

have a king. Haste thou therefore, Uthyr, and engage the enemy, for the whole island shall be thine. For it is thou, Uthyr, who art signified by this star with the head of a dragon. By the beam pointing over France is denoted a son of thine, who shall be great in wealth, and extensive in sway, and by that directed towards Ireland, a daughter, whose sons and grandsons shall successively govern the whole.[6]

It was a terrifying apparition, for comets are generally to be interpreted as negative auguries; however, in Tysylio's account this is neutralized by identifying the negative or baleful influence of the comet with the death of Emrys. A more optimistic spin is then put on events by equating Uther (Meurig) himself with the comet and his daughter Anna and son Arthur with its twin tails. To reinforce these positive links between himself and what is clearly seen as a death-star, Uther has two dragon talismans made for himself:

Uthyr recollecting the words of Merddyn, when the ceremony [his coronation after the death of Emrys] was over, commanded two dragons of gold, and exquisite workmanship, to be made, in form similar to that which he had seen on the head of the comet's beam of light. One of these he deposited in the principal church at Winchester, the other he made his standard to be carried before his army. From this circumstance he was thenceforward called Uthyr Pendragon[7] [Uther of the Dragon's Head].[8]

The connection between the king and the dragon-star carries on to the next generation, for later, before the Battle of Baedan, Arthur II himself wears a helmet in the form of a fiery dragon:

Arthur then put on a breast plate, worthy of a king; a gilt helmet, on which were the image of a fiery dragon, and another device called Prydwenn,[9] in which was the carved image of the Virgin, which Arthur usually wore when going to a perilous engagement. He also put on his sword, called Caledvwlch,[10] as it was the best in Britain and had been made at Afallach. He also took in his hand a spear called Ron-cymmyniad [the spear of command].[11]

We have here a description of objects: sword, shield, helmet and armour, each with its own talismanic power. Arthur, like his father

Utherpendragon, is portrayed as invoking the power of the dragon or comet as his birthright. As it is Arthur II, not Utherpendragon who wears a dragon-helmet, it seems more logical that it was during his reign that the dragon-star made its appearance. As he was middle-aged when his father died, it probably augured the start of Arthur's region. Yet all the romances are agreed that the golden age of Arthur ended in strange circumstances: his kingdom was brought to an end not by the Saxons, whom he had defeated, but by the supernatural events surrounding the appearance of the Grail and the wasting of his land with perpetual winter. Could there be anything behind these stories?

Many of the old histories, the cornerstones of our research, mention a terrible plague that swept through Britain round about the time of the later Saxon invasions. In the *Brut Tysylio*, and consequently Geoffrey's *History*, this plague is projected several generations forward to the time of a Cadwallader[12], who seems to have died around the year 689. What is described is something which even by medieval standards is clearly perceived as having been a very abnormal event, certainly much worse than the Black Death:

> During these disturbances, a pestilence and a famine, sent from God as a punishment for their sins, fell upon the Britons so grievously that food was not to be had, saving what the chace [*sic*] could afford; and the living were, through hunger, unable to bury the dead. Such as were able to go to other countries did so, exclaiming, 'O Lord! thou hast given us to be a prey to wolves.' Cadwallader had a fleet prepared for him, and set sail for Bretagne, exclaiming in like manner, 'Woe to us sinners! by the multitude of our sins have we provoked our God: when we had a time to return to Him, we returned not, therefore doth He disperse us abroad; whom not the Roman power, nor any, save Himself, could thus disperse.'
>
> With such lamentations, Cadwallader approached the dwelling of Alan,[13] by whom he was welcomed thither most kindly. In Britain there were left, by the pestilence and famine, those only who retired into the forests, and lived by hunting, and mostly in the recesses of Wales. This calamity continued for eleven years.
>
> When it ceased, those of the Saxons who had escaped it, sent information to Germany, that the island was destitute of inhabitants, and advised them to come and take a cheap possession of it. That people therefore collected an immense number of men and women,

who landed in the north, and settled in the kingdom from Norway[14] to Cornwall; there remaining no Britons to oppose them.[15]

Graphic as is this description of the Cadwallader's woes, there is little evidence or likelihood that a plague on this scale actually befell the Britons at the period he is describing: around the end of the seventh century. *The Anglo-Saxon Chronicle* records the sun as having been darkened and a pestilence raging in Britain during 664 but this was for only one year. This may be what prompted Tysylio to choose a date around this time for the legendary plague, but it is hardly on the scale he describes. It also conflicts with all accounts concerning the Saxon takeover of England, which was all but complete by this time. However, project things back a century and a very different picture emerges. There is only one entry in *The Anglo-Saxon Chronicle* between 556 and 565. This entry, for 560, simply says that Ceawlin inherited the West-Saxon kingdom and Aelle the Northumbrian. Whatever else happened in this period is a complete blank as far as the later Saxon historiographers were concerned, which is curious considering that this is precisely the time that the comet was supposed to have struck.

What seems to have happened is a misidentification of who the 'Cadwallader' was at the time of the comet. It is more than likely that the 'Battle Sovereign' in question is really Arthur II, and that the Alan referred to was a king called Alan Fyrgam who ruled in Brittany during Arthur II's reign. Alan had fought alongside Arthur II at the Battle of Baedan and later acted as the latter's host when he and surviving Britons crossed the Channel to escape the 'Yellow Pestilence'. The identification of Arthur II as the Cadwallader during whose reign occurred the terrible scourge of the Yellow Pestilence is to be found in 'The Life of St Teilo', as contained in the Llandaff Charters. Teilo was Bishop of Llandaff Cathedral after Dyfrig (Dubricius), who crowned the young Arthur. He therefore ministered during the later part of Arthur II's reign, *c*. 550–65. That he witnessed the pestilence confirms that it happened in the time of Arthur II, not a 'Battle Sovereign' or Cadwallader of the seventh century.

> St. Teilo received the pastoral care of Llandaff, to which he had been consecrated, with all the adjacent diocese, that had belonged to his predecessor Dubricius; in which however he could not long remain, on account of the pestilence which nearly destroyed the whole

nation. It was called the Yellow Pestilence, because it occasioned all persons who were seized by it, to be yellow and without blood, and it appeared to men a column of a watery cloud, having one end trailing along the ground, and the other above, proceeding in the air, and passing through the whole country like a shower going through the bottom of valleys. Whatever living creatures it touched with its pestiferous blast, either immediately died, or sickened for death. If anyone endeavoured to apply a remedy to the sick person, not only had the medicines no effect, but the dreadful disorder brought the physician, together with the sick person, to death. For it seized Maelgwn, King of North Wales [actually it was probably Maelgwn of Llandaff] and destroyed his country; and so greatly did the aforesaid destruction rage throughout the nation, that it caused the country to be nearly deserted.[16]

Virtually the same words to describe the Yellow Pestilence are used in the *Life of St Oudoceus*, contained in the Llandoff Charters. St Oudoceus was a nephew of St Teilo and another of the great ornaments of the Welsh church. He returned to Wales with Teilo and later, in turn, became Bishop of Llandaff. The date of their return must have been after 562 when the plague had ceased. The idea of a watery cloud with one end trailing along the ground sounds remarkably like the sort of mushroom cloud one might see after a nuclear explosion. To these descriptions may be added a number of others that seem to be talking about some great catastrophe with effects not too dissimilar to what we would today expect as the result of a nuclear strike. That the victims of this plague were 'yellow and without blood' implies they suffered from a condition where so many of their red blood cells were destroyed in such a short time that their liver and spleen couldn't deal with the resultant bilirubin. This could have been the result of an infectious disease; but could it also have been something else, perhaps even a radiation sickness brought on by the fall-out from a comet? This is what I now wanted to find out.

THE STAR OF DEATH

Until very recently it was fashionable to believe that the planet on which we live, once a boiling cauldron of molten rock, has long since settled down into peaceful middle age; that, give or take the occasional earthquake, or volcanic eruption, our planet leads an untroubled life. Today, as I write this, comet Hale-Bopp, the brightest this century, is lighting up the night skies. It is millions of miles from us and there is no possibility of a collision with it, yet in space terms it is a very near miss. Two years ago the planet Jupiter was not so lucky when the fragmented comet Schumacher-Levy slammed into it. The impacts, though not directly visible from earth as they took place on Jupiter's far side, caused noticeable changes to its system of atmospheric rings. We can only imagine the enormous explosions and firestorms that must have caused such visible changes to the giant planet. The question on every astronomer's lips since then has been: could the same thing happen to planet Earth? The discomforting answer is a resounding yes; the question being not is it possible, but when will it happen? As the consequences of such a 'strike' would be devastating, possibly leading to the extinction of the human race, there has been a refocusing of attention, at least by some astronomers, away from the obscure metaphysics of the 'Big Bang' theories of the universe to matters closer to home in our own solar system.

The remarkable renaissance of catastrophism (the theory that changes in the earth's crust have occurred in sudden and violent events) as a branch of astrophysics is something of which few people are aware. This is not surprising, as it has really only developed as a recognized discipline over the course of the last ten years or so. Agreeably, given our interest in Britain, it is the British school, headed by Dr Victor Clube of the Oxford University Astrophysics Department, that is at the forefront of research into these matters. Alan and Baram had quoted Dr Clube as an expert on the subject of cometary impacts with the Earth, and in particular on the event which they said took place in Britain during the sixth century. As there is little written about this,[17] other than one or two papers, I decided to ask Dr Clube if we could meet and discuss the whole subject in person. Thus it was that I found myself in the Department of Astrophysics at Oxford University with the man who is probably the world's foremost authority on the influence of comets on world history.

It very quickly became clear that behind Dr Clube's affable exterior lay a mind of great originality. Using the tools of physics he and his colleagues had examined the orbits of a large number of fragments from what was once a spectacular comet, which had, they believed, interacted with the Earth on more than one occasion, causing widespread damage. Could this, I wondered, have been the comet signifying the birth of

Arthur? Was it this which caused the strange yellow plague? These were questions I put to him as we sat together in his little office.

'Well,' he said, taking over the lead in our conversation, which till then had consisted mainly of the usual pleasantries, 'before we can talk sensibly about the Dark Ages, we need to set out the framework of what this is all about.' There is now little doubt, he continued, that it was a cosmic event that wiped out the dinosaurs. It has been suggested that a bolide of only about ten kilometres in diameter was responsible for their demise. If a rock this size, smaller than the Isle of Wight, struck the Earth it would have caused an explosion immeasurably greater than that of the nuclear bomb dropped at Hiroshima and raised a dust cloud that would have blanketed the sun for several years. Under these conditions most vegetation would have died and the cold-blooded dinosaurs would have been wiped out. When the clouds eventually thinned out, the coast would have been clear for furry mammals to inherit the earth.

'This, with some modifications, is the current view on how the Cretaceous Age came to an end and the Tertiary began. The discovery of a stratigraphic layer containing abnormally high amounts of the extra-terrestrial metal iridium corresponding to this event confirms that in essence this is what happened. Whilst we can take some comfort that events on this scale are rare – taking place on average once every fifty to one hundred million years as far as we can tell – we shouldn't be too complacent, as lesser impacts happen with much greater frequency.

'Modern scientific catastrophism is a space-age phenomenon. Until the late 1960s it was generally believed that there was little risk of the Earth being struck by anything larger than a meteorite. It was also believed that the visible craters on the moon were all formed long ago when the solar system was still young. The possibility that the Earth and moon are still, even today, liable to be struck occasionally by larger objects in the range of 100–1,000 metres in diameter was dismissed as unlikely in the extreme. Catastrophism was deeply out of fashion whilst its opposite, uniformitarianism (the theory that geological processes are always due to continuously and uniformly operating forces), held the field. As a result of the Apollo and other missions to the moon, this view has had to be radically altered. We now know that craters formed as a result of impact are being created on the moon all the time. Some of these, such as the Giordano Bruno crater, which has been shown to be the result of an event witnessed by one Gervase of Canterbury in 1178, are relatively large. The Giordano Bruno crater resulted from the impact of a bolide a few kilometres in diameter. Though this is much smaller than the body that caused the dinosaur extinctions, it would still have involved a release of energy equivalent that of a 100,000 megaton H-bomb, or about ten times the combined nuclear arsenal of the world. Had it struck the Earth and not the moon, then it would have caused a world-wide catastrophe – a cosmic winter. Viewing the event in this way we realize that we on Earth had a very lucky escape. Mercifully, such events are not that frequent, but the lunar landscape shows that smaller events than this, involving bolides between 100 and 1,000 metres, happen on Earth on average about once a century.

Dr Clube explained that to understand such events it is necessary to know a little bit about current theories concerning the origins of comets and what happens to them once they enter the inner solar system. New comets are being discovered all the time, though usually they are barely visible to the naked eye. The recent Hale-Bopp, which gave such a spectacular show at the start of 1997, is an example of a previously unknown comet. The current model – and there is good evidence for this – indicates that outside the orbits of the outermost planets there is a region called the 'Oort cloud'. In this region, which is still part of the solar system even though it extends to almost half the distance between the sun and our nearest stellar companion, comets are born. How comets are made is still a mystery. There are probably many thousands of them out there, each one capable of causing a dinosaur extinction should they collide with the Earth. These bodies follow more or less stable orbits around the sun but occasionally one is deflected out of the Oort cloud[18] and moves into an elliptical orbit that swings through the inner solar system. Mostly such comets are harmless visitors from outer space, but once in a while one moves into an orbit that crosses that of the Earth. It is then that we have the potential for collisions.

When people think of cometary collisions they generally imagine a single, large impact, but such events rarely, if ever, happen. New comets are largely made up of dust, ice and other volatile chemicals. Generally speaking, as a result of the gravitational pull of the sun or collisions with objects such as asteroids, they fragment into smaller pieces. Each time a comet approaches the sun, some of its ice melts, giving rise to one or more cometary tails. These are composed of water vapour, dust, charged ions and other volatile molecules blown away from the comet by the solar wind.[19] For this reason the tail or tails generally point away from the sun. However, sometimes, when a comet is exactly in the plane of the ecliptic (the sun's path), illuminated dust can give the impression of a silvery 'sword' projecting from the cometary head towards the sun. Dust particles spread throughout the orbit of the comet and these 'vapour trails' will produce showers of meteors or shooting stars should the Earth pass through such a dust cloud. Larger particles, say the size of peas, give rise to fireballs as they burn up in the upper atmosphere. These are spectacular events when they happen, rather like firework rockets exploding. Young comets – those which have not passed close to the sun very often – are generally much more luminous than older ones which have visited the inner solar system many times and thereby had their supply of ice and other volatiles burnt off. Some comets melt away entirely, whilst others have rocky cores like asteroids. As these comets get older so they break up into a swarm of rocks, boulders and other debris, becoming virtually invisible in the process.

Dr Clube and his colleagues have been examining such a 'swarm', which seems to be the remnants of a giant, earth-crossing comet that they think made its first appearance in the inner solar system around 30,000 years ago. The dust trail from this comet gives rise to the Taurid-Arietid meteor shower that occurs twice every year, around the end of June and November. Though this is no cause for alarm, larger remnants of this comet are life-threatening. Two of these fragments are comet Encke, which may be the core of the original proto-comet, and a body called Hephaistos. Though they now have different orbits from one another, Dr Clube and his colleagues have been able to show that these two bodies, as well as an asteroid called Oljato and several other objects of a few kilometres in diameter, were once constituent parts of the same parent comet. An encounter with one of these larger chunks of the original comet would be quite catastrophic but is fortunately unlikely. However, these larger chunks are accompanied by many smaller objects of perhaps only 100 metres or so in diameter. Encounters with these are relatively frequent and can be quite dramatic.

In 1908 a spectacular event took place at Tunguska in Siberia. As it came crashing down to earth, a large boulder, which Dr Clube thinks was a fragment about 100 metres in diameter of the former comet, exploded in the air eight kilometres above ground. The explosion and its accompanying fireball was the equivalent of a forty- to fifty-megaton bomb. The sky was lit up as far away as northern Europe and for nine days people were able to play cricket, read the papers and take pho-tographs at midnight. At the site of the explosion, fortunately in an almost uninhabited area of forest, there was complete devastation, trees being flattened for a distance of forty miles.

It is hits from boulders of this size that pose the greater danger to mankind, not the risk of a once-in-a-hundred-million-year chance of a strike by a large comet such as that which caused the dinosaurs to become extinct. On average we can expect one Tunguska-type event per century. This doesn't sound a lot but masks the fact that at certain times the risk is much greater than at others. The orbital period of the Taurid-Arietid swarm is stable at approximately three years, its elliptical path stretching out beyond Mars. Though the orbit of the swarm passes through that of the Earth, it does not always intersect with our orbit. This is difficult to explain in non-technical terms, but suffice it to say that there are periods lasting a century or so when the orbit of the Earth intersects that of the swarm. This does not mean that there will necessarily be a collision but it makes it possible, should the Earth and the swarm be at a point where their orbits meet. On average we would expect there to be a higher risk of collision with fragments of this comet for one hundred out of every six hundred years.

Recently Dr Clube's team have been able to analyse data concerning comets as observed by Chinese astronomers over the past two millennia. This shows peaks of activity roughly every five to six hundred years on average, confirming that their model is substantially correct. Now it just so happens that during the fifth and sixth centuries, at the start of the Dark Ages, there was such a peak of activity. Thus the idea that Britain was hit by one or more fireballs at this time, as a result of the Earth passing through the Taurid-Arietid swarm, is by no means far-fetched. In fact, the historical evidence is compelling. Gildas's assertion that the island of Britain was on fire from end to end may well have been the case, even though the scars of such a conflagration are hardly visible. If you go to Siberia today and visit the scene of the Tunguska strike there is little to show for it. The forest has long since grown back so that, although at ground level old trunks of trees can be seen facing the direction of the blast, nothing can be seen from the air. This event happened as recently as 1908. Clearly, then, any obvious traces of a conflagration in Britain dating to the sixth century will have long since disappeared. More work needs to be done on this but Dr Clube and his colleagues believe there is evidence that the British forests were much more extensive prior to this event than after and in many places they have simply not grown back. There was also a precipitous collapse in the population of Britain at this time, making it easy for the Saxons to move in afterwards and repopulate England. That shock waves and firestorms virtually destroyed the country also explains why there are so few above ground-level Roman ruins in Britain compared with the rest of the former Empire.

Dr Clube's statement that during the Tunguska strike for nine days people had been able to read newspapers and take photographs at midnight was intriguing, for later Alan was to inform me that Welsh records state that the sky was lit up to a similar extent when the comet struck Britain in the sixth century. As later historians couldn't believe that such a thing was possible, they tended to dismiss these records as myths.

Intrigued by the idea of a trailing cloud bringing death in its wake, I asked Dr Clube if there was any possibility that a bolide of the type he was considering could have deposited large amounts of chlorine, mustard gas or some other poisonous gas that is heavier than air. This he was unable to confirm, pointing out that really we know very little about the chemistry of comets other than what can be seen in the tail. As any complex molecules that might exist in the core would be broken down by the effects of solar radiation, it is difficult to say what might be hidden in a comet's heart.

Dr Clube also said that there is further evidence from dendrochronology that a fairly major impact occurred in the sixth century. In the normal course of events dust from both the bolide itself and the firestorm it causes when striking the Earth rises up into the atmosphere. In major events such as this, the dust blots out light from the sun, causing a sudden 'cosmic winter'. This is reflected in the growth pattern of trees, which effectively stop growing until the dust clears. The dendrochronological evidence confirms that since the time of Christ there has been only one episode of this sort and that occurred between 535 and 542. The dust would first have spread out in a band around the latitude where the strike occurred and then gradually spread out further south, where the effects would have been progressively weaker. The great famine and plague described by Gildas and in other historical records could have been caused partly by the conflagration but also by the mutation of viruses and other bugs that took in material from the comet. The wasteland would have been just that: a devastated landscape that for some years was under the icy grip of a cosmic winter that would not end, because virtually all sunlight was shut off by dust: without the light and heat of the sun, the land could not warm up, crops would not grow and this led to widespread starvation of both man and animals.

The people of Britain, those who survived, would have had little choice but to migrate to friendlier climes. But the whole of northern Europe would also have been affected. This could have been a motivating factor in propelling barbarian migrations from Scandinavia and Northern Europe. Certainly after the event, when the dust had lifted and things began to return to normal, Britain would have been relatively empty of people and therefore easy prey for Saxon migrants. This is what the records seem to be telling us: not that a few pirates in their keels were able to overthrow what till then had been a very prosperous and powerful state, but that the ancient Britons were reeling from a Tunguska-type – or even much larger – event. They were unable to repel the Saxons because they were so weakened by the disease and famine brought on by this natural catastrophe. It is little wonder, remarked Dr Clube, that Gildas and others preached that this was a punishment sent by God for their sins. What else could they believe when their state was destroyed by what we would still describe today as an act of God?

I left Oxford with much on my mind. Though Dr Clube hadn't been able to confirm the exact nature of the Yellow Pestilence, he did not say it was an impossibility and he had provided us with a plausible scientific theory for what really happened in Britain, showing that from a scientific point of view the evidence of Gildas and other records was credible.

In his book *The Cosmic Winter*, which he co-authored with Bill Napier, he postulates what would happen if a fairly small bolide, travelling at 60,000 miles per hour, should explode over Louvain in Belgium. The authors explain that it would vaporize before hitting the ground, reaching temperatures of 100,000°C and creating, for an instant, a pressure of some ten thousand tons per square inch. The force of the explosion would be equal to that of some 200 megatons of TNT – enough to wipe out Belgium and cause a major emergency in neighbouring countries. Could such an event, far, far more powerful than the bombs that destroyed Hiroshima and Nagasaki, be enough to trigger nuclear reactions in its core? It is noteworthy that one of the principal constituents of comets is water. Perhaps in the enormous temperatures and pressures at the heart of a fireball impact some of the hydrogen contained in the water is converted to tritium – that is, extra-heavy hydrogen. This is an extremely dangerous substance, which, if ingested

272

in any large quantity, would cause radiation sickness and leukaemia. It is also highly radioactive with a half-life of only thirty-one years. After thirty-one years only half the amount of radioactive water generated by the explosion would be left in the biosphere and in any case this would have been steadily diluted by mixing with ordinary water. In a few years there would be nothing to show for it.

Without further evidence we can only speculate as to whether the fire-ball that we believe to have hit Britain in the sixth century had a radioactive effect. Because so many people died and the survivors were by definition those who lived well away from the epicentre of the explosion, records of what really happened are scanty. What is clear is that whatever happened effectively destroyed the civilization of the Britons.

The Welsh who survived the catastrophe were unable to prevent the Saxons from taking over the prime lands of England. For while King Arthur took refuge in Brittany from the effects of the comet, his nephew Mordred, in an unholy alliance with the Saxons, attempted to usurp the kingdom. In time the story of the wasteland became no more than the background to the adventures surrounding the quest for the Holy Grail. The defeat and death of Mordred along with most of King Arthur's surviving knights in the Battle of Camlann is the *Götterdämmerung* of the Arthurian cycle. Its final chapter includes the strange story of King Arthur's burial – not at Avalon but in south Wales. Alan was now to show me his grave.

CHAPTER SEVENTEEN
MORTE D'ARTHUR

Throughout my discussions with Alan and Baram we frequently returned to the subject that had first brought their work to my attention: the burial of Arthur II. It was their claim to have discovered the probable site of his tomb that had led to the newspaper article I had read a year or so before we first met. Needless to say, I was keen to visit the site to see for myself the final resting place of Britain's most famous king. But first I wanted to hear from them, in their own words, what had drawn them to this site in the first place and why they were so certain that it was the right location. As we sat once more in Alan's front parlour, surrounded by the usual piles of books, manuscripts, photographs and jottings, he explained to me their reasoning and how it was they had come upon what they believe to be the greatest British archaeological discovery of the late twentieth century.

They knew that there were two King Arthurs and that only one of them could have been buried at Glastennen/Ynys Wydrin/Afallach. They also knew that that was the site of the burial of Arthur I, the eldest son of Magnus Maximus, not of Arthur II, or Athrwys, the son of Meurig. Although the second Arthur took the title of Pendragon of all Britain, he was primarily a king of Glamorgan. This is where Camelot was, where he endowed churches and where the Battle of Baedan took place. Logically, therefore, south Wales is where he would have been buried.

In *Le Morte d'Arthur* by Sir Thomas Malory the wounded King Arthur charges his loyal lieutenant Sir Bedevere with disposing of his magical sword, Excalibur, in a lake so that it should not fall into the wrong hands. Twice Bedevere fails in his duty and hides the sword, returning to the king and pretending that he has done as he commanded.

The third time he overcomes his desire to hang on to the sword and does the king's bidding. Though this is a mythical version of events, Alan and Baram believe there is possibly a substratum of truth behind it.

It was certainly customary amongst the ancient British, at least in the Bronze Age, to throw swords into lakes as offerings to the gods. A memory of this custom seems to be indicated here. More importantly, Sir Bedevere, or Bedwyr, was a real person. There is a famous Welsh poem contained in the 'Black Book of Carmarthen', dating from around 950–1050, called '*Englynion Beddau Milwyr Ynys Prydain*', which means 'The Songs of the Graves of the Soldiers of the Island of Britain'. Mistranslation in the past has obscured its real meaning. But by going back to the original Welsh and retranslating it using the oldest dictionary they could find, Alan and Baram believe they have been able to redis- cover what the bard who wrote it was actually saying. He was not writing poetry for its own sake but was setting down precisely worded clues for finding the graves of various warriors. Alan and Baram have followed the clues given and thereby traced the graves of a number of these personages, including that of Bedwyr.

The poem states that Bedwyr was buried at Din Dryfan, or Dunraven. Sure enough, when they went there they found a clearly visible barrow on a grassy slope overlooking the sea. Bedwyr was Arthur's seneschal and was in charge of the castle of Dunraven, so it is not surprising that he should have been buried here. It is certainly a magnificent spot for his final resting place. Incidentally, Dunraven, not Tintagel in Cornwall, as is widely assumed, is where Arthur II was born. The word 'Tintagel' used in the legends comes from the Welsh *din-dagol* and means nothing more than 'double-banked hill fort' – which Dunraven was. This, how- ever, is not where Arthur himself was buried.

In many of the later romances, it is said that Arthur never died but merely sleeps in a cave until such time as he is once more needed at the time of Britain's greatest peril. Other stories speak of him being ferried away by nymphs to Avalon after the fateful Battle of Camlann. There his wounds would be attended to and he would be nursed back to health. 'Using all the clues available to us,' said Alan, 'we have been able to work out what happened to his body after he died and, we believe, to pin- point accurately his final resting place.'

Once more I found myself driving along the M4 before turning off south onto the A473. We stopped at Coychurch, and Alan showed me in

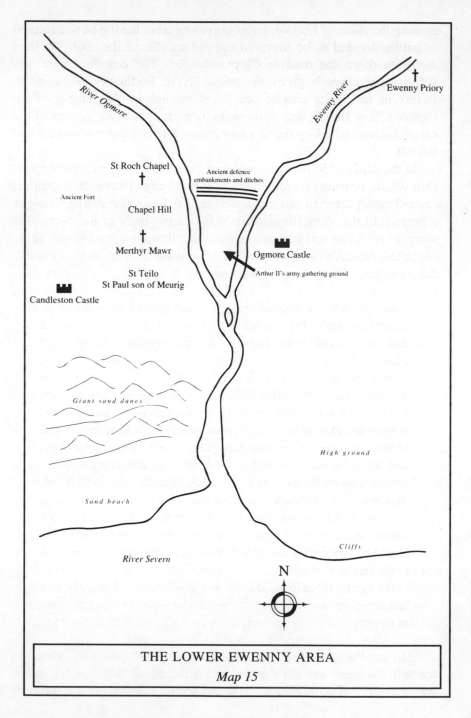

River Ogmore

Ewenny River

Ewenny Priory

St Roch Chapel

Ancient defence
embankments and ditches

Ancient Fort

Chapel Hill

Merthyr Mawr

Ogmore Castle

St Teilo
St Paul son of Meurig

Arthur II's army gathering ground

Candleston Castle

Giant sand dunes

High ground

Sand beach

Cliffs

River Severn

N

THE LOWER EWENNY AREA

Map 15

passing the stone of Ebissar, an Angle prince who, having been captured in battle, decided to be tonsured rather than die on the spot. We then drove on down the road to Ogmore-by-Sea. The coastline here was surprisingly unspoilt given the proximity of Porthcawl to the west. Before us was a flat area of beach, cut through by the estuary of the Ogmore River that flowed down from the hills above. We got out of the car and Alan picked up the story of Arthur's burial from where he had left off.

'In the "Life of St Illtyd",' he began, 'there is a story of a mysterious ship which, bearing an embalmed, wrapped body along with a magical "altar" stone, came to shore near where Illtyd was at the time living as a hermit. In the story Illtyd secretly buries the body in his cave. This story is retold in numerous other places, including an addendum to Nennius's *Historia Britonum*, called "The Wonders of Britain."' Here is the passage:

> There is another wonderful thing in Guyr, an altar is in the place called Loyngarth, which is held up by the will of God. The story of that altar it seems to me better to tell than be silent – It happened when St. Illtyd was praying in a cave which is by the sea which washes the land above the said place, the mouth of the cave is towards the sea – that behold a ship sailed towards him from the sea and two men sailing in it. And the body of a holy man was with them in the ship and an altar above his face, which was held up by the will of God. And the holy man of God [Illtyd] went forth to meet them and the body of the holy man and the altar was continuing inseparably above the face of the holy body. And they said to St. Illtyd, 'this man of God entrusted it to us that we should conduct him to thee, and that we should bury him with thee and that thou shouldst not reveal his name to any man, so that men should not swear by him. And they buried him and after the burial the two men returned to the ship and set sail.
>
> But that St. Illtyd founded a church about the body of the holy man and about the altar, and the altar held up by the will of God remains to this day.

Alan and Baram believe that the dead 'holy man' spoken of in hushed tones in the story was none other than Arthur II. St Illtyd, as we know, was a cousin of Arthur's and it would therefore have been natural to involve him in the burial of his king. By Alan's and Baram's calculations Arthur died around 579, at a time when Morgan, his son, was too young to inherit the kingdom. To maintain stability in the kingdom it was important for people to believe that Arthur was still alive and likely to return at any moment, his brother Frioc acting as regent in the meantime. It therefore makes sense that Arthur's body would have been secretly brought home by sea to be buried in a cave by his cousin Illtyd. Later, when Morgan was of an age to take the crown himself, the truth could be revealed and the body reburied elsewhere, as indeed the story tells us it was. The question is: where was he first brought to and where is he buried now?

Guyr, the place mentioned in the story, is *O-gwyr* – in general, Welsh names for places have not changed very much over the centuries – which is the region around the Ogmore River. Loyngarth comes from *llyfn-garth* and means 'smooth ridges'. This was, as Alan pointed out, an accurate description of the area of sand dunes where we were beside the estuary of the Ogmore River. In ancient times boats, even quite large ones, would have been beached on the sands here by the mouth of the river. If the tide was in, smaller craft could be rowed on up the river as far as Ogmore Castle, which stands just above the confluence of the Ogmore River with the River Ewenny. This castle was seized by the Normans in 1091 but it is very much older than that. It was to be our next port of call.

We climbed into the car and I drove back up the road we had come down for a couple of miles before parking by the ruins of an old castle. Unlike Caer Melyn, Caerleon or any of the other important Arthurian sites in the region, this castle was made of grey stone walls rather than earth ramparts. Though the present building probably dated from not long before the Norman invasion of 1091, since the site was clearly of strategic importance I could believe that there was probably a building here in the sixth century. We admired the ruins for a few minutes before walking over to a stone, with barely legible writing inscribed on it, standing on a small plinth.

Alan carried on his commentary. 'This is an extremely important memorial stone, though actually what you are looking at here is a facsimile – the original is now in a museum. Like others we have shown you, it carries an inscription, only this time it concerns ownership of land. You can read it better if you throw a bucket of water over the stone but it has been translated by Professor McAllister, who is very good on this sort of thing, as reading: "Be it known to all that Arthmail has given this field to God and to Glywys and to Nertat and to Fili the bishop."' Alan explained that Nertat was a daughter of Brychan of Brecon. Glywys was a son of Gwynlliw and a brother of St Cadoc. Both Nertat and Glywys were therefore cousins of Arthur II and they are mentioned on one of the stones at Margam. Fili the bishop is Ufelwyn, a grandson of St Gildas, and his name is on a stone at Merthyr Tydfil. Arthmail is of course 'Iron-bear', Arthur II. Ogmore was one of his castles and Alan and Baram believe that the flat area between the two rivers was the army gathering-ground prior to the Battle of Baedan.

'There is an amusing story,' Alan said, 'of how, prior to the battle, while the forces were assembling, one excited youth rode his horse into the river and splashed Arthur. He was a young man and hadn't met the king before so he was forgiven for his transgression. It's an interesting detail, for here at Ogmore the River Ewenny is fordable – this is actually the Ewenny and not the Ogmore you are looking at. Over there, where those children are playing on stepping stones, you can see where this incident probably took place. The triangular area between the two rivers is defended by triple banks of earth running across the area and was the place for marshalling the army prior to marching on to Mynydd Baedan. However, it is not the Ogmore River that interests us today so much as the Ewenny. It is along here that Illtyd had his cave and this is where we believe the body was first taken for burial. To see it we will have to follow the course of the Ewenny back up to the Coedymwstyr, "the Forest of Mystery".'

We drove back along the A473 to Pencoed, eventually parking by some playing fields. Close to the 'H' of a rugby goal were several old tumuli, mute spectators to Wales's national game. Crossing the field, we made our way into the woods beyond, which rose steeply up a hill. It was a hard climb along a slippery path over fallen trees and through tangled brambles before we eventually reached our objective: the entrance to a cave. I had been looking forward to seeing this cave for some time, ever since Alan had first mentioned to me that it may once have been used for the burial of King Arthur. On our way Alan explained that this was the cave that had once been the home of St Illtyd when he was living as a hermit and away from the comforts, such as they were, of his church foundation at Llantwit Major. What was strange was that it was much higher up than I had imagined, giving it an elevated quality that some-what mitigated its chthonic connections.

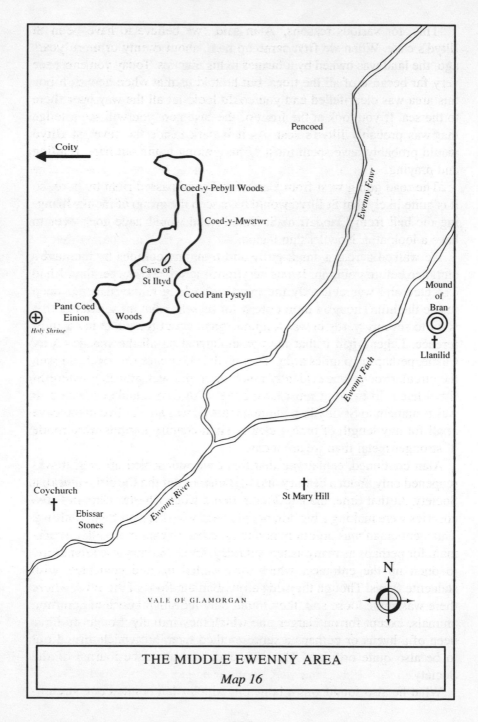

Coity

Pencoed

Coed-y-Pebyll Woods

Coed-y-Mwstwr

Cave of
St Iltyd

Coed Pant Pystyll

Mound
of
Bran

Pant Coed
Einion

Woods

Llanilid

Holy Shrine

Coychurch

St Mary Hill

Ebissar
Stones

Ewenny River

Ewenny Fawr

Ewenny Fach

N

VALE OF GLAMORGAN

THE MIDDLE EWENNY AREA
Map 16

'This, for various reasons,' Alan said, 'we believe to have been St Illtyd's cave. When we first came up here, about twenty or more years ago, the land was owned by a farmer in his nineties. Today you can't see very far because of all the trees, but he told us that when he was a boy this area was clear-felled and you could look out all the way over there to the sea. If you look at the front of the cave here you will see a ledge that was probably Illtyd's seat. As it is dark inside the cave, St Illtyd would probably have spent most of his waking hours out here, reading and praying.

'The road going west from Cardiff to Dyfed passed right by here, so it is quite likely that St Illtyd would have seen the group of monks bringing the bell from Llandaff to St David's and would have gone over to have a look at it. Now let's go inside.'

We walked across a small gully and took photographs by the cave's entrance before going in. It was very much larger and deeper than I had expected and was evidently the mouth of a long tunnel that ran deep inside the hill. Though I didn't see it for myself, Alan informed me that sixty to seventy yards in was a round room, about forty feet in circumference. Legend had it that the tunnel carried on all the way to Coity Castle, perhaps two miles away. Though the outer cave was cold and wet, the circular room was evidently much drier and was probably where St Illtyd lived. Even so, it must have been an uncomfortable existence. It was testament to St Illtyd's endurance that he was able to live in the cave at all for any length of time – clearly sixth-century hermits were made of stronger metal than we are today.

Alan continued, explaining that this cave was sealed up until it was reopened only about a century ago by a member of the Cardiff Naturalist Society. At that time, the late Victorian era when Charles Darwin's discoveries were making a big stir, people were very keen on fossil hunting. This gentleman was an old man and he came down here, with a workman, for perhaps as many as ten Saturdays in 1888. They used dynamite to open up the entrance, which was walled up and cemented with stalactite flows. Though they dug around on the floor of the cave, where there was some loose soil, they found only the small bones of common animals, except for one larger one which they initially thought to have been of a hyena or perhaps a sabre-toothed tiger, but which turned out to be also quite ordinary. This was documented in the journal of the Society.

What he also found was a large pit, which Alan pointed out, stretching from one wall to the other, maybe ten feet long, four feet deep and four feet wide. It was a man-made hole and, as the stone here is very hard, it must have taken a considerable amount of work to carve it out of the bedrock. The records of the Cardiff Naturalist Society show that the man who discovered this cave in the 1880s was quite sick and certainly incapable of digging it himself; in any case, he and his fellow only came up here for a few Saturdays and would not have had enough time to execute such work. Plans he had to carry on investigations the following year came to nought, as he died.

It has been speculated that this pit was some sort of animal trap, but Alan and Baram don't believe this, as an animal such as a bear, wolf or sabre-toothed tiger could easily have leaped across to the other side and would not have been deterred. They are sure that this was the original grave where St Illtyd first buried the body of King Arthur after it was secretly brought to shore, as described by Nennius and others.

Using the lights from my video camera as a torch, I examined the hole carefully. There could be absolutely no doubt that it was man-made as the corners were squared off, and it was certainly large enough to have contained a coffin. In fact it reminded me of nothing so much as the granite sarcophagus that sits inside the King's Chamber of the Great Pyramid. The idea that this hole could have been a burial pit made sense to me and tied in with Arthurian stories, not only those concerning King Arthur himself, but also of other burials within caves. Given the proximity of the cave to the road and the story of the bell, the cave was certainly a prime candidate to have been Illtyd's hermitage. This being so, it would have made sense for him to bury the body of his cousin Arthur here, given that it was necessary to keep his death secret. Without permission, nobody would dare to enter the cave of a saint, still less dig up the floor, and thus King Arthur's secret would have been safe.

Alan went on to explain their theories for what had become of Arthur's remains after they were taken from the cave. In 'The Life of St Illtyd' the mysterious body is disinterred from the cave and reburied elsewhere, along with the magical 'altar' stone. He and Baram considered various possibilities for where Illtyd might have reburied King Arthur. One obvious candidate was the Church of Merthyr Mawr, which lies on the Ogmore River less than a mile from Ogmore Castle. Like so many others in Wales, this was rebuilt in the nineteenth century, so gives the impression of being relatively modern. However, the original church to stand on this site was very much older and stood in a slightly different position from the present building. Because of this, an effigy that once lay within the church itself is now outside the walls. Merthyr Mawr means the 'Great Martyr' in Welsh, which makes you wonder in whose honour the church was built. It can't be Tewdrig, although he is considered to have been a martyr, as his church and grave are at Mathern. Alan and Baram wondered for a long time whether the effigy might have been Arthur's but are now of the opinion that it isn't.[1]

They examined 'The Songs of the Graves' for clues and found the line:

> *Bet y March bet y guythur*
> *Bet y Gugawn Cletyfrut*
> *Anoeth bit bet y Arthur.*

This translates as:

> The grave of the Knight, the grave of the wrathful one
> The grave of the angry red-sword
> A bare/exposed place is the grave of Arthur.

The second verse,

> *Bet Elchuith ys gulich glaw*
> *Maes Mauvetauc y danaw*
> *Dyliei Cynon yno y cunaw,*

is a little more complicated to translate. *Elchuith* is not a proper name, as it has been translated by the Rev. Robert Williams: it should be *ell chuith*, meaning 'extremely windy'. *Mauvetauc* is derived from *medd-digaeth*, meaning 'drunken helplessness'. *Cynon* can be a name but it also means 'chief' or 'chiefs'. In Alan's and Baram's opinion a correct translation of this verse is:

> An extremely windy grave in a narrow, wet place
> The field of reproach of drunken helplessness
> The duty of the chiefs to bear him hither.

The first verse is pretty much self-explanatory. It tells us that Arthur carried the angry red-sword, Excalibur or Caledvwlch, and is buried

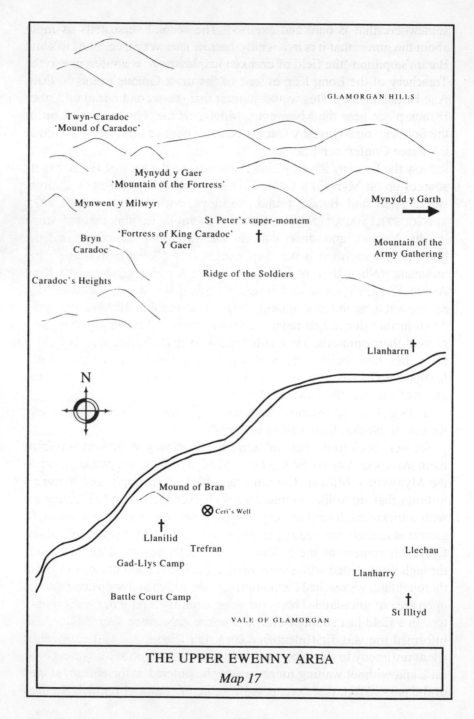

GLAMORGAN HILLS

Twyn-Caradoc
'Mound of Caradoc'

Mynydd y Gaer
'Mountain of the Fortress'

Mynwent y Milwyr

Mynydd y Garth →

St Peter's super-montem †

Bryn
Caradoc

'Fortress of King Caradoc'
Y Gaer

Mountain of the
Army Gathering

Caradoc's Heights

Ridge of the Soldiers

Llanharrn †

N

Mound of Bran

⊗ Ceri's Well

† Llanilid

Trefran

Llechau

Gad-Llys Camp

Llanharry

Battle Court Camp

St Illtyd †

VALE OF GLAMORGAN

THE UPPER EWENNY AREA
Map 17

somewhere that is bare and exposed. The second verse tells us more about the grave: that it is in a windy, narrow and wet place. In Alan's and Baram's opinion 'the field of drunken helplessness' is a reference to the Treachery of the Long Knives, one of the most famous events in Dark Age British history. This would suggest that the second burial of Arthur II took place near the Mynwent y Milwyr or the 'Grave Monument of the Soldiers' on Mynydd y Gaer, erected in honour of those who died at the Peace Conference of *c.* 466.

Now the Ewenny River, which flows near to the cave of Illtyd, has its sources up on Mynydd y Gaer. This is where stands St Peter's Church, where Alan and Baram found the stone with the inscription 'REX ARTORIUS FILI MAURICIUS'. It is therefore tempting to think that this stone is what Nennius and others call an 'altar' and that it accompanied the body of Arthur when it was first buried in the cave and later on the mountain. When they had the church excavated, they hoped to find Arthur II's grave close to where they found the stone. However, this proved not to be the case, though it is always possible that had they gone down further they might have found something. Accordingly, they have revised their opinions. They still think that he is buried on Mynydd y Gaer, but now believe he was not buried inside the church itself. Mynydd y Gaer is also significant because, as we have seen, it is the grave of Meurig, the father of Arthur II.

'Let's go back up the mountain,' said Alan, 'and I will show you where we now think that King Arthur is buried.'

We went back to the car and drove the short way to Brynna and from there made our way up the west side of Mynydd y Gaer, parking near to the Mynwent y Milwyr. The wind was blowing strongly and the wind turbines that stood like so many trees all over the summit filled the air with a melancholic call as they stripped it of some of its energy. Alan glowered at them and led me to where we could get a better view of the Grave Monument of the Soldiers. After trekking for some two miles through fields filled with sheep along a track that had once been a main thoroughfare, we reached the point where the old road disappeared into an open area of grassland. There, running north, lay a pass in the mountain top. In a field just south of this pass was a large stone slab, which Alan informed me was first identified by Brian Davies as a fallen menhir; silent testimony to the importance of the site. 'Do you see anything?' he said, and without waiting for an answer he pointed at the eastern slopes of the pass. 'Well, there seems to be a pile of stones,' I replied. He then explained that old as well as new maps named this place as the 'Pass of the Soldier' and that this was perhaps no accident, as Arthur II was frequently referred to as 'Arthur the soldier'. We were, in fact, just some 200 yards west of the ruined St Peter's Church and roughly the same distance from the Giant Circle of Llanbadfawr, where they believe Arthur II's father Meurig lies buried. Alan reiterated that the names of all the surrounding fields in the area were preserved on tithe maps and that these clearly told the story of the infamous massacre at the Peace Conference of c. AD 456. However, this one was called 'The Field of the Highest Ruler', which he and Baram believe refers to Arthur II.

We made our way up to the pile of stones. 'We didn't realize what this was until we came up here one evening by the long route we've just taken,' said Alan. 'On that day the sun was behind us, low in the sky, and as it shone through the clouds it made these stones glow like a shield made of copper or gold.' When we arrived at our destination it became apparent that what had looked at first sight like an innocuous pile of stones was in fact part of a large tumulus or burial mound. The position of the mound, either by accident or design, made it difficult to spot from a distance. I examined the stones and it became apparent that they were in fact a rough wall sealing off a concealed cave or overhang some three feet below the hilltop.

'There's another sealed-up cave over there,' said Alan, pointing to a second spot. 'Here we have everything described in the Arthur verses of "The Songs of the Graves",' he continued. 'The poem states that he is buried in an extremely windy place, and this is the windiest place on this notoriously windy mountain. We know all about the winds here, as in 1991 our excavation tents were wrecked by a 100 m.p.h. gale followed by two 70 m.p.h. storms. The "Songs" say the place is narrow, and this pass is narrow. They also say it's wet. Well, that bog is certainly very wet; in fact it's the source for the Nant Ilid, a stream which runs down to the village of St Ilid on the north side of the mountain. It may be a coincidence, but Ilid is generally thought to be the same person as Joseph of Arimathea, and he is closely associated with the Arthurian Grail legends. Further evidence that this is the right place for the burial of Arthur II is contained in the Perlesvaux manuscript, which cites three circular beehive hermitages at the grave site of King Arthur. We found one in the church ruins dating to c. AD 450–600 and here are the ruins of two more on each side of the pass.' We inspected them and also the remains of other walls, close to the grave mound, which were four feet thick. Whilst we couldn't be sure what these were, producing a compass from his pocket Alan was able to show that, in the fashion of a Christian church, they lay exactly east–west in orientation. We speculated that perhaps it was this building that Nennius referred to when he said that Illtyd built a church about Arthur II's grave.

Standing on the hilltop above the mound and stone wall, Alan reminded me that the 'field of drunken helplessness' was next to St Peter's Church, clearly visible only some two hundred yards away. He said he was both amused and exasperated that no one in living memory – perhaps for centuries – had noticed that a large tumulus lay perched on the side of the hilltop. If anyone had seen it, they had certainly not recognized it for what it was. 'Down there in the distance,' he concluded, before we made our way down, 'you can see the silvery streak of the Ewenny River, leading up to the Coed y Mwstyr woods, where lies the cave in which Arthur II was first buried. We are now about two hundred yards from the Giant Circle of Llanbadfawr, the same distance from St Peter's Church and one hundred yards from the ruins of Caradoc's castle. We have three major war-kings buried quite close together on this mountain: Caradoc up there to the west, Utherpendragon Meurig over there in the Llanbadfawr and Arthur II right here. The Wilson and Blackett view is quite simple: what we find here fits with what the records say. Mynydd y Gaer has to be Caer Caradoc.

'Of course,' Alan concluded, 'we can't be absolutely definite about any of this until such time as either we or someone else is able to arrange a proper archaeological investigation. We very much hope that if Arthur II is buried here there would be some identifying items with the body, perhaps even a death mask, or deerskins, as we know from several records that he was wrapped in deerskins (and DNA tests on these would reveal the species of deer). Then we will know once and for all what happened to Britain's "once and future king".'

THE SWORD IN THE STONE

On our earlier trip to the summit of Mynydd y Gaer, when Alan had pointed out the strange anvil-shaped stone and told me (and was later able to show a picture of this) that on the side now facing the ground there was the impression of a wide-bladed sword, we got talking about the old legends concerning Excalibur and other legendary swords. I little expected to hear that they had a picture of what may well have been the original 'Sword of Constantine', possibly even Excalibur itself. He now told me the strange story of how this had come into their possession.

A few years ago Alan was over in the US visiting a friend of his and Baram's, Professor Jim Michaels, who has been supportive of their work over many years. Curiously, although they have had much opposition from the academic community in Britain, the Americans, perhaps because they don't feel threatened by it in the same way, have always been much more interested in what they have discovered. Alan was sitting with him one day when suddenly his fax machine sprang into life. It received a message from someone Jim didn't know but who had somehow got hold of his number because of his acknowledged expertise on matters to do with epigraphy. What came through was a picture of a very old and strange sword that had recently been discovered in America. Because this is a sensitive matter, Alan was not at liberty to divulge either the whereabouts of this sword now or how it was discovered, but said it is certainly of extreme antiquity.

Etched into the sword was an inscription that Jim was unable to translate, so he showed it to Alan. It was immediately clear to Alan that this was in Welsh Coelbren lettering, but as it was difficult to make out from the fax, they asked the sender if they might be sent a proper picture. When this arrived a few days later, Alan was able to confirm that this was so, and to furnish Jim with a translation: 'The duty of the host is to him who holds the sword.'

What this sword might be we cannot be sure but it is clearly royal and Alan and Baram think it may be the fabled 'Sword of Constantine' that was once included in the Crown Jewels. This sword is recorded as having been given to King Athelstan of Wessex (c. 894–940), the grandson of King Alfred the Great, and as having disappeared during the time of Oliver Cromwell. How it arrived in America is anyone's guess but they suspect that it might have been brought over by a Puritan immigrant. The Crown Jewels were stolen in 1649. Rewards with guarantees of immunity from prosecution ensured that most of them were recovered, but not the Sword of Constantine, so it is possible that the sword was brought to America at this time.

I looked up references to the legendary Sword of Constantine in several of the books Alan had lent me and found mention of it in William of Malmesbury's *History of the Kings of England* as one of the gifts given to Athelstan when he betrothed one of his sisters to Hugh, King of the Franks. The chief of an embassy sent over to England was one Adulf, the son of Baldwin, Earl of Flanders and himself a descendant of King Alfred. William describes the costly gifts, writing:

> When he [Adulf] had declared the request of the suitor [Hugh] in an assembly of the nobility at Abendon, he produced such liberal presents as might gratify the most boundless avarice: perfumes such as had never been seen in England before: jewels, but more especially emeralds, the greenness of which, reflected by the sun, illuminated the countenances of the by-standers with agreeable light ... the sword of Constantine the Great, on which the name of its original possessor was read in golden letters; on the pommel, upon thick plates of gold, might be seen fixed an iron nail, one of the four the Jewish faction used for the crucifixion of our Lord: the spear of Charles the Great [Charlemagne], which whenever that invincible emperor hurled in his expeditions against the Saracens, he always came off conqueror; – it was reported to be the same which, driven into the side of our Saviour by the hand of the centurion, opened by that precious wound the joys of paradise to wretched mortals; ...[2]

Shrewdly, by presenting Athelstan with such important relics, Hugh was giving Frankish support to Athelstan's claims to the throne. Though a Saxon, Athelstan regarded himself as a successor of King Arthur and therefore the legitimate ruler over all of Britain. He was certainly the first Saxon king who could in any real sense claim to be paramount king of all England; this primacy of his throne is acknowledged in the *Brut Tysylio*. He is in fact the last king mentioned by both Tysylio and Geoffrey of Monmouth, forming a sort of bridge between the ancient world of the kings of Britain and the medieval world of Saxon and Norman England. This is what Tysylio has to say:

> The Saxons thenceforward [after the failure of the Britons to retake Lloegres following the calamity of the Yellow Pestilence] prudently kept themselves united; and built towns and castles: and having freed themselves from the power of the Britons, they under Athelstan, obtained possession of all England, and he was the first Saxon who had sovereignty of it.[3]

Athelstan's rule extended further than England alone. At Dacre in Northumberland he received the submission of a host of lesser kings, including Hywell Dda of Dyfed, Owain of Cumbria, Constantine of Scotland and Ealdred of Bamburgh (Northumberland). Later on, in 937, he defeated a united army of Scots, Norwegians and northern Welsh at Brunanburgh in Dumfriesshire, thereby confirming his overlordship of Scotland. Had he been Welsh he would have been termed a Pendragon but in his charters is instead called '*rex totius Britanniae*'.

There is a curious reference to the Sword of Constantine in a remarkable speech given by Athelstan's nephew, King Edgar. He calls upon the elders of the Church, the holders of the Sword of St Peter, to join with him in cleaning up the Church. He uses the following words: '*Ego Constantini vos Petri gladium habetis in manibus. Jungamus dextras: gladium gladio copulemur ut purgetur Sanctuarium Dei*. This translates roughly as: 'I have [the sword] of Constantine you the sword of Peter in [your] hands. Let us join hands, sword to sword and purge the Sanctuary of the Lord.' We must suppose that Edgar, the same king who later had a pang of conscience about stealing the bell from St Illtyd's church, was brandishing the sword at the time. The reference to a presumably hypothetical Sword of Peter is interesting, for the Latin word *Petri* can mean 'of the Stone' as well as 'of Peter'. Peter, of course, is the one Apostle recorded in the Bible as carrying a sword, with which he struck off the ear of the High Priest's slave. His sword would symbolize Apostolic authority. Peter's supposed seniority derived from the episode where Jesus changed his name from Simon to Peter, saying that he was the rock or stone on which he was going to build his church. We may infer that, to Edgar at least, the Sword of Constantine symbolized his authority as 'Defender of the Faith', a role deriving not from the Pope or Peter but from the sword's namesake: Constantine the Great. The legend that King Arthur drew another sword from a stone would suggest that the ancient kings of Britain believed that they, not the bishops of Rome, were in possession of Peter's (the stone's) sword as well as that of Constantine.

In the eleventh century, after Britain had been conquered by the Normans, the Pope hit upon the ingenious idea of directing the temporal power of European kings eastwards. The crusader movement to recover the Holy Land from the Muslims echoed the conquests of Constantine and it was no accident that it was conducted under the banner of the red cross, the symbol of England. The most famous, if not the most successful, of crusaders was Richard the Lionheart, Richard I of England, who in many ways modelled himself on King Arthur. In his equestrian statue in front of the Houses of Parliament in London and on his Great Seal of 1199 he is seen fully armoured and brandishing a sword, representing the heroic king *par excellence*. It is recorded by Benedict of Peterborough that Richard I made a gift of the 'Sword of King Arthur' to his ally, Tancred of Sicily. Where he obtained this sword we don't know but it seems unlikely that it would have been the Sword of Constantine. Later Tancred presented the same 'Sword of King Arthur' to the Church of the Holy Sepulchre in Jerusalem. Here there is a statue of the Virgin Mary holding a heavily jewelled sword, presumably a representation of this sword, in the crook of her arm. The Sword of King Arthur was of course called Excalibur in the legends.

Another very interesting sword, spoken of in great detail by Tysylio and Geoffrey of Monmouth, is called the *Mors Crocca* or 'Red Death'. The story of this sword may have been the origin of the idea of a special sword signifying the power of British sovereigns. Its history is much older than Arthur's legendary sword Excalibur, going back to before the time of Christ. Now when Julius Caesar made his first attempt at the conquest of Britain in 55 BC, he was met by a reception party of angry Britons. A charge led by Nennius, the brother of Caswallon, was launched at the Romans as they disembarked. In the course of the battle which ensued, Nennius engaged Caesar in hand-to-hand combat. The latter struck two resounding blows with his sword. The first hit the British prince on the helmet but as Caesar raised his sword to strike a second blow Nennius held up his shield in self-defence. The sword lodged itself so deeply in the shield that, try as he might, Caesar could not withdraw it. Just then the drift of the surrounding battle forced the combatants apart, leaving Nennius in possession of the opposing general's sword. Able now to prise it free from his shield, Nennius discarded his own sword and used it himself to great account, slaying many Romans. In fact, the sword proved so deadly that anyone struck with it that wasn't killed instantly died later from their wounds. The sword was therefore considered magical and earned itself the nickname of the Mors Crocca.'[4]

Unfortunately Nennius himself was not exempt from the magic of the Mors Crocca, passing away some fifteen days later from the wound he had sustained to his head. According to Tysylio, he was buried, along with Caesar's sword, in London by the 'northern gate', probably to be interpreted as Cripplegate. Other writers say that the sword of Caesar was kept on open display. E. O. Gordon, quoting from a Welsh manuscript preserved in Jesus College, Oxford, and translated by Lady Charlotte Guest, tells the Nennius story in slightly different words:

> Nennius attacked the 10th Legion. Caesar was assailed by Nennius in person. The sword of the great Roman buried itself in the shield of the British prince, and before he could extricate it, the tide of battle separated the combatants, leaving the weapon a trophy to be long afterwards exhibited to the inhabitants of Caer Troia [London]. Nennius died from the wounds inflicted by the famous 'Mors Crocca' and was buried in the Bryn Gwyn.[5]

The legend of the Mors Crocca or Caesar's sword has undoubtedly grown with the telling but there is no reason to believe that it is a total fabrication. People would frequently have lost swords in the course of battle and one can imagine that for the triumphant Britons Caesar's sword would have been a wonderful trophy. Being the general's own weapon, not only was it probably the finest in the whole Roman army, but it also had a deeply symbolic significance. As the weapon of Caesar it represented his power and by implication that of Rome itself as directed against Britain: Caesar losing his sword in the way that he did would have symbolized to the Britons that providence was preserving them from their enemies.

A possible likely scenario as to the subsequent history of Caesar's sword is this. According to Welsh records and traditions, a detachment of Londoners, disgusted at the way certain of their leaders had made peace with the Romans, went to south Wales to join the forces of Caradoc. These volunteers, under the leadership of Belyn, one of Gweirydd's brothers, were well received by the Khymry of Essylwg – in fact they attract particular praise in the triads because they asked for no pay. It seems very likely that they took Caesar's sword with them, it having become by this time an important totem of British power.

It is possible that a 'sword in the stone' episode (or something like it) may actually have taken place – not in south Wales but in London. Although Arthur II was, by heredity, the rightful king of Glamorgan, the ancient province of Essylwg, he needed to assert his authority over the entire island of Britain. Though the Angles, Saxons and Jutes had by then settled in eastern England, they did not at that time have control over London. Arthur, as a Glamorgan king, could not automatically expect fealty from the Britons outside his home kingdom of Glamorgan.

But if he arrived in London brandishing a sword that was believed to be the legendary Mors Crocca and used it to strike an oath on the Brutus Stone of London (more will be said about this in Appendix 1), this would have won him much support. This can only be an hypothesis, but were it correct it would make sense of the 'sword in the stone' story and weld it into known historical events.

Today the coat of arms of the City of London shows white or silver-coloured dragons supporting a white shield with a red cross emblazoned on it – the armorial bearings of St George (Arviragus) of England (Lloegres); the dragons too have red crosses on their outstretched wings, again signifying that they stand for England. Above the shield is a helmet sprouting dragon's wings, again with red crosses on them. The helmet seems to be representative of that of a 'pendragon', which by a play of words means a 'dragon head'. That the pendragon in question is Arthur appears to be indicated by the fiery plumage coming out of the helmet. This seems to symbolize the fiery tail of the comet, which in the legends was symbolized by a dragon. The design of the London coat of arms is probably based upon the histories of Geoffrey of Monmouth and Tysylio, where it is stated that King Arthur had a helmet in the form of a dragon made for him and wore it before the Battle of Baedan; likewise, he also adopted the red cross as his insignia. Hence the coat of arms of the City of London seems to be, in inspiration at least, pre-Saxon and to represent the coat of arms of King Arthur himself. If this is the case, then the fighting sword represented in the top left-hand corner of the shield is almost certainly meant to be his sword, Excalibur.

As the sword on the coat of arms is bright red in colour, it probably also represents the Mors Crocca, which may very well have been this same, legendary sword. As we have seen, the original Welsh name for Excalibur, as recorded in the *Brut Tysylio* and other documents, is Caledvwlch, meaning 'the Hard Cleft'. Since it was the fact that it was so sharp and made a deep 'cleft' in the shield of Nennius that caused Caesar to lose it in the first place, this name could imply that Excalibur and the Mors Crocca are the same.

The sword which has turned up in America, though it has lost its handle and ornamentation, certainly looks like a *gladius*, the type of double-sided, single-handed weapon used by the Roman infantry at the time of Caesar's invasion. The blade could have been etched by the Britons at any time subsequent to its capture in 55 BC, to emphasize its special identity. So the writing of the inscription in old Welsh

293

lettering does not necessarily preclude it from having originally been the sword of Julius Caesar.

Though the Mors Crocca could be the origins of the Excalibur legend, it clearly is not connected with the idea of a Christian 'Sword of Peter', which could be why in the legends Arthur acquires more than one sword, perhaps representing his authority in both temporal and spiritual matters. If so, the Sword in the Stone, with its pun on the name of Peter, would seem, because he is also known as 'the big fisherman', to have some connection with the legends of Joseph of Arimathea coming to Britain and the preservation of the Holy Grail in the castle of the Fisher King. Perhaps this is why in the legends it is said that Excalibur was forged at Afallach, the place given to Joseph by Gweirydd for his foundation of Glastennen. This takes us back again to the story of the Holy Grail and the legends of Joseph of Arimathea coming to Britain, a subject to which we now felt impelled to return.

CHAPTER EIGHTEEN

THE DYNASTY OF THE HOLY GRAIL

Throughout our period of collaboration leading to the writing of this book, our thoughts turned again and again to the story of the Holy Grail. We have seen that on one level the quest for the Grail, the subject of so many medieval texts, concerns the means by which the kingdom of Athrwys, Arthur II, stricken by the impact of cometary debris, can recover from its 'wasteland' condition: a search for a cornucopia of healing that can act as an antidote to the Yellow Pestilence caused by the comet. The peculiar irony of the story is that, far from reviving the British kingdom, the quest for the Holy Grail leaves King Arthur so bereft of quality knights that he is barely able to defeat his usurping nephew Mordred at the Battle of Camlann.

The exact nature of the Holy Grail, like the Philosopher's Stone of alchemy, is itself a matter of some conjecture. In Welsh, a *greal* is a collection of stories such as the Bible or the Koran. However, we have seen that in medieval literature it is sometimes described as a special stone, a *lapsit excilis* or 'paltry stone' with the connected meaning of *lapis ex caelis* or 'stone from heaven'. Elsewhere (and this seems to be the original meaning of the French word *graal*) it is a large, lidded dish or tureen, such as might be used for serving soup at a banquet. More usually it is said to have been the cup used by Jesus to consecrate wine at the Last Supper. According to the legends, this cup was recovered after the banquet by St Joseph of Arimathea and subsequently used by him to collect a few precious drops of the Saviour's blood when his body was taken down from the Cross. To the medieval mind this made it a relic of inestimable value – far more precious than the bones of any saint – and its loss in King Arthur's reign, therefore, was charged with significance.

Whatever the Grail (or Greal) may have been physically, in the legends it was believed to be a source of grace and nourishment for the soul; to be in its presence is likened to being fed with the food one most desires. Because it was such a holy relic, its custodian had to be the purest of the pure. Yet curiously these custodians are not bishops, monks or even priests, but rather knights whose destiny it is to find the Holy Grail and thereby restore the kingdom of King Arthur. In time the quest for the Holy Grail came to be the most popular subject of all for Arthurian romancers, and the doings of the Grail knights – Gawain, Lancelot, Bors and above all Perceval and Galahad – came to overshadow King Arthur himself in the affections of medieval readers.

There can be no doubt that most of what was written by the medieval romancers was historical fiction. The legends of King Arthur and the Holy Grail were used as themes to be elucidated, reworked and developed in the context of the world of the medieval knight. As they did so, certain themes concerning the Grail legend became the bedrock of an accepted canon and they were repeated, albeit with some alterations, by most writers and commentators. The most important of these themes concerns the worthiness of the Grail knight to achieve his mission. This depends not only on his good behaviour – which blended the very unsaintly attributes of the fighting knight with those of a spiritual obsessive – but on his pedigree. Jesus's own words, as recorded in the Gospels, that 'many are called but few are chosen' could have been uttered with the Knights of the Round Table in mind. For whereas all set out on their quest in hope, only the destined knight – usually Galahad or Perceval – is successful. The knight's right, indeed duty, to become a custodian of the Grail lies not so much in his own achievements, important as these are, as in his ancestry. He, like a king, is born to his task and becoming Grail guardian is therefore his special destiny.

The inner mystery of the Grail stories is hinted at only obliquely in the medieval legends, but that it concerns a secret bloodline is clear to anyone who makes a serious study of the subject. As is well known, San Greal (Holy Grail) is a pun and can also be written Sang Real or 'Royal Blood'. Thus the quest for the Holy Grail is also a search for this royal blood – that is to say, the holy bloodline. Invariably the successful Grail knight is, unbeknownst to himself, a scion of this royal household, which turns out to be the most necessary credential to become a custodian of the Grail. The question remains though: what is this dynasty? Or, as it is phrased in the legends themselves, who does the Grail serve?

In recent years a number of writers have attempted to answer this question. Several popular books have been written on the subject, the best-known being *The Holy Blood and the Holy Grail* by Henry Lincoln, Michael Baigent and Richard Leigh. Ignoring King Arthur and Britain entirely, the authors of this international bestseller presented a case for believing that the secret Grail dynasty was that of the Merovingian or 'long-haired' kings of France, who were supplanted by the Carolingians during the eighth century. According to them, the secret at the heart of the Grail legend was that Jesus Christ had been married to Mary Magdalene and that she had borne him a son – possibly the 'Barabbas' of the New Testament – who, with his mother, had gone to live in France and acted as progenitor to the Merovingians. That a marriage between Jesus and Mary Magdalene is nowhere stated in the New Testament and never seems to have been acknowledged by the Church did not deter them from presenting a thesis that was controversial. The authors based their arguments on several documents supposedly found in the little Church of Rennes le Château during the nineteenth century. These have now been shown to be modern forgeries (indeed, in a recent BBC documentary one of the forgers was even interviewed). They also completely ignored the fact that throughout the medieval period the Grail legends were understood as being part of the 'matter of Britain'.

Since *The Holy Blood and the Holy Grail* was published in 1982 there have been several other books presenting the same arguments, with variants, that Jesus was married to Mary Magdalene and had a son. Some of these later books have published spurious British genealogies which, not being based on authenticated lists such as those of Owain, the son of Hywell Dda, or on evidence such as the Llandaff Charters, only add to the general confusion surrounding the whole subject.

Having no wish to cause further gratuitous offence to practising Christians, we were of a mind to avoid this contentious subject altogether. However, given the situation as outlined above, we feel honour bound to address it, most especially as we seem to be in possession of at least some of the answers to the questions raised by these books. We therefore – and in all humility, recognizing that because the basic data is incomplete we are unable to fill in all the details – present what we believe to be the truth behind the mystery of the Grail and the link between the Holy Family of Jesus and the royal families of Britain.

THE HIDDEN LINEAGE OF THE GRAIL DYNASTY

The King List of Owain, the son of Hywell Dda, turns out to be, as on other occasions, an important document for tracing the Joseph of Arimathea connection. List 1 traces back to 'Abatlac son of Amalech'. Here there is a note that says in Latin: '*Amalech, qui fuit Beli magni filius et Anna mater ejus, quae dicitur esse consobrina Maria Virginis, matris Domini nostri JESU CHRISTI.*' This translates as: 'Amalech, who was the son of Beli the great and Anna his mother, of whom they say the Virgin Mary, mother of our Lord Jesus Christ, to be a blood-relative.' List 10 presents a different line to Owain's tree, but still terminating in Anna, going back to 'Eudos, son of Eudelen, son of Aballac, son of Beli and Anna'. It would seem that Abatlac and Aballac are one and the same person.

More information on this matter is supplied in the genealogies of St Cadoc, a sixth-century British saint and the son of Gwynlliw by Gwladys, a daughter of Brychan of Brecon. On his father's side, the tree traces back to 'Baallad son of Aballach, son of Beli, son of Anna'. We may therefore assume that Baallad is a brother of the Eudelen mentioned in List 10 of Owen. St Cadoc's mother's tree is more provocative still. It goes back to Battlad, son of Aballach, son of Beli and terminates with the Virgin Mary herself.

The Jesus College MSS No. 20, which again lists genealogies of Hywell Dda and his son Owain, also traces a lineage back to Beli and Anna; but this time there is a comment written in Welsh which says: '*Yr Anna hon oedverch y amherabdyr rufein. Yr Anna honno a dywedi wyr yr eifft y bot yn gyfynnithderb y veir vorbyn.*' The usual English translation for this is: 'This Anna was daughter to the Emperor of Rome. That Anna used to be said by the men of Egypt to be the cousin of the Virgin Mary.' However, it is not absolutely certain that the word *gyfynnithderb*, translated today as 'cousin', did not at the time of writing have a wider and more indeterminate meaning as 'kinswoman' or even 'lineal descendant'.

What is clear from all these family trees is that any connection between the Holy Family and the royal families of Britain was by virtue of a marriage between a woman called Anna and someone very important. More light is thrown on the identity of the couple involved by the statement in the Jesus College manuscript that 'Anna was a daughter of the Emperor of Rome'. In the British histories (Tysylio and the rest) there is only one recorded daughter of an Emperor of Rome who married a British king and that is Genuissa (or Gewissa), the 'daughter' of Claudius I, whom we met earlier. We put the word 'daughter' in quotes because she is not listed amongst his progeny, which suggests that she was a daughter by adoption and not blood.

Now this is not as strange as it may at first appear. The reason Roman Emperors adopted young foreign women (usually princesses) was so that they could decide whom they married. Marriage would give the woman's husband title over any lands they might inherit and even where the heiress had older brothers or sisters, their 'rights' could still provide the Romans with a pretext for interfering in what was really an internal matter of a foreign state. All over the ancient world the Romans interfered with royal successions as a first step in annexing the small kingdoms that lay beyond their Empire.[1]

Claudius I, invader of Britain, appears to have been only too knowledgeable of this tactic. He adopted Gwladys, the daughter of Caradoc, and, since Caradoc was king of the Khymry of Essylwg, therefore a potentially important pawn in the game of determining the succession to the kingdom of Essylwg, arranged for her to marry his relative, Aulus Rufus Pudens Pudentius. She changed her name to Claudia, so it is not at all unlikely that the Anna adopted by Claudius would also have had a name change. Since Anna is recorded as being the daughter of an Emperor of Rome who married a British king, and since Genuissa is the only person who could fit this description, we conclude that Anna was in fact Genuissa and changed her name. Whether Genuissa is a corruption of 'Venusia', as some writers believe, or means something else is not clear.[2]

What is important is that a princess of this name is said to have married Gweirydd or Arviragus, a marriage which could only have taken place around AD 51, subsequent to the capture of Caradoc and his family. Our researches indicate that the marriage between Arviragus and Anna/Genuissa is closely linked with the legend of Joseph of Arimathea bringing with him to the court of Arviragus not only the banner of St George but also the mysterious Grail containing the blood of Christ.

THE LEGEND OF JOSEPH OF ARIMATHEA

St Joseph of Arimathea is one of the peripheral characters to the Gospel story. He is mentioned in all four Gospels as being a rich man, evidently a secret disciple, who obtains permission from Pontius Pilate to take Jesus's body down from the Cross and have it buried in his own rock-hewn tomb.

> When it was evening, there came a rich man from Arimathea, named Joseph, who was also a disciple of Jesus. He went to Pilate and asked for the body of Jesus. Then Pilate ordered it to be given to him. And Joseph took the body, and wrapped it in a clean linen shroud, and laid it in his own new tomb, which he had hewn in the rock; and he rolled a great stone to the door of the tomb, and departed. Mary Magdalene and the other Mary [the mother of James and Joseph] were there, sitting opposite the sepulchre.[3]

St Mark's Gospel tells the same story, only adding that Joseph was an 'honourable councillor'. St Luke repeats that he was a 'member of the council' with a further qualification that he was also 'a good and righteous man, who had not consented to their [presumably the council's] purpose and deed, and he was looking for the kingdom of God'. St John's Gospel gives us the most complete account of all, indicating that Joseph was a secret disciple and that the tomb was in a garden – probably Gethsemene.

> After this Joseph of Arimathea, who was a disciple of Jesus, but secretly, for fear of the Jews, asked Pilate that he might take away the body of Jesus, and Pilate gave him leave. So he came and took away his body. Nicodemus also, who had at first come to him by night, came bringing a mixture of myrrh and aloes about a hundred pounds weight. They took the body of Jesus, and bound it in linen cloths with the spices, as is the burial custom of the Jews. Now in the place where he was crucified there was a garden, and in the garden a new tomb where no one had ever been laid. So because of the Jewish day of Preparation, as the tomb was close at hand, they laid Jesus there.[4]

The idea that Joseph of Arimathea, this peripheral character, might have led an apostolic mission to Britain seems a romantic myth until one begins to investigate the subject seriously. In *The Drama of the Lost Disciples* George Jowett, drawing on the work and researches of many others before him, has assembled much written evidence, mostly not from Britain itself, confirming both that Christianity came to Britain in the first century and that Joseph led the mission. He quotes Martin of Louvain and his *Disputoilis Super Dignitatem Anglis it [sic] Gallioe in Councilio Constantiano*, of 1517 which says:

> Three times the antiquity of the British Church was affirmed in Ecclesiastical Councilia. 1. The Council of Pisa, A.D. 1417; 2. The Council of Constance, AD 1419; 3. Council of Siena, AD 1423. It was stated that the British Church took precedence over all other churches, being founded by Joseph of Arimathea, immediately after the Passion of Christ.[5]

Much further back in time, Eusebius of Caesaria (*c.* 260–340) in his *Demonstatio Evangelica* says: 'The Apostles [unnamed unfortunately] passed beyond the ocean to the Isles called the Brittanic Isles.[6] As Eusebius was a contemporary of Constantine the Great and perhaps even one of those who met the Empress Helen on her pilgrimage to the Holy Land, he would have been careful to speak the truth on such matters.

Going back further still, Tertullian of Carthage (*c.* 208) says that the Christian Church of his day 'extended to all the boundaries of Gaul, and parts of Britain inaccessible to the Romans but subject to Christ.'[7] Sabellius (*c.* 250) writes in an even more illuminating way: 'Christianity was privately confessed elsewhere, but the first nation that proclaimed it as their religion and called it Christian, after the name of Christ, was Britain.'[8] Polydore Vergil, court antiquary to Henry VIII and one of the foremost scholars of his day, writes: 'Britain partly through Joseph of Arimathea, partly through Fugatus and Damianus, was of all kingdoms the first to receive the Gospel.'[9]

Gildas, the sixth-century ancient British historian whose work *Gildae sapientis de excidio et conquestu Brittanniae* is the jumping-off point for most Arthurian researches, writes that 'We certainly know that Christ, the True Son, afforded His Light, the knowledge of His precepts to our Island in the last year of Tiberius Caesar.' Elsewhere he amplifies this statement most revealingly to read: 'Joseph introduced Christianity into Britain in the last year of the reign of Tiberius Caesar.'[10] Tiberius died on 16 March AD 37, which gives the traditional date for the Joseph mission of AD 36. At that time all Britain was still outside the Roman Empire, the Claudian invasion not taking place until AD 43.

As we have seen, Joseph did not travel alone: he is generally recognized as having come to Britain with twelve disciples. According to Jowett, these were listed by Cardinal Baronius (quoting from Mistral in *Mireio* and another ancient document in the Vatican library) as: St Mary, the wife of Clopas; St Mary Magdalene; St Martha; Marcella, maid to the Bethany sisters; St Lazarus; St Maximin; St Eutropius; St Martial; St Salome; St Trophimus; St Clean; St Sidonius; St Saturninus; St Joseph of Arimathea.[11]

There are, of course, thirteen names here in addition to that of Joseph himself, so it would seem that Marcella the maid, who isn't named as a saint, doesn't count as a disciple. At that time it was probably expected that Tiberius was on the point of death and his mad nephew Caligula was poised to take over the Empire, so the inclusion of the Bethany sisters, Mary and Martha, who were Jesus's closest friends, suggests that Joseph's motive for going to Britain was partly to get them out of harm's way with the rest of the 'lost disciples'. There could, however, have been other less obvious reasons. We found further clues to what really happened when, on examining the New Testament carefully, we discovered that Jesus's own family tree was far more extensive than is generally supposed.

THE FAMILY OF JESUS CHRIST

Though in the course of the last century or so there has been a whispering campaign aimed at discrediting the New Testament, to the point where it is even considered intellectually respectable to believe that Jesus never even existed as an historical person, the Bible remains the bedrock of the Christian faith. Whatever uncertainties there might be about the authorship of the Gospels and when they were written, there can be no doubting that the Letters of St Paul were written soon after the Crucifixion and that within a very short time Christian missionaries were active all over the Roman world. These people and their immediate descendants would have vetted the material that later became canonical and therefore it makes sense to believe that the story of Jesus, as told in the Gospels, is substantially correct. Granted that there may be some inaccuracies of detail and that in part at least the Gospels are to be read allegorically, still there is no one else from his era as well documented as Jesus. We may not know everything we would like to about

Jesus the man, but we can be sure that, as far as they go, the Gospels are a faithful record of his mission.

That said, we have to understand that the Gospel story concerns real people with real relationships. Jesus was not an alien from another planet but a real man with a large number of relatives. Fortunately, identifying his relations is not as difficult as some would have us believe. For example, in Matthew 13:55 we are told that he had four brothers named James, Joseph, Simon and Jude. The reason that this is not better known is that the Church, in promulgating the doctrine that Mary was 'ever virgin', had to draw a veil over Jesus's kindred by pretending that the word 'brother' is being used in a wider sense to mean 'friends'. This is simply not true. The Greek word used in the original Gospel of Matthew is αδελφοι (*adelphoi*), which means 'brothers'. The Greek for 'friends' is φιλοι (*philoi*) and surely this is the word the Gospel writer would have used if that is what he meant. The doctrine of Mary 'ever virgin' was devised by St Jerome (*c.* 340–420) and though it was ratified at the acrimonious Council of Chalcedon in 451, it is not scripturally authenticated. In fact in the Gospels, as we shall see later, five brothers and at least one sister of Jesus are named.

To get to the truth of the matter it is necessary to realize that many of the people mentioned in the Gospels were Jesus's relatives and that they are often referred to in ways that assume the reader knows who is being talked about. Sometimes their identification isn't all that clear and the reaction of Biblical commentators has been to err on the side of caution and proliferate the numbers of people with the same name. For example, in the New Testament there is a large number of women called Mary. No less than seven are noted: Mary the mother of Jesus and wife of Joseph the carpenter, Mary Magdalene, Mary the mother of James and Joseph, Mary the wife of Clopas, Mary the sister of Martha and Lazarus, Mary the mother of John Mark (nephew of Barnabas) and a Mary who aided St Paul in Rome. Clearly Mary was a popular name at the time, but a close examination of the text reveals that at least some of these are duplicates and we can narrow down the number of Marys to four or five.

All the Gospels have something to say about the women who attended the Crucifixion. In Matthew 27:56 some of these are named as 'Mary Magdalene, Mary the mother of James and Joseph, and the mother of the sons of Zebedee'. In St John's Gospel,[12] it says that standing by the Cross of Jesus were 'his mother, his mother's sister, Mary the wife of Clopas and Mary Magdalene'. It is not clear from this whether or not

'Mary the wife of Clopas' is the sister of Mary the mother of Jesus, but this seems unlikely, as if so there would be two sisters both called Mary. In any case, Mary's sister was the mother of the sons of Zebedee and we have no evidence that Zebedee was the same person as Clopas. On the other hand, in Mark 15:47 Mary the mother of Joses (or Joseph) is described as accompanying Mary Magdalene to the rock tomb to see where the body of Jesus was laid. From these and other references it becomes clear that this Mary, the mother of James the younger as well as this Joses, was none other than the 'Virgin' Mary herself.

Further confirmation for this is in Matthew 27:56 and Mark 6:3, where Mary is described as mother to James and Joses (or Joseph) and as we have seen, they, along with Simon Zelotes and Jude are called brethren of Jesus: 'Where did this man [Jesus] get this wisdom and these mighty works? Is not this the carpenter's son? Is not his mother called Mary? And are not his brothers James and Joseph and Simon and Judas? And are not his sisters with us?'[13]

That Jesus had at least four brothers as well as sisters in the plural begs the question: where did they all come from? Even if we accept that Mary was a virgin when Jesus was conceived, there is nothing to suggest that she remained in this condition after he was born. We can only assume that she gave birth to her other children in the normal fashion as a result of sexual relations with her husband. The question is: which husband? Was it Joseph the carpenter, who in the same paragraph is described as Jesus's father?

Outside the story of the Nativity, not much is said about this Joseph in the New Testament. However, in the Apocrypha it is made clear that he was already an old man at the time of his marriage to Mary:

> The last rod was taken by Joseph, and behold a dove proceeded out of the rod, and flew upon the head of Joseph. And the high-priest said, Joseph, Thou are the person chosen to take the Virgin of the Lord, to keep her for him: But Joseph refused, saying I am an old man, and have children, but she is young, and I fear lest I should appear ridiculous in Israel . . .
>
> Joseph then being afraid, took her into his house, and Joseph said unto Mary, Behold I have taken thee from the temple of the Lord, and now I will leave thee in my house; I must go to my trade of building. The Lord be with thee.[14]

The mention of Joseph going to his trade of building is very apposite. Our word 'carpenter', which conjures up images of a small joiner's shop, gives an entirely wrong impression of his trade. In fact in the Greek original of the Gospels Joseph is described as a τεκτον (*tekton*), meaning 'builder'. At his age he was probably a head builder – what we would today call an 'architect'. As Herod's temple was begun in 20 BC, at a time when we may assume Joseph was in his prime, it is not unlikely that he was one of the builders, if not the chief architect employed on the project. This could explain how he was known to the high priests and how Mary, who, according to the Apocrypha, was a ward of the temple, was put in his charge. As he was an old man at the time of their marriage, which probably took place in 8 BC,[15] he probably died not many years later, leaving Mary a young widow. If this is the case, the suggestion that she married again is certainly not out of the question.

From other evidence contained in the New Testament, this does seem to have been the case. By putting together texts from different Gospels we can find out quite a lot about Mary's status at the time Jesus was preaching. For example, amongst the twelve apostles there are two named James. One of these is the brother of John and a son of Zebedee. The other, who must be the same as 'James the brother of the Lord', is described both in Matthew 10:3 and in the Acts of the Apostles as 'James the son of Alpheus' (actually spelt Αλπηαιοσ in the original Greek). As Mary was the mother of this James (Mark 15:47), it follows from this that his father, Alpheus, was her husband. If we look up further references to Alpheus we find that he is described as the father of Levi the tax collector, who seems to be the same person as Matthew (Mark 2:14), as well as of James.

From all of the above we can deduce that Jesus had five brothers (including Levi/Matthew) and at least two sisters. At least some of these, if not all, were sons and daughters of Alpheus, who, if he is not to be identified with Joseph the carpenter, is clearly Mary's second husband. We are also able to draw up a tentative family tree for Jesus, to which we may add his cousins, the sons of Zebedee by his mother's sister. As only James and Joseph are definitely stated in the Gospels as being sons of Mary and Alpheus, we cannot be sure that Simon, Jude, Levi (Matthew) and the sisters (one of whom seems to be the Salome who witnessed the Crucifixion) are not children either of Alpheus by an earlier marriage or of Mary by Joseph the carpenter. However, as this detail does not materially affect the argument that follows, we have included them all as

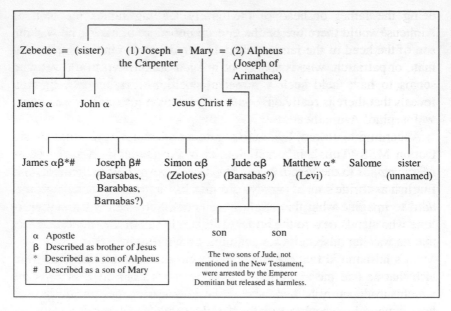

THE HOLY FAMILY OF MARY
as deduced from the New Testament
Diagram 13

children of Mary and Alpheus. In any case, they were all members of Jesus's extended family group, with Alpheus as patriarch of the household. A number of ancient Welsh poems state that Jesus was the son of Alpha – Alpheus.

The question now is: who was this Alpheus? Again we have no firm evidence but we can, by a process of deduction, draw reasonable conclusions. The name Alpheus is Greek and seems to have two possible etymologies, both of which are probably being hinted at, a pun being intended. The first would be a reference to the River Alpheus, the chief river in the Peloponnese which rises in central Arcadia. This river was special, for it was believed in ancient times that it flowed through hidden caves, passing under the sea, to rise again as a fountain at Syracuse, a city in Sicily. Thus by analogy the name Alpheus could be seen to represent a secret bloodline, or 'river', that came originally from overseas. We will say more about this later.

A second, simpler explanation is that Alpheus simply means 'chief' or 'head man', literally 'the Alpha' (*aleph* in Hebrew), the first letter in *abba* or Father. This would be a reference to 'Alpheus' (or the 'A' man) being the father or head of the family. Calling James the 'son of Alpheus' would therefore be the Greek equivalent of saying he was the son of the head of the family, which clearly he was. Who was this head man, or patriarch, who is spoken of in such oblique terms and yet who seems to have held such a powerful position? Further investigation reveals that there is really only one candidate: the man otherwise known as Joseph of Arimathea.

According to Jowett, there are a number of manuscripts, such as the Cotton MSS 'Titus', in which Joseph of Arimathea is referred to as *paranymphos* to the Virgin Mary. This Greek word is often rendered into English as 'bride's man' (implying a role like a bridesmaid, though it is hard to imagine what this might have been), but a literal translation is 'one who stands next to the bride'. This surely can mean only one thing: that he was her husband. One good reason for believing that Joseph was Mary's husband is that not only was he present at the Crucifixion but also that he had the authority to go to Pilate and ask for Jesus's body, which subsequently he had buried in his own grave. It is difficult to see how anyone but the head of the family would have had the status to demand such a thing, let alone to have his wish granted by the relevant authorities. Joseph was not one of Jesus's known apostles, and neither was he a surviving brother taking over the role of head of the family. Our opinion that Joseph of Arimathea is the Alpheus figure makes more sense than the suggestion that he was an otherwise unknown brother of Mary's, though it is possible that Jesus looked upon Alpheus as a sort of 'uncle' rather than as a father figure. Significantly, Alpheus or Joseph seems to have had at least two sons of his own by Mary, one of whom turns out to be very important for our story.

THE LOST APOSTLE

The original twelve apostles are named in the New Testament as Simon (Peter), Andrew, James, John, Philip, Bartholomew, Thomas, Levi (or Matthew), James (the less), Jude (perhaps also named Thaddeus or Lebbaeus), Simon (the Zealot or Cananean) and Judas Iscariot. It is obvious that they fall into two main groups: those who were former disciples of John the Baptist and those who were members of Jesus's extended family. Of the former group are Simon Peter, his brother Andrew, Philip, and probably Bartholomew and Thomas. Family members are Jesus's brothers James (the less), Jude, Simon the Zealot and Matthew/Levi, along with his cousins, James and John the sons of Zebedee. Judas Iscariot could be in either group as he is described as the 'son of Simon' and it is not clear if this means that he is a son of Simon Peter, Simon the Zealot (Cananean) or some other Simon that we don't know about. Thus at least six, possibly seven, of the original twelve were family members. However, there is one important name missing from the list of apostles and this is Jesus's other brother Joses (or Joseph) who, like James the less, is definitely named as being a son of both Mary and Alpheus. Why should he alone not have been included in the twelve?

It seems to us that the answer to this question is hinted at in several places in the New Testament, most specifically in the Crucifixion story. When Jesus is being tried by Pilate, the latter is clearly willing to release him, making use of an alleged custom among the Jews that a prisoner of their choice should be freed at the Passover. However, the crowd shout out for someone called Barabbas, with the result that he, instead of Jesus, is released. In the Gospel of St Matthew this Barabbas is described as a 'notable' prisoner (the adjective is actually επισημον (*episemon*), which means 'official', whilst St John calls him a 'robber'. The truth seems to be that he was a noted (that is, recorded) dissident, for in the Gospel of Mark it says: 'Now at that feast he released unto them one prisoner, whom they begged. And there was one named Barabbas with the rebels having been bound, who in the rebellion murder had done.'[16]

The rebellion being spoken of was probably the event recorded by Josephus the historian of the Jews when Pilate, shortly after his appointment in AD 26, caused widespread commotion in Judea because he insisted on bringing Roman insignia into Jerusalem. Alternatively, it may have been another insurrection, also mentioned in Josephus, that occurred shortly afterwards on account of Pilate's having spent 'sacred treasure' on building a new aqueduct. This event led to many deaths when an angry crowd of demonstrators was clubbed into submission by Roman soldiers. It is possible that the Barabbas of the Bible was one of the ringleaders of this demonstration. In any event, the name Barabbas, which means 'son of the father', is surely a 'surname'[17] that is intended to be understood descriptively and not as a personal name. The question is: what was Barabbas's personal name and who was the father of whom he was the son?

Now according to Lincoln *et al.,* Barabbas's father was Jesus, the

Jews being given a choice between father and son: the suffering Messiah or his heir.[18] It seems to us that the 'father' in question is the patriarch of the Holy Family: Alpheus. We have seen that Jesus is a son of Mary but not of Alpheus, and that Mary had at least two sons, Jude and Joseph (Joses), who are stated as being Alpheus's children. The 'son of the father' could therefore seem to be one of these and his most likely identity – indeed as we shall see the only possibility that makes any sense – is Joseph. If this is so, the choice being offered to the Jews by Pilate was between two brothers, one an unorthodox prophet (Jesus), the other a political prisoner (Joseph Barabbas, son of Alpheus). If this is so, it makes sense that Joseph is not included in the list of apostles, for, unlike his brothers James, Simon, Levi and Jude, he would have been in gaol throughout most, if not all, of Jesus's ministry; not only that, but if he had indeed been the 'black sheep' of the family (a robber or even a political murderer), he may have been considered unsuited to the task of apostle. The next question, then, is: what happened to Barabbas after he was released?

A possible answer to this question can be found in the first chapter of the Acts of the Apostles, which describes how the disciples gathered together to elect a new apostle to take the place of Judas Iscariot, who, following his treachery, hanged himself. Two candidates present themselves: one is Matthias (who wins when the disciples draw lots) and the other is 'Joseph called Barsabas, who was surnamed Justus'. In Acts 15:22 there is a 'Judas surnamed Barsabas', who is one of the 'leading men among the brethren'.[19] He is sent out with Silas to accompany Paul Antioch. If, as seems reasonable, we assume that Joseph and Judas Barsabas were brothers, it is worth looking at their surname, which is almost exactly the same as Barabbas. We also know that Joseph, the son of Mary, had a brother called Jude, who was also a son of Alpheus or 'the father'. It would seem, therefore, that the Joseph Barsabas who applies for the seat vacated by Judas Iscariot, and Barabbas, the now free former revolutionary, are one and the same person. He is Joseph, son of Alpheus and brother of St Jude.

There is, however, another candidate for the identity of Joseph, the brother of Jesus, and this is someone called Joses (Joseph) Barnabas. He also asked to be made an apostle, and to persuade the others to accept him, he sold a field and laid the money he received for it at their feet: 'And Joses, who by the apostles was surnamed Barnabas, (which is being interpreted, The son of consolation,) a Levite, a Cypriot by birth, having land sold it, and brought the money, and laid it at the feet of the apostles.'[20]

The story of how Barnabas became an apostle is deeply symbolic, for when Judas betrayed Jesus, he did so for a payment of thirty pieces of silver. Feeling remorse for what he had done, or perhaps realizing that no amount of money would make up for the fact that he was now an outcast, Judas sought to return the silver to the priests who had paid him: 'And he cast down the pieces of silver in the temple, and departed, and went and hanged himself. And the chief priests took the silver pieces, and said, It is not lawful for to put them in the treasury, because it is the price of blood. And they took council and bought with them the potter's field, to bury strangers in.'[21]

The sale of a piece of land by Barnabas and his giving the money as a donation to the apostles would seem to be some sort of recompense, a recognition that the debt of Judas needed to be paid off if he were to take over his seat. It seems likely that Joseph Barsabas and Barabbas are one and the same person. If so, we can understand why his surname may have been changed again to Barnabas, meaning 'son of consolation'. A clue to this is a curious scene that takes place at the end of Jesus's Crucifixion, in which he apparently gives away his mother for adoption to a disciple, who is generally recognized as being St John the Evangelist.

> Now there stood by the cross of Jesus his mother, and his mother's friend Mary, the wife of Cleophas, and Mary Magdalene. And when Jesus therefore saw his mother, and the disciple standing by, whom he loved, he saith unto his mother, Woman behold thy son. Then he says to the disciple, Behold thy mother. And from that hour the disciple took her to his own home.[22]

There are several things to be said about this scene. First of all, the word translated as 'home' does not mean this. In the Greek it is ιδια (*idia*), which seems to be a play on the word ιδε (*ide*), meaning 'behold'. A more correct translation might be that the disciple in question took Mary to his own 'beholding' – that is, he recognized her for what she was: his mother. Second, we don't know that it was John, the author of the Gospel, whom Jesus was addressing as the disciple 'whom he loved'. John was in no more need of adoption than Jesus's mother, Mary, who had other children to turn to. However, if the beloved 'disciple' in question was really Jesus's brother Joses and he is identified as Barabbas, this passage makes sense. Having been recently released from a death sentence, he would probably still have been in a very emotional state. We can imagine him being filled with guilt and remorse at seeing Jesus's death and hesitating from coming too near the Cross. Mary, meanwhile, would have been torn in half. On the one hand she would have been filled with grief at seeing the Crucifixion; on the other she would have been relieved that her wayward son Joseph/Barabbas had been set free. Neither son nor mother would have known how to deal with each other in these difficult circumstances. In our interpretation, it appears that in calling on his 'beloved disciple' to behold his mother, Jesus is effecting a reconciliation. Having Joseph, her lost son, back with her would indeed have been some considerable 'consolation' for Mary and we can see why his name would have been changed from Barsabas (or Barabbas) to Barnabas (son of consolation).

In any event Joses Barnabas later accompanied Paul on many of his journeys, including the one to Antioch when they went in a party that included Jude Barsabas. This makes it seem even more than likely that Joses Barnabas was the same person as Joseph Barsabas, who was a brother of this Jude.

Identifying Barnabas as Joseph, son of Mary and Alpheus, raises the question of how he could also have been a Levite Cypriot. The amendation that Barnabas was a Levite could mean that he was a priest, rather than of a different tribe; and it is not impossible that Joseph, son of Mary, was born in Cyprus.

THE MARRIAGE TO ARVIRAGUS

As we have seen, the British genealogies record that someone called Anna, a relative of the Virgin Mary, was an ancestor of several royal dynasties and she is clearly to be identified as the same person as the 'Genuissa', adoptive daughter of Claudius I, who is recorded as marrying Arviragus. Now whilst we can't be too definite about her exact lineage, it would seem likely, given the timescales involved, that she was not a cousin but a granddaughter of the Virgin Mary.[23] However, we cannot be sure who were her actual parents. She could have been the daughter of any one of Mary's children and still have been connected with the Josephian mission to south Wales. It seems to us that the most obvious candidate for her mother is Mary the wife of Clopas, who is listed as attending the Crucifixion and is described by John as a 'friend' of the Virgin Mary. The question then is: who was Clopas? Once more we seem to be faced with a name that is really a description. It seems to be derived from the Greek word κλοπη (*klope*), which means 'theft' or 'robbery'. Though the usual Greek word for thief is κλεφτησ (*klephtes*), it seems likely that 'clopas' was an alternative. On the other hand it might be that 'clopas' means something that has been stolen or taken away. In either case it is likely that Clopas is in fact Barabbas, whom John describes as a robber ληστησ (*lestes*) and who had himself been taken away (stolen) by the Romans. It seems likely, therefore, that Mary the wife of Clopas was the Virgin Mary's daughter-in-law, being married to her son Joseph 'Barnabas'.

As we have seen, according to Cardinal Baronius and others, this Mary travelled to Britain as a member of Joseph of Arimathea's party and, as a married woman, it is not at all impossible or even unlikely that she was either a mother or pregnant at the time. If so, the child – quite possibly the Anna of the royal records – would have been brought up in the court of Caradoc until AD 51. If this girl Anna grew up in the Essylwg kingdom, where Joseph is said to have founded the Cor Eurgain, then it is very likely that she was taken prisoner by the Romans with Caradoc. His adoption of her, thereby making her an imperial ward, would have made her a valuable pawn in his subsequent negotiations with Arviragus, who we may assume was by this time a Christian and a disciple of her grandfather Joseph of Arimathea. Following this line of reasoning, it is Mary the wife of Clopas, who herself attended the Crucifixion of Jesus and helped with his burial – and on whom, therefore, Jesus's blood may have spilt – who may be understood to be the 'receptacle' of the Holy Blood. She is the 'Holy Grail' brought to Britain by Joseph of Arimathea. The child that she carried in her womb was Anna, the daughter of Joseph the brother of Jesus, and, therefore, of the Holy Blood.

Further confirmation of the link between Anna, Joseph of Arimathea and Barnabas is more than hinted at in the Welsh version of the Grail story, 'Y Seint Greal'.[24] This links the Grail dynasty with both Joseph, the son of Joseph of Arimathea, and the island of Cyprus, which, according to the Bible, was the homeland of Joseph Barnabas. The passage in question concerns a king of Sarram called Evalac, who is given a shield with a cross on it by Joseph, the son of Joseph of Arimathea. With the

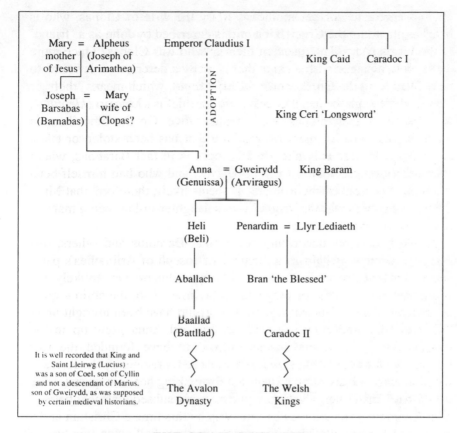

Mary = Alpheus   Emperor Claudius I
mother | (Joseph of   King Caid   Caradoc I
of Jesus | Arimathea)

ADOPTION

Joseph = Mary
Barsabas | wife of   King Ceri 'Longsword'
(Barnabas) | Clopas?

Anna   = Gweirydd   King Baram
(Genuissa) | (Arviragus)

Heli   Penardim = Llyr Llediaeth
(Beli)

Aballach   Bran 'the Blessed'

Baallad
(Battllad)   Caradoc II

It is well recorded that King and
Saint Lleirwg (Lucius)
was a son of Coel, son of Cyllin
and not a descendant of Marius,   The Avalon   The Welsh
son of Gweirydd, as was supposed   Dynasty   Kings
by certain medieval historians.

THE GRAIL DYNASTY
and its relationship with the kings of Britain
Diagram 14

aid of this shield, Evalac defeats his enemy, Tolomeus (Ptolemy). Later this same Evalac comes to Joseph's assistance when the latter is imprisoned in Britain by a cruel king:

> . . . when Joseph of Arimathea came; he who buried Jesus Christ, and drew him down from the cross; and he set out from Jerusalem with his kindred, and proceeded, by the will of God, until they came to an island called Sarram, where there was the King of Sarram, who was called Evalac. And at that time there was war between Evalac and another powerful king called Tolomeus. And when Evalac was

prepared to go against Tolomeus, Joseph, the son of Joseph of Arimathea, said to him: If thou wilt go to war so unadvisedly as thou art going, I will pledge myself to thee that thou wilt not return. How dost though advise me, says Evalac, to go to war? I will gladly tell thee, says Joseph. Then he related to him the best points of the Gospels, and the form of the new faith, and about the passion of our Lord Jesus Christ on the cross tree. And then he made a shield with a cross on it of red sendal; ... And thereupon Evalac departed against Tolomeus. And when he came to such a danger that he thought for a certainty that he would die, he uncovered the cross and his shield, and there he saw as he supposed, a man on the cross full of blood; and then he said the words that Joseph had taught him, by which he obtained victory and honour, and mastery over Tolomeus. And when he came again to the city of Sarras, he declared to the people how he obtained victory by following the advice of Joseph. And he did so much as to accept baptism, he and Naciens his son-in-law by his sister ... The name given then to Evalac was Moradrins. And so good was he in his Christianity that God loved him, as will be known hereafter. And afterwards it happened to Joseph, and Joseph his father, and a number of his family with them, to set out from the city of Sarras, and they came as far as Great Britain. And when they had come to Britain, there came against them a savage and cruel king.[25] And after imprisoning Joseph and his father, the news spread over the isles, and it came at last to Sarras.

And then Moradrins summoned his power together, he and Naciens the red, his son-in-law by his sister. And they came even to Great Britain against the king that had imprisoned Joseph; and it was not long before they overcame the king that owned the country, and the people. And so they conquered through their Christianity the whole extent of Great Britain. And so greatly did Moradrins love Joseph, that neither he nor Naciens, nor his host, ever wish to return to their country, but continued there with Joseph and his companions, and went the way they went also.[26]

Tolomeus or Ptolemy was a common name in the royal houses of Syria and Egypt in the years prior to the Roman takeover of the region. Its inclusion in the story helps us to identify the island in question as Cyprus, since Cyprus is the nearest large island to the Holy Land and close to both Egypt and Syria. The history is slightly garbled. At the time of Joseph of Arimathea, Cyprus was inside the Roman Empire and governed by pro-consuls, and therefore not a crusader kingdom. Therefore the reference to Joseph, son of Joseph, giving the king a shield with a red cross upon it was probably inserted by the writer, because in his own day the island of Cyprus was a crusader kingdom with strong links to the Knights Templar.

Cyprus was at that time an important island on account of its mineral wealth. In Roman times it was the most important source for the metal copper, which indeed derives its name from the Latin *aes Cyprium*, meaning 'ore of Cyprus'. A possible link between Joseph of Arimathea, Britain and Cyprus is that by tradition Joseph is supposed to have made his money as a trader in mineral ores. The legends in Britain refer to his coming to Cornwall to purchase tin, but this would have been of little use without copper as well, for the two metals were generally amalgamated to make bronze. Though the Roman world knew about and used iron, bronze was still in great demand for statues, jewellery and practically anything else where a high degree of resistance to corrosion was of greater value than strength. If there is any truth in the British legends of Joseph as a metal-ore trader, it is highly likely that he would have visited Cyprus on a regular basis. This could explain how he might have a son who was born there.

At the time in question (the first century) there was a large Jewish population in the city of Salamis, a port under the 'shoulder' of Cyprus and therefore facing towards Syria. This could be the origin of the 'Sarras' (or Sarram) in 'Y Seint Greal'. It is interesting that in the story the conversion of the 'King of Sarram' is undertaken not by Joseph of Arimathea himself but by his son Joseph. We know from the Acts of the Apostles that this Joseph, whom we have identified as Joseph Barnabas, went to Cyprus with St Paul in AD 46. Later, after a disagreement with St Paul over whether or not they should take Barnabas's nephew John Mark with them on a trip round all the churches they had preached in before, they went their separate ways. The last we hear of Barnabas is his sailing away to Cyprus with John Mark. There can be no doubting that Joseph Barnabas was and is regarded as the apostle of Cyprus: indeed his tomb is supposedly to be seen in Salamis to this day.[27] Even so, it is certainly not impossible or even improbable that Barnabas went from Cyprus to join Joseph of Arimathea in Britain: it would be only natural for him to do so if they were father and son.

That Barnabas had a wife is more than hinted at by Paul in his first

Letter to the Corinthians: 'Do we not have the right to be accompanied by a wife, as the other apostles and brothers of the Lord and Cephas? Or is it only Barnabas and I who have no right to refrain from working for a living?'[28] As Paul himself was neither married nor a brother of Jesus, this would suggest that he was alluding to Barnabas – otherwise why would he raise the subject of marriage at all?

The name Evalac, given to the King of Sarram by the writer of 'Y Seint Greal', is, of course, very similar to Aballach or Afallach, which is the name of both a grandson of Anna in the king lists and the original name for Avalon, and perhaps even the origins of that name. The name 'Aballach' could be derived from Alabarch, the name by which the head man of the Jewish community of an important city, such as Alexandria, was known in Roman times. The suggestion that Evalac was 'King of Sarram' could simply mean that he was the Alabarch of Salamis. If Aballach were a descendant, through Anna, of her father Barnabas, it is possible that he would have inherited property in Cyprus. This being so, he would have had a strong incentive at least to visit the island. It is perhaps interesting to note that there was an uprising by the Jews of Cyprus, Egypt and Cyrene in 116–7, during which a large part of Salamis was destroyed. The uprising was suppressed by Hadrian, then still only a general, and all surviving Jews (presumably including any who were Christians) were expelled from Cyprus. If Aballach had been there at the time – perhaps even directly involved in the troubles as the Alabarch of Salamis – it is not unlikely that he and some of his followers would have returned to Britain, which was then more or less outside the Roman Empire. This seems to be borne out by his given name of Moradrins, which would seem to be composed of two Welsh root-words: *mor* meaning 'sea' and *adrefu* meaning 'to return home'; he is therefore the one who returns home from overseas. As this time would have been about sixty-five years after the marriage of Arviragus and Anna, it would have been the correct generation for the time of their grandson, Aballach, Abattlac or Avallac. There might therefore be a degree of truth in the strange legend of a King of Sarras coming to Britain, even if other events in the story have become garbled.

Of course it is possible that it was the island city of Tyre that is being referred to as Sarram by the author of 'Y Seint Greal'. This does not materially affect our argument, except possibly the identification of Joseph Barnabas with Joseph Barsabas/Barabbas, for that island too would have had a Jewish population and an Alabarch.

DESCENDANTS OF THE GRAIL DYNASTY

As we have seen, the Welsh records are emphatic that St Cadoc, Owain, the son of Hywell Dda, and many other saints and kings of Britain were descended from Anna and Beli, who is to be understood to be either Beli the Great (whose real name was Annyn (Aeneas) the Rugged), ancestor of Gweirydd, or Anna's son of the same name. Since dynasties by their very nature tend to proliferate, whilst in the first generation there may be only two or three brothers and sisters with this genealogy, by the fourteenth generation the brothers and sisters sharing the genealogy could number hundreds or even thousands. In this way the Empress Helen, being a British queen by origin, was descended through Anna from the Virgin Mary, and so therefore was her son Constantine the Great. This goes a long way to explaining their determination not only to make the Roman Empire Christian but to seek the Holy Cross on which Jesus was crucified: for Helen this was not just a holy relic but a family heirloom. In the same way, anyone who could show a lineage back to Constantine was also of the Sang Real, including both King Arthurs. As regards the claims of the long-haired Merovingian kings of France, they too had a link with the Holy Blood, not as claimed by Lincoln *et al*, through Rennes le Château or any supposed lineage from Mary Magdalene, but by virtue of a marriage with the Grail dynasty of Britain.

Like the Britons, the royal dynasty of the Franks believed themselves to be descended from the House of Troy, through Antenor, son of Hector. In Anderson's *Royal Genealogy* there is a marriage that links the Frankish kings with the line of Anna. It was between the Frankish King Marcomir IV, who is listed as the twenty-third after Antenor, and Athildis, a daughter of the British King Coel, father of Lucius. It took place in 129 and gave rise to a son, Clodomir IV, who died in 166. Dagobert, who died in 317 and is listed seven 'generations' later (we have put the word 'generations' in quotes because we cannot be sure that we are dealing with father-to-son relationships and not with brothers, uncles and nephews), had two sons, from whom sprang the kings of the western and eastern Franks. Five kings further down the list brings us to Pharamond, Duke of the East Franks. Eighth after Pharamond brings us to Pepin of Herstal, Duke of Brabant, who died in 717. He was the father of Childebrand, ancestor of the Bourbons, and of Charles Martel, the grandfather of Charlemagne. Thus, by the Frankish marriage into the

British royal family, not only the Merovingians but other French, and indeed other European houses, were also descended from Anna.

Dagobert II, last of the Merovingians, is said to have come to Britain to study at a monastic college. Subsequently he broke with Roman Catholicism and adopted the Welsh brand of Christianity, which was decidedly Gnostic in character. It is not clear who his wife was but it seems likely that she was British and of the royal lineage. This would have reinforced the Anna–Sang Real connection.

To summarize our findings, then, it would seem that the legend that the Grail symbolizes – the Sang Real or 'Holy Blood' brought to Britain by Joseph of Arimathea – concerns his bringing with him 'Mary the wife of Clopas', the wife of his son Joseph. This son was known variously as Joseph Barsabas, Barnabas or simply as Barabbas, the 'thief' who was released by Pilate instead of Jesus. Like Jesus and his brother James, he was a son of Mary, whose second husband, Alpheus, can be identified as Joseph of Arimathea. Later, because of the association of the Grail dynasty with the idea of Royal Benediction or healing power, it was linked with the idea of the Philosopher's Stone (obtained by alchemy) and, indeed with meteorites and comets – symbols of God's power.

The wife of Barabbas (or Clopas) gave birth to a daughter called Anna, who was raised in south Wales. Following the capture of the British King Caradoc by the Romans with nearly all his family, this Anna was brought back to Rome. Recognizing her importance as a bargaining counter, the Emperor Claudius adopted her as his own daughter and then betrothed her to the British King Arviragus as part of a peace settlement. She subsequently gave birth to several children, so becoming the matriarch of royal Christian dynasties, which, because of her lineage, link back to Mary the mother of Jesus. We leave it to others to judge whether or not this be the case.

EPILOGUE

For me the quest had come full circle. After a long course of what can only be called initiation, I now had no doubts that the history of Britain from before the time of Christ to the collapse of the Arthurian kingdom around AD 684 was very different from how it is generally portrayed in modern textbooks. Drawing together the conclusions of all the chapters of the book, I was able to combine in one narrative the events of the story of what really happened in Britain at that time.

Throughout this long epoch and even during the Roman occupation, which was neither as unchallenged nor as complete as most people think, Britain was administered by local kings who believed themselves descended from the legendary Brutus. These British royals intermarried with the Roman Caesars to produce an imperial dynasty and at least some of them ruled over the entire Empire. The Joseph of Arimathea of legend, otherwise known as St Ilid, came to Britain in the first century AD with a group of companions. Joseph is thought to have brought with him a cup from the Last Supper, the Holy Grail of legend, but, more importantly, according to some accounts his party included Mary, the wife of Clopas, who was probably the mother of Anna.

St Ilid found a welcome in south Wales and established the first *cor,* or choir, of the saints at Llantwit Major, under the patronage of Caradoc's daughter Eurgain. Later he went to the court of Arviragus, the Lloegrian king who led the resistance to Roman domination from his stronghold in the Midlands. This king later married Anna, who had been adopted by the Roman Emperor Claudius I and given the name Genuissa. In reality she was a descendant, probably a granddaughter, of the Virgin Mary. A second *cor* of the saints was set up at Glastennen or Afallach, which was not, as supposed by some, Glastonbury in Somerset but a foundation near Lichfield in the Midlands, which endured until it was destroyed in the sixth century. In the tenth century, at the time of Dunstan, people misidentified the legendary church founded by Joseph at Afallach with Glastonbury Abbey in Somerset. The mistake was compounded in the twelfth century when the monks of Glastonbury, knowing that Arthurian legends referred to a place called Afallach, discovered bones in the precincts of their Abbey and took them to be the bones of the legendary King Arthur.

In the fourth century Constantine the Great, who was himself at least half British, made Christianity the state religion of the Roman Empire. His mother was Empress Helen, daughter of King Cole 'Godebog'. She went to Jerusalem to recover what she believed to be the Holy Cross, which she subsequently brought back to Britain. This may very well be hidden to this day in a sealed cave marked by a cross at Nevern in Dyfed.

Magnus Maximus, generally referred to as a usurper of the Empire, was probably no such thing, but rather the lost grandson of Constantine by his eldest son Crispus. Had his invasion of the western Empire in 383 succeeded, it is possible that the barbarian invasions of Britain in the fifth century may have been contained and the Roman Empire of the West have endured, as did that of the East. As it was, he was defeated, but not before his son, Andragathius or Arthun (Arthur I), had killed Gratian, the Roman Emperor of the West. Arthur I was later buried at Atherstone, the real Afallach, near Old Lichfield or Wall. Later his career was confused with that of his direct descendant, Athrwys or Arthur II, causing scepticism concerning the career of this later warrior-king. The identities of these two became merged as one 'King Arthur'.

In reality Arthur II was a sixth-century Glamorgan king – son of Meurig, grandson of Tewdrig. He was crowned at Caerleon by Bishop Dyfrig and his glittering court of Camelot was at Caermelyn near Cardiff. As Pendragon, or commander-in-chief, of all Britain, he fought a series of battles against Angle, Saxon and Vandal invaders, the most notable being the Battle of Mount Baedan. This took place on a hill still called by that name in Glamorgan. He established his rule over the whole island of Britain, but this was shaken when Britain was hit by fragments of a comet, causing widespread destruction and initiating a strange malady, the Yellow Pestilence. Large areas of the island became a total wasteland, experiencing a winter that went on for nine years. In the aftermath, the Saxons were able to take over most of Britain. Thereafter the ancient kingdom of the Britons was largely confined to Wales. Here the old language, genealogies, stories, legends and traditions of Britain were preserved, some of which were later rediscovered by the Normans to be celebrated and elaborated in the medieval literature concerning 'King Arthur'.

For centuries the history of Britain, as set down by Tysylio and his translator, Geoffrey of Monmouth, was assumed to be substantially correct. However, with the advent of the Hanoverian dynasty in the early eighteenth century there was a turning away from traditional histories in favour of a more 'politically correct' approach which emphasized the Roman point of view. This tendency to play down the ancient history of Britain, particularly Wales, no doubt increased in the wake of the Scottish rebellions of 1715 and 1745 and the French Revolution of 1789. As a result, when, in the late nineteenth century, the historian Bishop Stubbs carried out a root-and-branch pruning of allowable history, his work was widely applauded.

A loss of confidence by the Welsh, whose culture and language was at that time under attack and who were custodians of many of the British records, meant that this new interpretation of the past went virtually unchallenged. Unlike Scotland, which, having come later into the United Kingdom, retained its own legal and academic infrastructure, Wales had no academic institutions left of its own, its ancient schools of learning having been closed down centuries earlier. It was left to independent scholars such as Edward Williams (Iolo Morganwg) and other members of the Welsh Manuscript Society to collect, publish and comment upon traditional Welsh historical texts.

It was by following the clues indicated by these texts, such as the 'Songs of the Graves' and ancestral lists of Owain, the son of Hywell Dda, that Alan and Baram were able to find real artefacts such as the memorial stones of the two Arthurs. Unfortunately, the divide in opinion concerning traditional history between the established centres of learning and outsiders such as ourselves is still evident. In the 1980s Alan's and Baram's ideas were treated with hostility by the establishment. It is possible that the reception they would have received today would be different. With an elected assembly in the offing and almost certain development of some sort of autonomy for Wales, the time is right for a reassessment of Welsh – which are properly British – historical records. The rediscovery of Arthur I in the Midlands and Arthur II in Glamorgan

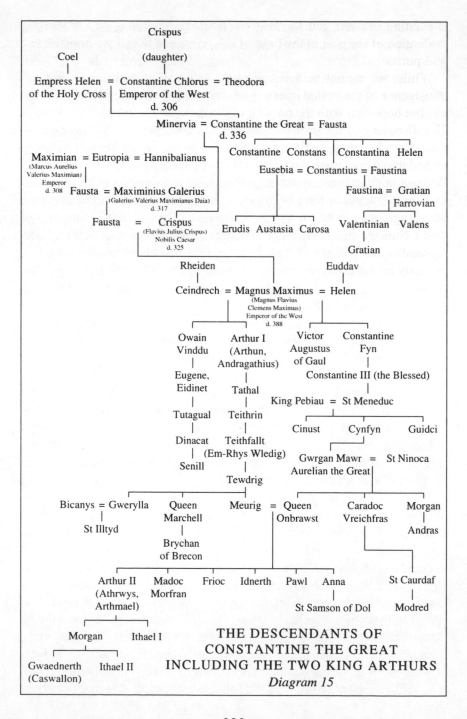

THE DESCENDANTS OF
CONSTANTINE THE GREAT
INCLUDING THE TWO KING ARTHURS
Diagram 15

is exciting in itself, but for us it was also the beginning of a whole re-evaluation of the past in the light of new evidence which we hope others will pursue.

Whilst we cannot be too optimistic about the future, given the intransigence of the vested interests who control so much of Welsh life, we can but hope that with the passing of the generations things will change. The discovery of the probable burial site of Arthur II on the hillside of Caer Caradoc may just be enough to stop the mountain itself being turned into a coal mine, but only if the people of Britain take an interest. Without such interest, much of what we have described in these pages may, in a few years, have become no more than a memory. That would be a tragic way to begin a new millennium. It is our hope that events won't come to this, but rather that a new generation of historians and archaeologists will see fit to take the traditional histories seriously and properly investigate the remains of 'King Arthur's Holy Kingdom'.

The Stone of Brutus

There is one other story, concerning some tentative investigations of my own, that is worth telling – which suggests a need to re-evaluate our capital, London.

In the course of our studies, Alan drew my attention to another curious 'sword and stone' story. This concerned the rebellion that took place in 1450, when Jack Cade of Kent, with an army numbering at one point 40,000 men, rose in revolt against Henry VI. The causes of the rebellion, like the Peasant's Revolt of half a century earlier, were many but are mainly said to have concerned maladministration and corruption. Though the revolution was ultimately suppressed and the leaders hunted down, for a time the rebels held London. To justify his rebellion, Cade is said to have drawn his sword and struck with it a particular object known as the 'London' or 'Brutus' Stone, which thereafter stood in solemn witness to his oath.

The London Stone, which ought to be of immense interest not only to Londoners but also to all Englishmen, is still in the capital. Having read about Jack Cade and suspecting that the stone he struck could be significant for our story, I determined to examine it at the soonest opportunity. Thus it was that on a cold winter's day I took the Underground to Cannon Street and began searching the area where my map assured me I should find it. After about an hour of fruitless questing, I realized that my map, being an historical representation of London as it had looked in the Middle Ages, took no account of Cannon Street railway station and the fact that the stone had been moved. Eventually I found it behind a cast iron grille, on the other side of the road. Barely visible behind a pane of dirty glass and buried deep within the wall of a foreign bank, the stone was much smaller than I had expected. On top of the grille, confirming that this was indeed what I sought, was a bronze plaque. It was clear that the person who had written the text had taken considerable trouble to play down the significance of what ought to be regarded as one of the great treasures of London. In language that is extremely 'economical with the truth' it says:

This is a fragment of the original piece of limestone once securely fixed in the ground now fronting Cannon Street Station.

Removed in 1742 to the north side of the street, in 1798 it was built into the south wall of the Church of St Swithin London Stone which stood here until demolished in 1962.

Its origin and purpose are unknown but in 1188 there was a reference to Henry, son of Eylwin de Londenstane, subsequently Lord Mayor of London.

The use of important stones as witnesses to oaths is an old custom that goes back to the Bible. In Genesis it is said that Jacob raised his Pillow Stone to bear witness to a covenant with God. In Wales people often took oaths whilst sitting on the grave of an important ancestor; where this was not practicable, their memorial stones served a similar purpose. In the same vein, British monarchs, even today, take their coronation vows whilst sitting on a throne containing the Stone of Scone, otherwise known as the 'Stone of Destiny' and believed by many to be the original 'Jacob's Pillow Stone'.[1]

Jack Cade's striking of the London Stone seems to have been done for a similar purpose. He claimed to be descended from the recently extinct line of the Mortimers, Earls of March and Ulster, the last of whom, Edmund, had died in 1425. Certainly Cade had served in France with the English army and it is not impossible that he was a son, perhaps illegitimate, of Edmund, who had fought along side Henry V at Agincourt. Roger Mortimer, the father of Edmund and a descendant of Edward III, had been declared heir apparent by Richard II. If it was true that Cade was descended from Edmund, he would have had a claim not only to the extensive lands of the Mortimers but also to the throne of England and Wales. As the Mortimers were Lords of March and were descended, on the distaff side, from Llewellyn the Great, he could, had he been able to prove his ancestry, have expected support from the Welsh.

Alan confirmed that Cade was probably a son or grandson of Edmund Mortimer, the 5th Earl of March, who had died in 1425. Around that time there was a mysterious Welsh poet named Sion O'Caint, which translates as 'John of Kent'. His identity remains a mystery, but if he was a Mortimer and came from the Marches this could be the answer. *Caead* means 'covered over' in Welsh, and this could be the origin of the name Jack Cade, referring to his identity as a secret Mortimer. Edmund Mortimer married the fifth daughter of Owen Glyndwr in 1402 and it is not impossible that Jack Cade was born of this union. If this were the case, he could have claimed royal descent through Roger Mortimer and backwards to Lionel of Antwerp, second son of Edward III, making him a legitimate claimant to the English throne.

In any case, since Edmund Mortimer's grandfather Ralph had married a daughter of Llewellyn the Great, the Mortimers may have had their own lineage going back to the Brutus kings, which would of course have been true of any descendant of Edmund's. It is therefore quite likely that Jack Cade's striking of the London Stone was an invocation of Brutus, legendary founder of London – or rather Trinovantum – as his witness. Given his ancestry, this would no doubt have gone down well in Wales, though the significance of the act would not have been entirely missed by Londoners either, who seem to have been well aware of the antiquity and importance of their city's foundation stone.

As on my first visit I had no time to take the matter further, when I returned to London a few months later I made a beeline for the London Stone and then walked onwards to the Museum of London, where I felt sure it should be possible to get more accurate information on what had actually happened. There large hoardings explained the history of London in graphic form, from its primitive beginnings, through its glorious 'Roman' period, its decline with the fall of that mighty Empire, its colonization by the Saxons, on through the Middle Ages, the Tudors and finally to the present day. As seems to be the current trend, exhibits were laid out not so much for their own intrinsic value and interest but as cultural elements illustrative of the orthodox version of history being championed by the museum.

Though the Trinovantes were mentioned in passing as the British people who, prior to the Roman invasion, lived in the area now occupied by London, there was no mention of their great city of Trinovantum, or of London being founded by Brutus, or of the Trojan migration – not even as a romantic myth. The Trinovantes were depicted as semi-savages who lived in wattle-and-daub huts. Though there was plenty of evidence of the Trinovantes' skill in the use of iron and other metals, they were clearly not regarded as being capable of building themselves a city, minting coins[2] or any of the other crafts one associates with city dwellers. It was clear that, as far as the museum was concerned, there never was such a place as Trinovantum, and the City of London or Londinium owed its origins to the Romans. This despite the fact that Nennius writes that Julius Caesar fought a great battle 'near the place called Trinovantum', or that Tacitus says that in AD 60, a mere seventeen years after Claudius's invasion, London 'did not rank as a Roman settlement, but was an important centre for business-men and merchandise'.

As there was absolutely no mention of the London Stone either, I decided to ask if there was an archaeologist available who could answer some questions on this subject. Accordingly, I soon found myself speaking on the telephone to a very helpful young lady, the Roman curator. Though she sniggered at the idea of London having been founded by the Trojan Brutus and having originally been called 'New Troy', she nevertheless agreed to come down to the lobby and show me some books with references to the London Stone. The first of these was entitled *The Roman City of London* by Ralph Merrifield. In a chapter called 'The Topography of Roman London' he describes an excavation carried out by a Professor Grimes in 1961 on the site of St Swithin's Church, Cannon Street.

> The edge of this roadway, with a drainage gulley to the north of it, was found on the site of St. Swithin's Church in an excavation by Professor Grimes, and again further west in the builders' excavation. On its southern side stood – and perhaps in part still stands, deeply embedded beneath the middle of the modern road – the mysterious London Stone, made of Clipsham Limestone, of which the top alone, shaped like a tea-cosy, is still preserved in a niche on the site of St. Swithin's [now the Overseas Chinese Banking Corporation]. Camden [a sixteenth-century historian] believed that it was a Roman mile-stone, and he may even have been right, although there is no certainty of its Roman date. All that we know is that it was a venerated antiquity in the Middle Ages, when it seems to have taken on something of the character of a fetish stone. Its original purpose had evidently been forgotten as early as the twelfth century, when it was simply called 'Londenstane'. If it had been an Anglo Saxon wayside or market cross, as is sometimes suggested, some memory of this origin would surely have been preserved in its name at this early date. It is also unlikely that it was a sacred stone of the pagan Saxon period, like the one overthrown by St Augustine at Canterbury (and since set up by the Ministry of Works), for it was a stone shaped by masons and not a natural monolith. It is therefore feasible that it was a roadside monument of some kind, set up in the Roman period, although the use of Clipsham limestone might suggest a later date.[3]

More details concerning the London Stone and of Professor Grimes's dig on the site of St Swithin's Church are contained in the Gazetteer in the same book:

> *268 Cannon Street, former position of London Stone*
> A small portion of London Stone was until 1960 incorporated in the S. Wall of St. Swithin's Church, but until 1742 it stood on the south side of Cannon Street in approximately the position shown – now in the middle of the widened road. It is not unlikely that the base, and perhaps even the main part of the stone, is still buried here. The portion removed from the church wall is shaped artificially to a rounded top, and is evidently merely the upper part of the great stone which Stow describes as being deep-rooted in the ground. It is of Clipsham Limestone, and is quite featureless apart from two grooves worn at the top. From the time of Camden [c. 1586], it has been suggested that it was a Roman milestone, possibly the central milestone of the Province, from which all distances were measured. Modern archaeologists have been sceptical of this, and there is no evidence of a Roman date, though the stone was certainly in existence in the early Middle Ages, and according

to Stow it is mentioned in a Gospel book given by King Athelstan to Christ's Church, Canterbury. In excavations for rebuilding after the Great Fire [1666], mosaic pavements and other Roman remains were found in the adjoining ground to the south, and the stone certainly stood beside a Roman road.[4]

This entry is preceded by the following:

> *267 Cannon Street, site of St. Swithin's Church, 1960–1*
> Excavations by Professor W. F. Grimes showed that the natural surface was overlaid by 4–6ft. of Roman deposits. A burnt layer containing daub, tile-fragments, plaster and pottery suggesting a date in the second century rather than the first, was observed. The Roman road was located near the south edge of the site, with gravel metalling about 4ft. thick, and a gully along its N. edge, which was 5 ft. inside the church, in the eastern part of the site. Post holes along the N. side of the gully suggested an early timber building. This had been succeeded by a Roman building with foundations of knapped flints, cut into the burnt level and therefore of a later date. It had a corridor 11 ft. wide internally, on its south side adjacent to the street. To the north were small compartments, much damaged by the church vaults.[5]

An earlier description of the London Stone, prior to the demolition of St Swithin's Church and its rebuilding as a bank, is contained in an inventory of the historical monuments in London, by the Royal Commission on Historical Monuments, published in 1928.

> Set in a stone case in the front S. Wall of St. Swithin's Church is the large rounded block of stone known as London Stone. It stood formerly on the S. side of the street 'near to the channel,' says Stow, pitched upright, fixed in the ground very deep and fastened with bars of iron. In building operations after the Great Fire, it was found to have a large foundation, and 'in the adjoining ground on the S. side (upon digging for cellars . . .) were discovered some tessellated pavements, and other remains of Roman workmanship'. In 1742, the stone was moved to the N. side of the street, and reset close to the wall near the S.W. door of St. Swithin's Church. It was again moved in 1798. Its original position is recorded on Strype's plan of Walbrook Ward. The block is now quite formless, and there is no evidence of its original use. Camden considered it to be a Roman milestone, but as Stow[6] says: 'the cause why this stone was set there, the time when, or other memory hereof is none.'[7]

I have quoted the above extracts in full partly to provide the reader with contemporary knowledge concerning the stone but also to illustrate how this information is usually presented in a biased way. The RCHM extract, though clearly true in as far as it goes, gives the impression that the whole stone and not just part of it was placed in the wall of the church in 1742. Thus the reader could be excused for thinking that the small block is all that there is of the stone. In fact, as the extract from Merrifield's book shows, this is only the top of the stone, which was cut off in 1742 so that Cannon Street could be widened. Thus there is every likelihood that the main body of the stone, which by all accounts was very large and fixed upright with iron bars, is still buried under Cannon Street.

What excited me, though, was that, unintentionally, these descriptions of excavations provided evidence for Trinovantum. Professor Grimes says he found a 'burnt layer' into which the foundations for a later Roman building were cut. Without saying why, he suggests that the burnt layer dates to the second century. Yet we know from the histories, Roman as well as British, that London was burnt down by Boudicca c. AD 60. Could not the layer of destruction refer to this event? Could it have been the timber building, represented by the post holes and probably of pre-Roman construction, that was burnt down then?

This is an intriguing possibility, but even more exciting is what is implied by another snippet, which I have not had time to explore further and leave to others to follow up. Merrifield's Gazetteer records that massive walls were found, a few yards south of Cannon Street by what is now the station, whilst sewers were being built in 1840–1.

> At the Junction of Bush Lane and Gophir Lane (formerly Cross Lane) was found a massive wall 20–22 ft. in width crossing Bush Lane diagonally (approximately to N.N.W.). It was built of flints and ragstone, with occasional masses of tiles, the flints prepondering on the N. side and the ragstone on the S. – suggesting two dates. The top of the wall was 6 ft. below the level of the modern pavement, and the sewer excavation continued to depth of 15 ft., apparently without reaching the bottom.[8]

Though again he doesn't say so, such a thick structure could only be part of either a citadel or city wall. If Grimes's excavations of St Swithin's revealed that the Roman levels were only four to six feet below the present pavement level, who built this wall that goes down more than fifteen feet? Could the structure be part of the original walls of Trinovantum, initially raised by Brutus in memory of Troy and later rebuilt by King Llud shortly before the invasion of Julius Caesar? This is an intriguing thought, for it means that archaeologists may have already, unwittingly, stumbled upon the ruins of 'New Troy', which was probably quite a small city originally, or even perhaps just a citadel in the immediate vicinity of the London Stone. According to the histories, it was only much later, under the famed King Llud, that a curtain wall was extended to enclose what we now call the Square Mile.

> NEw Troy my name: when first my fame begun
> By Trajon Brute: who then me placed here:
> On fruitfull foyle. where pleasant Thames doth run
> Sith Lud my Lord, my King and Lover dear,
> Encreaft my bounds: and London (far that rings
> Through Regions large) he called then my name
> How famous fince (I ftately feat of Kings)
> Have flourifh'd aye :let others that proclaim.
> And let me joy thus happy ftill to fee
> This vertuous Peer my Soveraign King to be.

SURVIVAL OF THE BRUTUS TRADITION IN SEVENTEENTH-
CENTURY LONDON

What then could the London Stone really be? Tysylio tells us that when Brutus and his fellow Trojans arrived in Britain they circumnavigated the island in search of a suitable site on which to build their capital. Eventually, perhaps guided by dreams or other portents, they chose this site on the north bank of the Thames as the right spot for their New Troy. Assuming that this story is true, it would seem natural that they would have raised a memorial to celebrate both their lucky escape and new beginnings in Britain. All evidence from the triads and other early writings indicates that the Trojans were a very religious people – at least as much as the Irish, who had their Lia-Fail or 'Stone of Destiny' as a symbol of their covenant with God. It seems reasonable to suppose, therefore, that the London Stone was put up by Brutus and his fellow Britains to symbolize the new covenant between them and God. This would explain why, though its real significance would have been lost to memory after the Saxon takeover of London, it was a 'fetish' in the Middle Ages. As the omphalos (that is, a stone marking the central point) of the capital city, it would have been considered the central spot of the kingdom and accordingly all distances would indeed have been measured in relation to it. In this sense it would have been, as Camden suggested, the central milestone.

Though it may be many years before we are able to demolish the buildings on Bush Lane to take another look at the walls of Trinovantum, it would be relatively easy to retrieve the rest of the London Stone from its tomb beneath the road. That in itself would be a great day for London. Who knows – we may even find some writing on it: evidence that this was indeed the foundation stone of the city. It is a curious irony that since the start of the 1960s, the decade which many now believe to have been the time when Britain lost its direction, the head of the stone has been housed not in a church but in the walls of a bank. Symbols are not everything, of course, and one shouldn't be superstitious, but that does sound like bad Feng Shui, to borrow an oriental term; it is like pawning the Crown Jewels. Perhaps it is time, now that Scotland's stone has been sent north to Edinburgh, that the English stirred themselves to attempt to retrieve the main body of our own sacred stone and reunite it with its cap. Who knows, maybe then we will see a turnaround in the fortunes of this island, which Edward III termed Troylebaston, the 'bastion of Troy'.

Summary of the findings of the 1990 excavations of the Church of St Peter's-super-Montem

The excavations of autumn 1990 of the ruins of St Peter's Church were intended (a) to probe the antiquity of the building, which the Welsh Ancient Monuments Commission believed to date from no earlier than the thirteenth century and which Alan Wilson and Baram Blackett believed to be of more ancient origin; and (b) to seek proof of the burial of Arthur II. By its very nature excavation works backwards, the most recent structures being encountered before the more ancient lower layers; however, for the sake of clarity this report begins with the earliest structures and works forwards in time.

STAGE 1

On the top of the mountain a great mound monument was built at an early, unknown period. The site is a patch of marshland and is the sump from which three streams break out. This monument is a vast boat-shaped mound and ditch, some 180 yards long by 96 yards wide. We believe this 'ship' to be a site of Christian worship, the Cor Emrhys (as explained in Chapter 13).

STAGE 2

It appears that some time later a rectangular building was erected, downhill and to the south-west of the original swampy *cor*. This building had a rough floor of flat stones compacted into the earth. It appears to have been 35 feet long by 16 feet wide. As there are only vestigial traces of what might have been wall footings, it would seem to have been a timber building over the rough flagstone floor. The reason for choosing this lower site rather than building in the *cor* itself is obvious. It is a fairly flat, dry plateau shielded from the north winds and open to the southern sunshine. Old photographs show that the church was once surrounded by trees, which would have acted as a windbreak.

The St Peter's Church at Cor Emrys is recorded as having been burnt during the Saxon revolt and the subsequent massacre at the Peace Conference that took place in c. AD 466. The findings of the excavation were consistent with this. Significantly, there were traces of burning on these first, flat stones. Later excavation revealed further areas of burning in several places over the now exposed, ancient floor. A trial hole, dug two feet down in the south-west corner of this floor, showed further evidence of burnt vegetable matter and charred stones.

STAGE 3

The main floor of the Stage 1 building lay three and a half feet below the level of a later (1610) church, though there were some architectural features at the eastern end which were only one and a half feet below. A small circular building was found immediately adjoining these areas of raised stonework. This appears to have had its entrance to the west and was slightly elliptical, being some 8–9 feet across and 10 feet long. This circular building was typical for a fifth- to seventh-century 'Celtic hermitage', as these were usually shaped like beehives. The crudeness of the remaining stonework would suggest that the resident hermit or saint probably lived in a circular leather tent, which would have looked rather like a Mongolian yurt. The 'Life of St David' and other sources suggest that Welsh saints of this era often did live in structures of this sort.

It was thought at first that there might have been some sort of apse added to the circular beehive structure, until it was realized that the western end had simply been removed when the church had been enlarged centuries later.

STAGE 4

At some later date a solid rectangular stone building was erected. This enclosed both the very early platform building (Stage 2) and the beehive hermitage of Stage 3. It was evident from this that the builders of this new church knew precisely where the former churches had stood. The Stage 3 building had walls that were approximately two and a half feet thick, with flat stone faces and rubble infill. It bore little or no resemblance to what is considered to be typically Norman walling. There was a surviving lancet window in the wall, in a style that is generally referred to as 'Early English' and was in use between AD 650 and 850. As the Normans did not reach Cardiff, which is twenty-four miles away, until 1091 and were excluded from the uplands of Glamorgan for a further two hundred years, we can say with confidence that this window, and therefore this stage of the church, was pre-Norman.

Once more there were extensive signs of burning all across the level of the floor associated with this building. This matches historical records of Mercian raids into the area, and of other raids by the 'Black Horde' (Vikings from Normandy and Dublin), which took place from 826 and during which churches were the main targets.

STAGE 5

Evidence shows that the Stage 4 building was later expanded uphill to the east. Because the extension was on a higher level, it became necessary to raise the floor level throughout. This undoubtedly helped in preserving the evidence of the earlier structures.

One side of a new south-facing door was built in the south-east corner of the previous Stage 4 building. A new lancet window was inserted to the west of this door. This lancet window, however, differs in style from the Early English window of the previous stage. The altar, which had probably been moved several times already, was also moved to the east of the building, inside the new extension.

STAGE 6

It would seem that in *c*. 1400 a chancel was added to the Stage 5 building, again being attached to the east end. This entailed going further up the hill and again the floor level of the main structure was raised to accommodate it. By this time the level of piled earth at the west end of the church was about four feet high, creating a pressure on the walls that must have been huge. The chancel had another, as yet unexplained, feature: in the north-west corner and below the floor level there was a separated area, covered by two stone slabs of roughly 6 feet by 2¹/₂ feet. Under here was a sandy soil infill, unusually free of bones from its shape and other detritus. It was in this area that the stone of Arthur II was found and a niche in the wall looks to have been where it was once housed. Accordingly, a pit was dug to a depth of about five feet, but as there was a danger that further excavation could undermine the neighbouring wall, it was not possible to dig deeply enough to confirm, once and for all, that this was not where Arthur II lies buried.

STAGE 7

A large porch was added onto the southern doorway. This was equipped with stone benches and measured roughly 10 feet by 10 feet. A flight of steps was found inside the porch leading into the church from the lower, outside ground level. The raising of the floor level of the church with its successive expansion to the east made these steps necessary.

STAGE 8

The final building effort took place in the seventeenth century. At this time the building was shortened by sixteen feet, by removing a length of walling from its western end. It would seem that this had been done because over time the piled-up earth inside the walls, exerting an outward pressure, had seriously weakened the walls and necessitated the demolition of the western end of the church. This theory was further supported by the fact that some sixteen feet of the original Stage 2 platform floor lay buried in rubble outside of the ruins of the present church.

Edward Lluyd visited the Church of St Peter's in 1697 and reports the building as having been derelict. It was, however, brought back into use and was finally abandoned only in 1838. Thereafter it became the scene of constant graverobbing and vandalism, resulting in the present sorry state of the building.

The Great Stone Port and the Welsh Dykes

The River Severn, the longest in Britain, poses particular difficulties for navigation. Principal among these is its extraordinary tidal variation of up to forty feet, which gives rise to its famous 'bore' (a wave caused by the incoming tide at certain times of year that can run up river as far as Tewkesbury). In the Cardiff area, which is typified by mudflats, the variation of the tides means that the sea retreats for a very long way at low tide, leaving ships beached and therefore useless for military purposes.

Before land was reclaimed in order to build the Alexandra and Roath docks, the shoreline between the Taff and Ely estuaries was long and straight, corresponding to today's high-water mark for spring tides. Beyond this high-water mark there is a low, flat shelf of mudflats extending for well over a mile to the Orchard ledges where the shelf ends and the water deepens sharply. When the tide is out the mudflats are exposed. It was on the edge of these flats that we believe the ancient British kings built a great stone port in the sea, to overcome the problems created by the tides. Until recently there was a long, straight road running down through Splott in south-east Cardiff, called Portmanmor Road, a name deriving from either Porth-Maen-Mor, meaning 'the Port of Stone in the Sea', or Porth-Maen-Mawr – 'the Great Port of Stone'. It points directly at the centre of the harbour whose ruins, although not marked on modern Ordnance Survey maps, were included in those drawn up by local cartographers in the nineteenth century. The harbour is shaped like a gigantic horseshoe with its mouth facing outwards towards the deeper water of the Severn Estuary. The bulk of the harbour sits on the mudflats with its entrance stretching over the shelf. The distance across its opening is approximately 400 yards, and it is 500 yards deep. Using this manmade harbour, ships could come and go as they pleased, regardless of the tides. It was certainly a remarkable structure and deserves to be explored archaeologically, for if there is anywhere in the British Isles where we could expect to find Dark Age wrecks, then this is it.

East of Cardiff the ancient Britons exploited the mudflats in other ways. Stretching all the way to Newport and even as far as the new Severn Bridge they reclaimed the land by means of a remarkable system of dykes. Behind these dykes and below sea level is rich farmland intercut with a system of canals and drainage ditches. There is much evidence that this system of dykes is much older than the Victorian pumping stations now to be seen in the area. In the *Legenda Sancti Goeznovii* (*Life of St Genovesius* – printed from a manuscript by A. de la Borderie) is a statement that Genovesius worked as one of 2,400 monks building dykes under the direction of St Illtyd 'in the land of Arthur'. Illtyd, of course, was a cousin of Arthur II and was a military commander before becoming a saint and refounding the Church of Llantwit Major in the sixth century. Thus the dykes must be as old as this at least and in fact Roman-inscribed stones have been found in the fabric of the dykes. St Andras, son of Morgan, son of Gwrgan Mawr, and therefore another cousin of Arthur II, built a chapel on a recorded site at Castleton – which is reclaimed land – further confirmation that the dykes were in existence during the sixth century.

The Normans used the Big Rill, the largest of the canals, to bring in ships and wine from France. The ridge of hills above this major canal is called the Cefn Mably, after Mabilia, the daughter of Robert Fitzhammon. She lived with her husband, Robert the Consul, on the site of Arthur II's old castle of Caor Melyn or Camelot. The recovered land below the castle is known as the marshfields, with a village called Marshfield in its centre. That the system of dykes was still in existence in Norman times is confirmed by the fact that at least one family from Marshfield, with ancestral roots going back to AD 1100, traditionally had the job of maintaining them. In 'Y Seint Greal' and other medieval texts the 'Lord of the Marshfields' is said to have made war on the 'Widow Lady of Ca'Melot'. Whatever else may be said of this story, the geography is correct.

In recent years, since the Second World War, both the harbour at Cardiff and the dyke system have come under attack by developers. Near Newport some of the dykes are actually being demolished at the moment to make way for new houses, factories or whatever. How the sea is to be contained without these defences we don't know. Presumably whoever lives there must resort to prayer instead. For the present at least the dykes are fulfilling their ancient role, but we would advise anyone interested in seeing this authentic Arthurian landscape, as envisioned by Tennyson in *The Lady of Shalott*, to visit the area soon before it, like Lyonesse, once more sinks beneath the waves.

The Ancestors of Owain, son of Hywell Dda, Prince of Dyfed

Hywell Dda of Dyfed was a great ruler and lawmaker, who had these king lists prepared for his son Owain's wedding. As the intention of producing such lists was to show noble descent, they traced the subject's ancestry back to someone important – preferably with some good names on the way. In this case, although Owain was born around AD 900, some of the lists go back as far as Anna, who the lists say was related to the Virgin Mary. There are thirty-three of these lists, some much longer than others, and they are arranged so that they begin at the present and go steadily back in time. The following are the most relevant to this book.

LIST 1

This concerns Owain's paternal descent from the kings of Gwynedd, going back through Maelgwn Gwynedd and Cuneda to their remote ancestors.

1. Owen the	d. 988	Owain (Owen)
2. son of Higuel	d. 950	Hywell Dda (Howell the Good), the Prince
3. son of Catel	d. 909	Cadell, Prince of Ceredigion and Ystrad Tawi
4. son of Rotn	d. 876	Rhodri Mawr (the Great), King of Wales
5. son of Mermin	d. 843	Merfyn Ffrych, King of the Isle of Man
6. and Ethel		and by marrying Ethel, King of Gwynedd
7. daughter of Cynas	d. 817	Cynan Tirdaethwg, King of Gwynedd
8. son of Rotin	d. 755	Rhodri Maelwynog, King of Gwynedd
9. son of Intguiaul	d. 720	Idwal Iwrch, King of Gwynedd
10. son of Catguelant	d. 686	Cadwallader, King of Gwynedd
11. son of Catgallaun	d. 660	Cadwallon, King of Gwynedd
12. son of Catman	d. 630	Cadfan, King of Gwynedd
13. son of Iacob	d. 603	Iago, King of Gwynedd
14. son of Beli	d. 599	Beli, King of Gwynedd – son of Einiavn

15. nephew of Rhun d. 586	Rhun, King of Gwynedd
16. son of Mailcun	Maelgwn Gwynedd, Dragon of Britain
17. son of Catalaun Lawhir	Cadwallon Longhand
18. son of Emiaun Girt	Emiaun
19. son of Cuneda	Cunneda Wledig
20. son of Oetern	Eternus
21. son of Patern Pesrud	Paternus 'red robe'
22. son of Tacit	Tacitus

After 'Tacit' there are a further fourteen names, which makes seventeen before Cuneda, who is estimated to have been born between AD 360 and 370. This means that, allowing for equal generations, the list goes back at least a further 350 years, which takes it back to around the time of Christ.

The names after Tacit are: Cein, Guorcein, Doli, Guordoli, Dumn, Guordumn, Amguoloyt, Amguerit, Oumun, Dubun, Brithguein, Eugein, Abatlac and Amalech. Then there is a note which says: 'Amalech the son of Beli the Great and his mother, whom they say was a blood-relative to Mary the Virgin, Mother of our Lord Jesus Christ.'

LIST 2

This lists Owain's ancestors on his mother's side.

1. Owein the	Owain (Owen)
2. son of Elen	Helen
3. daughter of Loumarc	Llywarch
4. son of Hineyt	Hyfaidd
5. son of Tancoyslt	Tancoyslt (inherited at Owain's death)
6. daughter of Owein	Owain (brother of Iddon and Regin)
7. brother of Margitiut	Mareddydd, King of Dyfed
8. son of Teudos	Tudor, King of Dyfed
9. son of Regin	Rhain (Rheinwg) King of Dyfed
10. son of Catoguon	Cadwgan
11. son of Catheu	
12. son of Cloten	
13. son of Nougey	Noe
14. son of Arthur	
15. son of Pets	Pascent, son of Vortigern?
16. son of Ciricar	Categan, son of Vortigern?
17. son of Guortepir	Vortiporix son of Aircol Lawhir (here confused with Vortimer, son of Vortigern)
18. son of	c. AD 470–540
19. son of Aircol (Lawhir)	Agricola Longhand c. AD 450–520

20. son of Triphun
21. son of Clotin
22. son of Cloitguin
23. son of Nimet
24. son of Dimet   Probably Eidinet, son of Arthur I
25. son of Maxim Guletic   Magnus Maximus, d. AD 388
26. son of Protec   Probably Emperor Theodosius
27. son of Protector   Probably General Theodosius
28. son of Ebiud   Possibly King Erbin
29. son of Eliud   Possibly King Euddav
30. son of Stater
31. son of Pincr Misser
32. Constans   d. 350   Constans, son of Constantine
33. Constantini Magni   d. 337   Constantine the Great
34. Constanti   d. 306   Constantius

This list appears to be correct for the first twelve, possibly fourteen, entries. After that, however, it appears to have become muddled by including all the sons of Vortigern. Pascent, Categan and Vortimer were sons of Vortigern by Servilla, who was a daughter of Magnus Maximus. If the Arthur who is listed as father of Nougey is really Athrwys, son of Meurig, there should be seven generations between him and Maxim Guletic (Magnus Maximus), but instead we have ten. The rest of the list appears to be little more than a recitation of important rulers of Britain going back to the time of Constantius.

An important note after the last entry refers to Constantius's wife: '*Et Helen Lu reduncque de Britan nia exiuit ad crucem Xr'i querendum usque ad Ierusalem et in de attulini se cum usque ad Constantinopolis et est ibi usque in Lodiernum diem*'. This translates roughly as: 'And Helen Lu (Linyddog?) who went out of Britain on a circuitous journey to search for the cross of Christ as far as Jerusalem and from there she brought it to Constantinople and it is there in "Lodiernum" [which could mean "in hiding" or, literally, "under a blanket"] today.'

LIST 4

(I)udgual
Tutagual
Anavaunt
Mermin
Anthec
Tutagual
Run
Neithon
Senill

Dinacat
Tutagual
Eidinet
Arthun   Arthur I or Andragathius
Maxim Gulc   Magnus Maximus
tic qui occidit   who killed Gratian the king
Gratiancum regum   of the Romans
Romanorum

LIST 10

Morcant
Coledauc
Morcant Bulc
Cincar Craut
Bran Hen
Dumngual Moilmut
Garbaniaun
Coel Hen Guptepauc   Coel Hen Godebog *c.* AD 400
Tecmant
Teuhant
Telpuil
Urban
Grat
Iumetel
Titigirn
Oudecant
Outigirn
Ebiud
Eudos
Eudelen
Aballac
Beli and Anna   This list descends from Anna

LIST 12

(G)urci ha Peretur mepion   Gwrgi and Peredur, brothers, died around
Eleuther Cascord Maur   AD 580. They were sons of Eliffer (Oliver)
                                 Gosgordd Fawr (which means 'of the great
                                 retinue')

(Gurgust) Letlum
Ceneu
Coyl Hen

341

The 'great retinue' to which Eliffer and his sons belonged must have been that of Arthur II. Eliffer was in fact King of Britain for six years around AD 585, just after Arthur II.

LIST 25

Iudnerth	(Kings of the West Midlands?)
son of Morgan	
son of Catgur	Possibly Gwrgan Mawr, father of Morgan, Caradoc and Onbrawst, mother of Arthur II
son of Merguid	
son of Moriutned	Friend of Vortigern
son of Morhen	
son of Morant	
son of Botan	
son of Morgen	
son of Mormayl	

Glast Unum (A 'Glast' – a man of Glastennen?)

Sunt Glastenic qui venerunt qu vocatur Loytcoyt

This last translates as 'Glastenic they are who come from what is called Loytcoyt [Wall or Old Lichfield].'

LIST 28

Iudhail	Ithael
Atwys	Athrwys (Artorius or Arthur)
Fernmail	Fernfael
Iudhail	Ithael (mentioned on Samson Stone)
Morcant	Morgan
Atwys	Athrwys (King Arthur II)
Mouric	Meurig (the Uthyr-Pendragon before Arthur)
Tendubric	Tewdrig (Theodoric, the martyr-king of Mathern)

This may well be the most important list of all as it concerns the Dynasty of South Wales, confirming the relationships between the kings as found in the Llandaff Charters and other places.

NOTES

PROLOGUE

1 Sir Thomas Malory, *Le Morte d'Arthur*, p. 1242.
2 I was later to discover that in Wales opposition to their ideas was not just passive but had at times been vociferous, leading to libellous statements in the press and even court actions. Clearly their work had touched some raw nerves and made them a number of powerful enemies.
3 The preserving of history is listed in the ancient triads as having been one of the duties of the bards.

CHAPTER 1. THE ONCE AND FUTURE KING

1 Known as Gryffyd ap Arthur in Wales.
2 Troia Newydd in Welsh.
3 That is, 'Llud's City' – after a king of that name.
4 A comet? This possibility will be explored in Chapter 16.
5 The name of this famous battle, also known as the Battle of Badon Hill, has a variety of spellings, e.g. Badon, Baedan, Baidan.
6 Athelstan (*c.* 894–940), grandson of Alfred the Great, was the first English king who could claim to rule over the entire island of Britain, including Scotland and parts of Wales. Athelstan ruled from 925 to his untimely death in 939. The Battle of Brunanburgh, by which he subdued Scotland and thereby made himself undisputed master of the entire island, was fought in 937.
7 Introduction to Geoffrey of Monmouth, *The History of the Kings of Britain*, trans. Lewis Thorpe, p. 17, Penguin Books, 1966.
8 The Welsh Chronicles, known as the *Brut Tysylio*, named after a St Tysylio

who is thought to have compiled them, are still in existence. This book was translated from Welsh into English by Peter Roberts and published as *The Chronicle of the Kings of Britain* (E. Williams, 1811). It is clear to any impartial reader that this is the book translated by Geoffrey of Monmouth.

9 E. O. Gordon, *Prehistoric London*, p. 4, Covenant Publishing Co., 1946.

10 John Morris, *The Age of Arthur*, p. 118, Weidenfeld & Nicolson, 1992.

11 Wolfram von Eschenbach, *Parzifal*, ed. André Lefevere, p. 124, Continuum Publishing Co., 1991.

12 Matt. 21:42.

13 It was first published by Polydore Vergil in 1525 but with many admitted changes and alterations. In tone it is strongly pro-Roman and anti-British – a very curious state of affairs for a book allegedly written by a British cleric of the sixth century at a time when the Church in Britain was divorced from Rome. Its avowed advocacy of the Roman position on all controversial matters, and the way it portrays the Britons as idle, helpless weaklings who are dependent on Roman favours, fly in the face of Welsh traditions. The suspicion is that the present text is really the work of a Roman Catholic monk writing not in the sixth century but more probably in the tenth.

14 John Morris, *The Age of Arthur*, p. xviii.

15 Geoffrey Ashe, *King Arthur's Avalon*, p. 9, Fontana, 1973.

CHAPTER 2. THE SECRET INHERITANCE OF WALES

1 'Cymry' is an alternative spelling. In either case the pronounciation is the same: come-ree.

2 In Wales Asser is known as the 'Blue Bard', his name being derived from the French root *azure*.

3 John Morris, *The Age of Arthur*, p. xv, Weidenfeld & Nicolson, 1973.

4 As he was of the Roman Church, brought to England in the wake of the Saxon invasions by St Augustine in AD 597, and many of these documents would have referred to the teachings of the original British Church founded centuries earlier, his motives appear to be suspect.

5 There is also a whole corpus of bardic material that was once preserved orally. The charge that this material is all of relatively recent composition flies in the face of tradition and grossly underestimates the ability of trained bards to memorize poetry.

6 It is interesting to note that Malory's *Le Morte d'Arthur* was first printed by Caxton in 1485. It is probably its early availability in printed form that

has made Malory's text so famous in comparison with older versions of the Arthurian legend.

7 Lloegres is the Welsh name for a region of Britain whose borders roughly correspond to present-day England.

8 Triads, of which there are literally hundreds, are a particular form of verse whereby diverse subjects, usually pithy sayings, are discussed in threes. These mnemonic triplets bear some comparison with the Haiku tradition of Japan.

9 The danger in using Williams's translations as source material has been recognized by some scholars and was even pointed out by W. J. Thomas when he gave the Rees Memorial Lecture in 1958. He noted, for example, that in the highly important poem 'Songs of the Graves' Williams had identified vague references to some 200 ancient kings and princes when there were only 70 to 80 named in the 'Songs'. For example, Williams renders the Welsh word 'Elchwyth' as a person of that name instead of translating it properly as 'extremely windy': thus what should be an accurate description relating to the place of Arthur's grave becomes gibberish.

10 Foreword to *Myvyrnian Archaiology of Wales*, eds. O. Jones, E. Williams and W. O. Righe, Thomas Gee, 1806, entitled 'A short review of the present state of Welsh manuscripts'.

11 The system of Coelbren writing predates the adoption of the Roman alphabet as the means of writing down Welsh. It is the original script in which Khymric was written and is still used, ceremonially, by modern-day bards.

12 Ibid.

CHAPTER 3. THE LLANDAFF CHARTERS

1 In Welsh the term 'ap' means 'son of' or 'successor to', the equivalent of the Scottish 'Mac' or Irish 'Mc'.

2 *The Liber Landavensis*, trans. Rev. W. J. Rees, pp. 602–3, Welsh MSS Society, 1890.

3 Ibid., pp. 576–7.

4 St Chad was a later, English bishop who fixed his see at Lichfield and died in AD 672.

5 Nearly twenty-seven acres.

6 *The Liber Landavensis*, pp. 381–2.

7 The Rivers Wye and Towy would mark the eastern and western boundaries of his diocese.

8 *The Liber Landavensis*, pp. 390–1.

9 The Gower peninsula is a district in western Glamorgan.

10 *The Liber Landavensis*, pp. 386–7.
11 Ibid., p. 411.
12 Ibid., pp. 383–4.

CHAPTER 4. FORGOTTEN STONES OF HERO KINGS

1 The time here alluded to must have been *c.* 1758.
2 It has since been moved back into the church itself and is placed next to the north wall.
3 By 'Etruscan' he is referring to writing in the Coelbren alphabet of the bards.
4 *Iolo MSS*, eds. Edward Williams and Taliesin Williams, pp. 363–4, Welsh MSS Society, 1848.
5 Ibid. In the edition published by Edward Williams, the last word is represented as *tecani*, interpreted by the Rev Thomas Price as *decani* and translated as 'deacon'. Other people read it as *tecain*, which seems to be an alternative spelling of *teyrn*, meaning 'ruler'. It is really three, abbreviated root words: *te-ca-ni*.
6 Later we visited the church in question and I saw this stone too.

CHAPTER 5. THE QUEST BEGINS

1 Iestyn (Justin) ap Gwrgan was the King of Glamorgan at the time of the Norman invasion of 1091.
2 The *Mabinogion*, plural of Mabinog, is the title of a collection of Welsh folk tales from the fourteenth-century 'Red Book of Hergest'.
3 Caesar, *The Conquest of Gaul*, trans. S. A. Handford, p. 28, Penguin Books, 1951.
4 He is more usually listed as his great-grandson.
5 Nennius, *Arthurian Period Sources*, ed. and trans. John Morris, vol. 8, pp. 18–19, Phillimore & Co, 1980.
6 Ibid., p. 22.
7 The kings of the Franks made similar claims of descent from Trojans through Antenor, a great-grandson of Hector, son of Priam, son of Laomedon, son of Ilus the brother of Assaracus. Again, like the British, they preserved royal genealogies going back to a Trojan War at around 650 BC (see note 3, Chapter 7). This date fits the Roman record as set down by Virgil in his epic poem the *Aeneid*, which concerns the migration of Aeneas from Troy to found Rome. Other ancient records of Frankish

marriages with daughters of British kings also match up very well. In any case, it was always understood until quite modern times that the followers of Brwth/Brutus were Brythons, their island, known to Arab writers like Gregory Bar Hebraeus as Brutus Land, later being called Britain.

8 Shakespeare makes an oblique reference to the Trojan origins of the Welsh in his play *Henry V* (V. i.), where the rascally Pistol twice refers to his Welsh companion Fluellen as a 'base Trojan'.

9 Hu Gadarn means 'Powerful, the Mighty One'.

10 Lloegres roughly corresponds to the province of Britannia Superior and Cymry to Britannia Inferior. Most of the region of Albyne (what we now call Scotland) lay outside the Roman Empire altogether, though in the fourth century a new province of Valentia was formed between Hadrian's Wall and the Clyde.

11 *Fir* means 'man' in Irish and *Bolg* is from the same root as the Latin *Belgae*.

12 It is possible that these Belgic tribes are the real 'Lloegrians' identified in the triads as being related to the British and as coming from the Loire region. In reality they probably came over from northern France and Belgium.

13 According to the Rev. Peter Roberts, translator of the *Brut Tysylio*, the name London could have been derived from *lliant* meaning 'strand' or 'shore' and *daln*, the old Welsh name for the Thames. Caer Lliant Dain or 'the Castle on the Shore of the Thames' would certainly be descriptive but there is no further evidence for this derivation.

14 E. O. Gordon, *Prehistoric London*, p. 106, Covenant Publishing Co., 1946.

15 Ibid.

16 Essylwg, the home of the 'Silures' (south Welsh Khymry), was in south-east Wales and roughly comprised the totality of what is now the counties of Glamorgan, Gwent and Brecon plus western Gloucester and eastern Carmarthen. It means 'abounding in prospects', a description of the land, not the people.

17 Following its invasion by the Picts, the territory of Albyne, or Scotland, tends not to feature much in the histories except as a source of trouble. Its kings are never mentioned as becoming pendragons of Britain.

CHAPTER 6. THE INVASION OF BRITAIN

1 This is not really a name but a title. It means 'ruler of the separated state'.

2 Rome, like Britain, had a colourful foundation legend closely linked to the aftermath of the Trojan War. According to this legend (most fully expounded by Virgil in the *Aeneid*), Aeneas, who as we have seen was a prince of the junior branch of the ruling house of Troy, escaped first to Africa (where he broke the heart of Dido, Queen of Carthage) and then to

Italy. Arriving at the mouth of the Tiber he was befriended by Latinus, the king of Latium, and married his daughter, Lavinia. In her honour he founded the city of Lavinium, the forerunner of Rome. Other, probably connected legends, indicate that in the sixth century BC the city was ruled by an Etruscan house of kings known as the Tarquins. They came from the Etruscan city of Tarquinia, slightly to the north of Rome, and supplanted the native line. The last of these kings, Lucius Tarquinius Superbus, was a proud, arrogant man who acted like a tyrant. He was very unpopular with the citizens of Rome and, following the rape by his son of a high-born lady called Lucretia, the citizens of Rome rose in rebellion and drove the entire Tarquin family into exile. Rome became a republic and over a period of centuries evolved a very sophisticated constitution based on a subtle balance of power. Though they no longer had kings of their own, the Romans did not forget Aeneas and the Trojans. Caesar was clearly intrigued by the British connection.

3   *Brut Tysylio*, pp. 74–5.
4   Caesar, *The Conquest of Gaul*, pp. 102–3.
5   This name, as so many others, is really an acronym and comes from the Welsh *Man-ddu-bradwr*, meaning 'the One Marked as the Black Traitor'.
6   Caesar, *The Conquest of Gaul*, pp. 113–14.
7   Geoffrey of Monmouth, *The History of the Kings of Britain*, p. 100.
8   Caesar, *The Conquest of Gaul*, p. 111.
9   Strabo.
10 Geoffrey of Monmouth, *The History of the Kings of Britain*, p. 111. Remnants of these defences have been found recently, the base of the stakes indeed being sheathed in lead and sunk into the mud of the river-bed.
11 Today Westminster Bridge stands roughly on the site where this battle would have taken place. It is no doubt not a coincidence that here, guarding the north bank of the Thames, is the famous bronze sculpture of Boudicca, whose rebellion in AD 60 held up Roman expansion into Britain.
12 Caesar, *The Conquest of Gaul*, p. 113.
13 Ibid.
14 Population figures for ancient Britain are being revised upwards all the time. Collingwood in 1929 estimated that the population was 'probably half a million, at most one million'. Mortimer Wheeler in 1930 changed this to 'one and a half million'. In 1955 W. G. Haskins said this was too low and should be two million. Professor Frere said it was 'over two million' in AD 100. Since 1973, with the discovery of many more ancient sites and the development of new tools such as aerial photography, this figure has been further revised. Christopher Smith and Barry Cunliffe in their book *The Iron Age in Britain* admit that 'It may be necessary to revise

the estimate of the Romano-British population to 5 or 6 millions'. Since then even more sites have been discovered, revealing just how densely populated Britain was even before the Romans arrived.

15 Cynfelyn was a son of Nennius, another brother of Caswallon, who died from his wounds following hand-to-hand fighting with Caesar himself.

16 Tacitus, *The Annals of Imperial Rome*, trans. Michael Grant, p. 265, Penguin Books, 1977.

17 Confusingly, some accounts make Caradoc the son of Bran. This is a mistake. There were two 'Caradocs': Caradoc ap Arch and Caradoc ap Bran (see Genealogy of Iestyn ap Gwryan).

18 Vespasian and Titus were later to become Emperors of Rome.

19 The Brigantes were another Khymric tribe occupying virtually the whole of northern England.

20 Tacitus, *The Annals of Imperial Rome*, p. 267.

21 Ibid.

22 *Iolo MSS*, p. 345.

23 Tacitus, *The Annals of Imperial Rome*, p. 332.

CHAPTER 7. THE ROMANS IN BRITAIN

1 Percy Enderbee, *Cambria Triumphans or Britain in its Perfect Lustre*, Book III, 1661.

2 Jane Williams writes: 'There is no record or mention of any Roman governor of Britain between Sallustius Lucullus, who was put to death by Domitian, and Neratus Marcellus, who was a *praefect* (i.e. not a *propraetor* or governor) under Trajan about the year 106, and superintended the making and alteration of roads throughout the subjugated part of the island. Hadrian ascended the imperial throne (AD 117), and little is known of Britain between the departure of the great *Propraetor* Agricola (AD 84) and the arrival of that emperor, AD 121.' Jane Williams, *A History of Wales*, pp. 42–3, Longmans, Green & Co., 1869.

3 The traditional Greek date of 1200 BC for the Trojan war is looking increasingly suspect in the light of new evidence. A date of *c*. 750 BC is now being openly talked about, with *c*. 650 BC not being impossibly late. For more information on this see Peter James, *Centuries of Darkness*.

4 A province more or less corresponding to modern-day Romania and Transylvania.

5 Jane Williams writes: 'The legions were regularly recruited from Britain, even when the country was but partly conquered; and the levies of men increased, not only with the extent of territorial subjection, but, from the days of Vitellius, with exigencies consequent upon the foreign and civil

wars of the empire. Many military cohorts and squadrons entirely composed of Cymry and Lloegrwys, were also reckoned among the standing armies of Rome, and served in Egypt, Armenia, Illyricum, Spain, Gaul, and other lands, without a prospect of ever returning to their homes . . . During the long period of bloody strife which preceded the fall of the Western Empire, Britain furnished a fourth part of the Roman armies.' Jane Williams, *A History of Wales*, pp. 58–9.

6 Percy Enderbee, *Cambria Triumphans or Britain in its Perfect Lustre*.

7 *Brut Tysylio*, pp. 47–8.

8 Ibid., p. 53.

9 Scythia here denotes not southern Russia, the original home of the Scythians, but northern Europe and Denmark in particular, to which they had long since migrated.

10 *Brut Tysylio*, pp. 89–90.

11 In reality Severus was the Emperor and certainly didn't take orders from the senate!

12 *Brut Tysylio*, pp. 91–2.

13 In Geoffrey of Monmouth's *History* he is more correctly called Sulgentius, the result of the usual confusion of 'f' and 's' in the English language. In the original Welsh of the *Brut Tysylio*, though, he is Sylien, which properly translates as Julian.

14 Percy Enderbee, *Cambria Triumphans or Britain in its Perfect Lustre*, Book III, pp. 142–3.

15 Ibid., p. 143.

16 He means Bassianus, who adopted the name Antoninus out of respect to the earlier Emperors Antoninus Pius and Marcus Aurelius Antoninus.

17 After Julius Caesar, Claudius and Hadrian.

18 Elagabalus's mother is recorded by Spartians as having been Julia Soaemia Bassiana, a niece of Julia Domna.

19 Gaius Iulius Verus Maximinus was Emperor for three years, from AD 235–8. He is said to have been a Thracian shepherd before joining the army, though this seems unlikely.

CHAPTER 8. THE ROYAL COLLEGE OF THE CHRISTIANS

1 Traditionally St Ilid became the chaplain of King Bran, often referred to as Bran the Blessed. The exact position of Bran within the Khymric dynasty is not clear. Some records seem to identify him as Caradoc's father Arch, others as King Ceri's great-grandson. The truth seems to be that he was the latter and was a young boy at the time St Ilid came to Britain.

2 Much more will be said about Magnus Maximus later.
3 There are two other circles in neighbouring fields, now almost completely obliterated by the plough.
4 This dating comes from Gildas, who writes that Christianity was brought to Britain 'in the last years of the emperor Tiberius, at a time when Christ's religion was being propagated without hindrance: for, against the wishes of the senate, the emperor threatened the death penalty for informers against soldiers of Christ'. Tiberius died in AD 37, but this extraordinary statement seems to suggest that he was not only tolerant of the new religion but actively encouraged its promulgation.
5 *Iolo MSS*, pp. 343–4.
6 In Latin writing the same symbol is used for 'v' and 'u', so her name is really Genuissa.
7 Just to the north of Fortress Mountain.
8 Unfortunately, though the stone is on display at the British Museum, it currently stands with these pictures turned inwards towards a display case, which itself is only about a foot away from the stone. To make it even harder for the interested observer to examine the pictures properly, the stone has been turned upside down. Thus anyone not knowing what they were looking at would probably walk straight past without giving the stone a second glance. One could be excused for thinking that the way this important stone is displayed is part of a conspiracy to conceal its significance; however, it is more likely a matter of simple carelessness on the part of its custodians, who don't realize its true significance.
9 G. F. Jowett, *The Drama of the Lost Disciples*, p. 83, Covenant Publishing Co., 1980.
10 At the time these would have been occupied by the Picts, who came from Scandinavia and were enemies of the Khymric British.
11 *Brut Tysylio*, p. 86.
12 In another version of the Welsh Chronicle her name is given as Gwenisa.
13 Geoffrey of Monmouth, *The History of the Kings of Britain*, p. 121.
14 G. F. Jowett, *The Drama of the Lost Disciples*, p. 86.
15 Details of her trial are contained in Suetonius, lib. vi, Ch. 16; in Pliny, *Epistles*, lib. x. epigram 98, and in Tacitus, the *Annals of Imperial Rome*, xv.
16 2 Tim. 4:21.
17 Rom. 16:13.
18 Martial, lib. ii, epigram 54.
19 Martial, lib. iv, epigram 13.
20 G. F. Jowett, *The Drama of the Lost Disciples*, p. 126.
21 *Irenaei Opera*, 3:1, Ivancus.
22 As the Romans called the River Dart the Ravenatone, it seems likely that

'Raphinus' refers to Totnes, a likely port to cross to from Brittany.
23 G. F. Jowett, *The Drama of the Lost Disciples*, p. 189.

CHAPTER 9. THE CROSS OF CHRIST

1 Percy Enderbee, *Cambria Triumphans or Britain in its Perfect Lustre*, Book I, p. 166.
2 The reason why her reputation was blackened by St Ambrose, and by inference the legitimacy of her son Constantine called into question, will become apparent later.
3 Night-hawks are people who come out to archaeological sites with metal detectors under the cover of darkness, usually looking for Roman coins or other trinkets. They have a very uneasy relationship with orthodox archaeologists because they often end up destroying the science of a site in their pursuit of metal objects.

CHAPTER 10. THE PIRATE KINGDOM AND THE CONSTANTINE SUCCESSION

1 This can only be conjecture.
2 Evans, *Glamorgan, History and Topography*, 1936, p. 316.
3 Not only was he an appointed Augustus but he was also the great-great-nephew of the Emperor Claudius II, who briefly ruled between 268 and 270.
4 Victorinus and Tetricus were probably close relatives and may even have been brothers, as the former's mother, Victoria, ensured that the Empire passed to the latter after her son was murdered.
5 Valerian was co-emperor with Gallienus. He was captured by the Persians at Edessa and ended his days as the slave of Sharpur II, acting as the latter's footstool when mounting his horse. After he died his body was flayed, the skin dyed red and hung up to be shown as a warning to visitors. That the Romans were powerless to save their Emperor's skin perhaps illustrates the essential weakness of the Empire of his day.
6 Claudius II is named as Gloyw Gwalltir in a Welsh genealogy contained in the Jesus College Manuscript 20. This document contains another illuminating gloss that 'this man here made on the edge of the Severn a town and his name he carefully concealed in "Caer Gloyw" [Castle of Claudius]'. This is clearly a reference to the founding of Gloucester, which, curiously enough, Geoffrey of Monmouth had attributed to Claudius I. The name Gloyw is probably the root from which is derived Clovis, the ancestral

name of the kings of the Franks, which in its later form became 'Louis'. Whether Clovis, the first of the Frankish kings to be crowned at Reims, claimed descent from Claudius II, who died some three hundred years earlier, is something that needs further research. The Welsh version of the name Louis is, of course, Lewis. Perhaps this name also owes its origins to the legendary founder of Gloucester.

7 *Iolo MSS*, p. 352.

8 *Brut Tysylio*, pp. 94–5.

9 The story that these Romans were massacred in cold blood and their heads thrown into the Walbrook seemed fictional until the excavations of General Pitt-Rivers revealed evidence for this gruesome event.

10 Matthew Paris makes this AD 315.

11 '*At Octavius in Britanniam reversus, regnum Romanis dissipatis occupavit, et illud annis multis pacifice gubernavit.*' Matthew Paris, 1. 157.

12 It is estimated that while Magnentius lost 24,000 men, Constantius suffered losses of 30,000, which severely weakened his forces in the face of the ongoing threat from Persia.

13 He had briefly been made Caesar in 351, presumably to recover and run the western Empire.

14 G. F. Jowett, *The Drama of the Lost Disciples*.

CHAPTER 11. THE GLASTONBURY HOAX

1 *Glastons* means 'place of oak trees' in Breton and Cornish (which are languages closely related to Welsh; *Glastennen* means 'scarlet oak' in Welsh). 'Bury' means earthwork or burial mound. Presumably the monks took the interpretation of Glastonbury as 'earthwork or burial mound among the oak trees' to mean that Glastennen was Glastonbury. However, such a description could apply to many places.

2 King Alfred ruled Wessex 871–99, King Edgar 959–75.

3 He is also the same monk who later would pour such scorn and invective on the work of Geoffrey of Monmouth, accusing the latter of blatant lying. He loathed the Welsh and greatly applauded the expulsion of their entire community from Exeter over the Devon border into Cornwall.

4 Also founded by Alfred as a nunnery following his victory over the Danes.

5 According to these legends, Jesus visited Britain with his 'uncle' Joseph of Arimathea whilst still a boy. He is said to have stayed for a while at Glastonbury and to have built his own hut of wattle and daub. This hut is later said to have been turned into a church by St Joseph and dedicated to the Virgin Mary after he returned to Britain following the Crucifixion.

CHAPTER 12. THE SEARCH FOR ARTHUR I

1 Also spelt Lectoceto or Letoceto in later texts such as the 'Ravenna Cosmography'.
2 The 'learned Llwyd', who was writing around the time of William and Mary and Queen Anne.
3 By the Weights and Measures Act of 1878.
4 A name possibly indicating fields belonging to Glastonbury.
5 The hart or deer, especially one that is white, is considered lucky amongst the Welsh.
6 *Vinddu* or *finddu* means 'black-lipped' – that is, he had a moustache.

CHAPTER 13. THE CHURCH ON THE HILL

1 A fuller archaeological report is included in the appendices.
2 The province of Erging was on the River Wye, encompassing the area between it and the River Severn, which today lies in the counties of Gloucester and Hereford & Worcester. Euas or Ewyas, adjacent to Erging, was the upper part of Gwent and Monmouth, to the east of the Black Mountains.
3 According to this account, Constans had two brothers, Ambrosius Aurelius and Uatherpendragon. Tysylio does not seem to have realized that 'Ambrosius Aurelius' is really two people: Em-Rhys Wledig and Gwrgan Mawr, nor that 'Uatherpendragon' is a title held by many different kings.
4 *Brut Tysylio*, pp. 109–10.
5 *The Anglo-Saxon Chronicle*, trans. Anne Savage, p. 25, Macmillan, 1982.
6 Presumably Valentinian III, who was, nominally at least, Emperor of Rome and the western Empire from 425 to 455. What kingdom they received is not clear. It could not have been Britain as this was already outside the Empire and had its own ruler in the person of Vortigern.
7 In east Kent, just south of Ramsgate.
8 Presumably it was Vortigern and his party of Britons who were apprehensive of Ambrosius – that is, Teithfallt.
9 The promontory on the north-east tip of Kent, which, though now contiguous with the rest of the county, was then cut off by rivers.
10 Presumably the origin of the name Ramsgate for the principal port of Thanet.
11 Nennius. As King Edmund of Wessex reigned from 939–46, this would mean that the Saxons first arrived in 397, two years after the death of Theodosius. Hengist must have met Vortigern fifty years later, 447 years after the birth, rather than the passion, of Christ.

12 Nennius, *Six Old English Chronicles*, Ch. 31, ed. J. A. Giles, Henry G. Bohn, 1848.

13 Ibid., Ch. 37.

14 Ibid.

15 Ibid., Ch. 46.

16 Though Nennius puts it before, Geoffrey and Tysylio place this event after the disaster of the Peace Conference.

17 This was built in an almost inaccessible valley near Llithfaen on the Lleyn Peninsula.

18 Merlin means 'little horse', a title which implies wisdom in the Welsh Gnostic tradition. The 'Merlin' of legend, the counsellor of the Utherpendragon Meurig and his son Athrwys, was Taliesin. He is remembered for his wisdom as one of the very greatest of the Welsh bards.

19 As explained in Chapter 4, he was in fact son of Teithrin, successor to Nymaw.

20 *Iolo MSS*, p. 353.

21 Contained in the *Iolo MSS* is a list called 'The Genealogies of the Saints of the Island of Britain' collected by Iolo from 'The Book of Mr Cobb of Cardiff'. This includes the entry 'Teithvalch, the son of Nyniaw, called also Tudvwlch, the son of Nyniaw. His church is Llandudvwich, in Gower.' This must be the same as Llandyfodwg, with 'Gower' being read instead of 'Ogwyr' where the church stands. A common error.

CHAPTER 14. ARTHUR II, KING OF GLAMORGAN

1 Nennius, *British History and Welsh Annals*, ed. and trans. John Morris, Phillimore, 1981.

2 A large iron-age hill fort guarding the middle reaches of the River Stour.

3 In Welsh the first letter in a word often mutates, in this case from 'c' to 'g', when words are combined.

CHAPTER 15. THE COMING OF THE KING OF AFRICA

1 *The Mabinogion*, trans. Geoffrey Ganz, Penguin Books, 1976.

2 In 'The Genealogy of Iestyn the Son of Gwrgan' she is recorded as having been martyred by heathen Saxons – quite possibly Vandals. The place of her martyrdom was Merthyr Tydfil, and her stained-glass window is to be seen in Llandaff Cathedral.

3 In the *Bruts of England* it says of this (in places I have rendered the text into modern English): 'When Gurmonde had wasted and destroyed all the

land throughout, he gave the land to the Saxons; and they took it with good will, for the Saxons long time had desired it, for-as-much as they were of Engistes [Hengist's] Kindred, that first had all the land of Britain, and they let them be called Englishmen, for as much as in his time it was called Engistes lande, when he had conquered it of Vortiger that had spoused his daughter. But from the time that Brut came first into Engeland, this land was called Britaigne, and the folk Britons, till the time that this Gurmonde afterwards conquered it and gave it unto the Saxons, and they anon right changed the name, as before is said.' *Bruts of England*, Early English Text Society, Oxford University Press, 1960.

4   The invasion of Wessex, that is the region of central-southern England, is problematic to say the least. Place names described in the *Chronicle* are unknown and the kings, Cerdic and Cynric, who led the invasion of Wessex, have British names.

CHAPTER 16. THE LOST CITY

1   In Latin 'u' and 'v' are the same letter.
2   A. L. F. Rivet and C. Smith, *The Place Names of Roman Britain*, pp. 505–6, Batsford.
3   *Brut Tysylio*, p. 86.
4   Geoffrey of Monmouth, *The History of the Kings of Britain,* p. 121.
5   There is some confusion here with names, for, as we have seen earlier, Tysylio is rather mixed up concerning identities. He imagines Em-Rhys (Ambrosius) and Uther to have been brothers. In fact Merddin himself is the real Em-Rhys Wledig and the 'Uther' in question would have been his grandson, Meurig, the father of Athrwys or Arthur II. These reservations apart, which stem from Tysylio's lack of access to all the genealogies, we can see that he is making an important statement about a comet.
6   *Brut Tysylio*, pp. 131–2.
7   In fact Tysylio seems to be wrong in this. According to Alan, 'Utherpendragon' was a title that meant 'Wonderful Head of the Dragons', meaning commander-in-chief or field-marshal.
8   *Brut Tysylio*, pp. 131–2.
9   Presumably his shield or breastplate.
10   This seems to be the original name for Excalibur, which Geoffrey calls Caliburn. According to the translator, Caledvwlch means 'the Hard Cleft' – a good name for a sword.
11   *Brut Tysylio*, pp. 131–2.
12   Cadwallader is a title rather than a name, meaning 'Battle Sovereign'.
13   King of Brittany.

14 Probably a province of Scotland settled by Scandinavians.

15 *Brut Tysylio*, pp. 187–8.

16 Llandaff Charters, p. 75.

17 The book *The Cosmic Winter* by Dr Clube and his associate Bill Napier (Oxford University Press, 1990) mainly concerns earlier events at the time of ancient Egypt and Sumeria. Since its publication in 1990, their work has extended to encompass the Arthurian period.

18 The mechanism by which this happens is rather too complicated to explain here.

19 The sun itself emits a steady stream of charged particles, which blow out into space as a highly attenuated 'wind' that buffets everything in its path. On Earth the solar wind causes compression of the magnetosphere on its sunward side, as well as the Northern Lights.

CHAPTER 17. MORTE D'ARTHUR

1 I had visited Merthyr Mawr with Alan on one of my first trips. On that occasion what had attracted our attention was a large collection of memorial stones in a corrugated-iron shelter behind the church. Most of these were only a few hundred years old, but amongst them were some that appeared to be quite ancient, including one with the inscription 'PAVLI FILI M . . .' Alan informed me that this 'Pavli' or Paul was a brother of Arthur II and therefore a son of Mauricius or Meurig. However, he didn't think Paul was himself the 'Great Martyr'.

2 William of Malmesbury, *History of the Kings of England*, trans. P. H. Norman, p. 119.

3 *Brut Tysylio*, p. 190.

4 Sometimes this sword is referred to as 'the Red Death' and at others as 'the Yellow Death'. The confusion seems to be because of the colour of saffron, which, though it stains cloth yellow, is itself dark red in colour, like dried blood. 'The Red Death' is probably the more accurate translation.

5 The Bryn Gwyn, or White Mound, lay at the centre of what later became the castle complex of the Tower of London. It is now surmounted by the Norman keep known as the White Tower.

CHAPTER 18. THE DYNASTY OF THE HOLY GRAIL

1 They did this in Judaea – for example, when Caesar recognized the claims of Herod by virtue of his marriage to Mariamme, sister of Aristobulus III

and granddaughter of Hyrcanus III.

2 Genuissa appears to mean 'of the gens [family] of Issus [Jesus]'. Alternatively it could simply mean 'jewess' – the 'j' being substituted by a 'g'.

3 Matt. 17:57–61.

4 John 19:38–42.

5 G. F. Jowett, *The Drama of the Lost Disciples*, p. 80.

6 Ibid.

7 Ibid., p. 81.

8 Ibid.

9 Ibid.

10 Ibid., p. 82.

11 Ibid., p. 70.

12 John 19:25.

13 Mark 6:3.

14 From The Protevangelion, *Lost Books of the Bible*, trans. William Hine, Gramecy Books, 1979.

15 See *Magi* by Adrian Gilbert (Bloomsbury, 1996) for a detailed discussion of how this date is arrived at.

16 Mark 15:6–7.

17 There are other examples of such 'surnames' in the New Testament, the most obvious being that of Cephas or Peter, meaning rock or stone, for Simon the fisherman.

18 See *The Holy Blood and the Holy Grail* by Lincoln, Baigent and Leigh.

19 Acts 15:22.

20 Acts 4:36–7.

21 Matt. 27:5–7.

22 John 19:25–7.

23 If Mary was twelve at the time of her engagement in 8 BC, she would have been seventy-one in AD 51 – old enough to have a grown-up grand-daughter.

24 As mentioned earlier, 'Y Seint Greal' is probably also the oldest version of the story.

25 The 'savage and cruel king' is clearly not Arviragus but rather a reference to the Roman emperor then in control of much of the island.

26 'Y Seint Greal', pp. 448–9.

27 Interestingly, the Church of Cyprus, though Orthodox, has always stressed its independence from all others, including those of Antioch and Constantinople.

28 1 Cor. 9:5–6.

APPENDIX 1

1 The Stone of Scone was brought to England by Edward I but was returned to Scotland in 1997.
2 Though pre-Roman coins have been found in London, these are described as having been minted in Kent, presumably because Julius Caesar said that the men of Kent were the most civilized in Britain.
3 Ralph Merrifield, *The Roman City of London*, pp. 123–4, Ernest Brown, 1965.
4 Ibid., pp. 271–2.
5 Ibid., p. 271.
6 Presumably in his *Survey of London* published in 1598.
7 *Royal Commission on Historical Monuments 1928: An Inventory of the Historical Monuments in London*, vol. 3, 'Roman London', HMSO, 1928.
8 Ralph Merrifield, *The Roman City of London*.

GLOSSARY OF WELSH
PRONUNCIATION

In Welsh there are seven, not five, vowels. These are a, e, i, o, u, y and w. The 'y' sound is either like an 'ea', as in dear, or a short 'u' as in bun. The 'w' sound is usually like an 'oo', as in fool. Consonants are mostly more or less the same as in English, except that there are some special sounds: 'dd' is pronounced like 'th'; 'f' is pronounced like 'v', whereas 'ff' is like the single 'f' of English; 'll' has no equivalent in English but is rather like pronouncing 'sh' with the tongue kept pressed against the upper gum behind the front teeth (like the start of 'l'). There are other more subtle differences, but these are the main ones. Pronunciation of some of the words used in this book is as follows. These are approximations, as many Welsh sounds simply do not exist in the English tongue and cannot be properly translated.

Welsh word	Pronunciation
Afarwy	Avarwee
Arwystli	Ar-oo-weestlee
Athrwys	Arthroo-wees
Brut	Brute
Brynllywarch	Brin-loo-warch
CADW	Cadoo
Ceri	Kerry
Cybwr	Keeboor
Cynfelyn	Kin-velin
Dindryfan	Din-druv-an
Dyfrig	Duff-rig
Gloyw	Gloyoo
Glyndwr	Glin-doo-wer
Glywys	Glue-wee-s

Gweirydd	*G-why-reed*
Gwrgan	*Goorgan*
Iestyn	*Yestin*
Iolo Morganwg	*Yolo Mor-gan-noog*
Khymry	*Cumree*
Llangynwydd	*Langunwith*
Lleirwg	*Lie-roog*
Llydaw	*Lud-au*
Mawr	*Mau-er* (as in Mau Mau)
Merddyn	*Merthin*
Merthyr	*Merther*
Meurig	*My-rig*
Mynwent y Milwyr	*Munwent uh Milweir*
Mynydd	*Munith*
Onbrawst	*Onbrowst*
Pencoed	*Pencoid*
Powys	*Powis*
Tewdrig	*Tuedrig* (as in Tuesday)
Twrch Trwyth	*Two-rch Troo-ith*
Tysylio	*Tu-silio*
Uthyr	*Utheer*
Wledig	*Wuh-led-ig*
Ynys	*Unis*

SELECT BIBLIOGRAPHY

PUBLISHED MATERIAL

Ammianus Marcellinus, *The Later Roman Empire*, trans. Walter Hamilton, Penguin Books, 1986.

Ashe, Geoffrey, *King Arthur's Avalon*, Collins, 1957.

Birley, Anthony (trans.), *Lives of the Later Caesars*, Guild Publishing, 1992.

Blackett, A. T. and Wilson, A., *Arthur and the Charters of the Kings*, M. T. Byrd & Co., 1981.

Blackett, A. T. and Wilson, A., *King Arthur King of Glamorgan and Gwent*, M. T. Byrd & Co., 1981.

Bligh Bond, Frederick, *An Architectural Handbook of Glastonbury Abbey*, RILKO, 1981.

Bligh Bond, Frederick, *The Gate of Remembrance*, B. H. Blackwell, 1918.

Bradley, S. A. J. (ed. and trans.), *Anglo-Saxon Poetry*, J. M. Dent, 1982.

Brie, Friedrich W. D. (ed.), *The Bruts or the Chronicles of England* (edited from MS Rawl B 171, Bodleian Library etc., Part 1), Oxford University Press, 1906 and 1960.

Brooke, Christopher, *The Saxon and Norman Kings*, Fontana, 1979.

Caesar, *De Bello Gallico and Other Commentaries of Julius Caesar*, trans. W. A. MacDevitt, J. M. Dent.

Caesar, *The Conquest of Gaul*, trans. S. A. Handford, Penguin Books, 1951.

Chambers, E. K., *Arthur of Britain*, Sidgwick & Jackson, 1927.

Clube, Victor and Napier, Bill, *The Cosmic Winter*, Oxford University Press, 1990.

Davies, Edward, *Celtic Researches – on the origins, traditions, and languages of the ancient British*, 1804.

Dill, Samuel, *Roman Society in the Last Century of the Western Empire*, Macmillan & Co., 1899.

362

Enderbee, Percy, *Cambria Triumphans or Britain in its Perfect Lustre*, 1661.

Eschenbach, Wolfram von, *Parzifal*, ed. André Lefevere, Continuum Publishing Co., 1991.

Evans, D. Delta, *The Ancient Bards of Britain*, Educational Publishing Co., 1906.

Evans, J. Gwenogfran, *The Book of Aneurin*, 1908.

Evans, Sebastian (trans.), *The High History of the Holy Grail*, James Clarke & Co., 1969.

Flavius Josephus, *The Complete Works of Flavius Josephus*, trans. William Whiston, T. Nelson & Sons, 1852.

Ganz, Geoffrey (trans.), *The Mabinogion*, Penguin Books, 1976.

Garmonsway, G. N. (trans.), *The Anglo-Saxon Chronicle*, J. M. Dent, 1953.

Geoffrey of Monmouth, *The History of the Kings of Britain*, trans. Lewis Thorpe, Penguin Books, 1966.

Gerald of Wales, *The Journey Through Wales*, trans. Lewis Thorpe, Penguin Books, 1979.

Gilbert, Adrian G., *Magi: the Quest for a Secret Tradition*, Bloomsbury Publishing, 1996.

Gordon, E. O., *Prehistoric London*, Covenant Publishing Co., 1946.

Hanna, Ralph III (ed.), *The Awntyrs of Arthure at the Turne Wathelyn*, Manchester University Press, 1974.

Hone, William (trans.), *The Lost Books of the Bible*, Gramercy Books, 1979.

James, Peter, *Centuries of Darkness*, Jonathan Cape, London, 1991.

Jones, Edward, *Musical and Poetical Relicks of the Welsh Bards*, 1794.

Jones, O., Williams, E. and Pughe, W. O. (eds.), *The Myvyrnian Archaiology of Wales (including Welsh Laws and Musical Records by Edward Jones)*, Thomas Gee, 1870.

Jones, Thomas, 'The Black Book of Carmarthen: "Stanzas of the Graves"', Sir John Rhys Memorial Lecture to the British Academy 1967, Proceedings of the British Academy, Vol. LIII.

Jowett, G. F., *The Drama of the Lost Disciples*, Covenant Publishing Co., 1980.

Luard, Henry Richards (ed.), *Flores Historiarum: the Chronicles and Memorials of Great Britain and Ireland during the Middle Ages*, HMSO, 1890.

Malory, Sir Thomas, *Le Morte d'Arthur*, ed. A. L. Pollard, Medici Society, 1929.

Marshall, Dr Alfred (trans.), *The Interlinear Greek–English New Testament*, Samuel Bagster & Sons, 1975.

McAllister, *Glamorgan, History and Topography*, 1936.

Merricke, Sir Rice, *A Book of the Antiquities of Glamorganshire*, reprinted by James Andrew Cobbett, 1887.

Merrifield, Ralph, *The Roman City of London*, Ernest Brown, 1965.

Morris, John, *The Age of Arthur*, Weidenfeld & Nicolson, 1992.

Morton, H. V., *In the Steps of St Paul*, Methuen & Co., 1937.

Nennius, *Arthurian Period Sources*, vol. 8, trans. and ed. John Morris, Phillimore & Co., 1980.

Peter, Rev. David, *Hanes Crefydd yn Nghymru or The History of Religion in Wales – From the Arrival of the Cymry to the Present Times*, 1810.

Powell, David (using the translation of H. Lloyd), *The History of Cambria now called Wales*, 1584 and 1811.

Rees, Thomas, *History of South Wales*, 1815.

Rees, W. J. (trans.), *The Liber Landavensis*, Welsh Manuscript Society, 1890.

Rhys, Ernest, *Atlas of Ancient and Classical Geography*, J. M. Dent.

Rivet, A. L. F. and Smith, C., *The Place Names of Roman Britain*, Batsford.

Roberts, Rev. Canon, *The History of Rome*, vol. 1, J. M. Dent, 1912.

Salway, Peter, *Roman Britain*, Clarendon Press, 1981.

Savage, Anne (trans.), *The Anglo-Saxon Chronicle*, Macmillan, 1982.

Sawyer, P. H., *From Roman Britain to Norman England*, Methuen, 1978.

Stephens, *The Literature of the Khumry – The Language and Literature of Wales*, Longmans, Green & Co., 1876.

Tacitus, *The Annals of Imperial Rome*, trans. Michael Grant, Penguin Books, 1990.

Tacitus, *The Histories*, trans. Kenneth Wellesley, Guild Publishing, 1989.

Tysylio, *The Chronicles of the Kings of Britain*, trans. Peter Roberts, E. Williams, 1811.

Warrington, Rev. W., *The History of Wales* (2 vols.), reprinted 1791.

William of Malmesbury, *History of the Kings of England*, trans. P. H. Norman.

William of Malmesbury, *Chronicle of the Kings of England*, Bohn, 1847.

Williams, David, *History of Gwent*, 1784.

Williams, David, *History of Monmouthshire*, 1796.

Williams, Edward and Taliesin, *Iolo MSS*, Welsh Manuscript Society, 1848.

Williams, Edward (ed.), *Myvyrnian Archaiology of Wales*, Welsh Manuscript Society, 1806.

Williams, Jane, *A History of Wales*, Longmans, Green & Co., 1869.

Williams, John, *An Ecclesiastical History of the Khymry*, Welsh Manuscript Society, 1846.

Williams, Rev. J., *Barddas*, Welsh Manuscript Society, 1862.

Wilson, A. and Blackett, A. T., *Arthur the War King, Founder of Britain*, M. T. Byrd & Co., 1982.

Wilson, A. and Blackett, A. T., *Artorius Rex Discovered*, M. T. Byrd & Co., 1986.

Wynne, William, *The History of Wales* (8 vols.), 1697, 1702 and 1774.

MANUSCRIPT SOURCES

The British Library contains several massive archives. The most important from our point of view are the Cottonian and Harleian collections. The following are just some of the important manuscripts contained in these collections.

Cottonian MSS

Cat. A. vi 1, 'A Chronicle of Wales from King Cadwallader to Llewellyn Son of Griffith ap Llewellyn' by Humphrey Lhywd, 1559. (This is really a history of north Wales.)

Cat. A. vi 217, 'Ejusdem Fragmentum ex Chronico Wallico ab ipso Wallice scripto'.

Domitian 1. 157.b. and Julius D. x 28, 'Collections of Very Early Brecon Genealogy and Pedigree'.

Domitian viii 24.b, 'Notula quando Cantredae sive Centurae Walliae primo inceperint'.

Domitian viii 119, 'Cantredae Walliae'.

Titus A. xix 101, 'Versus Rhythmici de Wallis'.

Titus D. xxii, 'Ecclesiastical Chronicles of Llandaff'.

Titus F. ii 214, 'History of the British Kings, chiefly Arthur'.

Vespasian A. xiv 1.B, 'Calendarium in quo Sancti Wallicipraecipus memorantur'.

Vespasian A. xiv 12B, 'Vitae Sanctorum Wallensium'.

Vespasian A. xiv 10.b, 'De situ Brecheniauc'.

Vitelius C. x 97, 'The Register and Calendar of Llandaff, the Popes, and the English King'.

Vitelius C. x 26, 'Excerpts of Llandaff Antiquities'.

Vitelius C. x 47, 'Life of St Oudoceus and various Charters'.

Vitelius C. x 92, 'Nomina regum Brittaniae, et episcoporum Landavensum, cum variis recordationibus, Gallice'.

Harleian MSS

310, 'Fragmentium Vitae Sti. Davidis Menevensis Archiepiscopi'.

368, Sir Edward Stradling of St Donat's, 'The Winning of the Lordship of Glamorgan etc.'

624, 'Giraldus Cambrensis de vita Davidis Menevensis Episcopi Historia'.

838, 'Various Annals of Llandaff'.

1143 and 1370, 'The Descent of Welshmen who Obtained Great Title, Honour and Worship in England'.

1386 and 1441, 'The Arms of the Founders of Welsh Families'.

1933, 'Arms of Welsh Families'.

1933, 'Pedigrees and Arms of Welsh Families'.

1935, 'A Collection of Welsh Pedigrees'.

1946, 'The Arms of Old founders of Welsh Families Beginning with Brutus'.

1949, 'The Descent of the British Kings and Princes from Brutus to Rhese Gryg who Died in 1233 AD'.

1961, 'The Arms of Divers Old Welsh Families'.

1969, 'Descents of Many Welsh Families Including Those of the Fifteen Tribes of North Wales'.

1970, 'The Arms and Descents of Several Welsh Families'.

1975, 'Descents of the Many Nobility and Gentry who have Resided or Possessed Lands in Pembrokeshire, Caermarthenshire, Glamorgan, Brecon, Cardiganshire, etc.'.

1976, 1977, 1978, 1995, 6102, 6122, 1412, 'Descents of Divers Old Welsh Families'.

1979, 'Descents of Some Welsh families'.

1997, 'A Collection of Welsh Descents Including the Names of the Conquerors of Brecon and Glamorgan'.

2218, 'Pedigrees of Some Welsh Families Including Mansells of Margam'.

2273, 'Excerpts from the Library of the Abbey of Neath of 1595'.

2288, Hugh Thomas, 'A Collection of the Pedigrees of Welsh Families'.

2289 and 128, 'Collections of Very Early Brecon Genealogy and Pedigree'.

2289, 'The Letters of Edward Lluyd to Dr William Nicholson'.

2291, Hugh Thomas, 'A Collection of Welsh Pedigrees'.

2299, 'A Large Collection of Welsh Pedigrees'.

2300 and 128, 'A Collection of Carmarthenshire Pedigrees'.

2414, 'Pedigrees of Some Welsh Families'.

3325, 'A Short History of Wales from 668 to 936'.

3538, 4031 and 6153, 'Various Welsh Pedigrees etc.'.

3859 includes the Wedding Lists of Owain the son of Hywell Dda, Nennius's *Historia Britonum* and other texts.

4181, 'The History of Welsh Heroes by Threes or Triads in Welsh and English'.

4291, 'Arms of Welsh Families'.

4776, 'Extenta terrarum Ecclesiae Leges et Consuetudines Walliae'.

4872, John Lewys of Llynwene, 'A History of Great Britain from Noah's Flood to Cadwalladr', 1661.

5058, 'Genealogies of Welsh Families'.

6068, 'A Collection of Records Concerning Wales and Pedigrees of Glamorgan, Monmouth and Others, the Book of George Owen'.

6108, 'A History of Brecknock and Glamorgan from the Time of Meurrick King of Brittaine until the Year 1606'.

6823, 6831 and 6870, 'The Genealogical History of the Ancient and Present Nobility and Gentry of Wales' (the planned work of Hugh Thomas).

7017, 'A Geographical Description of Brecknockshire', and 'The History of Brecknock from Meyrick King of Britain until 1603'.

Other important manuscripts are contained in the Bodleian Library, Oxford (e.g. Laud 610 and Rawlinson 502, 3468), the Library of Jesus College, Oxford, Cardiff Library, the Welsh National Library at Aberystwyth and the Welsh School in London.

The principal manuscripts used by Taliesin Williams in compiling the 'Iolo Manuscripts' are:

The MS of Hafod Uchtryd.
MS of Watkyn Giles of Penyfai, Glamorgan.
'The Long Black Book of Thomas Trueman of Pant-y-lliwydd, Glamorgan'.
'The Book of Thomas Hopkin' of Coychurch, Ogwr, Glamorgan'.
MS of Thomas ap Evan of the Bryn (transposed *c.* 1670).
'The Book of Mr Cobb of Cardiff, Glamorgan'.
MS of Twrog.
MS of Anthony Powell of Tir Iarll, Glamorgan.
Ieuan Deulwyn (The royal line of Coetty, *c.* 1150 70), Glamorgan.
The Peniarth MS.
The Hengwrt MSS.
The Harleian MSS.

In addition to the above there are over 20,000 pages of handwritten material recorded and copied by Iolo Morganwg (Edward Williams) languishing in the National Library of Wales, Aberystwyth. An embarrassment to those who have sought over the years to discredit his work, this fact is not advertised. Another collection lies generally ignored in the Cardiff Library.

INDEX

368